Peasants in Socialist Transition

PETER D. BELL

Peasants in Socialist Transition

LIFE IN A COLLECTIVIZED HUNGARIAN VILLAGE

UNIVERSITY OF CALIFORNIA PRESS
BERKELEY • LOS ANGELES • LONDON

University of California Press
Berkeley and Los Angeles, California
University of California Press, Ltd.
London, England
© 1984 by
The Regents of the University of California
Printed in the United States of America
1 2 3 4 5 6 7 8 9

Library of Congress Cataloging in Publication Data

Bell, Peter D
    Peasants in Socialist Transition.

    Bibliography: p.
    Includes index.
    1. Kislapos, Hungary—Social conditions.
2. Hungary—Rural conditions—Case studies.
3. Villages—Hungary—Case studies. 4. Collective
farms—Hungary—Case studies. I. Title.
HN420.5.K56B44   307.7′2′09439   80-25126
ISBN 0-520-04157-7

Contents

Illustrations

Preface

This work is the social history of a small collectivized agricultural community in Hungary after World War II. It describes the political, social, and economic transformation experienced by the Hungarian countryside under the farreaching and sometimes revolutionary policies of a socialist government led by the Communist Party. These postwar years have been turbulent. They have been marked by large-scale land reform, by the nationalization and collectivization of most of the economy, by political repression followed by an armed uprising in 1956, by the introduction of an extensive New Economic Mechanism, and by a gradual and considerable expansion of freedom in all spheres that has extended to the present.

Nowhere in Hungary have the changes wrought by these events been as great as in the countryside. Early land reforms directly affected the lives and fortunes of most village dwellers. The economic policies and repression of the early 1950s had as negative an effect in rural areas as anywhere else, contributing greatly to the flight from agriculture. Collectivization, at first unpopular and unsuccessful, has with increased support and economic backing from the government brought villagers' incomes to equal those of city dwellers, a striking development considering the "three million beggars" of the Hungarian prewar countryside. Villages are becoming increasingly integrated into a modern, developed, industrial Hungary. The goal of this book is to describe and analyze the effects on the countryside of these postwar events and processes by examining their impact on the people and social institutions of one Hungarian village.

The book's plan has undergone numerous changes since I first began work on it. Its origin stems not only from academic institutional necessities, but from several factors. The first is a general interest in Hungary, partly derived from having been raised as a second-generation Hungarian-American (albeit one who until his first contact with Hungary as a visiting relative/tourist had relatively *little* interest in that country and little knowledge of things Hungarian). The second is curiosity about what life is actually like in a socialist or communist society—an area about which Western media and even the academic world have been largely remiss in providing adequate and objective coverage. Finally, both my undergraduate years as a psychology major and my graduate years in anthropology have fostered an interest in interpersonal perception, in how people think about one another.

I set out for Hungary in late August 1974 with the plan of studying the effects of agricultural collectivization on villagers' lives and on the way in which they perceive one another. As I began to realize the importance of other postwar events and processes besides collectivization in the lives and thinking of the villagers, these events and processes began to assume greater significance in my thinking. I also came to realize that in order to understand the categories and models for behavior that people use to judge and interpret the actions of others I would have to have a greater background knowledge of local (and national) events and processes. Gradually the emphasis in the study shifted to these more general events and changes, and the present work resulted.

Many individuals have contributed in many different ways to the transformation and completion of this book. First, I should like to thank the people of Kislapos. The patience with which they met my many questions and my general intrusiveness, their many small acts of kindness and the general hospitality they extended to me, and the friendliness and openness with which many greeted my presence despite doubts bred by unpleasant memories from the past have endeared them to me and made my stay a pleasant and profitable one. I am especially grateful to the couple in whose home I spent my months in the countryside. Their ability to accommodate one who is used to different ways and their usual good humor and directness eased many a difficult time for me.

My relatives in Budapest were my frequent gracious hosts, confidants, nurses, and advisers. They were witness to my many moods during the stay in Hungary and undoubtedly became more involved in my visit than any of us had planned. For this and much more I am grateful.

My close friends in Budapest played similar roles. Their insights, stores of knowledge, forceful perspectives, and desire to help me see and appreciate a different way of life bred, nurtured, and sustained a wider appreciation and knowledge of, and a greater interest in, Hungarian society and culture. Personal kindnesses too numerous and varied to mention can never be adequately acknowledged.

To Tamás Hofer, of the Ethnographic Museum in Budapest, my research adviser in Hungary, I am indebted for encouragement to work in Hungary and for *Proper Peasants* (which he co-authored), a work whose breadth and depth of scope I am constantly appreciating anew. I thank Ferenc Bakó, director of the Castle Museum in Eger, for his efforts in helping me choose a village to study.

The exchanges of ideas with friends and colleagues in the Ethnographic Research Group and the Sociological Research Institute in Budapest are much appreciated. The computer time made available by friends in the latter, in addition to that provided by the Institute for Cultural Relations, was most useful for my work.

I thank Catherine Károlyi for making available a place for me to begin writing in beautiful surroundings among congenial people at the Fondation Károlyi in Vence, near Nice.

In the United States, I wish to express appreciation to the International Research and Exchanges Board and to the Office of Education, without whose funding and sponsorship this research enterprise would have been impossible.

For the opportunity to work with and learn from Roy D'Andrade, I am grateful. Through his stimulating thought, manifested in teaching and research, he awakened my interest in interpersonal perception as an important cultural area. Fred Bailey has inculcated in me a growing appreciation of "political man"—one that, undoubtedly, he *and* I wish would develop even more. His general supportiveness, kind understatement, and careful reading have contributed to my understanding of village actors. David Jordan deserves special thanks for his close reading, unflagging enthusiasm, and good humor in the face of some god-awful turgid and convoluted prose. His detailed and pointed comments are most appreciated. Meryl Lanning of the University of California Press deserves similar thanks for putting this prose into a more polished form. The work's limitations are my own.

Introduction

Eastern and Western Europe have for centuries taken divergent historical paths. While the latter was developing into an incipient capitalist society, the former was in the middle of its "second feudal era." Through to the middle of the twentieth century, Eastern Europe was the poorer step-child on the periphery of the more developed West, a producer of raw materials and foodstuffs subject to the market demands of the dominant North and West. The end of World War II saw Europe divided into two vastly different political blocs and the East transformed into a set of socialist states.

This has led to many changes in Eastern Europe. Its transformation has been one of the greatest examples in history of large-scale social engineering (exceeded in magnitude only by that in the Soviet Union and China). Although in Western Europe, too, there have been efforts to better the conditions of large segments of the population, to encourage modernization and industrialization, and to quicken the development of agriculture, compared to Eastern Europe these efforts have been limited in scope and have depended mainly on economic incentives. Eastern Europe has witnessed far stronger efforts.

Yet, how different have the changes been in Eastern Europe from those occurring in the West? To examine this question it is useful to look at the peasantry. Before the war this group comprised the majority of the population in most Eastern European countries; it was this group that underwent some of the greatest changes in countries where private agriculture gave way to collective and state farms. The economic structure of agriculture in Eastern Europe has been radically altered. Yet there are in these countries many of the same patterns common in Western Europe. There has been large-scale migration to the cities from the countryside and a rapid reduction in the size of the farming population. The "moral community" (Bailey 1971) has remained an important element of rural communities in the East just as it has in the West; many of the dimensions of judgment and social perception common in Western rural communities are found in those of the East despite changes that are at least partially intended to produce the "socialist man."

This work aims at describing and explaining just what has and what has not changed in the East European countryside, an area that has received all too little attention from Western social scientists and even less close ethnographic scrutiny. The book examines the postwar transformation of the Hungarian countryside and describes how national policies and processes have been translated into social existence in one Hungarian village, Kislapos.[1]

In the past forty-five years, Hungary has undergone a momentous social, economic, and political transformation. As a result, a primarily agriculturally oriented capitalist country with enormous social and material inequalities has been transformed into an industrially oriented socialist state. Taking a broad historical perspective, this study explores the ways in which the social structure, the lives, and the perceptions of Kislapos's inhabitants have been affected by farreaching post-World War II events in Hungary.

With the notable exception of the excellent work of Fél and Hofer (1969, 1973), Hungary has remained largely uncharted in English language ethnographic literature. Even these two writers have dealt only with the precollectivization Hungarian village. Hence, there is currently an almost complete lack of ethnographic literature in English on contemporary rural (or urban) Hungary, on the life of villagers in a socialist country, and particularly on the changes that the collectivization of agriculture has wrought. This lack is particularly unfortunate given the general absence of studies of this type in Eastern Europe.[2] Although the circumstances leading to the dearth appear to have changed in a positive

---

1. This name is a pseudonym, as are all names given to nearby villages, to some of the geographic sites, and to all villagers.

2. Indeed, this is unfortunately true, though less so, in the Hungarian language. In recent years there has been considerable sociological survey research and often insightful sociography continuing in the tradition of the reform-minded writers of the 1930s, but little extended, firsthand observation and analysis of a modern Hungarian rural community. Hofer (1968; Fél and Hofer 1969: 3–6) traces some of the reasons for this to the tradition- and folklore-oriented nature of Hungarian ethnography (*néprajz*). The political sensitivity of the postwar rural transformation has also played a part. A recent heartening exception to this pattern has been the work in the village of Varsány by the Ethnographic Research Group of the Hungarian Academy of Sciences (Bodrogi 1978).

With the exception of Yugoslavia, for which there is a large body of published material, opportunities for such research by foreigners have only recently opened up in Eastern European countries. Published works include those of the Romanian Research Group of the Department of Anthropology at the University of Massachusetts (Cole 1976a, b; Beck 1976; Kideckel 1976; McArthur 1976; Randall 1976; Sampson 1976) and the ethnography of a contemporary Czech village by Salzmann and Scheufler (1974). Additional studies are under way now in these and other Eastern European countries.

manner and more Western anthropologists are conducting research in Hungary, few English language readers are yet familiar with the complex and extraordinary sociohistorical background of today's rural Hungary.

CENTRAL THEMES

This work emphasizes two broad sets of themes in a historical perspective: 1) those of hierarchy and 2) those of ties of reciprocity, between both equals and unequals. These were central themes both in the prewar organization of rural Hungarian society and in the thinking of rural villagers. Despite great upheavals and the radical restructuring of Hungarian society, they continue to be important elements in both social organization and social perception in the village.

Pre-World War II Hungary was a highly stratified society, remarkable both for extremes of wealth and poverty and for the large number of finely differentiated gradations in the rural and urban status hierarchy. Unlike most Eastern European countries, Hungary had not experienced a major land reform after World War I, and the extremes of social differentiation related to marked variation in landownership had not yet been ameliorated. In the countryside, landed wealth was a central and pervasive factor in villagers' lives and thought. The social status and prestige of most families was directly related to the amount of land they owned. Landownership largely determined one's work opportunities and one's level of education. Thus, landownership indirectly influenced the individual's level of refinement, an important component of prestige. Finally, such wealth meant power, both economic and administrative. Indeed, the law guaranteed control of the village administration by the wealthiest villagers. Lack of land, on the other hand, meant subservience to and dependence on those more wealthy.

The policies of the post-World War II years were aimed at destroying this system of stratification and at eliminating the huge social and material inequalities that existed and replacing them with a far more egalitarian and just society. After much tribulation, many of these goals have been largely achieved. Land reform eliminated the most glaring inequities. The policies of the 1950s, including the anti-kulak measures and the compulsory delivery of agricultural goods at low prices, eliminated the wealthy peasant stratum and made private agriculture much less attractive. The collectivization of the vast majority of farmland in the late 1950s and early 1960s virtually eliminated the importance of landed wealth in the village political and status hierarchy.[3]

Nonetheless, themes of hierarchy and inequality, of power and depen-

3. Such agricultural policies, including collectivization or cooperativization, have been common to all Eastern European countries, although Poland and Yugoslavia have deemphasized the establishment of cooperatives, allowing a majority of agricultural land to remain in the hands of small farmers for at least some

dence, remain important factors in the Hungarian experience. A relatively integrated dimension of hierarchy, status, and power is still central to villagers' considerations of their fellowmen. This is reflected not only in the salience of this dimension in formal tasks given to villagers, and in the agreement over the sharp dividing line between the leaders and the led, but also in the frequency of reference to questions of hierarchy, the leadership, and the use and abuse of power, and to themes of dependency and subordination and of the importance of (and material rewards ensuing from) good relations with the local leadership.

Many of these themes have found form in complaints about the village leadership, particularly that of the local collective farm. Some of this stems from certain contradictions widely manifested in Eastern European socialist societies and present in this village. First, there is frequently a conflict between the egalitarian ideology of communism and the requirements arising from the leadership. The strong emphasis on egalitarianism and the ideology of equality has left a positive mark and considerably reduced differences of wealth and income. It has also, however, increased sensitivity to small differences and made more difficult the introduction of hierarchy and leadership necessitated by a large organization like the collective farm, which has many members, handles complex affairs, and requires a division of labor and delegation of authority. This egalitarianism, the high value traditionally placed on independence by the rural peasantry, and the competition for positions and resources in the emerging cooperative farm have made some kinds of dissatisfaction inevitable, especially where there exist few widely accepted, clear-cut bases or rules for the selection of leaders and the allocation of positions.

Another major contradiction has been that between, on the one hand, the ideal of popular participation and personal innovation inherent in the ideology of revolution so central to communism, which is an important part of everyone's ideological education, and, on the other hand, various barriers to popular participation in decision-making, including the strongly centralized decision-making structure of Eastern Europe (see Neuberg 1973). Thus, the leadership of the local collective farm has been placed in a double-edged position of role conflict, as both the representative of the membership and the transmitter of policy originating in a highly centralized political and administrative structure.

This dissatisfaction has been exacerbated by some leaders' use of their considerable power for their own material benefit. Moreover, some con-

---

years to come. While the timing, pressure and details of collectivization have varied from country to country, the basic phases and forms have exhibited broad similarities. The claim by Cole (1976a: 249) that Romania's "agricultural reconstruction programs are not to be confused with policies elsewhere" seems somewhat exaggerated. For comparative data on East European agriculture and agricultural policies, see Sanders (1958), Karcz (1967), Enyedi (1978: 156–190), and Francisco, Laird, and Laird (1979).

temporary leaders have made it general practice to follow the models of leadership manifested by some prewar—and postwar—wealthy peasants and estate managers. This posture has done little to endear them to workers; themes reflecting it have found their way into the language of claims against leaders. Some leaders have paid only lip service to the democratic principles on which these agricultural cooperatives are to be run, principles whose application was already reduced by limitations of extreme centralization. Many have used their positions as sources of patronage for other members, allocating jobs to relatives and close friends.

On the other hand, the emphasis on references to universalistic norms in the language of claims used by some members to criticize leaders should not blind one to the fact that many would just as soon see an application of particularistic norms more beneficial to themselves. The issue is often less one of disagreement on values and more one of envy.

Another striking continuity between past and present is the importance of reciprocity and social exchange in rural life. In the past, mutual obligations of work, help, and favors were important organizing principles of village life. Family and kin relations, based on the family as the primary economic and production unit, were the prime focus of this social exchange. At the same time, patron-client relations based largely on the power associated with landed wealth and the dependence accompanying its absence were a central element of political, economic, and social relations. This often involved political support given implicitly in exchange for mutual political support or economic aid within the framework of kinship and other social relations (for example, of neighbors, or of landowner and sharecropper). Political ties were strongly reinforced by the fact that most of the wealthiest villagers were close kin.

Today the family is no longer the unit of production, and landed wealth has ceased to have any importance. Power relations within the family have changed a great deal; children are leaving home and establishing independent existences outside agriculture at a rapid rate. Yet family and a slightly reduced circle of kin are at the center of a still vital system of social interaction and mutual exchange of labor, favors, and other kinds of aid. Patron-client relations, though differently based, are an important element of concern for many villagers, and the reciprocity underlying them is reinforced by the continued importance of kin-based reciprocity. Indeed, even recently there has been considerable overlap between the systems of family- and kin-based reciprocation and the system of power-dependency relations. Within change there have been powerful strains of continuity; these will be closely examined here.

FOCUS

The focus of this study is on the collectivization of agriculture. It is this process, more than any other of this period, that has had the greatest influence on the lives and fortunes of Hungary's rural population, affecting the very basis of their existence. That it has been such a critical factor is not hard to understand. Though there were also hundreds of thousands of landless agricultural laborers in prewar Hungary, rural Hungarian society basically took a traditional peasant form. In the peasant economy the family can be viewed as a self-sufficient production unit whose purpose is to provide basic necessities and work for its members based on land owned and/or leased (rented, sharecropped, and so on) by the family.[4] Collectivization has radically altered the fundamental status of the family's relationship to land and, in so doing, has played a considerable role in the transformation of Hungarian rural society, in whose organization family, kinship, and land were central.

Although the collectivization of agriculture and the changes that took place after 1959 are the primary focus of this study, it is a longer-based and more historically oriented analysis for several reasons. The first is the difficulty in establishing a precollectivization base for the purposes of comparison. There was no one such base period of relative normalcy. Collectivization did not take place all at once, but rather in two significantly different phases. The first period, lasting nationally from 1949 to 1953, saw the establishment in Kislapos of two relatively small collective farms in 1949 and 1950, whose membership consisted primarily of formerly landless agricultural laborers and whose success could be characterized as limited. The latter period, 1958 to 1961, included the almost complete collectivization of the village's farm land in 1959 through the establishment of two more collective farms and the enrollment of the village's more successful peasants in the collectives. The further consolidations that have taken place since then have resulted in ever-increasing strength and success of the collectivization movement. Although the second phase is of perhaps greater significance for more people, it is clear that the first was important for the whole process of collectivization.

Further contributing to the lack of a clear precollectivization base period are the events of the 1940s and 1950s, which have not at all been conducive to stability for a peasant economy and society. Thus we have the forced deliveries and depleted manpower of the war, followed by the serious losses of animals and general devastation of the countryside at its end. This period was succeeded by reconstruction in the late 1940s to reach prewar economic levels and exaggerated industrialization and repression in the early 1950s, typified in the countryside by forced deliveries of agricultural goods at low prices and anti-kulak measures, and capped by the 1956 uprising. The following two years of relative stability and prosperity were witness to a rural society already considerably changed from that of fifteen years past.

4. For a thorough discussion of this view of the peasant, see Franklin (1969).

These events highlight the second reason for the broader, more historical scope of this study. The collectivization of agriculture did not take place in a sociohistorical vacuum but had other important social, political, and economic antecedents and concomitants. Besides those referred to above, there were the farreaching postwar land reform, which greatly enlarged the ranks of the smallholders while eliminating the holdings of the enormously powerful latifundia and wealthier gentry; the flood of workers from the countryside to the city due to rapid industrialization, the lure of urban areas, and temporarily depressed conditions in agriculture; and the general modernization and increase in living standards following the war. If the process of collectivization and its effects are to be understood, clearly an understanding of other events and ongoing processes of the period is essential.

A more thorough look at these events and processes is necessary for a third reason as well. The fact that they are closely interwoven with collectivization makes it more difficult, perhaps impossible, to isolate the effects of collectivization alone. It is also clear that these other events and processes have had important consequences of their own for presentday rural Hungarian society, affecting both social structure and social perception. In order to illuminate these changes, it is necessary to look closely at the social history of Kislapos and the countryside in general.

A BRIEF OUTLINE

This study begins with an introduction to the village of Kislapos in Chapter 1. In Chapter 2 the social and economic hierarchy of Kislapos in the 1930s is outlined in detail; the village's social strata are described and their economic and social interrelations analyzed. The emphasis shifts in Chapter 3 to an analysis of family structure and of the central organizing role of family and kinship in village life; other important relationships are also sketched. Chapter 4 describes the more important political, religious, social, and economic institutions and associations of prewar Kislapos and examines the relationship between social stratification and power, authority, and leadership.

Having set up a basis for comparison with this analysis of Kislapos's prewar peasant society, and having set the stage for the years to follow, the book continues by setting forth the historical events and upheavals and the social, economic, political, and demographic process of the extraordinary 1940s and 1950s in Kislapos (Chapter 5). With the description of the formation of the collective farms in 1959, the curtain has been drawn on the age of private farming in the village, and the period of socialist agriculture has been entered. The history and organization of the village's early collective farms are treated in Chapter 5, and the structure and operation of today's collective farm are examined more closely in Chapter 6. This background makes it possible to analyze contemporary Kislapos's social structure, in which the collective farm plays a central role along with the continuingly influential family and kinship structures. In Chapter 7, the still important, though somewhat altered role of family and kinship in today's village is discussed and important changes in the structure of relations within the family are noted. Other socially salient avenues of interaction are also treated. Chapter 8 analyzes recent developments in power relations in the village, including the resurgence of the former middle peasantry and the continued importance of patron-client relations, as well as the villagers' views of those in power and of the road to success.

The final section takes a look at the cognitive social world of Kislapos's inhabitants. Chapter 9 presents the basic sets of categories into which they sort their fellow villagers and the characteristics, attitudes, and feelings they associate with these categories of people. Major components of social status and behavior are examined, along with the more salient stereotypes and motivational themes attributed to others. Categories of the past are viewed as retaining great importance in today's social perception; these themes are traced to their present and past experiential bases. One effect of demographic shifts in the village, the recent influx of a hundred Gypsies into a community almost totally devoid of them and proud of it, is discussed in Chapter 10. This chapter outlines the stereotypical reactions of villagers to the Gypsies, examines the degree of fit between these reactions and reality, analyzing the bases of discrepancies, and traces the development of relations between the villagers and the despised newcomers. The cognitive approach of these two chapters enriches our understanding of the themes of hierarchy and reciprocation in contemporary Hungarian society.

THE RESEARCH

The data on which this work is based were collected while I lived in Kislapos during the thirteen months from January 1975 to February 1976. Unless otherwise stated, the end of this period, January 1976, is the ethnographic present in this work. During these months I lived in the household of a retired railroad worker and his wife, a couple who in the past had taken in boarders. Having a childhood background in Hungarian and having studied the language both in the United States and for several months in Budapest prior to my fieldwork, I was able to communicate effectively with the villagers and to understand what they were saying.

During the first few months in Kislapos I became acquainted with the village and its inhabitants, making myself known and accustoming people to my inquiring presence. This period was spent largely in observation, informal conversation, and longer talks with a few villagers whom I began to know well. The latter started filling me in on local history and provided sketches of other villagers so I could place them better and begin to understand local social networks. This observation, informal conversation with a large number of villagers, and longer talks with an increasing number of people continued throughout my stay.

After this opening phase I conducted large numbers of structured and unstructured interviews, gathering numerous life histories and eliciting descriptions of fellow villagers and close kin. Several different formal elicitation tasks were used to obtain more specific data on social perception. I also collected considerable genealogical data—for the vast majority of villagers, in fact—so that I could better understand their various social ties.

Relatively little attempt was made to conduct truly random sampling, but interviews, conversations, and formal tasks alike were conducted with members of all social levels, of both sexes, and of all adult ages (though there were relatively few interviews with youths at school or working elsewhere and living primarily away from home).

Informants who played leading and subordinate roles in prewar and precollective village institutions, who held important posts in the party and village administration, were interviewed to construct a more detailed picture of the past and of the historical processes leading to the present. A great deal of relevant information was also obtained through interviews and conversations with many other villagers.

Village and collective farm records were perused several times, mainly to double-check villagers' recollections and claims about the past. These were obtained less often than would have been ideal, for several reasons including general bureaucratic reticence and uncertainty on all sides about the scope of my freedom of inquiry, as well as my own lack of tenacity.

Fieldwork in a socialist country was in many ways no different from that elsewhere. No explicit limitations were placed on my range of inquiry. Problems of suspicion and anxiety on the part of some villagers were no doubt similar to those in other countries where inquiries are made by outsiders whose affiliation with local leaders, fellow villagers, the local police, and foreign information-gathering services is unclearly perceived by informants. Memories of harsh years in the past inhibited some.

As a researcher from a country that was for years officially vilified, but upon which many look with sympathy and envy, and in which a number have relatives, I met with a variety of responses. Friendliness and warmth were the norm and openness was common.

ONE VILLAGE OUT OF MANY

Although Kislapos cannot be said to represent rural Hungary fully, as indeed no village can be said to be a typical community of a country, much of its past and present social structure and the historical events and processes unfolding there do reflect the societal conditions of much of the Hungarian countryside. The whole cannot be typical, but many aspects mirror well what is and what has happened in some, many, or most Hungarian villages. Some aspects, of course, are more singular. In order to put Kislapos and its history and social order into proper perspective and to shed light on more general Hungarian conditions, an effort will be made throughout this work, in both text and footnotes, to place Kislapos's social and historical conditions within the larger range of possibilities of other communities in Hungary. However, the questions this work treats and the themes of hierarchy and reciprocity it emphasizes are important and useful for all Hungarian communities.

To begin this clarifying, qualifying process let me explain the reasons for the choice of Kislapos as a field site. As I was originally most interested in the impact of farm collectivization on the backbone of Hungarian agriculture—the smallholders and middle peasants, the *Proper Peasants* of Fél and Hofer (1969)—it was important that I study a village in which this group once formed a relatively large percentage of the population and in which agriculture is still the primary occupation. Kislapos met these requirements. Moreover, it has a relatively successful collective farm, though not a showcase one, giving it some typicality in this respect. Its small population of nine hundred, a manageable size for my purposes, and the collective farm's past history of merger from smaller farms, a process that suggested some interesting group divisions within the village, made it even more appealing. A final point in its favor was the recent arrival of a hundred Gypsies due to floods in a neighboring village—an invasion greeted with considerable displeasure by Kislapos. This presented an interesting case of attitudes toward, and stereotypes of, Gypsies and their assimilation into a community.

Later I found that some of these factors favorable for my research, such as the high percentage of agricultural workers, the recent arrival of the Gypsies, and the relatively small population, were due to the village's poor position in the rural transportation network and the lack of other local work possibilities. But that situation is not unique to Kislapos. The village is a somewhat extreme and accelerated example of a migration toward urban centers that is taking place in Hungary, much of the rest of Europe, and, for that matter, in much of the world. In Kislapos's case the acceleration is partly a result of the very success of the collective farm, as well as other local factors.

In any case, the above circumstances and Kislapos's position in the ranges of variation presented throughout this work should be taken into consideration in generalizing to the rest of the countryside. It is hoped that this book will broaden the Western view of Hungarian village society, past and present, and facilitate such generalization.

Chapter 1

The Village

Kislapos is a small, flat village of about nine hundred people in north-central Hungary. It consists of a core of houses and gardens, farm and public buildings, and a Roman Catholic church, surrounded on all sides by fields, meadows, and pasture (see Map 1.1).

GEOGRAPHY

Lapos, as the villagers call it, sits on the northern edge of the Great Hungarian Plain, about twenty kilometers south of clearly visible mountains, just below a well-known wine-growing band on the foothills of two mountain ranges. It is located in the northern part of the region between the Danube and the Tisza rivers and lies on the bank of a large stream called the Farkas. This river, originating near the Czechoslovakian border, flows south between two mountain ranges to enter the plains and joins with other rivers south of Kislapos to flow ultimately into the Tisza.

The village is well suited and situated for agriculture. It enjoys a temperate continental climate with some snow in the cold, dry winters and extreme heat only rarely in the wetter summers. With total precipitation averaging about 550 mm. per year, this region can produce a good grain crop. A tapable water table makes it possible to raise vegetable crops requiring more moisture.

Another factor contributing to this suitability for agriculture is the Farkas. In the past the untamed river frequently flooded, leaving the area a rich semimarshland with good soil. But this contribution has been somewhat double-edged. Flood waters still threaten occasionally, even though the river's channel was straightened and moved out of the village proper and its embankments built up in the years just before World War I to prevent flooding (thus providing the highest ground for some miles in an otherwise flat terrain). More important, a high water table often makes large areas of farmland near the river virtually useless. Fields further to the east, however, with equally good soil and the advantage of being a little higher, are very productive, while those still further east, at the border of

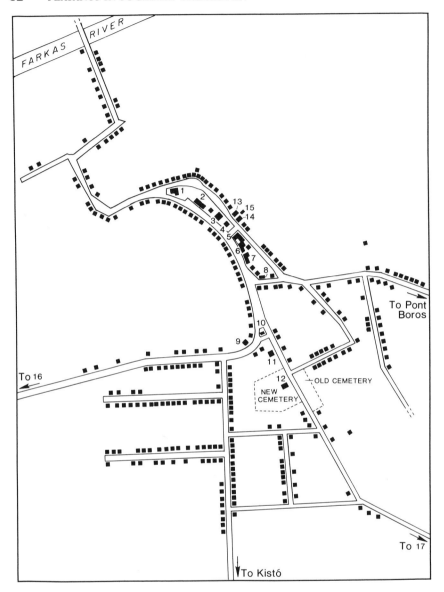

To Pont Boros
To 16
To 17
To Kistó

MAP 1.1   Kislapos Today
Community Buildings
  1. Roman Catholic church
  2. School
  3. Cultural house (Népház)
  4. Water works
  5. Hangya general store and tavern
  6. Council hall and medical consulting room

7. Post office, butcher shop, and fire station
8. Creamery collection point
9. Mill
10. Weigh station
11. Hangya storage building
12. Mortuary
13. Collective farm headquarters (old Kossuth)
14. Grain storage barns
15. Preschool
16. Collective farm cattle barns (old Petőfi)
17. Collective farm cow, calf, and horse barns and horticultural greenhouses (old Gold Spike)

the village, are sandier and suited only for grape and wine production—never economically important in Lapos.

Administratively, Kislapos is part of Homok District, the seat of which is Boros, ten kilometers to the southeast.[1] Both, in turn, look to Eger, seat of Heves County (in which they both lie) for higher administrative authority.

In other ways it is not so easy to place Lapos into larger geographical and social groupings. It is in a transitional region, part of neither the hilly grape-growing region nor the mountains to the north. Yet its strongest connections, both economic and social, have been with these areas. On the other hand, while it is part of the Great Plain, it does not share in the settlement pattern so typical of the plain. Lapos lies five to ten kilometers north of the edge of the region of *tanya*-s,[2] scattered farmsteads spread over the countryside, so characteristic of southeastern Hungary. Before World War II there were only four or five such farmsteads in the fields of Kislapos; since then their residents have either moved into the village or died, so that an inhabited core only has resulted.

Lapos also does not belong to any of the ethnic-like groupings surrounding it. It is not a *palóc* village (one of a large grouping of villages in the hills and mountains of north-central Hungary exhibiting broad similarities in dialect, family structure, house style, folk art and other areas), nor is it one of the *jász* or *kun* (Cuman) communities to the south and west (an area partly populated by descendants of tribes entering the Danube basin after the initial Magyar migration).

1. Átány, the village of the fine studies by Fél and Hofer (1969, 1973), is not far from Kislapos. Despite the short distance separating them, there has traditionally been little contact between the two villages. The fact that Kislapos is solidly Roman Catholic, whereas Átány is Calvinist, has undoubtedly contributed to this.

2. For simplicity, following the example of Fél and Hofer (1969), the plurals of all Hungarian nouns in this text will be indicated by the nominative singular form followed by a -s and not by the appropriate Hungarian plural form.

A view of flat Kislapos from winter snow-touched fields. The Roman Catholic Church is on the left and the old collective farm headquarters, with its small steepled cupola, is visible at the right.

It is a small, predominantly agricultural community that, at least in the view of its inhabitants, has for greater than half a century prospered somewhat more than its neighbors. Throughout the period of study, Lapos has had a population numbering only one-half of those of its nearest neighbors, Gödör, Barnaföld, and Kistó, and only one-fourth or one-fifth of the larger Pont and Zöldfa, a little further away.[3] In terms of size it is relatively even smaller, encompassing only 1,803 *hold*-s (1,038 hectares or 2,560 acres; 1 hold = 0.57 hectares = 1.42 acres). The areas of the nearby communities are all considerably larger; each has 1.4 to 1.8 times as much land per person as Kislapos.

Agriculture has always been the main form of employment in this peasant village. In the 1930s all of its inhabitants, with the exception of only a few storekeepers, tradesmen, teachers, and railroad workers, derived

3. Taking Hungary as a whole, Kislapos's size ranks near the median for villages. Extrapolation from 1973 data places it somewhere between the fortieth and forty-fifth percentiles in terms of community size. However, communities as small as Lapos constitute less than 10 percent of Hungary's population and less than 20 percent of its village population (Andorka 1979: 25–26).

their livelihood from the land. Government census figures indicate that even in 1970 more than two-thirds of the male and four-fifths of the female active earners acquired their income through agriculture. Both these ratios are higher than in any of the nearby communities; in fact, they are the highest for all villages in Lapos's district and higher than in most Hungarian villages (see Table 1.1).

The peasants have been fairly successful at their livelihood. When in the years 1974 and 1975 the village's collective farm merged with the farms of five other settlements, Kislapos's premerger collective was found to have been the most successful and financially solvent of them all. This relative prosperity has not been limited to the post-World War II period. Although at the turn of the century a sizable part of Lapos's fields was owned by outsiders, by the end of the war the village residents, expanding their holdings, had bought considerable land in the fields of Kistó and Gödör to the west and in Pont and Dombos to the north. Even by the 1930s, Kislapos had gone successfully into raising pigs and cattle for meat, milk, and quality breeding and had adopted intensive agriculture to a greater degree than its neighbors.

This agricultural success cannot be explained by any special natural quality of Kislapos. Its soil, though good in some areas, is not extraordinary, nor is it on the whole significantly better than in neighboring communities. It is rather due to the villagers' hard work, resolution, and willingness to innovate in intensive farming—as well as, perhaps, the necessity of taking on such work-intensive practices because of the village's small size and relatively high population density—that the village has performed so well in the agricultural sphere.

Lapos has remained so predominantly an agricultural settlement because it has a somewhat isolated position in the transportation and industrial network of the area. This is especially important because of its relatively great distance from any major industrial or mining concentration. The village lies in one of the few areas of Hungary outside a fifty-kilometer radius of any major industrial or mining center. Its neighbors, Kistó, Barnaföld, and Gödör, lie along a well-traveled, well-surfaced main road between the larger towns of Boros and Gyöngyös. Pont to the north is on the major railway line connecting the industrial cities of Budapest and Miskolc, and this fact has for a long time predominated in its economy. Kislapos, on the other hand, has only a paved but badly potholed, narrow spur road leading in one direction to Kistó and in the other to an equally bad route going to Pont or to a road leading to Boros. For many years workers commuting weekly to industrial jobs in centers like Budapest and Miskolc were left with no other option than to plod along the Farkas embankment to and from the Pont railway station in the dark in both summer and winter. This they did from the late 1940s on in increasing numbers. Though infrequent daily bus service to Pont and Boros, introduced in the 1950s and 1960s, has improved their plight, the lack of

Table 1.1   Population Distribution by Principal Occupation,
1900–1970

Year of Census	Location	PERCENTAGE OF TOTAL POPULATION					
		Agri-culture	Industry	Com-merce	Trans-port	Civil Service	Other
1900	Kislapos	93.18	1.17	1.27	0.10	2.53	1.75
	Homok District	83.22	7.60	1.15	0.75	1.76	5.52
	Contemporary Hungary	60.8	16.0	4.8	2.9	3.6	11.9
1910	Kislapos	95.19	1.54	1.13	0.00	1.43	0.72
	Homok District	82.82	8.33	1.24	1.36	1.56	4.69
	Contemporary Hungary	55.9	19.3	5.4	3.8	3.6	12.0
1920	Kislapos	93.26	3.14	0.55	1.11	1.11	0.83
	Homok District	84.11	7.63	1.26	1.60	1.37	4.04
	Contemporary Hungary	55.7	18.6	5.6	4.3	4.3	11.5
1930	Kislapos	91.81	3.52	1.06	0.09	1.41	2.11
	Homok District	81.15	8.89	1.78	1.62	2.03	4.53
	Contemporary Hungary	51.8	21.0	5.9	3.7	4.6	13.0
1941	Kislapos	88.89	5.60	2.12	0.59	1.44	1.36
	Homok District	79.39	9.27	2.55	1.95	3.54	3.30
	Contemporary Hungary	49.1	23.1	6.0	4.0	4.5	13.3
1949	Kislapos	84.82	6.96	1.95	3.14	2.37	0.76
	Homok District	78.64	8.76	1.84	2.37	2.67	5.73
	Contemporary Hungary	49.1	23.1	4.8	4.8	7.0	11.2
1960	Kislapos	67.34	17.55	2.45	5.68		6.99†
	Homok District	58.96	20.06	3.49	5.72		11.77†
	Contemporary Hungary	35.5	33.0	5.3	7.0	6.8	12.4
1970	Kislapos	75.79	12.53	1.89‡	4.95‡		4.84†‡
	Homok District	53.65	28.23	3.78‡	6.05‡		8.30†‡
	Contemporary Hungary	28.7	41.5	6.4	8.2		15.2†

NOTE: Population includes dependents.

† Includes "civil service."

‡ Approximate. Although 1970 census figures had "active earners" and their dependents divided into the five categories listed here, "inactive earners" and their dependents were divided merely into "agriculture," "industry," and "other." These inactive "other" were broken down into the categories of "commerce," "transport," and "other" on the basis of extrapolations drawn from their respective numbers among active earners and their dependents.

nearby industry has continued to dampen the appeal of working in factories while living in Lapos. The necessity of spending whole weeks away
from home and family in rented rooms or workers' quarters and the psychological and monetary cost of doing so have caused most of Lapos's
residents living in this way ultimately to move nearer the place of work or
to come back to agricultural life in the village.

Kislapos's small size has brought with it the disadvantages of small
communities. For example, it has never had its own doctor. In years past
doctors have been called in from Kistó, Pont, or other villages. Even now
Lapos's doctor, who lives in Kistó, has office hours only twice weekly in
Lapos, though he comes at other times when called. Occasionally in
recent years paramedics living in the village have assumed some health
care duties, including giving shots. Only sporadically has Lapos had its
own veterinarian, despite its considerable livestock.

Lapos has never had its own priest, at least as far as anyone can remember, although its Roman Catholic church dates back to about 1790. It has
traditionally shared Kistó's priest. Before World War II, Sunday masses,
which alternated between Lapos and Kistó, were held biweekly in the
village. Now both villages have weekly masses despite decreased attendance; the priest rushes to Kislapos following the worship in Kistó.

RECENT DEMOGRAPHIC CHANGES

The recent decline in Kislapos's population has further accentuated
these disadvantages. In 1969 the village was judged too small to support
its own town council president, and that position was eliminated. Several
years later its nursery school was closed because of the paucity of pre-
schoolers, and in 1974 the upper four grades of the eight-grade village
elementary school were moved to Boros because of declining enrollment.

Kislapos has not always had a declining population, not even throughout the period studied. Nor has it been alone among local villages to have
lost some of its population in recent years. In fact, for the past hundred
years its population curve exhibits strikingly the same tendency as all its
nearby neighbors in the district (see Figure 1.1). With minor interrup-
tions there was a steady growth of population until a peak was reached in
the 1930s and 1940s (and in Zöldfa's case in the 1950s), followed by a
considerable decline in the 1960s through to the present.[4]

For the most part, the peak around the war and the subsequent decline
can be traced to a few major factors. First is the war itself, with an enforced

4. Roughly the same broad pattern has been exhibited by Hungarian villages as
a whole except that, as in Zöldfa, total Hungarian village population increased
until 1960, dipping only afterward (Andorka 1979: 23).

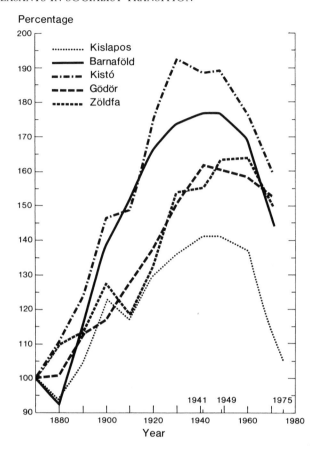

FIGURE 1.1   Population Change for Local Villages

social and economic disruption that brought a significant drop in the birthrate. The second is the too rapid forced industrialization of Hungary by the Stalinist government of the early 1950s, which created a tremendous demand for labor to fill new factory and construction jobs, particularly in the cities. Like most such industrial spurts in the rest of Europe and the world, it generated a tremendous migration of hundreds of thousands to the cities, both as new inhabitants and as commuters. The effects of this policy would not have been as dramatic had it not occurred simultaneously with other policies seriously dampening the motivation of peasants to continue working on the land. This third reason, the neglect and subordination of agriculture in order to build up industry, took a number of forms, including forced deliveries of agricultural goods to the state at low prices, an aggressive drive against wealthier peasants, "peace" loans, and a general lack of government investment in and support of agriculture.

To these can be added the final phase of farm collectivization, completed in the early 1960s. Its attendant uncertainties for peasants and the continuing attraction of more secure and usually better-paying jobs in the still rapidly expanding industrial and construction sectors maintained or even increased migration from the countryside.

The importance of the lack of nonagricultural work opportunities for people living in Lapos becomes especially clear when one realizes that from 1941 to 1970 the population of rural communities or villages in Hungary declined by only about 5 percent, whereas the agricultural work force was sharply reduced, by one-half. In 1949, fully 73 percent of the village work force was employed in the agricultural sector, whereas by 1970 this proportion had dropped to 40 percent (Andorka 1979: 23, 65–66).

In Lapos the growth in the early part of the period was, both in absolute terms and relative to its size, smaller than that of its neighbors; the later decline was relatively greater. The slower growth has several possible causes. One is the high population density at the turn of the century in Lapos, a village capable of keeping only a portion of the considerable natural increase. Indeed, Lapos throughout the twentieth century has had a high outflow of people, an outflow that the birthrate matched until the 1950s (see Table 1.2). In addition, Lapos's inhabitants have been willing to take somewhat more risks than those of its neighbors. Besides their greater willingness to try the innovative techniques of intensive agriculture in the 1930s, some of them were far more venturesome, trying to improve their situation by working in America for a time in the early years of this century. In 1910, for example, more than 3 percent were in America, compared to less than 0.5 percent for the rest of the district (though villages to the north and in other parts of the country showed higher ratios than Lapos). Thus, Lapos's inhabitants may have been more willing or, due to economic circumstances, felt more impelled to try to improve their fortune elsewhere.

Kislapos's relatively faster decline has been due to other reasons, including its poor position in the transport network, its lack of services, its size, and its lack of local nonagricultural work opportunities in an age when agricultural labor is increasingly looked down upon.[5] Ironically,

5. These factors seem to be important nationally as well. Erdei (1971: 168), dealing with the demographic future of villages in the area around the city of Szeged, indicates that the future of some villages depends on the development of transit connections to Szeged. He predicts that, if these improve sufficiently, there will be more commuters and the villages' populations will decrease but little; if they do not improve, the loss of population will accelerate. Andorka (1979: 26)

the financial success of its collective farm, enabling parents to educate their children and to buy housing for them in the city, may also have contributed to the outmigration and population decline.

Lapos's population curve, in summation, is a resultant of two trends. The first is a birthrate that with the exception of the two world wars has shown a steady decline throughout this century (see Figure 1.2 and Table 1.2). The other is a continued high outflow of people. Reflecting the increased flight of the village's youth and the resulting increased age of its population (see Table 1.3), the first trend has accelerated and the second increased in recent years. Thus, we have a somewhat unusual picture. Kislapos is a village whose people are prospering, partially because of its size and location and the extra effort its inhabitants have made because of these factors and partially due to the success of the collective farm. At the same time it is a village that appears to be dying precisely because of its size and location and the nature and success of its collective farm.

MATERIAL IMPROVEMENT AND PHYSICAL EXPANSION

Kislapos has also changed physically in the years since the war. The quality of its buildings has improved significantly. Many old houses have been torn down and new, healthier, and more comfortable ones built in their places; others have been significantly renovated. Thatched roofs have been almost totally replaced by tile, straw-filled dried mud bricks by fired clay ones, open chimneys and smoky rooms by better heating and cooking arrangements and ventilation. There is running water in many houses, and indoor toilets have replaced outhouses in some. Fresh piped water is at most only a few steps away from all houses and has completely replaced often polluted well water. Electricity has reached every house.

---

points out that nationally from 1960 to 1975 villages with less than 500 inhabitants lost population most rapidly; those with 500 to 3,000 decreased more slowly; medium-sized villages of 3,000 to 5,000 remained largely unchanged; and those of larger rural communities actually grew. He notes that "the lack of a nearby city is one of the most important factors in the decline of villages" (ibid.: 27).

The latter factor looms especially important when one takes into account that, in 1970 in Hungary, 40 percent of those in industry (including white-collar workers) lived in smaller towns and villages, but only 22 percent worked in industrial plants located in these towns and villages; the situation is even more extreme in construction. Thus, in 1970 more than one-third of the active workers living in towns and villages commuted to work in another town, the majority daily (ibid.: 94–95). These general tendencies and the movement of people out of the agricultural sector underlie Lapos's demographic problems—problems heightened by the fact that Boros, the district seat, though relatively large, is still inadequately developed as an urban center (ibid.: 29) and offers few industrial and service jobs for potential commuters from Lapos.

Table 1.2 Population Fluctuations in Kislapos

A. BIRTHS, DEATHS, AND POPULATION CHANGE, KISLAPOS, 1900–1968

	1901–10	1911–20	1921–30	1931–41	1942–49	1950–60	1961–68
Live births	403	298	373	321	185	220	73
Deaths	213	217	197	198	125	136	105
Net outflow†	239	−25	124	79	60	118	124‡
Net change	−49	106	52	44	0	−34	−156‡

B. AVERAGE ANNUAL BIRTHS, DEATHS, AND POPULATION CHANGE, KISLAPOS, 1900–1968

	1901–10	1911–20	1921–30	1931–41	1942–49	1950–60	1961–68
Live births	40.3	29.8	37.3	29.2	23.1	20.0	9.1
Deaths	21.3	21.7	19.7	18.0	15.6	12.4	13.1
Net outflow†	23.9	−2.5	12.4	7.2	7.5	10.7	15.5‡
Net change	−4.9	10.6	5.2	4.0	0	−3.1	−19.5‡

C. AVERAGE ANNUAL BIRTHS AND DEATHS BY HISTORICAL PERIOD, KISLAPOS, 1900–1968

	1901–14	1915–19	1920–40	1941–45	1946–56	1957–68
Live births	39.4	22.2	34.3	19.4	25.1	9.9
Deaths	21.9	22.2	18.7	17.8	12.8	12.8

NOTE: Calculated from the 1970 government census (indicating the population of Kislapos at census times dating from 1870 to 1970) and from the census records of annual births and deaths in Kislapos from 1901 to 1968.

† Negative figures indicate a net inmigration for the period in question.

‡ The net population change and net outflow from 1961 to 1970 were multiplied by 0.8 to reach this figure.

Several of the main streets, in the past frequently a sea of mud for half the year, have been paved, and sidewalks have been laid along all streets.

Several new public buildings have gone up in recent years, including a new school, nursery school, and a waterworks; others have been modified to expand the services they offer. The number of antennas visible reflects the fact that most homes in Lapos now have television, a far cry from the 1930s, when but one wealthy peasant had a radio. Changes in the way of life associated with all of the above improvements have been even greater. Finally, Kislapos has expanded greatly both in size and in the

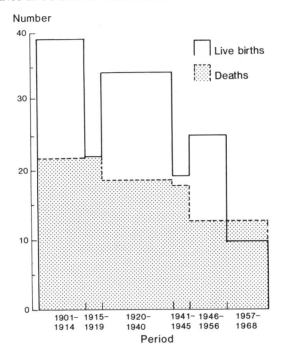

Number

FIGURE 1.2   Average Annual Number of Births and Deaths,
Kislapos, 1900–1968

number of houses. There are now around three hundred houses, compared to 167 in 1900, though the village is actually losing population.

At the turn of the century Kislapos was only a small nucleus of the
present core, with the major part extending away from the old banks of
the Farkas, surrounding the church and public land. A few other houses
were scattered along the other bank (see Map 1.2). This nucleus was
much more densely packed than the present core. Frequently twenty or
thirty people lived in one yard, cramped into four small dwellings lined
up in one long building or located in two shorter structures facing one
another. By the end of World War I some expansion of the nucleus was
evident, as houses appeared on the side of the street connecting the old
core to the new Farkas and on the beginnings of streets leading away from
the core. Even a few scattered farmsteads appeared on the edge of the
village center. Aiding this expansion were a number of factors, not the
least of which was the desire for greater living space and room for barns
and other farm buildings for growing peasant enterprises. Another was
the consolidation in 1911–12 of villagers' scattered small parcels of land

Table 1.3   Population Distribution by Age Group, 1900–1970

Year of Census	Location	PERCENTAGE OF TOTAL POPULATION			
		Age 0–19	Age 20–39	Age 40–59	Age 60+
1900	Kislapos	50.19	26.32	17.64	5.85
	Homok District	47.99	26.58	18.39	7.03
1910	Kislapos	47.59	24.97	19.65	7.78
	Homok District	47.63	26.36	18.23	7.78
1920	Kislapos	44.60	28.07	18.47	8.86
	Homok District	44.97	27.95	17.88	9.20
1930	Kislapos	41.41	29.07	18.24	11.28
	Homok District	41.13	30.58	18.39	9.90
1941	Kislapos	38.08	27.48	23.58	10.86
	Homok District	40.37	27.04	21.47	11.13
1949	Kislapos	32.57	30.28	25.28	11.87
	Homok District	35.27	28.26	23.53	12.94
1960	Kislapos	29.26	28.38	25.68	16.68
	Homok District	33.78	27.82	23.13	15.26
1970	Kislapos	25.58	23.37	27.05	24.00
	Homok District	31.63	24.65	24.30	19.41

into larger units, which made desirable the relocation of one's house at least nearer to, if not on, one's main holding. A third was the return of some of the villagers from America with valuable earned dollars, as well as the arrival of newcomers eager to acquire land and new houses.

Events following World War I further contributed to this expansion. Land reform had been long overdue in Hungary. With two or three million landless agricultural laborers living in poverty and much of its land concentrated in the hands of several hundred families and the Roman Catholic Church, Hungary was a nation of great inequalities. The defeat in World War I and the demise of the Dual Monarchy in 1918, along with a groundswell among the people brought about the formation of Mihály Károlyi's democratic republic.[6] Among other policies the government

6. Customary English usage has been followed with respect to personal names: the surname follows the Christian name. In Hungarian, the surname precedes the Christian name. Thus, Mihály Károlyi (or Michael Károlyi, as he is known in English) is known as Károlyi Mihály in Hungary.

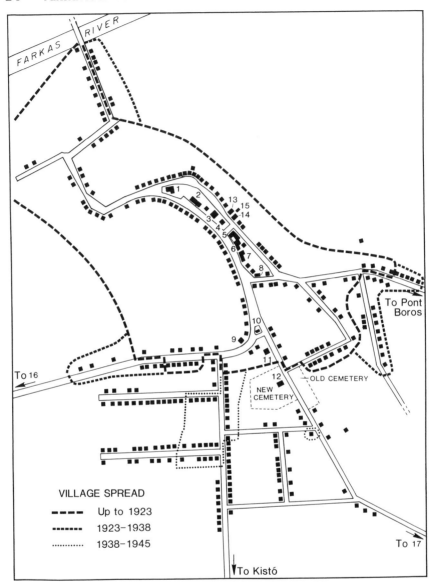

MAP 1.2   The Growth of Kislapos

ultimately instituted land reform, which President Károlyi himself started by dividing his own sizeable estates near Pont.

The land reform was short-lived, however, because of the government's inability to deal with the intransigent Allied Powers and the resulting takeover by Béla Kun's Soviet Republic in March 1919. The Soviet government canceled most of the land reform so that large landholdings could be easily converted into collective farms. This decision was unpopular with the peasantry and made it easier for large landholders to reclaim their lands following the demise of the equally short-lived Soviet Republic and the reactionary takeover of power.

To placate the land-hungry peasantry, the new leadership instituted a limited land reform in 1920, affecting only a small fraction of the country's arable land. Under its terms, big landholders selected from their own holdings land to distribute in return for compensation. Larger parcels of land went to members of the army, the gendarmerie, and the military Heroes Order. Less than a third of the allotted 948,000 hold-s was offered to the landless and small landowning peasants, who constituted almost three-quarters of the 411,000 recipients. This amounted to only slightly more than one hold per person (Berend and Ránki 1973: 461).

Kislapos, without any large landholders of its own, received land from the holdings of Mihály Károlyi to the north, in particular from the estate called Puszta. When the reactionary takeover seemed imminent, Károlyi fled Hungary in exile. Because he was considered a traitor by the new rightist government, his holdings and land were taken over. In 1922–23 many poorer peasants in Lapos received "proletarian land," one or two hold-s of low-lying land to the north of the river, for which they had to pay. In the following two or three years, small plots of land for future housing and perhaps a hold of land for cultivation and pasture were allotted from land near the central core to poorer families, who, of course, paid for it. The former owners of this richer land were compensated with double the amount of poorer-quality land on the Károlyi estate on the other side of the Farkas. In this way the village spread toward the Farkas, and a number of new streets on the other side of the town were opened up (see Map 1.2).

In the late 1930s and early 1940s, "children's" land was distributed, again from the Károlyi holdings, to those landless and smallholders who had three or more children and who could meet the stiff credit terms for repayment—terms that were stiffest for those least able to afford it. Again, small plots of one or two hold-s were offered. At the same time in the New Settlement part of Lapos, furthest away from the river, house plots were distributed. As in the past "reform," local owners of this land were compensated with land from Puszta.

With the end of World War II, the driving out of the Germans, occupation of the country by Russian troops, and the establishment of a more democratic leadership, real land reform was finally instituted nationally in March 1945. In Lapos it was largely carried out in the months following, although there were numerous revisions in the next year or two to correct injustices. Again, there was no big landholder in the village, so attempts were made to obtain land elsewhere. Puszta's land was no longer available because a settlement had been established there in 1941, so leaders turned to Kistó, where there had been several large landholders. They managed to obtain several hundred acres of plowland for Kislapos's poorest, although the land remained part of Kistó. At this time, numerous houseplots were distributed in what was called the New Settlement and owners were compensated from the village common land. Little real payment was demanded for these plots. The years since then have been spent building on these pieces of land and continuing Lapos's physical expansion.

Chapter 2

Social Stratification

Hungary prior to World War II was a nation of great inequalities. In the countryside there were on one extreme estates of thousands of hold-s in the hands of a few members of the old aristocracy and the rising rich capitalists; on the other hand, as the agricultural historian Péter Gunst (1976: 381–391) has demonstrated, there was a mass of three million agricultural proletarians, two-thirds of the agricultural population and a third of the nation's, who had little or no land. In between was a relatively small number, about a fifth of the total agricultural work force, who can be called self-supporting peasants.

A look at the breakdown of landholdings in 1935 will make clear just how great were these extremes. Those owning over 1,000 hold-s comprised less than one-tenth of 1 percent of the landholders, yet their holdings made up just less than 30 percent of the land; those with over 100 hold-s made up about seven-tenths of 1 percent of the landholders but owned over 48 percent. On the other end of the scale, fully 38.5 percent of the landholders owned under one hold but accounted for only 1.5 percent of total holdings. Only 10.2 percent of the land was owned by the 72.7 percent of the landholders with five hold-s or less.

Much of this extreme fragmentation was due to the government's land "reform" of the 1920s, which aimed not so much at a true reform but rather at appeasing and coopting the recipients. Revolutionary events at the end of World War I and land reforms in the nearby countries,[1] not to mention the existing inequalities in Hungary, had raised to a peak the thirst for land action among the rural poor—a thirst that even the leaders of the right, newly returned to power and looking to the past, knew could not be quenched by words alone. This led ultimately to the actions of the 1920s, by which hundreds of thousands of minuscule plots were sold to

1. For example, in Poland, where pre-World War I conditions of landownership were almost as extreme as in Hungary, land reform led to significant changes. There 77 percent of those engaged in agriculture in 1931 were landowning peasants, and only one-fifth of the landowners were smallholders (Andorka 1979: 59).

the landless and the smallholders at unfavorable terms. No limits were put on the largest landholdings, nor did the plots given out enable the recipients to be anywhere near self-supporting. The intention of the ruling classes was to preserve the present landholding structure as much as possible by introducing the greatest number of people at the least cost into the strata of landholders, thus inducing them to support the continuation of the landholding system through their "common" interests as landholders. Indeed, the terms of the sales did for the following decade make land reform less appetizing for the poor (Gunst 1976: 381–385).

Kislapos was no exception to this pattern. Though it had no large estates within its small boundaries, it was bounded on several sides by them. Throughout the 1930s and into the years of World War II, many of Lapos's poorer laborers earned their income on them. Lacking such estates itself, Lapos was in some ways a truncated version of this society, with the wealthier peasants filling the topmost stratum in most village affairs. On the other hand, Lapos was well entrenched in the surrounding social network with its concentrated wealth and its laboring poor, and the village society reflected it.

PRELIMINARY DISTINCTIONS

Landownership was the foundation on which Kislapos's peasant society rested. Land has always provided (and even today under a vastly different social system continues to provide) the main source of nourishment and income for villagers. Just as important, a family's relation to land (that is, its possession of it or relation to those who did possess it) largely determined its social and economic status in the community and, for the most part, its way of life.

Acquiring land was a major goal of almost every family in Lapos. Land was the chief form of wealth in the countryside as well as the main income producer. As a limited and relatively scarce means of production, it served as a major basis of power. But to most people who had little or no land, this was not its chief meaning. They, too, desired land for its wealth and were quite capable of ranking their fellow villagers in terms of it. Moreover, they clearly felt the power that others' landownership exercised over them. But ultimately they viewed land from a different perspective. For most it was not only the source of their daily bread; it also provided the opportunity for a family to be self-sufficient, to be independent of the orders and whims of others.

Thus it was that in the Hungarian countryside landownership provided the basis for social stratification. Male villagers and their families could easily be ranked according to the amount of land they owned. A first approximation of these rankings in Kislapos would produce the following classification: wealthy peasants (*nagygazda*-s) owning 20–25 hold-s

Table 2.1   Pre-World War II Status Categories

gazda	cselédtartó (keeps cseléd-s) team-owner	wealthy —— nagygazda middle	magángaz-dálkodó (private farmer)
arató-napszámos (harvester/ day laborer)	részes munkás summás cseléd	smallholder — kisbirtokos landless —— nincstelen	

(about 28–35 acres or 12–15 hectares) or more; middle peasants (*közép-paraszt*-s) with 5–20 hold-s (7–28 acres or 3–12 hectares); smallholders (*kisbirtokos*-s or *törpebirtokos*-s) with 5 hold-s (7 acres or 3 hectares) or less; and the landless (*nincstelen*-s).[2]

These quantities, of course, are not arbitrary. They represent differences in the abilities of families owning such amounts to support themselves, subject to extremes in the sizes of families. For example, middle peasant families were able to support themselves on their own land and with their own labor.[3] They generally could neither hire laborers to work for them for long periods nor rent their land to others for share-cropping, as did the wealthier peasants. Nor did they have to supplement their income from the land, as did the smallholders, by working as laborers or harvesters for others or by renting or sharecropping land. They were mainly self-supporting.

2. Strictly speaking, not all these categories were used by the villagers in the past. They are categories that official sources (e.g., agricultural census reports and agricultural experts) used even before World War II. They have come into common usage by the postwar government, which has placed emphasis on men owning as much land as they could work themselves, and by analysts of the rural past. They are commonly accepted throughout Hungary today and are used even by older villagers in characterizing their fellowmen of prewar days. I use them because they reflect useful distinctions made by villagers themselves. The villagers' own categories map nicely onto them, keeping corresponding distinctions. See Table 2.1 for a rough portrayal of the correspondence of the villagers' categories to those I utilize. Explanations of the villagers' categories are given in the text.

3. However, the ranges of acreage offered above are approximations. Sárkány (1978: 67) suggests that in the hillier Varsány, a community northwest of Lapos, six or seven hold-s was the lower limit of land from which one family could earn a living; twenty hold-s was the upper limit for a holding which did not require regular outside help.

Wealthy peasants, on the other hand, had more than enough land for their own needs and more than they were able to work by themselves. At least some of their land was worked by the labor of others, whether hired laborers, tenants, or sharecroppers. Moreover, the work role of the wealthy peasant differed considerably from that of the middle peasant. For the wealthiest of peasants—those with 50 or more hold-s—the emphasis was on directing the labor of others, not on working oneself.

The smallholders were in just the opposite situation, owning some land but not enough to support their families with it. Surplus family labor had to be channeled into other income-producing activities. Though the members of some families went off to the mines, factories, and railroads in order to supplement the production of the limited land cultivated by the rest of the family, most people in the prewar period in Lapos were forced to turn to the land of others. Under fortunate circumstances, they might rent or sharecrop land. Otherwise they could work as wheat harvesters or day laborers, or even contract themselves out as farm workers for longer periods.

The lowest stratum was that of the landless, whose plight was often worse because they lacked their own housing. Because of this and other circumstances, they were frequently not considered full members of the community; and indeed, they often were only transient inhabitants. Several possibilities were open to them. Some would hire themselves out as farmhands for a year, at a large estate or for one of the wealthy peasants, receiving mainly payment in kind and living quarters. Some primarily tended animals or worked as teamsters; others did more general work. There were more specialties on the large estates, including better-paying barrel-making and blacksmithing. Others, with more specialized knowledge of valuable crops like tobacco and melons, which required considerable care, preparation, and intensive labor over a long period, would work these crops for larger landholders for a year in return for payment in kind and living quarters.[4] Additional full-time positions open to this stratum were such denigrated ones as swineherds for the community and maids for the wealthier peasants. Some chose a combination of seasonal jobs, including contracted labor, harvesting, day labor, and sharecropping.

This preliminary classification is not exhaustive. First, there were several positions in the village that did not belong to any of these strata. These included members of the village intelligentsia, such as the village notary-secretary and the school principal and teachers; then there were

---

4. Gyula Illyés (1967: 260), in his widely acclaimed *Puszták népe* (People of the Puszta), a partly autobiographical sociographical description of life on these estates, notes that the tobacco growers' status in the estate hierarchy was near the bottom, despite the knowledge necessary for the work. In some ways the estate's hierarchy was a reversal of the hierarchy outside it.

storekeepers, craftsmen, blacksmiths, and road maintenance men. Since the former group received its income from the use of village land, and the latter often owned small plots of land with which they supplemented the income from their trades, all can still be relatively easily placed into a framework derived from the approximations by landownership.

A more serious classificatory problem is that, although each of these categories was distinct, the situations in which the members of different categories found themselves often shaded into one another, particularly at the lower end of the scale. This overlap was often caused by such factors as the number of members in the family, the death of the male head of the household, and the marriage status of younger adult members of the household—factors that even today are of supreme importance in determining a Hungarian family's living standards. Land quality was also a factor.

A more basic overlap was that between members of the smallholders and the landless. There was often little real difference between owning one hold of land without a team and some of the implements to work it, and not owning any land at all. Thus, the standards of living of these two groups frequently offered few differences.

Second, members of both types of households often varied their sources of outside income (supplementary in the case of smallholders, main and supplementary in the case of the landless) from year to year. In fact, different members of the same family in both groups could be engaged in different forms of outside labor; some of these forms were shared by both groups.[5]

This, in turn, leads to the third overlap and a cross-cutting distinction, that between *részes munkás*-s and *cseléd ember*-s (literally, share workers and servant people, respectively). The former were essentially sharecroppers and laborers hired for tasks like harvesting and hoeing for a share of the crop worked. The latter were hired hands, whose labor was contracted for a period of a year or less by a wealthier peasant or landowner with a set payment, mostly in kind, as well as housing. A prime distinction between these two categories is the degree of independence they enjoyed. The cseléd-s (hired farm hands) were under the constant direction and orders of the proprietor, whereas részes munkás-s, though working under the basic directives of the landholder or his subordinate, found more scope for their initiative. This was reflected in the methods of their payment. Though dependent upon weather and soil for the amount of their income, by dint of their hard effort and care részes munkás-s (especially sharecroppers) could play a direct role in increasing their own incomes. Cseléd-s, on the other hand, received a fixed annual pay-

5. In view of these similarities between the landless and smallholders, Erdei (1940: 145) argues that fully three-quarters of the Hungarian rural population consisted of "proletarians and semi-proletarians."

ment independent of the year's production; thus, they were not motivated to produce or achieve more.

This distinction found its way into the characteristics attributed to the two groups by landholders in Kislapos. Many considered the cseléd-s to be lazy, to like easier work, to like to take orders, and to do what they were told but not to concern themselves with the results of their work. One old smallholder said that "on the large estates, if the work did not progress, they yearned for the sun to set," and that "they were used to being told that they should go plow the corn land, and the next day would get up, harness the oxen and go wherever the oxen wanted." In contrast to this was the non-cseléd, who was said to like being independent with no one above him and who was motivated to work hard and improve his own situation.

Of course, the decision to be a cseléd or to take on other kinds of work was not based solely on such alleged characteristics but also depended on a family's material situation and other circumstances beyond the control of the family members. For example, death or prolonged illness of the father often profoundly affected a family's livelihood. Occasionally poorer villagers developed close multistranded relations with those better off and afforded themselves a wider range of economic and social opportunities. Thus, two broad considerations must be taken into account in order to understand the structure of rural Hungarian society. The first is the complexity of the arrangements in which members of different strata found themselves. The second is the amount of land owned by families and the relationships of people with little or no land to those with larger holdings.

These same considerations are important even today. Though land itself is no longer central, past relationships and attitudes associated with the various strata form the basis for attitudes and relationships in contemporary village society. A thorough grounding in the distinctions and relationships of the past is vital for a sound grasp of the present.

MIDDLE PEASANTS

It is the stratum of middle peasants (középparaszt-s) that one associates with the Hungarian countryside and with peasantry in general. In some ways this is misleading and in others quite appropriate. It is deceiving in that this was by no means the most numerous stratum in the countryside prior to World War II. That distinction was shared by the smallholders and the landless poor. Nationwide in 1935 those with five to twenty-five hold-s totaled less than one-quarter of the landowners (not to mention those with no land at all) and in Lapos somewhat closer to one-sixth.[6] In many

6. According to the national agricultural survey of 1935.

Table 2.2   Distribution of Farms by Size, Kislapos

Size of Farm in Cadastral Hold-s	1941		1949	
	Number of Farms	Percentage of Total	Number of Farms	Percentage of Total
Under 1	26	12.2	20	7.0
1 to 5	95	44.6	142	50.0
5 to 10	59	27.7	70	24.6
10 to 20	21	9.9	43	15.1
20 to 50	7	3.3	5	1.8
Over 50	5	2.3	4	1.4
Total	213	100.0	284	100.0

NOTE: Based on the 1941 and 1949 government censuses.

ways this was not the typical situation of the rural Hungarian family (see Table 2.2).

On the other hand, it was the ideal type, the norm for the "proper peasant."[7] It constituted a self-sufficient, independent status free of constant intrusions into one's daily life, subservience to the wealthier, and the economic uncertainty so characteristic of the life of the smallholder and, in particular, the landless. This status, though not as high as that of the wealthy peasant, served as the goal for most of those less prosperous, for it at least had the appearance of being accessible to them. Moreover, its pride, if not always admired by those poorer, was envied by them. Indeed, the economic situation and to some degree the life style of the groups just above and below the middle peasants can be viewed as variations on the central ideal type of that group. This group provided much of the stability of village society, and its interests were perhaps most firmly entrenched in daily village life.

This self-sufficiency mirrors Franklin's (1969) peasant ideal type, in which the family is the basic economic unit, whose goal is to provide not only the basic necessities for its members from its land but also to provide work for each of them. With "full employment" the family attempted to maximize its production, if not necessarily its production efficiency, on its own land. Virtually all family members capable of work labored in the family enterprise.

The husband and wife were the mainstay of the operation, handling the bulk of the work in the fields. Work was differentiated by sex with the men

7. The primary subject of *Proper Peasants*, by Fél and Hofer (1969).

tending to take on the heavier (though not necessarily harder) tasks like plowing, wheat harvesting, working with the teams, and caring for the bigger animals. In the fields women did most of the "foot work" (*gyalog-munka*) of constant hoeing, harvesting of vegetables and fruits, and collecting cut wheat; at home, cultivation of the garden and care of the smaller animals and poultry were their tasks, as well as the cooking, cleaning, washing, canning, and other household work, which was their exclusive domain.

The division of labor within a particular middle peasant family was a function of this overall sexual division of labor and of the composition of the household. The latter was subject to births, deaths, illness, and migration from the family, all part of the household lifecycle.

Typically, a young married couple in this stratum was unlikely to form a nuclear household of its own. This is not to say that individuals did not form nuclear households of their own via marriage. Many did. Indeed, given the large number of children in many families and the waning of the custom of living together as an extended family, it became increasingly common for such couples to strike out on their own and live apart from their families and the domination of their parents. However, due to the custom of inheriting parental property only at the death of the parent and not at marriage, these couples often found themselves without land of their own, or with only a hold or two. Until their later inheritance their position resembled more closely that of the landless or of smallholders than of their siblings at home.

The typical situation was the two- or three-generation stem family. In these families the older couple, and particularly the male, held greater power and stayed closer to home, while the younger couple handled much of the field work. When more labor was needed, the older couple or the older male would join in. Children were introduced to family labor from an early age. As they grew older and their grandparents aged, they were expected to take on an increasing share of labor in the family enterprise, especially at times of greater work, often at the expense of their schooling. At the death or illness of an adult, a youth might well take over his work. The division of labor and distribution of power within the family are treated more thoroughly in Chapter 3.

Because of nonideal age and sex composition of the stem family and unexpected absences, illnesses, and deaths, it was often necessary for family members, particularly women, at some time to take on sex-typed work tasks of the opposite sex. Children learned almost the whole gamut of farm tasks in their youth and were frequently prepared for such an event even if they were not always strong enough to take on the full responsibility. Thus, if there was work to be done in the family enterprise, the necessary labor could be found within the family. Indeed, if there was extra labor strength in the family, work would be found on the family land for it.

In general this self-sufficiency of the middle peasant family on its own land is the keystone of this stratum. There were exceptions to the rule, however, mostly caused by wide variations in the size and composition of the family. It is unclear whether all the families, particularly in the lower ranges of the stratum (those families with only five or ten hold-s), were able to support themselves from their land alone (Gunst 1976: 385). Although intensive agriculture in the form of raising and breeding quality cattle for milk, meat, and further breeding, and the cultivation of tomatoes and melons for export, had gained ground in Kislapos in the 1930s, extensive farming methods still were the rule. Except among the wealthier peasants, cash crops played a small role in the peasant economy. Moreover, by decreasing the circulation of money, the depression of these years only aggravated the difficulties of intensive farming, both in obtaining labor and in marketing (Gunst 1976: 388). Thus, larger families in the lower ranges of the middle peasant group using extensive methods were unable to make full use of their labor resources beyond a certain point on their own land. They, too, turned to renting and sharecropping more land to increase production and to utilize their own labor more fully. Smallholders were the stratum that most often resorted to these practices.

Occasionally even prosperous middle peasants worked additional land. Some, particularly if they were well equipped with a team and implements, may have seen this as an easier way to augment their income than working their own land harder. Others may have looked to the day when their holdings would be split among several siblings; they tried to increase their incomes in order to buy more land, or to compensate a daughter with a rich dowry for her later inheritance.

Some families were in far different circumstances. Widows with small children were often forced to give out their land for rent or sharecropping or to work it with the aid of hired day laborers and harvesters. Elderly childless couples and those couples or individuals whose children had left them alone with their land found themselves in similar situations. Other families with more land and with a temporary loss of labor from sickness or death resorted to the hiring of a year-round laborer (cseléd), who lived with the family.

One well-to-do peasant with over twenty hold-s was hardly able to work for several years because of a debilitating sickness. His wife, with an infant child, and his parents, who were in their fifties, could not work the land fully by themselves. For several years until he recovered his health they hired a cseléd. In another, somewhat poorer family, the four older children (three of them women) had already left home when the father died, leaving his wife and barely adolescent son. They employed a widower with three children as cseléd until the family's labor situation had improved as the son grew older and married. Still another peasant, with close contacts to the village mayor, obtained the positions of village postmaster and collecter at the dairy. He gave out most of his land for sharecropping and hired an adolescent boy as cseléd to look after his cattle.

The self-sufficiency of the middle peasant and the interchangeability of family work roles does not mean that these peasants did not seek the temporary help of relatives, friends, and neighbors when they had a short-age of a particular type of labor. Cooperation and reciprocation were common, both within the stratum and among it and those below it. Middle peasants, who almost invariably owned a team of horses or oxen, frequently did cartage or plowing for teamless smallholders. They could count on "foot work" in return at a future time when they needed more hands. Sárkány (1978: 77–78) reports that in Varsány, a community north-west of Lapos, four days of "foot work" were considered equivalent to one day of team work in the early 1930s—a ratio that dropped to 3:1 by the end of the decade. Other traditional forms of cooperation and reciprocation, discussed in detail later, were also utilized. All of them not only provided opportunities for socializing and reducing boredom, but helped to allevi-ate the problems caused by discrepancies in the composition of families and to make better use of their work forces.

SMALLHOLDERS

Smallholders (törpebirtokos-s) in general did not have enough land to support their families; they had to look to other means to augment their income and use their labor. One factor that determined how they did this was whether they had a team, be it horses, oxen, or even two cows. The more land they owned the more likely they were to have a team. If a team was available, in turn, it was much more likely that the family would take on more land through renting or sharecropping, or take on carting in exchange for labor or produce, or do both. Without a team, chances were greater that they would turn to harvesting wheat for wealthier peasants in the peak harvest season and/or take on day labor.

Renting and sharecropping land were favored because either method gave greater opportunity to earn more, to save, and to acquire more land. Harvesting, day labor, and other peak-season temporary labor often pro-vided only enough income to stretch over the unemployed part of the year, nothing more. Renting and sharecropping also gave the peasant who was working the land more freedom from the daily orders given to day laborers and harvesters. On the other hand, these methods were also riskier than at least that of the day laborer, whose daily wage was insured. There was no guarantee the crop would be good. Though the harvesters' income also depended on the crop, unlike the others, they invested noth-ing in it.

Terms for renting land were relatively simple. A payment, such as the delivery of two or three quintals (two or three hundred kilograms; 1

quintal = 100 kilograms) of wheat per hold, was fixed in advance. In return, the renter was entitled to plant the land with whatever he wanted and to harvest the crop all for himself.

Sharecropping took several forms. These differed in the share retained by the sharecropper for himself, in the work required, and in the assumption of associated expenses. The two usual shares were one-half and one-third. In the former case, for his half of the crop the sharecropper provided the seed, did all the work, paid taxes on the land just as he would had he rented the land, and planted the crops agreed upon with the owner in advance. In the latter case, for his third of the crop the sharecropper did all the work on the crops; the owner supplied the seed and paid the taxes. With certain crops like maize and beets, for which frequent hoeing was required, the workers were given one-third of the crop for the hoeing and harvesting alone. In all these cases frequent consultation with the owner was required. He often directed the work and closely followed its progress. If a step was taken without his say, it could be cause for anger on his part. Some owners were less particular, concerned only about getting their fair share of the crop.

Owners of teams were in a better position to take on the former two sharecropping arrangements because both plowing and seeding were required; even harvesting required a team for hauling away the crop. In a few cases a good relationship developed between the sharecropper and the owner, who gave the sharecropper the use of his own team, presumably in return for feeding and tending it. For example,

the church cantor, who received the use of village land in exchange for his services, and in this case who had some land of his own, had developed a broad relationship with a village smallholder's family having five children. The wife as a child had occasionally washed for the cantor's family and cared for his children, and now her children continued to help out with washing and cleaning. Because of this relationship the cantor let the peasant use his horses for the land he rented. Later, when he moved away from the village, he loaned the peasant money to buy a house.

Though this latter arrangement was unusual, and renters and sharecroppers ordinarily needed a team of their own, the example gives an idea of how complex such sharecropping and renting arrangements could be and the number of different types of them. The ideal type was one in which a widow or an older couple, unable to work all their land, gave some out to a smallholder with several children. One example, which occurred right after World War II, illustrates this well.

The death of his father earlier in fighting during the war had left a twelve-year-old boy, an only child, living alone with his sick mother and fraternal grandmother. When the battle front came to the area in the late stages of the war in a skirmish between the retreating Germans and the advancing Russian troops, a shell hit their house and caused his mother a severe head injury. Following on the death of her husband, this led to a mental breakdown from which she never fully recovered. With over twenty hold-s, the young boy gave out the land that he could not work for one-third and one-half shares, depending on the terms, and also hired harvesters. He frequently carted and plowed for others with his team and thus received badly needed field work in return. One of the families sharecropping this land was that of a smallholder with a wife and three children. Having only four hold-s and a team, they were able to sharecrop much of the other family's land for several years.

Clearly, such arrangements often presumed another earlier relationship. Sometimes they led to one that, even if mostly economic, continued for years. Thus sharecropping and renting agreements, though fixed for only one year at a time, were frequently renewed year after year. They sometimes involved as little as one-quarter hold with work-intensive crops and sometimes as much as fifteen or twenty hold-s. In fact, some families rented and/or sharecropped as much as thirty or forty hold-s at a time from several different owners. In these latter cases, many families were interested in acquiring more land of their own and worked even more land than was needed merely to make fuller use of the family work force and to sustain the requirements of food and clothing. Outside of essentially nonagricultural work, this was the only opportunity for most rural poor to acquire further land.[8]

The chief work available to the poorer smallholder was harvesting and day labor. Here, too, there were numerous possibilities for labor and

---

8. One possibility was working in industry, which paid quite well compared to the wages of landless workers and favorably compared to smallholders' earnings. This can be seen in estimates of the differing annual per capita incomes in 1930–31 of various social categories cited by Andorka (1979: 118–119):

agricultural laborers	183.4 pengő-s
agricultural cseléd-s	204.6 pengő-s
smallholders with 1–10 hold-s	227.2 pengő-s
landholders with 10–100 hold-s	431.7 pengő-s
independent tradesmen	319.5 pengő-s
mining and smelting workers	427.3 pengő-s
industrial, construction, transport, and other workers	376.4 pengő-s

After the depression, industry, which had suffered greatly, experienced a boom in the late 1930s and the early years of the war. Commenting on the shoes, clothing, and other items industrial workers could buy, the agricultural poor sometimes referred to them as "gentlemen" (*úri ember*) compared to themselves. The other great opportunity, working as a factory or agricultural worker in North America for several years, was grasped at by hundreds of thousands of Hungarians along with other East Europeans at the turn of the century. This, however, was largely closed off by the 1930s with the new immigration policies.

The above data also make clear just how little real difference there was between the incomes of landless agricultural laborers, cseléd-s, and smallholders.

considerable variation in the terms of work agreements. One of the two major possibilities was harvesting wheat on the large estates just outside of Kislapos, particularly that at Puszta, which was within easy walking distance of the village, just across the Farkas River, two or three kilometers to the north. A representative of the estate would come to the village to recruit men for the coming wheat harvest or would do so through a harvester leader, who represented and led the harvesters at work. As many as thirty or more pairs were recruited annually from the village. Each pair consisted of an adult male harvester with scythe and a companion, sometimes a child or relative, usually an adolescent boy or girl or a woman, who followed behind him picking up the cut wheat, tying it into bundles, and stacking it.

The harvesters customarily received a share of the harvested wheat. This varied locally from one-eighth to one-eleventh and was most commonly one-tenth.[9] For his share, the harvester also had to help in threshing the grain, provide his own meals (cooked meals prepared by the harvesters' wives were usually brought out by a wagon from the village), and arrange to have his share hauled home. He would have to pay his working companion a share of his wheat, sometimes as much as a third, sometimes a fixed quantity agreed upon in advance. The harvester might also be given the opportunity to, or be required to, work at other times of the year as a day laborer at a fixed daily wage. For those of the smallholders and especially the landless for whom harvesting provided a major source of income, this was a chance to add to an income otherwise insufficient to sustain a family throughout the year. For others, it meant being occasionally called away from other work, which was either more important or paid better, for an insured, if not high, wage.

The other major possibility in the late 1930s was harvesting for one of the wealthier peasants who were unable by themselves to harvest their wheat. The wealthiest of them, owning around one hundred hold-s, hired four or five harvesters each; others hired correspondingly fewer. Altogether, this group may have hired as many as twenty to twenty-five harvesters with helpers. They received the same share as the estate harvesters, but the remaining terms differed considerably. Instead of having the chance to work as day laborers, they were given the opportunity to sharecrop (one-third) up to a hold or two of the peasant's land, usually growing corn, thus augmenting their income in a different way. In addition, however, they were required to contribute five or six days of free labor to the wealthy peasant at whatever time he might need it. Many village informants felt that some landholders had exacted this labor in the hardest tasks.

9. Sárkány (1978: 77) reports that with the shortage of labor during the later stages of the war, rates of one-eighth were more common.

Some found employment as harvesters for middle peasants who, because of a labor shortage in the family, found themselves unable to harvest their crop alone. In such cases, opportunities for day labor or sharecropping were rarer. Occasionally even some of the middle peasants with more children had some family members harvest for others. A few harvesters worked for wealthier peasants in neighboring villages.

Thus day labor frequently went hand in hand with harvesting; in describing their positions in the prewar period, many men referred to themselves and others with a single expression: harvester/day laborer (*arató-napszámos*). Day labor, however, frequently could be and was obtained apart from harvesting. Many teamless smallholders worked a number of days at various tasks (cutting grass, stacking hay, hoeing, shoveling manure) for another peasant in exchange for the plowing of their own fields, cartage, and other tasks requiring a team. Families short of labor or missing a member often hired day laborers to help them out in their work. Wealthier peasants hired day laborers relatively infrequently; more often they would count upon their own hired farm hands or use their harvesters to take care of extra work.

The major opportunity for day labor other than harvesting was outside the village: on the estate at Puszta, on several larger estates in Kistó, and on some of the larger vineyards in the sandy soil on the way to Zöldfa, to the east. Each day during the spring and summer, scores of people from Lapos walked together to and from a day's labor at one of these places, particularly Puszta (that is, until 1941–42, when the estate was distributed to settlers from all parts of the country, including former farmhands there). Women and children were by no means rare; the latter sometimes took on adult tasks, though at a reduced rate and wage, or less physically demanding ones, like thinning out seedlings, pasturing geese or ducks, and carrying water to the laborers. Hoeing was by far the most common work (along with harvesting of crops like corn, beets, and alfalfa). At the vineyards there was hoeing, tying of the shoots, spraying, and so on.

All these jobs offered a small daily cash wage, occasionally supplemented for the men by some brandy in the morning and wine for lunch. Around harvest, consumption of the crop (for example, grapes, fruits, and vegetables) at work and minor theft provided minor benefits to laborers. But because the wheat harvest lasted for little more than a month, and day labor took up another five or six, for half the year there was little work available. In general, the income from harvesting and day labor was by itself just enough to keep a family going.

For the many landless, for whom this was the main source of income, it was enough to keep barely afloat, but not to buy land and improve their position. After several years of such an existence, many of them strove to save enough to buy at least some animals, which they could use to sharecrop a little land. Others worked even harder to scratch together a tiny plot of land for themselves. It was often this first bit of capital that was most important to a potential landholder; and, given the possibilities for obtaining it, it was also one of the most formidable obstacles to be overcome. It was easier to earn an income from one's own land than through labor for others; and, just because of the low income from the latter, it was difficult to acquire that first bit of land. For many it was only the minor land reforms of the 1920s and 1930s, and even more the farreaching land reform following the war, that enabled them to achieve this first step.

LANDLESS WORKERS

This group (nincstelen-s) was Hungary's agricultural proletariat, the rural masses who constituted the nation's "three million beggars" between the world wars. Although their situation was not one of starvation, their opportunities did not far exceed that level. During the growing season, in which they strove to procure the family's basic requirements for the year, especially foodstuffs, through hired labor, the roof above their heads was often only that of a barn, the shoes on their feet were nonexistent, and the clothes of some were more patches on rags than anything else. The health of the group was poor, and there was a high death rate, especially among young children. They had one of Europe's highest rates of tuberculosis, a distinction shared with the country's urban poor. Of food there was enough, even if it did not have much protein content and was monotonous: mostly grain, bacon, fat, and other foodstuffs that agricultural laborers received in payment.

It was this group whose members most gladly fled from the village to the opportunities of the industrializing cities. And it was the landless whose position was least secure among the major village groups; even with the whole family working, the wages of several months of contracted agricultural labor were little more than enough to keep its members poorly clothed and fed with a roof over their heads. To achieve even this, younger children were put to work and therefore received a bare minimum of schooling. During the boom of the 1920s, many jobs opened up in the industrial sector for this stratum; but the depression of the 1930s largely wiped out this possibility for a decade. In the meantime, the continued availability of work depended mainly on the continued delay in introducing more modern machinery on the large estates; unfortunately, this state of affairs was in turn dependent on the continued availability of a mass of manual laborers at low wages.

Three major possibilities were open to the landless earning their bread through farm labor. There were the harvester/day laborer positions and the possibilities of being a *summás* (a hired hand on a large estate for two to six months) or a cseléd. Of the three, harvesting was the most favorable in many respects. With about six weeks of hard work plus additional day labor, a worker could acquire most of his family's food necessities for the following year. Frequently working together in a band with fellow con-tracted harvesters under the direction of a familiar band leader, these workers suffered relatively little from the often stinging leadership of the wealthy peasant or the estates' officials. On the other hand, their pay was subject to the vicissitudes of crop yield. During the late 1920s and early 1930s a series of bad wheat crops, in which many harvesters saw a sizable portion of their meager wheat share go to their helpers, forced many of them to join the ranks of the summás-s.

Summás-s worked during the growing season, from the beginning of May. The first few months were usually occupied with thinning out crops and hoeing, the next couple with the harvesting of various crops, and the last part of the season with the preparation of fields for the next crop. Wages included daily rations of bacon and milk, flour for bread, and a lump sum payment in kind (wheat, bacon, and various commodities) upon expiration of the contract. Some contracts, in lieu of daily rations, provided monthly payments of flour (for example, three quintals) and other commodities, distributed at more frequent intervals. Also included in payment was housing, which usually consisted of crowded barns with several families to a room, all sharing the same scanty quarters and cook-ing facilities.

It was not unusual for Lapos's residents to go off to distant estates for months at a time. Many families went at one time or another to estates in Fejér, Somogy, and Veszprém counties, 150–200 kilometers to the west, where large estates were more common than in the Great Plains region, or to Hajdú-Bihar County to the northeast. As many as thirty or forty persons would contract together to work on these distant estates. Some went as individuals, others as families.

Lapos's residents working as summás-s on the nearby Károlyi estates walked back and forth daily. Frequently those who worked on neighbor-ing estates, particularly the young, would walk to and from work together, joining in singing tunes and general merrymaking. In many ways the existence of the summás-s was the province of the young and the very poor. Although a sure, steady income and housing were provided for as long as six months, the pay was not high, and even if a family put together enough money in this manner to live for the rest of the year, the problem of winter housing was by no means solved. Only the leaders of summá-s bands of workers contracted with estates were able to acquire houses and land by their efforts. They did relatively little physical labor, mainly di-recting others (Sárkány 1978: 87). Although many whole families went to estates either nearby or far away, the pay of the summás-s was viewed more as supplementary income for a family.

When whole families went to an estate to work, virtually everyone actually did work, so that the family income would be that much greater. It was not unusual for eight- or nine-year-olds or even younger children to carry water buckets or watch the geese for a small share of an able-bodied worker's pay. Even more frequent were young adolescents who, from the age of twelve on, were officially permitted to work for half the normal wage. Known as one-row (*egy soros*) or half-share (*fél részes*) workers, they took on half the work of their two-row (that is, hoeing two rows of corn at once) adult colleagues.

As the wages of a summás were supplementary, it was not unusual for one or two members of a family to go off for two to six months to obtain additional income for the family, while other members stayed home to scrape out an existence from a tiny parcel of land or pursue the life of harvester/day laborers. This was facilitated by the existence of the bands: it was thus much easier for males or children to go off as summás-s and still have someone to look after them and prepare meals while other family members stayed at home. As a result, children as young as twelve (sometimes younger if they lied about their age) went off without their families for periods of up to six months to an estate in the company of a relative or godparent, or even a neighbor family, in order literally to bring home some extra bacon (and flour) for their families. Other adolescents went daily to the nearby Károlyi estates taken over by the state, not so much to earn the necessities as to be able to buy some more fashionable clothing or to have some spending money for Sunday afternoons in nearby Pont.

The summás existence was also temporary in the long run. Many youths took it up for a few years, attaining adult strength and work status at it, but because of the relatively low wages giving it up for more promising labor when the time came to establish a family. They would then seek positions as cseléd-s and harvester/day laborers or try to become smallholders. Rare was the individual who stayed at it for a decade. In many cases, it was only particularly bad circumstances that forced individuals to be summás-s. One mother with five children became a day laborer and her children summás-s for a summer when her husband suddenly died, leaving the family temporarily with no other means. Another informant and his brothers went to work as summás-s and water boys during World War I, when their widower father was called up as a soldier.

Many families aiming for more secure and gainful employment sought the position of cseléd on an estate or for a wealthy peasant or middle peasant who lacked hired hands. Quite a few poor laborers envied the position of the cseléd, and even some of the better off thought the benefits quite good. It was not unheard of for a harvester/day laborer with a house of his own, or perhaps even a smallholder, to seek a position as cseléd on one of the larger estates, renting out his own home in town in the meantime. Indeed, some of these positions were so contested for that, for example, on the Károlyi lands they could be acquired only through acquaintances already working on the estates.

But the position of cseléd was far from completely rosy; it meant considerable subservience to the landowner or manager of an estate. Indeed, in rural Hungary, where independence and self-sufficiency were the watchword of the peasantry, the situation of cseléd was synonymous with subservience. Of course, treatment of the cseléd varied considerably and to a degree was a function of the type of employment situation he occupied and the temperament of his employer. Many considered the situation of the estate cseléd, where the contractual terms were relatively favorable and the cseléd was not directly under the thumb of the owner, the best.[10] Less sought after were positions working for wealthy peasants. The work was generally done under the direction of the peasant himself, who frequently tried to get as much work as possible out of his cseléd-s by constantly pressing them, trying to increase their hours and responsibilities, and ignoring their private lives. Somewhat easier, or at least more relaxed, was the position of the cseléd living with the family of his employer. Here his treatment was much the same as that of the family members: subservient to the will of the family head. Though treated little differently, the cseléd was conscious of his different status (Ortutay 1977, vol. I: 479), and in this situation he received less pay than cseléd-s elsewhere.

The pay of cseléd-s on the larger estates and with wealthier peasants was standardized in the form of the *kommenció* (payment in kind). The most important elements received by an adult working for the whole year were the following: housing for his family plus several quintals of wood for heating; twenty to twenty-four quintals of grain, mostly wheat with lesser amounts of barley and/or rye; salt, vinegar, and other preservatives and spices; one hold of land plowed and sown by the owner, usually with corn; clothing, such as boots; and a small sum of money. Another aspect of the pay open to negotiation was the keeping of pigs and cows by the cseléd. Some cseléd-s were allowed to keep a cow of their own, sometimes with those of the owner, sometimes fed on his feed; others lacking cows (or lacking this term in their contract) were given, for example, two liters of milk per day. In addition, cseléd-s were allowed to keep pigs and poultry, feeding them on corn grown on their allotted land.

There were minor differences among the wealthier peasants in Kislapos in the wages they paid. Generally the issue of keeping animals proved important to the cseléd-s, as it was through animals that they could both improve their diet and, more important, raise money to buy land or a

---

10. Gyula Illyés (1967), however, paints a somber and not very favorable picture of the cseléd's life on the manor and describes in some detail the manager's exploitation of the workers and women.

house. In several cases cseléd-s left a peasant's hire at the end of the year because they could not reach agreement over the issue of keeping animals—how many, who was to provide the feed, and so on. The Károlyi estates provided both a couple of quintals more grain than did the local peasants and allowed the keeping of animals: another reason their positions were highly desired. But it was usually the quality of work by the cseléd and the treatment by the owner that determined whether one moved elsewhere or continued with the same employer after the year's end.

Sometimes several members of a family worked as cseléd-s for one landowner. In these cases they were given several times the kommenció of one cseléd. In the case of the Kis family in the 1920s, where five sons worked alongside their father for one of Lapos's wealthiest landholders, the six received a total of four full shares, including three and one-half hold-s of corn land. The father and two eldest sons received full shares, the third son a half share, and the two youngest a quarter share each. The latter two did not receive any corn land in their small shares; and altogether the family received only the housing reserved for one cseléd and his family. Not having many animals, they could not take full advantage of the animal-keeping provisions.

Frequently the wife also worked, particularly if the employer was a wealthy peasant. There were washing, housecleaning, perhaps even cooking to be done in the household of the employer or in other households in Lapos. Many stayed home to do their own family's cooking and housekeeping and, as a result, were compared to smallholders' and middle peasants' wives, who sometimes worked in the fields, and shared (perhaps unfairly) in the "lazy" epithet often used by the better-off to characterize cseléd-s.

Bennkosztos (eating in) cseléd-s, who lived and ate with the family of their employer much like family members, usually were boys up to eighteen or nineteen (or old men) unable to start off independently or get well-paid work—men whose material needs were not too great but who were still capable of putting in a good day's work. Although no such cseléd-s were ever so highly honored by the family that they were taken in as sons-in-law, as occurred in nearby Átány (Fél and Hofer 1969: 132, 141), there were cases where a young wife or other family member complained that the household head gave the cseléd the choice pieces of meat ahead of her. Besides room (for much of the year this meant a place in the barn at night looking after the animals) and board, they received a small sum of money and some clothing, plus miscellaneous items. Like other family members, their work was varied, though, as with cseléd-s for wealthy peasants and on estates, it centered around the larger animals—the horses, cattle, cows, and oxen.

Work for wealthy peasants, where there were as many as four or five agricultural cseléd-s, and particularly on estates was more specialized.

The cseléd's work was almost exclusively with the animals—plowing, feeding the animals, cleaning up around them, hauling goods with horses or oxen, milking. In these larger enterprises much of the field work was done with day laborers and summás-s. On the large estates even work with animals was divided up among the cseléd-s, so that there were milkers, teamsters, perhaps even a liveried coachman, each with different rank; there might be in addition a blacksmith, a mechanic, and other skilled workers who ranked higher than cseléd-s socially and economically.

Unlike being a summás, a position very few people held for more than a few years, being a farmhand was a way of life for many. Although the pay was not high, it included housing and was enough to live on, thus providing a certain security. Some viewed being a cseléd as a temporary position in the struggle to put together some money to acquire a house and land of their own. With the possibility of raising animals and saving money there was also the chance of establishing a more independent existence free of the servility characteristic of the farmhand's status.

But despite the possibility of advancement and saving money, the farmhand's position was not admired; in Kislapos the cseléd-s were frequently looked down upon. Coming as they almost always did from outside the village (had they lived in Lapos they probably would have had their own housing and would not have taken the position in the first place), they remained unknown for a long time, since their work occupied much of their time and, especially if they lived on the farmstead of two (in particular) of the wealthiest peasants in Lapos, kept them from coming into the village.

Even more important was the subservient status of the cseléd, in contrast to the independent ideal of the Hungarian peasant. Rural folk strove to achieve the latter status, to get away from having to take orders from someone else and out from under the feet of others. Cseléd-s, on the other hand, especially those apparently destined to remain farmhands for life, could not muster the pride of the peasant; it was assumed that they lacked motivation to alter their situation, that they preferred to take orders rather than to strike out on their own, that they were lazy and tried to avoid real work. Moreover, they had to tolerate the often relentlessly harsh treatment of superiors who exploited their ignorance and even beat them. Many who sympathized with them or pitied them at the same time held them beneath themselves for taking that treatment and not seeking to improve their situation.[11]

Much was dependent on the personality of the employer; but, as some informants said, the economic and social position of the wealthier peas-

11. To understand these views fully one must take into account pre-World War II Hungary's highly stratified society, in which relatively small differences in social levels were very important.

ants was such that they could afford to be supercilious with their fellow-men. Their treatment of their cseléd-s was unlikely to be ideal. Some drove their farmhands night and day, trying to get them to get up earlier to work, to spend still more time with the animals, to do more work for the same pay. The more explosive did not shrink from trying to beat them, the more amorous from trying to couple with their wives and daughters, the shrewd from cheating them and exploiting their gullibility. One wealthy peasant for years did not officially report his employment of Sándor Orbán as cseléd, nor did he sign the farmhand's work book. In this way he avoided paying the meager social security premium then required and could more easily renege on his wage promises, since there was no legal contract. Each year around St. Michael's Day in late September, when the cseléd-s could give notice, Sándor Orbán threatened to quit.[12] His employer tried to tempt him back with promises of more pay. If that did not work, the employer's wife threatened to give St. Anthony two pengő-s (a couple of day's wages for a day laborer) so that he would break the cseléd's legs. The latter was enough to block the farmhand's plans to change employers!

It was also difficult for the cseléd to endure some of the peasants' cheapness and attempts to get more work for less pay. The nagygazda's wife would give the cseléd's family milk with almost all the fat content removed by the dairy's machine, instead of whole milk desired for their growing children; one wealthy peasant refused to raise the pay of the aforementioned Kis family despite the growth of the number of animals they had to tend; the same peasant gave the adolescent János Kis two quintals of wheat at the end of the year instead of several more for tending the pigs, arguing that, since the Kis family's pigs ate along with his own, they ate up the difference.

The *szolgálónő*-s, women who lived with the families of the wealthy peasants and did their washing, cleaning, sometimes their cooking, and assorted tasks like gardening, milking cows, and even caring for their children, frequently had a difficult time. Unlike the "eating in" cseléd-s, they were driven harder than family members and sometimes were begrudgingly given even the poor fare to which they were entitled.[13]

12. The cseléd-s would move around New Year. Because of the difficulties in moving in such cold weather, the length of the advance notice required was later shortened and the moving day was changed to a more suitable, warmer period.

13. The reason for this may be that they were directed by the wives of the peasants. Sárkány (1978: 92) notes that in Varsány the peasants' wives often treated their hired labor and members of lower strata more harshly than did their husbands, who sometimes evinced a paternal attitude toward their workers. He explains this by the fact that, while the employers often directed the work of the laborers, many of them put in equal effort working alongside them and developed a better relationship with them than did their wives, who did not work in the fields. Sárkány argues that this joint work may have provided some cohesion for a rural society that was becoming increasingly stratified and differentiated.

Moreover, they were often young single women away from home, so they had little moral support to fall back on. Many of them took these positions in Lapos or in cities to improve on the summás existence, but they were frequently disappointed.

Several other possibilities were open to the landless, though generally they were even less tempting than those above. These included being the village swineherd or cowherd and growing tobacco or melons on one of the larger estates or for one of the wealthy peasants. All these jobs provided some sort of housing, in the former cases from the village grazing association, in the latter from the estates and peasants providing employment. But all were socially looked down upon; the former occupied the bottom rung on the village social ladder, the latter on that of the estate.

A few sought escape from this stratum by learning a trade. This was a difficult path because, aside from room and board, apprenticeship provided virtually no material rewards. A family in immediate need of income was more likely to send a boy to be a summás or to help with harvesting or the cseléd's work.

Finally, though relatively few from Lapos went this route, there was the possibility of pick-and-shovel (*kubikus*) work during the warmer months. This was usually earth-moving or construction work on roads and river embankments, on which hundreds and thousands of men labored with wheelbarrows, picks, and shovels. Though the pay was better than that of day labor, like that of the summás-s the work often involved bands of men contracting work for longer periods of time in distant parts of the country. Housing was provided only for the period of employment. Therefore even this was only a temporary solution and a rather difficult one.

WEALTHY PEASANTS

The nagygazda-s could be divided into two subgroups: those owning fifty or less hold-s, who, unable to work their land completely by the labor of their families, worked alongside their hired laborers; and those with more land, who generally assumed a directing role in its management, doing little if any physical labor while supervising and inspecting the work of their help. Both had more land than needed for subsistence, and both participated more heavily in the market economy of the countryside, selling a considerable amount of grains, produce, cattle, and dairy products for profit. Indeed, those in the latter group bore greater resemblance to farmers as we know them than to their poorer peasant compatriots, making use of and even buying such machines as tractors, threshers, and a variety of smaller machines and devices that smallholders and even most middle peasants could not afford.

Due to their wealth and the economic power associated with it, their greater time available outside of work, and perhaps a greater interest and expertise in civic affairs coming from a wider range of social and economic contacts, the wealthy peasants played a greater role in the village's political, economic, religious, and social institutions than members of any other stratum. This will be examined in further detail in Chapter 4; it suffices to say here that the nagygazda-s occupied a far more dominant place in the village social structure than their numbers would indicate—indeed, they were the dominant force in the village.

With this wealth they were also able to offer their children greater opportunities for maintaining and improving their relatively high status and living standards. Though many wanted their sons to take over the family property, both sons and daughters were given opportunities for schooling. In contrast to the rareness with which youngsters in less fortunate circumstances finished even the basic six grades of elementary school,[14] children of nagygazda-s often finished the eight grades of *polgári* schools (advanced elementary school: the four grades of elementary school in Lapos were followed by four grades of *polgári,* available only in Pont). They were better prepared eventually to enter the more respected and better-paying civil service, administrative, and teaching positions.

Those staying in farming, on their own, with their parents, or with their husbands or wives, also benefited from the custom of marrying people of roughly equal means, of wealth marrying wealth. Large families still led to fragmentation of holdings, but the inherited holdings of a spouse cushioned the fall. Already equipped with the first few hold-s ordinarily unavailable to the landless, and considerably more (both in land and in the implements and animals needed to work it), scions of the wealthier peasants found it easier than the landless to expand their holdings if they desired.

It is difficult to generalize about an average day spent by a nagygazda's family due to their luxury of choice. It was open to them how much work they should do themselves and to what degree they should supervise others. Fifty hold-s was the rough dividing line between primarily directing and supervising tasks, but there were exceptions in both directions: the owner of fifty or sixty hold-s, who had made his fortune working for ten years as a boilerman in America, continuing to work in the fields alongside his one cseléd at most and his day laborers; the forty-hold nagygazda staying mostly at home or involving himself with other matters while his cseléd-s finished his work; another peasant with forty hold-s renting out his land as he grew older.

There were broad differences in the ways nagygazda-s supervised their workers, differences that could be attributed to temperament. The appellation of blood-sucking (*vérszívó*) was applied to some of the

14. Poor children rarely went further unless a teacher or the village priest recognized some outstanding talent and championed their cause.

wealthiest nagygazda-s who constantly checked on the work of their cseléd-s and day laborers and tried to get as much as possible out of them, never being satisfied with their work. Others were more content to sit back and occupy themselves with other matters while their cseléd-s followed the basic orders and took care of the work. The brothers József and Ferenc Kovács, two of the wealthiest peasants in Lapos, reflected this difference well. Sons of a horsebreeder and trader who had acquired his wealth around the turn of the century through selling horses to the Austro-Hungarian army, they were considered by the villagers as exemplars, respectively, of the blood-sucking, hard-driving nagygazda on the one hand and the easygoing, considerate one on the other. József was known for his selfish, aggressive nature and his frequent altercations, especially with his cseléd-s, who often did not stay with him for more than one year. He constantly checked on their work, complaining about it, and was even known to beat them in a fit of temper. His main concern was to acquire more land.

Ferenc was known for his lenient treatment of cseléd-s, many of whom stayed with him for years. Though he was concerned with his farm and bought modern implements, including a tractor, he was often occupied with his passion for horses and their training and the trading and fairs that went along with this. Thus he was sometimes away for days at a time. When present, he conveyed a relaxed tone, encouraging his workers to take their time eating or during a work break and sometimes even joining them.

Between these extremes there was a general norm of trying to get as much work as possible from cseléd-s, harvesters, and day laborers—keeping their pay low while increasing workloads, exactingly following the progress of their labor, and criticizing "unsatisfactory" results (sometimes even when the cause was the weather or, unknowingly, the nagygazda himself).

The tasks of the nagygazda-s' wives varied. Their work was also frequently supervisory, for a number of them had servant girls to help with or assume the household tasks. The wife's domain was roughly the same as that of the middle peasant's wife, minus the work done in the fields but plus some tasks like cooking meals for day laborers.

Children were expected to help out and learn the operation of the farm or, in the case of girls, the appropriate sex-linked tasks and the organization of the household. But their participation in family work was not as crucial as in lower strata. Because of this and because of the availability of money for further schooling, the wealthier peasants' children were able to continue their formal education for a longer time than their poorer counterparts. The actual amount of work they did was more a function of their parents' stand on the matter than it was a necessity. The role of childrens' work in the families of less wealthy nagygazda-s was more important.

Most of the nagygazda-s used all three types of hired labor in the village—cseléd-s, day laborers, and harvesters—and sharecroppers. The use of sharecroppers and the renting out of land were largely dependent on the age and sex composition of the family; old age and the absence of a man in his prime were the chief causes for resorting to these forms of cultivation. With the introduction of intensive cultivation of tomatoes and paprika in the 1930s, sharecropping also brought good profits on small plots of land. The most common sharecropping, however, was part of the contract of the harvesters, since the wealthier peasants could usually use day laborers, cseléd-s, and harvesters to work land that they themselves could not handle.

The particular mix of the nagygazda's hired labor depended mainly on the crops grown and the number of animals kept. Grains, for example, made more use of harvesters, while various vegetables and fruits required more day laborers or sharecroppers. Cseléd-s were chiefly hired to tend and work with various animals. Their numbers were dependent on the presence of housing (separate or rooming with a family) and barns to keep the animals.[15] An average of four or five cseléd-s and harvesters each was needed per one hundred hold-s.

Despite the pride of many nagygazda-s in their farming skills and knowledge, it seems significant that most of them or their direct ancestors did not acquire their large landholdings through wise management or cultivation of smaller holdings. Some large holdings were purchased with funds earned through working in America or through large-scale horse breeding and trading. Fortuitous inflation after both world wars helped others to acquire larger holdings (see Chapter 5, note 1). One family benefitted from a combination of these. The husband had worked in America for a decade in order to buy land in Hungary. He had sent his earnings home in dollars, which had been converted to Hungarian pengő-s and then sat in the bank untouched. Runaway inflation in the 1920s wiped out these savings before the man's return to Hungary, but fortunately his family had bought considerable land in anticipation of the funds—land that was then easily paid off in inflated currency. Others saved larger sums through commercial trading of agricultural produce and by serving as managers on smaller estates. Farming one's own land was not the common way of achieving nagygazda status.

15. One reason for sometimes requiring the cseléd-s to sleep in the barns was to ensure that no problems befell the animals unnoticed at night. Though this was not an unusual practice even for concerned peasants themselves, cseléd-s sometimes felt that the hard-driving nagygazda-s took advantage of it to get even more work out of them and to further reduce their few hours off.

CRAFTSMEN AND ENTREPRENEURS

This group never constituted more than 2 or 3 percent of Lapos's population before World War II. The village usually had a blacksmith, a carpenter and a stonemason and frequently a shoemaker, a barber, a tailor, and a wheelwright, and two or more of some. Some, such as the blacksmith, were contracted by the village council to work there and were provided with a house and a workshop; villagers paid them individually for services rendered.

Most had only intermittent demand for their services and were forced to supplement their income by working a few hold-s of privately owned or rented land or by hiring themselves out as day laborers. Much of the barber's work came late Saturday night and early Sunday morning, when men were preparing for Sunday mass. The mason and (to a lesser degree) the carpenter were limited in the amount of work they could do in winter; others found not so much seasonal as market limitations on the demand for their work. Judging by the fluctuation in craftsmen over five prewar censuses and by informants' comments, there sometimes was so little demand for services that craftsmen were forced to move elsewhere.

Much the same could be said of the entrepreneurs who ran various shops in the village. Most could not eke out a living from commerce alone and worked their parcels of land in addition. Indeed, the National Hangya (Ant) Cooperative, which ran a general store and sometimes branch stores in the village, often employed local smallholders to keep shop. Though the storekeepers employed may well have had or thus acquired sufficient commercial spirit to open their own shops after termination of employment, they continued to work their own land and sometimes used the positions as a springboard for acquiring further land. For example, when dikes were raised next to the Farkas River in the early part of the century and hundreds of construction laborers from Szabolcs and Békés counties converged on the area to work, the local Hangya storekeeper, along with his father, who ran the tavern in the same building, made enough money selling them provisions to buy land, thus raising his status and that of his children from smallholder to prospering middle peasant.

Aside from the main Hangya store and the local tavern, both of which provided their proprietors with steady business, most stores did not last longer than a few years. The community was simply too small to support such concerns on a steady basis. Though there were as many as seven stores open in Kislapos directly after World War II, five of them branch stores of the Hangya, few were full-time operations and few lasted long. One independent general store survived for several years and probably would have gone on, had not the war caused shortages and the front ultimately brought its destruction, but Kislapos could not long support such enterprises as a store for animal chains and harnesses.

Besides these enterprises, there were motor-driven mills in the village for grinding grains and corn and two or three presses to extract oil from sunflower and rape seeds. Most were owned by wealthier peasants. One exceptional jack-of-all-trades combined his strong mechanical bent and entrepreneurial spirit with his small landholdings to outfit himself ultimately with a mill and press and later to build a truck for himself and acquire a tractor. Although his prewar success at partially nonagricultural enterprises in the village was definitely an exception in the community, he does illustrate the general tendency of this group to maintain a foothold in agriculture, indeed, to identify themselves ultimately as agriculturalists. Had the war and the ensuing radical restructuring of village society not intervened, he might well have gone over more completely to a nonagricultural enterprise; but it is equally likely that he would have reached the position of a wealthy peasant.

Members of these categories enjoyed a status in the village based on their landholdings and the degree to which their craft or enterprise was a full-time specialty; it was also dependent upon the applicability of their special skills in other social spheres. One keeper of the Hangya store for nearly fifteen years soon afterwards opened his own small general store and later was treasurer of several village organizations, including the collective farm. Despite his small landholdings, which he continued to work, and the fact that his siblings and only son all stayed in agriculture, he was considered primarily a commercial person and was known by the nickname of Boltos (storekeeper).

Carpenters in the village, who combined casket-making and even funeral preparations with their house construction work, also remained identified as craftsmen despite their small holdings. The blacksmith, also a full-time worker, was known as just that. A tailor, who for years was also an active participant in the leadership of the local Peasants' Circle, an organization promoting village social occasions and agricultural development, derived his stature from his work and his civic activity, not from his small holdings and his limited agricultural work.

On the other hand, one stonemason member of a poor smallholder family, who was unable to find enough mason work for a decent income and therefore worked his land (as well as being, at other times, an unsuccessful stock clerk for the local coop, the Hangya's postwar successor, and a mine worker), never really changed his status in the eyes of his villagers. The same is true for various short-term storekeepers and bartenders.

It may also have been the case that craftsmen and entrepreneurs moving into Kislapos were more likely to be identified fully as such, despite their agricultural work, than similarly occupied natives. This view is supported by the observation of Fél and Hofer (1969: 243–245) in nearby Átány that many of the craftsmen were outsiders and thus were less likely to have land of their own or to occupy the "amateur" status of an established teamless farmer who occasionally practiced some specialized skill.[16]

Such a description of the established craftsmen's status also corresponds to Fél and Hofer's (1969: 245) comparison with that of the more prosperous teamless peasants. In a ranking the craftsmen lay between the better-off middle peasants, who looked down upon them because of their lack of land, and the teamless farmers, whom they themselves regarded as inferior due to their own control of a specialty. Given their limited numbers, both craftsmen and entrepreneurs played a greater role in village civic life than that to which their wealth would ordinarily have entitled them.

Lacking their own land and having a perspective somewhat different from cultivators, full-time craftsmen and storekeepers were more likely to educate their children further, to raise them for a craft or for opportunities outside the village. Other strata sometimes gave their children for apprenticeship in a craft, but such decisions were sometimes also based on the physical unsuitability of a child for agricultural labor. The aforementioned tailor with smallholder parents had only one fully developed arm; a barber from a family with very small holdings went lame and then learned his craft. Such children who showed aptitude might also receive more schooling than otherwise, as did the poorer middle peasant's son with a malformed hand, who served as a village clerk for several years before he moved away.

INTELLIGENTSIA

This even smaller set was made up of the village notary-clerk (*jegyző*), the cantor-teacher (*kántor-tanító*), who served as the church organist and as teacher in the church-run village school, and sometimes others. The priest would have been a member, but Kislapos did not have its own priest.

All these categories were paid by the village. Part of the payment was the use of village common land: eight hold-s for the priest (in addition to the eighty or so that he received from Kistó), two each for the cantor-teacher and the notary, and some for the school administrator. All, except the priest, also received payments in grain—part of the proceeds from renting fifty hold-s of the village common land to villagers—as well as the use of village-owned houses. Some of the priest's and perhaps the cantor-teacher's income also came from the church's "couple tax," the annual assessment of married couples of a bushel of wheat (about twenty-two or twenty-three kilograms). Their incomes through these measures enabled

16. Interestingly, though the landless in Lapos sometimes considered a factory worker a "gentleman," Sárkány (1978: 91) reports that those with land in Varsány considered factory workers equal to the landless proletariat if they owned no land.

them to maintain a life style that was in accord with the respect given them by the villagers for their learned status. Most gave out their land for rent or sharecropping and did not actually farm themselves. The notary and the cantor-teacher each maintained a servant woman to do much of the washing and cleaning for their households, greatly relieving the workload of their wives—a privilege otherwise accorded only to nagygazda-s.

As Fél and Hofer (1969: 246, 412) point out, these categories were considered úr-s (lords or gentlemen), to be looked up to by the peasants. Their income, education, and important role in village civic affairs gave them a status roughly equal to that of the wealthiest nagygazda-s. Nevertheless, they were generally outsiders and representatives of higher levels in the Church and governmental hierarchies and therefore were looked upon with misgivings by the local nagygazda-s who held power in Lapos.

Chapter 3

Prewar Family and Kinship

Family and its kinship extension occupied central roles in the traditional social and economic structure of Hungarian peasant society prior to World War II.[1] Indeed, the social and economic spheres were strongly interwoven through the fabric of the family.[2] This becomes clear when one views peasant labor as not just an occupation, but a way of life. Peasants past and present are as eager to maintain family work opportunities as to maximize production and profit; they do not separate economic from kinship spheres (Franklin 1969; Bailey 1971: 29–30).

We have seen how villagers strove to provide family members a living from their own land and the variations this took given the unequal distribution. We also examined the economic interrelations existing between strata because of these inequalities. Of course, these hardly exhausted the social and economic ties of individuals. What is significant is the degree to which these, too, were kin- and family-based. Reciprocal economic aid, work exchanges, socializing, celebrating, recreation, giving and receiving aid and comfort at times of crisis and need, and a host of other activities and relationships largely occurred within the framework of family and kinship. To understand rural Hungarian society one must understand the organization of the family. Because the family has retained a central role in the contemporary village, this is as true today as it was in the past.[3]

---

1. For justification of the use of kinship here as an "extension" of family relations, see the section "Kinsmen." It can also be noted that such kin group concepts as *had, nemzetség,* and *atyafiság* discussed in Fél and Hofer (1969: 151–158) have little application in contemporary Kislapos.

2. It should be emphasized that social and economic spheres were and still are by no means distinct. Treating them as analytically distinct allows one to see better their great overlap and integration within the family and extended family circles.

3. This chapter adds to Fél and Hofer's (1969) excellent portrait of prewar and precollective family and kinship relations in nearby Átány and applies it to Kislapos.

DIVISION OF LABOR WITHIN THE FAMILY

Put simply, prior to World War II, work was apportioned into two spheres: the domestic, focusing on the home and household activities, and the economic-agricultural, producing for subsistence and market. The former was generally regarded as the women's, the latter the men's world. There were numerous exceptions to this, however. Women usually cared for poultry and small animals, often milked the cows, and sold eggs and milk for pocket money. They also frequently joined in work in the fields, particularly when labor was most needed in the agricultural cycle. This distinction can be refined to apportion to men the prestigious heavy work of tending and working with the larger animals and doing field work involving greater strength, while leaving women with almost all domestic chores and less desirable "lighter" (though not easier) agricultural labor, like hoeing, singling, and harvesting fruits and vegetables.[4]

The division of labor by age and sex was a function both of the family cycle and of potential structural deficiencies of the family. In the middle peasant stem family, the ideal case, it was common for the newly married young couple to reside with the parents of the groom. At the marriage of a younger brother, a married older brother and his family were expected to find a place of their own. This usually involved renting a home elsewhere in the village. At the turn of the century it was still common for two or more married brothers and their families to remain living together in one household with the men's parents; but by the 1930s this custom, the joint family household, had waned.

Depending upon the workload, the men in the stem family would perform the field work and care for the animals; with a greater load, the women might also join in—first the *meny* (the daughter-in-law), then the *gazdasszony* (the head woman in the family).[5] Whether the married women worked was also dependent upon the presence of brothers and sisters of the married son, who would be expected to join in before the women. Indeed, if there was sufficient young labor in the family for field work, the *gazda* (the "ruling" male in the family) might leave most of the

---

4. Apparently men and boys were more sensitive about doing low-prestige women's work than were women about doing men's. One informant related how during World War I, when his father was called up, his mother plowed and sowed the grain and his older sisters harvested. His job as a nine-year-old was to gather the swaths of cut wheat. He refused and sat down in the shade: "What would the people of Gödör say, if they saw the man picking the swaths and the girls harvesting!" Similarly, Sárkány (1978: 75) says that hoeing and gathering the sheaves of cut wheat were defined as female tasks and were strongly shunned by males. Even as summás-s males tried to show their inability to hoe.

5. As this category and its male counterpart, *gazda*, are laid out in more detail in the section on distribution of power, I shall temporarily refrain from greater elucidation of terms where it is not yet necessary.

work in the fields to them, picking his own work closer to home and handling the family's "business" affairs, while maintaining a directing role.

In fact, in some stem families the gazda opted for this role early on. In such cases, the young couple would do most of the family's field work. In the summer they might go out with the wagon to the fields even before sunrise to gather moist fodder for the cattle, while the elderly couple took care of the work around the house, the milking of the cows, and the feeding of the other animals. As long as the elderly male was strong, he would also go into the fields to work with the younger couple, but with age his role would be more of direction and less of actual involvement.

His wife tended to remain at home to cook and handle the daily household chores and affairs. She would have the midday meal ready for the other household members when they came in from the fields; and at busier periods of the crop cycle she might take the meal to the fields and handle the noon feeding of the animals herself (at less busy times this would be shared more equally by all members of the family). At the busiest times of the year, such as during the wheat harvest, when the family would frequently be out in the fields from before dawn until nightfall, she, too, might help gather the cut wheat. In the evening and during the less busy times of the year, such as in winter, the women under the direction of the gazdasszony might handle household tasks like sewing, ironing, and washing. At these less busy times the men could spend time in the barns talking and tending the animals.[6]

The births of the younger couple's children did not significantly alter this arrangement. After infancy they were watched over mainly by the elderly woman in the family while their mother again went out to the fields. It was not unusual for a healthy young mother to be out in the fields in the last few weeks before birth and to be back within a few months thereafter. In the meantime, her mother-in-law often spelled her in the fields.

The children soon entered into the work of the family enterprise. Around the time they entered school, at age six or seven, many children took the geese out to pasture and began to share in the feeding of the piglets and other small animals. Within two or three years they would be helping to thin out crops of vegetables and would be learning other tasks, like the handling of larger animals by boys and the hoeing, reaping, and gathering of harvest by both sexes. Girls were expected to play a significant role in household work, often almost completely taking over cook-

6. However, unlike nearby Atány (Fél and Hofer 1969, 1973)—where the stables were quite distant from the homes—*tanyázás,* holding regular nightly male gatherings in the barns, was not common. However, see the discussion on the village's prewar Peasants' Circle in Chapter 4.

ing and care of smaller children in nuclear households when both parents' work was required in the fields.

Ultimately, children were assigned work appropriate to their sex; but up until a little before puberty they tended to do the tasks that best corresponded to their age, strength, and skills. It was not unusual for older, stronger girls to help with plowing or other predominantly male tasks, while a younger brother would pitch in, albeit unwillingly, with work normally assigned to women.

Often, though by no means always, by the time the children had become teenagers, their grandparents were no longer able or willing to put in their accustomed heavy work in the fields. This made it necessary for the children to join in as full working members in the peasant enterprise. By this age, most children no longer attended school; few went beyond the standard sixth grade. Even when they were in school, attendance was frequently interrupted at busy times of the agricultural cycle when their help was needed. Indeed, because of the illness or death of the father or his absence from home due to war, boys as young as ten could be required to take over a man's work. With the approach of marital age, the stage was set for the family cycle to begin anew.

But the stem family and middle peasant family were hardly universal in Kislapos. In the families of the nagygazda-s, even when farmhands were hired, sons were expected to participate in the field work. Women, particularly the gazdasszony, concentrated mostly on household tasks and cooking for day laborers. Children in these families were not expected to take on much of the agricultural work. They could concentrate more on acquiring an education and on learning to direct others. One nagygazda, an exception, occasionally ordered his two daughters and son into heavier agricultural work to make sure they did not get too "soft." If hay had to be gathered quickly he called the girls out to work, even paying them a half day's wages.

Teenage members of smallholders' families were often expected to go to local estates or, less frequently, to the nagygazda-s to do day labor, or to work as sheaf gatherers alongside harvesters. Because these households, those of the children of middle peasants with large families, and those of the landless were more often nuclear, the wives had to take on more of the heavier agricultural labor; in turn, older children were expected to stay at home caring for younger siblings and assuming more of the domestic chores while parents worked in the fields.

The situation was similar but more extreme for landless families. When they took on day labor and harvesting, their children were expected to help more than did other children. When they went off as summás-s, children also took on full-time tasks on the contracting estates for partial pay, while women did both domestic and agricultural work. In the case of cseléd-s the split between domestic and agricultural work was more clearly along sexual lines. Men and boys did the contracted agricultural work for their employers for full and partial pay, respectively, while women and girls took care of the poultry and domestic work at home and often did similar work for the employer's wife, the wives of other nagygazda-s, or the foreman's family on an estate.

The situation among the village intelligentsia resembled that of the nagygazda-s; that of the craftsmen was closer to the middle peasants' division of labor. Children in both statuses had more emphasis placed on their formal education and/or learning a trade or profession than did children of other family types. In all families, as Fél and Hofer (1969: 114, 119–120) note, it was the gazda's task to teach at least the boys how to do the work around the farm, while the more formal and moral education of both sexes remained in the hands of the gazdasszony, as did the teaching of domestic tasks to girls.[7]

These differing relationships of men and women to their children and grandchildren are reflected in their treatment of their children. As Fél and Hofer (1969: 113–115) point out, the gazda was often quite authoritarian in his decisions about a child's future and even concerning the youth's potential spouse. The man was the "agent of discipline" and, though he showed occasional tenderness toward children, he felt "that they 'ought to be loved unnoticed.' " The gazdasszony, though she also exacted discipline, enjoyed a closer emotional relation to her children and grandchildren. Exemplifying this were the felt lifelong duty of the mother to care for her daughter when sick and especially at childbirth, even if the daughter lived in another village (ibid.: 121), and the money given by mothers to sons to help cover bachelor expenses (ibid.: 118, 198). The following quotation summarizing the differing foci of male and female orientation in Átány applies equally well to Kislapos and other villages and by analogy to relations within the family as well as outside it:

Whereas the esteem in which the family is held by the village is a function of the status and character of the *gazda*, friendly relations with neighbors and kin are maintained largely by the *gazdasszony*. Her daily interest, small acts of kindness, and participation in the custom of widespread lending and borrowing are the components of good social relations and a guarantee of help in case of need (ibid.: 120).

Besides being the managers of all household funds, charged with frugally and wisely apportioning household supplies, women were responsible for domestic matters, helped significantly in agricultural work when needed, and provided emotional tenderness in contrast to male authority.

7. In more prosperous families the girls were spared much of the domestic and field work common to their poorer counterparts. Thus, it was often the mother-in-law who was responsible for teaching these tasks or reteaching them to suit her demands (Fél and Hofer 1969: 120).

DISTRIBUTION OF POWER

Power within the family, that is, the possession of control, authority, and influence over members of the family and its material resources, was generally in the hands of the elder couple in the household. In particular, it was invested in the status of the gazda—usually the oldest married man or widower in the stem or nuclear household (as well as the joint household, though there were few cases of this by the 1930s in Kislapos)—and the gazdasszony, who was usually his wife. His position was due him because of his sex and his ownership and proprietorship of the family estate (Fél and Hofer 1969: 113–133, 408–409).

The old gazda made the farming decisions, directed the agricultural work, and even played a determining role in the work and career choices of his children and grandchildren. Although he often made decisions in consultation with his wife and not infrequently with his son as well, his voice was final. This was his prerogative until death or the time at which he handed over the reins to his son, who then became gazda with the same rights and privileges. As gazda-s held onto their power as long as they could and did not usually surrender it to their sons until death or until they became feeble, it was not unusual for the gazda to be a grandfather in a three-generation family, making important decisions about his grandchildren's futures. In cases where the gazda died young, a son as young as ten or twelve might assume the gazda position, although he did not really have full authority over the household as his father had had. If the children were too small, the widow would assume gazda status.[8]

The gazdasszony directed the household affairs; money for nonfarming expenses was in her care. The meny (daughter-in-law) was under her control, and their relationship was often strained because of the meny's lack of say in household affairs, including those directly affecting her own marriage; the often overbearing guidance of the gazdasszony; and the stigma of "outsider" that could remain with the meny for years. Though gradually the gazdasszony handed over more tasks and responsibilities (for example, cooking meals and baking the family bread) to her daughter-in-law, she, too, kept her power until she died or relinquished it.

The gazdasszony was not always the gazda's wife. An older widower often decided not to remarry if he had a meny in the household and

8. "Gazda" has other glosses as well. Fél and Hofer (1969: 408–409) report it as also being "(1) a peasant owning a farm which enables him to support his family without additional income (at least 15 to 20 hold-s of land); (2) a farmer by birth, upbringing, and experience; (3) the head of a family—e.g., 'the woman is gazda in that house'; (4) an elderly man, a well-to-do head of a family who lets his son or a servant do the work while retaining direction for himself; (5) in labor bands, the entrepreneur, organizer, leader." These definitions all give the idea of a financially self-sufficient individual and/or a leader and organizer or head, while offering a fuller view of the gazda status to which at times many of the definitions applied simultaneously.

wanted to continue living with his family. He would accept his meny as gazdasszony in order not to disrupt relations with his family.[9] If he had younger children, remarriage was far more likely.

Parental (or grandparental, as was often the case when the elder couple retained their power) authority was important and was maintained in overlapping economic and social spheres. Generally children were brought up to continue in the footsteps of their parents and, in the case of boys (or at least the eldest son), to succeed the father in the family enterprise. They were trained in agricultural practices, and little thought was given to their missing school if parents needed their help at home or in the fields. If a trade or craft was considered, it was the parents (or grandparents) who determined the matter.

Although by 1935 parents usually no longer picked out their children's spouses, they still exerted considerable impact on the final choice, frequently maintaining a veto via control of the land that would later be the young couple's livelihood. In cases where the couple chose to live separately—because of parental dissatisfaction with the selected marital partner or because of the young couple's inability to live under the dominance of the older one—lacking their own land, they often found themselves impoverished.

Besides age- or generation-based power, male dominance was also built into the family structure. Formally males had ultimate authority in family decisions, although women were often roughly equal partners in the enterprise, particularly if they did a great deal of the agricultural labor or if the husband had little land. Indeed, in cases where a man's weak will or his wife's particularly dominant personality resulted in a shift of household authority into her hands, she was referred to as the gazda in the house (Fél and Hofer 1969: 114).

Two other factors reinforced the cultural ideal of male dominance: 1) the younger family usually started out in the household of the husband's family; 2) despite laws in Hungary calling for equal inheritance for both sexes, a daughter often inherited less land than a son, partially because her trousseau at marriage was subtracted from her total inheritance. Moreover, any land received at marriage by the meny was often treated separately from the land of the rest of the family if there were children

9. As I have no data on the subject, and Fél and Hofer's report (1969: 121) does not treat it, speculation on the position of the son in those cases where the meny became gazdasszony but the father retained his gazda status is interesting. Did this lead to considerable father-son conflict or even son-wife conflict because of the elevated status of the meny compared to her husband? Were gazda-s more likely to step down at this time or soon after and hand the reins to their sons? If so, was this because of this discrepancy and the strains (cognitive and interpersonal) it may have introduced into the family, or was it due to the already advanced age of the gazda?

other than the son (Fél and Hofer 1969: 134). This, plus the fact that she usually received her share of inherited land only at the death of one or both parents, thus later in the family cycle, diminished for some time the importance of her inheritance to the new family. That much of her trousseau remained unused until she took over the gazdasszony role did not enhance her situation.

A typical case is that of Mária Harangi, wife of a peasant with seven hold-s. She describes the beginning and transformation of her life as a young meny:

You know what the custom is here in Hungary? When the little meny goes there, for a long time they don't buy her anything. Nothing at all. Those things that she brought from home were what she had to use for clothes, for shoes, for everything. Well, a good long time passed, I'd say eight or ten years, before a person really felt herself at home. Then in later years I also inherited one cadastral hold of land from my father and then I also had something to resort to, because we worked that separately, since my father-in-law allowed me to put its price aside. Out of that the two of us began to speculate. Right away we bought two little calves. We gave them out to be raised and when we got them back, they came back to the tune of 4,800 forint-s . . . When my father-in-law died, then the situation changed completely. Then my husband completely took over the enterprise and was able to make more headway.

The situation of the son-in-law (vő) or daughter-in-law (meny) moving into the household of the spouse's parents also illustrates the importance of age and sex in the family power structure. Less frequently it was the husband who moved in with his wife's family. This occurred particularly when the bride's family was much better off, the bride was an only child or one of several sisters, or, due to the bride's father's death, a man's labor was much needed in the bride's family. The position of the new household member was generally a difficult one, especially if he or she came from another village and, thus, had little contact with his/her own family. The spouse moving in had to become accustomed to different family customs, a new home environment, new kin, and frequently suspicion toward oneself by, and subordination of oneself to, the members of the receiving household. This subordinate status was compounded by the fact that the elder couple in such a household held virtually all the power in the family. They made almost all the decisions regarding the running of the agricultural enterprise, the direction of work, expenditures on food and clothing for all members of the household, and most other aspects of the young couple's life.

Although in real terms the position of the vő moving in with his wife's family was probably no worse than that of the meny in her husband's, his status was considered lower. Such a son-in-law was the exception to the norm and an even greater contrast to the position of the male ultimately as head of the household and economic enterprise. The real position of such a son-in-law was a function of the degree of economic need that the parents-in-law had for him, and it improved with greater need. Thus, his status within the family was better in the latter situations mentioned above than in the first few.

It should be emphasized, however, that it was often the older couple who maintained a solid front of authority over the younger; and it was not only the new member of the family who bore the yoke of their rule, which could be quite severe. The wife of a man with seven hold-s characterized her parents-in-law:

Like a little meny I had to dance the way the old ones played. They dictated things—in everything. They were the gazda-s. If I had to go to the store, I had to ask. If they didn't give anything for clothes, there wouldn't be any—and for that there wasn't very much. They went to the fair and they bought what they wanted for the little meny. My husband had to dance to it, too. We went out to hoe; the old man put the money into his pocket and went to the saloon.

Another woman, the daughter-in-law of a smallholder who had once been a harvest band leader on the Károlyi estates, told why she and her husband left the home of her father-in-law but two months after their marriage:

We went there because the children were small there. Two girls had already gotten married and my father-in-law was the only earner. He thought that we could help out. The relationship turned out so that we had to do everything; he didn't want to do anything. And the old one was a bit cantankerous, as they used to be in those days.

More usual was for the meny to feel powerless and discriminated against, for she was the newcomer, the one who had to learn the new ways and who was most cut off from outside support. As she was primarily under the direction of the gazdasszony, the greatest conflict developed there. It is not unusual for women informants in talking about their aged or dead parents-in-law to give highly contrasting pictures of the fathers- and mothers-in-law, with the former more positively judged. That the father-in-law was really more sympathetic is uncertain, but it is clear that this is partly a result of the older woman's greater role and dominance in the meny's existence. Conflicts between these women were the leading cause of the breakup of stem families.

INHERITANCE AND THE FAMILY CYCLE

The process of inheritance was closely intertwined with the family structural cycle. Both played a role in the dominance structure and, in turn, were influenced by it.

For the past fifty years, the family cycle has primarily involved a repeating pattern of stem and nuclear families, three-generation and two-generation families, or a combination of the two, with all but one child leaving the home to form a new household or live with in-laws. This was not always the complete list of pattern components. At the turn of the century the joint family, with two brothers and their families living together with their parents, was not uncommon. A one-time villager's depiction in her memoirs of childhood years in Kislapos around 1900 frequently mentions joint families, or at least brothers living with their respective families around the same yard and perhaps in the same building, although maybe not in one household (Berényi 1975). Several informants mention childhood households with as many as seventeen members. One such household consisted in 1914 of the informant, Sándor Tóth, then a boy, and his six sisters, his parents, his uncle (separated from his wife), his grandfather and the grandfather's third wife, that wife's two children from an earlier marriage, and his father's three step-sisters (from the grandfather's third marriage). Another family had twelve in the household in 1931: the informant and his sister, his parents, his father's brother with his wife and two children, his grandparents, and the two children of his father's older brother, who died in World War I (his widow had remarried).

There was a range of possible living arrangements for joint families. These two families could actually have lived in the same house and been "on one bread," pooling their resources, including food. They could also have lived together and worked the land collectively but not have been on the same bread. They could have lived in two different homes in the same yard, worked the land together, and not been on the same bread. Or they could even have been divided into a stem and a nuclear family, or two nuclear families (of brothers) in the same yard but have worked the land separately. There were other possibilities, but, like the last two examples, they are getting out of the realm of the joint family. Some of those possibilities survive in modified form even in today's collectivized farming village.

There had been much larger families in the early 1900s, more joint families, and many more families per yard than in later years. What happened to change matters? In general this was a nationwide development. The birthrate has declined throughout this century, for example, which has led to a smaller family size.[10] It has been argued that members of the

---

10. In southwest Hungary the *egyke*, or one-child system of birth limitation, dates back to the early nineteenth century. This birth limitation, practiced primarily by Calvinist Hungarians, served to stave off impoverishment of families over time because of continued division of small holdings among several heirs, and helped consolidate holdings of the families (Andorka 1975; 1979: 38–39). However, in extreme cases it led to severe population reduction and corresponding loss of influence of these groups in the areas where they lived.

middle and wealthy peasant strata were squeezed by economic and demographic pressures out of these strata into the ranks of either the smallholders and landless or the large landholders (Gunst 1976: 384–387).
Greater conformity to legal norms of equal inheritance for sons and
daughters undoubtedly exacerbated this tendency.[11]

There was also an increased desire of children throughout Hungary to
seek independence from their parents. Both nationwide and locally, the
minimal land "reform" of the 1920s gave some incentive to sons with
children to strike out on their own. Of perhaps greater importance were
the building sites parceled out through these reforms. With increased
opportunities for building separate homes, the process of setting up a
truly independent household was eased. This pattern continued after the
post-World War II land distribution.

Finally, the migrations to America in the late nineteenth and early twentieth centuries brought increased opportunity to seek a fortune or at least
a living outside the joint family circle. It is very unlikely that those who
came back, either enriched or no better off, were eager to return to a joint
family after the risk, hard work, and independence they had experienced
to improve their lots. And second, Lapos was always quite densely populated, making it difficult to maintain a large family on the land available.[12]
When the village "took off" financially in the 1930s due to the prosperity
brought on by animal breeding, and villagers were able to acquire considerable land outside its boundaries, the possibly greater opportunities for
such joint families were offset by the already large population and by the
well-advanced process of joint family splits, which by then had eliminated most of the joint families. Indeed, the last real joint family enterprise in Lapos ended in 1948 when the father of two young married sons
died; the two young couples split their share of the inheritance (some of it
went to other older siblings, leaving less total land anyway) and farmed
separately, although they continued until 1959 to live in opposite ends of
the same building.

11. There was little such economic pressure for birth limitation among landless
agricultural laborers. Additional children did little to decrease the already relatively poor chances for upward mobility; their taking on employment, frequently
when very young, may even have provided some additional income. As a result,
unlike landowning peasant families, the birthrate of this stratum decreased little
until after World War II (Andorka 1979: 39–40).

12. For this reason Chayanov's type of analysis (Kerblay 1971), taking into
account the ratio of working strength within a family to the number of consumers,
does not apply fully. The supply of land available to individual families was relatively inelastic because of the high price of land. Thus, socioeconomic status was
more closely related to land owned (as in Chapter 2) than the relative number of
working members (though both depended on the stage in the family life cycle, in
the case of nuclear families).

In typical cases, therefore, all but the youngest son left home at marriage or shortly thereafter. A daughter, unless she was an only child or one of the exceptions noted above, went to live with her husband's family or in a nuclear household with her husband. Older sons usually left home at marriage, establishing nuclear households or going to live with their wives' families. Among the landless and near landless it was not unusual even for only sons to leave home after, or even before, marriage. Occasionally older sons stayed home with their wives immediately after marrying until their younger brothers married. At that time they would usually leave "so that there would not be two young brides [and presumably greater conflict] at home."

It was not necessarily an advantage, however, for the younger brother to stay at home. In some cases he left instead of the older brother. For one thing, inheritance was partible and, as time went on, became more equally divided among all children. Though the son who went off after marriage to form an independent household may have been quite poor, he enjoyed other advantages. First, he was relatively independent of his parents and did not have to accept the often grating authority of his father. His brother at home might have to endure even his father's wasting the family property on drink or mismanaging the farm. Second, as one now elderly son of a smallholder expressed it: "He who stays with the parents when there are many [children] stays a beggar. He who goes separately gathers the strawberries because he works for himself, the other for the collective. For when the parents die, those who have already gone away take everything."

Though an exaggeration, this does reflect the basic truth that all children shared roughly equally in the inheritance even if they had not contributed to the common good for years since leaving home. The son remaining at home was expected to fill out his siblings' shares of the inheritance if they had received nothing or merely partial shares or a trousseau at marriage. If he wanted to keep his parents' land, he was expected to acquire more land to satisfy his siblings.

The case of informant Sándor Tóth, quoted just a few lines back, illustrates this principle well. Though continuing to live near his parents after marriage, he maintained a separate household and a separate peasant enterprise and thus avoided having to split his small and hard-earned landholdings among his siblings at his father's death.

In 1914 his father took his wife and seven children, along with his divorced brother, to live in the village separate from the rest of the originally seventeen member family. A year later they came back to live together but were no longer on one bread. By the time Sándor Tóth married, his father had seven and a half hold-s. Sándor and his bride stayed at his family's home for a year on one bread. Because his widowed mother-in-law constantly harangued them to go live with her and her other daughter, they did so. Much to her surprise, they moved into the back part of the house and did not live on one bread with her. At the time, Sándor Tóth reasoned that if his father had not mistreated him, and he went to live elsewhere (especially since he was the only boy in the family, with six sisters, and his whole family had asked him as sole son not to go), he would not go to live on one bread with someone else. Finally, after less than a year the couple moved back to his parents' home, living in a small storage room, but not on one bread because they wanted to be separate. Sándor Tóth worked as harvester for local peasants, including his father. His parents worked their land, and when they were no longer able to, he sharecropped it. He also sharecropped others' land and, before his father's death, acquired about four and a half hold-s on his own—one hold through the land reform after World War II, a little less than a hold bought or received from his father, and two and a half hold-s inherited by his wife.

To forestall such separatist tendencies, the son staying home was (and still is) sometimes given a larger share of the land or was credited with the house or a larger share of it for taking care of his parents in their old age. For example, the two brothers remaining at home in Lapos's last joint family each received five and a half hold-s out of a total of eighteen, although they had four considerably older siblings (two of each sex) who had left home earlier.

Women marrying out of the home had their share reduced by the value of the trousseau (for example, if they had been given furniture when establishing a separate home) and sometimes received a less than equal share anyway. Children leaving at marriage occasionally received a small piece of land to help them get started. This, too, was subtracted from their later inheritance.

On rare occasions an older gazda might parcel out a substantial part of his holdings to his sons even before his death. For example,

when Béla Gazsó's parents decided that eleven people [this is the previously mentioned family of twelve—one son of the dead uncle had since died from tuberculosis] were too many in their little house, they built a small house elsewhere in the village and moved there in 1933. They sold the mother's share of her parents' house to complete the building. The grandfather split up his land, giving five hold-s to each of his two surviving sons and keeping five for himself. Later, in 1940, the grandfather came to be with them so he could live with his son; his wife had died in 1936 and his other son had also died. He farmed his land together with the surviving son.

As another story has it:

One of Lapos's largest landholders in the 1920s and 1930s remarried after his first wife died, leaving nine children, most of them adults. His children protested the remarriage, perhaps because they feared that any half-siblings would reduce their share of the inheritance. To mollify them he split up most of his remaining land at the remarriage and gave the children land when they married, leaving himself with a small share of his once large farm. One of the two sons who remained in the village (the two others bought a tanya in a village ninety kilometers away) still had a house next to his father and fifteen or twenty hold-s of his own.

In general, older children did not favor a widowed father's remarriage because they feared a situation of the following type:

Ferenc Kis's wife died in 1916, having given birth to seven children, of whom five boys survived to adulthood. His second wife, after their marriage in 1917, gave birth to one girl. When Ferenc Kis died in 1945, his five sons shared equally in one-half of the inheritance of the house and the little land the father owned. Ultimately the half-sister alone inherited the other half through her mother's half-share of the property.

When one parent died, the other frequently retained control of half or all the property. Often this took the form of lifetime usufruct, although for-mal ownership might already have passed into the children's hands. These rights could be sold or traded.

In some cases, when the inheritance allocation had already been agreed upon before the gazda's death, rights in it could be traded even while he was still alive. Thus

István Kalicz, when he was about eighty in the mid-1930s, did not want to hand over control of his twenty-two and a half hold-s to his five surviving children (out of fifteen) until he died; he did agree, however, to give each child four and a half hold-s. By this time his eldest child Margit was approaching sixty. Long married to a poor smallholder, she was increasingly anxious to get her share of the inheri-tance. Her youngest brother, Gyula, in turn, wanted to preserve as much of his father's property in one piece as possible (this was much better than working scattered fields). Since Gyula himself had already acquired almost three and a half hold-s in small scattered parcels, he agreed to trade these fields for his sister's share of the inheritance and to pay the appropriate inheritance taxes as well. Since he was also able to buy the shares of his two brothers (one went to America, the other to Ózd, an industrial town to the north), he was able to keep eighteen hold-s of his father's land intact and later bought a few more to bring his total to twenty-three hold-s.

Another case illustrates several relevant factors.

Vilmos Kassa's two older brothers married in 1913; the eldest stayed home, the youngest left. His older sister married and left home shortly thereafter. By far the youngest child, Vilmos Kassa married in 1927 and lived on one bread with his widowed mother and his brother's family. When his brother remarried after his first wife died, they continued to live on one bread for two more years. When there began to be some dissension between the two couples, the brothers split up because "neither wanted to take orders from the other." Everything was split two ways: the land, the tools, and the house. Since there was only one kitchen between the front and back halves of the house, they continued to share it though no longer living on one bread. As was traditionally the case, the younger couple lived in the front end of the house, the older in the back half. Their mother lived with Vilmos Kassa. Because he took care of her, he used two-thirds of the land and his brother one-third. When his mother died in 1936, the land was split four ways among the four siblings. Because the older brother who had left home had died at an early age, his widow demanded his share. Since there were no surviving children, she received the right of use of her husband's land; when she died, the land was split equally among the three surviving siblings.

Although in this case the older brother somewhat atypically stayed home, this can be explained by the fact that his father had died. With the middle brother leaving home at the same time, the eldest brother's absence would have meant that his mother would be alone to work the land with her ten-year-old son. (Typically, when families split up, the mother lived with the younger son.) Moreover, when this split was made—much like other cases mentioned so far—the mother gave the right of use of her land (it was under her control following her husband's death) to her sons, retaining control over a share. Interestingly, the rights that the sons thus received were not ownership rights; when the mother died, ownership of the land was split evenly among all siblings, though possibly that of the house was not.

Five aspects of the family cycle and inheritance that recur above deserve further comment and emphasis. First, given the power of the gazda and his widow, as they grew older much of the disposition of land in their remaining years depended on their personalities and the quality of their relationships with their children. Some placed considerable demands on the children who stayed at home with them, demands that the children often could not successfully resist except by leaving home. Others were less anxious about holding on to their control of the land and even gave out shares to their children before they died. When relations were not so good, some gazda-s and widows gave their land for sharecropping or rent to others or perhaps to their own children.

Second, an assumption in the cases above, thus far unstated, is that equals would marry equals. That is, people were expected to select marriage partners of roughly the same strata or, perhaps, with roughly the same inheritance. Maximally there might be a difference of one stratum, although occasionally even this was thought too great. Temporarily ignoring all other factors, one can see that such a tendency would become increasingly important over the years as daughters shared more of the inheritances. Indeed, Fél and Hofer (1969: 139) point out that "until World War I—the son of a *gazda* [here taken as someone with at least fifteen to twenty hold-s] could marry a poor girl, since all daughters, even those of wealthier families, were allotted a minimum of the inheritance."

Much as in Átány (Fél and Hofer 1969: 139–141), considerations of property were secondary only when they were outweighed by physical, moral, or mental deficiencies in one partner or when a vő was sought to marry the daughter in a one-child family and to live with his parents-in-law. People with such flaws in the former case and such single daughters in the latter were likely to find spouses only in strata lower than their own. Even in these cases, land was seen as neutralizing such social markers. Otherwise, when a youth chose a spouse of a different status, conflict often developed between parents and child; the parents would try to dissuade their offspring or even to practice their veto. Sometimes this was successful, but sometimes a family rift resulted.

The number of potential spouses for a villager in the lower strata was much greater than for a wealthy peasant's child. This was due partly to the pyramid-shaped population distribution and partly to the similarity of the life circumstances of the lower strata. Thus, as in Átány, the wealthy peasant "stratum is closely linked together by intermarriages. 'Those who own more than twenty hold-s . . . are all related, all . . . in-laws' " (Fél and Hofer 1969: 285).

In Kislapos in the 1930s, the seven wealthiest gazda-s were Béla Magyar, József Kovács, Ferenc Kovács, Gáspár Fehér, András Magyar, László Gyarmati, and Sándor Pető. József and Ferenc Kovács were brothers, as were András Magyar's paternal grandfather, Béla Magyar's father, and László Gyarmati's father-in-law (he and his wife, childless until then, adopted the wife's sister's orphaned daughter). József Kovács married Sándor Pető's youngest sister, Sándor Pető married Béla Magyar's oldest sister, and Béla Magyar married József Kovács's younger sister, thus forming a marital circle. In addition, Ferenc Kovács married Gáspár Fehér's daughter; and the first wife (who died in childbirth) of Gáspár Fehér's son was Béla Magyar's paternal cousin, András Magyar's paternal aunt.

Another tendency manifesting itself in the first half of the century was the marriage of cousins "so that the estate wouldn't go apart." Fél and Hofer (1969: 141) point out that, while in the nineteenth century marriages even between third cousins were viewed as incestuous, the attempt "to balance status and maximize property" led to marriages even of first cousins in Átány (and Lapos), with special permission granted by the clergy. Another practice that kept property within the larger family was that of brother and sister marrying sister and brother "in exchange." Sometimes the marriages were celebrated together, sometimes years apart.[13]

---

13. Of course, the practice of visiting married siblings and cousins undoubtedly increased this tendency, as it did that of sisters or girl cousins marrying into the same neighboring village or into Lapos from outside. The practice of holding multiple wedding ceremonies in a family to save on reception costs also had a role. The occasional practice of levirate and sororate also reflected this tendency to keep the estate together (although it may well have predated it).

Third, one's share of parental inheritance was highly dependent upon the number of siblings in the family; given the high birthrates of many families in the area, that was one of the prime determinants of ultimate wealth. A middle peasant's estate divided up among six children would produce as many smallholders, whereas the only child of a middle peasant contracting a good marriage could end up a wealthy peasant.

Fourth, the life of a middle peasant's son or daughter establishing a nuclear household at marriage consisted of two quite different phases. The first was that of a relatively poor existence before a share of the family inheritance had been received. In this period the son might lead the existence of a poor harvester/day laborer or smallholder (if, for example, he or his wife received some small preliminary share of their respective inheritances), scraping together money to buy a house or a little land. Following the death of their parents, children might well reenter the higher stratum of their birth and start a far more comfortable existence.

Last, it should be pointed out that there were exceptions to many of the norms of remaining in or leaving the childhood household. Some of these can be explained by other semiconflicting norms, others by family conflicts, and still others by the chain-reaction effect of one exception leading to others. Thus,

Ilona Tóth and Albin Nagy were married in 1950. Both were the eldest children in their families. Ilona Tóth was Sándor Tóth's daughter; his four hold-s would ultimately be divided up among four children. Albin Nagy's father was a middle peasant and a postman; having only one younger sister, Albin could eventually count on a larger inheritance. However, because his parents did not approve of his bride, partly because they had hoped for someone better off, the couple rented a house for themselves. (This for an only son was not typical. Albin was a soldier at the time and remained so for thirteen more years before going to work in Budapest in an elevator factory. It is not clear whether he reenlisted before the decision to be married or afterward. Such a decision may have depended on his possibly not being able to or not wanting to count on the use of his father's land. This and the conflict made setting up a nuclear household easier, if not more pleasant. Interestingly, he continued until 1959 to come home at harvest to help his wife with the work on their little plot and sharecropped land.) Although relations improved with the parents to the point where they helped the younger couple build a house, the couples remained separate.

Albin's sister Anna married György Burom in 1956. György Burom was the youngest in his poor middle peasant family of four sons and three daughters. Of the latter, the eldest never married but died a spinster at forty in 1958, while the other two left home after marriage. One of the older sons died in World War II, and the eldest son left home; György Burom's directly older brother married in 1952 and stayed home, perhaps because his mother had died a year before, leaving his widowed father, older sister, and drafted soldier, younger brother György. In 1956 the brother's wife gave birth to their first son. Because the older brother was already at home, perhaps because of the new child, and because there was no one home with Anna Nagy's parents, György Burom and Anna Nagy moved in with them; they had thought of living alone, but the latter fact changed their minds. Finally, about four years later, just after the main collectivization drive in Kislapos, they bought another house into which Anna Nagy's parents moved, leaving them with their own house and a house in the future for their child.

KINSMEN

Relatives played a major role in the life of a rural villager. A substantial part of the annual cycle was conducted either alongside them or with their help. Their comfort, presence, and company were expected in times of family crisis and celebration, and their help was sought in times of need. Much of one's social circle was made up of relatives. Of course, relatives were not the only ones turned to for help. Generally, those people were sought with whom one already had some sort of relationship or connection: blood relatives, in-laws, neighbors, koma-s (godparents of one's children and/or childhood friends), and so on.

In two ways, relatives could be considered an extension of the family or household. First, many of those considered close kinsmen were in fact people with whom one might have lived or did live in earlier years, before the breakup of joint families or the exodus of daughters and older sons from the household. Similarly, they included those with whom one's parents had lived in earlier years. Thus, siblings and their children; one's own children, parents and grandparents; and uncles, aunts, and cousins were included—literally the extended family that in the past had often lived together. However, not only collateral and lineal relatives were included in the broad notion of relatives, but affinal relations as well. These were not in the full sense relatives, but they often occupied roles relative to oneself similar to those of blood kin.

In addition, relatives fulfilled many of the same functional roles in relationships that household family members did. It was culturally expected that when the family by itself could not take care of certain matters, relatives would help out. They were sought out except when it was much more convenient to do otherwise.

Let us look first at the day-to-day reciprocal economic and working relationships existing among related families. Probably the most common was reciprocal aid by relatives in the threshing of the grain harvest. From the 1920s on, several villagers (usually wealthy peasants) owned large threshing machines, which they hired out to local peasants. They provided the machine and an operator to handle controls, adjustments, and repairs; but the gazda provided the work force, which, depending on the size of the machine, ranged from fifteen to thirty hands, typically twenty to twenty-two. Many tasks were involved, including cutting the sheaves, heaving them up to the loader, feeding them into the threshing machines, pulling out the straw, carrying away the grain, straw, and chaff, carrying water for the steam boiler, and firing the boiler (Sárkány 1978: 75). The work force, known locally as the *kaláka*, consisted of relatives, neighbors, and perhaps koma-s and *nász*-s (the parents-in-law of one's child). Among the relatives might be both spouses' siblings and their respective spouses, cousins, uncles and aunts, and even parents. Less often in-laws' parents and more distant affinal and collateral relations came. In return, the workers would receive a meal and similar aid when their respective harvests were threshed. Attempts were made to equalize the work given, although there was no strict accounting. If one gazda had more land than another and thus required more threshing time, he might send more members of his family to help out with a poorer gazda's threshing. Sárkány reports (ibid.) that wealthy peasants also engaged in the work reciprocation, but the number of people involved was larger; harvesters joined in the threshing, as did day laborers, who were repaid with other kinds of work (carting, for example).

House-building was done in a similar fashion. Whereas later work like plastering could be done at leisure by the owner's family, the walls and roof had to be put up quickly, requiring a large work force. Almost invariably, both spouses' siblings and their mates helped out, and often parents and cousins. Neighbors, too, usually helped, and koma-s and good friends were frequently present. In addition, many others came to help out to reciprocate for similar help already given or with the expectation that they, too, would benefit from such aid when they eventually built. Team owners helped bring building materials; this was also reciprocated in kind or with other work.

Other frequent work, like husking maize, harvesting and pressing grapes for wine, and harvesting sugar beets and turnips for cattle, involved smaller groups of close relatives. Still other tasks, some in the more distant past, are mentioned by Fél and Hofer (1969: 161), such as washing homespun yarn in lye or hoeing and haying (which involved still fewer people, usually brothers and first cousins and possibly parents of both spouses).

More rarely, siblings and brothers-in-law worked together on their lands, living independently and keeping their harvests separate. For example,

in 1931 Károly Kelemen, the youngest of three brothers, left home to live with his wife and widowed mother-in-law, leaving his older brother at home with his parents. Since he lacked larger animals for plowing, he and his brother and brother-in-law worked their lands together, using the three or four horses of his parents. Although Károly Kelemen had less land than his brother cultivated at home, and the sister's husband had even less, relatively little thought was given to who had more land. Later he, his brother, and another machine-minded villager bought a tractor, and all used it for the two years they had it, along with his brother-in-law.

This degree of mutual aid was somewhat unusual. More typical were the tasks mentioned already and occasional help requested and given for tasks of short duration, that required more work strength than an individual family could muster. It was also common for a teamless individual to ask a relative to cart some produce or grain or to plow his land in return for other work. This did not differ significantly from relations between nonrelatives.

At times of need when help was required for lengthier periods, one turned to relatives. Thus, when his father was called up in World War I, Sándor Tóth together with his brother-in-law plowed both their fields, each contributing one horse. When Béla Kelemen's father was called up in World War II, his father's brother, Károly Kelemen, and his brother-in-law helped the ten-year-old boy with the plowing and the rest of the field work. Sometimes, after the death of a grown sibling, other siblings would help out their in-laws or nephews and nieces with the work for a while.

Relatives played an important role at family crises and celebrations. At the birth of a child, the mother's mother provided much of the care for the new mother and child. Siblings and cousins were expected to provide meals for the young mother for several weeks after birth, bringing them from home. At the christening feast of a firstborn child both spouses' parents, grandparents, and siblings were invited along with the godparents.

Virtually all relatives, even beyond second cousins, attended weddings. Most of those who settled outside the village tried to attend and similarly invited relatives in Lapos to attend their own family weddings. Like everyone invited, relatives were expected to bring chickens, wine, and other food for the reception; closer relatives, along with neighbors, took part in preparation of the food for the receptions at the bride's and groom's homes. In addition, brothers, sisters, cousins, uncles, aunts, and grandparents gave gifts of "kerchiefs, dress material, kitchenware, and table sets" (Fél and Hofer 1969: 159, 211–212).

Funerals were also widely attended by relatives. Smaller groups of closer relatives took part in the various rites associated with the death, mourning, and funeral. For example, only the closest relatives, the sons-in-law, brothers-in-law, and nász-s, and the group of mourning women who as close female relatives were almost constantly around the deceased, attended the closing of the coffin. Sons-in-law, brothers-in-law, and nász-s helped dig the grave, and they, along with the close relatives, attended the funeral feast following the burial (Fél and Hofer 1969: 222).

The annual pig-killing, usually near Christmas and invariably in winter, involved a smaller circle of kin. Usually siblings, parents, children, grandparents, sons- and daughters-in-law, brothers- and sisters-in-law, and nász-s were invited for the feast in the evening after the butchering and processing of the slain pig. Fewer kin took part in the actual work. As this was one of the important annual family social occasions, close relatives living in other parts of the country made an effort to be present.

It is noteworthy that middle and wealthy peasants were able to reckon and cultivate a wider circle of kinship ties than their poorer fellow villagers. Nagygazda-s, for example, were able to invite a greater number of relatives to their pig-killing feasts (Fél and Hofer 1969: 280), which also enhanced their prestige. While the children of nagygazda-s were often forced to look outside the village for potential spouses of equal wealth and standing, they were more able to keep up ties with their relatives and close family than were the poorer cseléd-s, who probably married outside their village of birth equally as frequently but were less able to maintain ties with their kinsmen.

In general, much of one's social activity was with relatives. Although some activities like house-building and threshing (given the limited availability of the threshing machine) had to be done quickly and, thus, required many hands, it is clear that in these activities—and even more so in others involving material labor obligations—much of the impetus for working together came from the opportunities to socialize. The tedium of the work was reduced and the time seemed to go faster.

Family and kinship relations were very important in work that did not involve labor exchanges. Bands of harvesters and summás-s contracting with large estates were often comprised of individuals and families bound by kin and kinlike relations: brothers, male in-laws, uncles, more distant relatives, and koma-s (Katona 1962; Fél and Hofer 1969: 285–287). Where obtaining such work for a few months was vital for a poor smallholder or landless laborer, such connections were very important.

NEIGHBORS

Although relationships with neighbors were not as deep as those with kinsmen, they, too, were multifaceted and involved a variety of economic and social cooperation. Neighbors were also involved, though in more limited ways, in family crises and celebrations and were very important in everyday activities.

Before going into some of these areas of cooperation, it should be pointed out that, although neighbors were often lifelong neighbors, neighborhoods were by no means permanently constituted. Families did move within the village. Young couples establishing nuclear households often moved several times into rented houses before buying or building more permanent homes of their own. With the distribution of building sites in the 1920s and 1930s, and as part of the postwar land reform of the 1940s, there was an increasing tendency for long-established families to build outside the old village core, and particularly for poorer ones to do so. The steadily decreasing birthrate, along with continued outmigration and, from the late thirties on, increased work opportunities outside Kislapos, led whole families to leave the village; this left empty houses into which new neighbors could move. The tendency toward change has probably gained in tempo up until the present.

Neighbors sometimes were relatives, but only in a minority of cases. In the late nineteenth and early twentieth centuries this may have been more common, especially in the more densely populated core, where several families lived in one yard with several siblings—or father and son—living in adjoining houses, albeit not together. As the population spread out in the village, this became less common, although siblings sometimes did build or buy houses next to one another or to their parents, or have parents buy, build, or make available houses neighboring their own homes. There was not even the infrequent presence of truncated clan-like (*had*) groupings of relatives living in one neighborhood, as there was in Átány (Fél and Hofer 1969: 155–156). More often than not, neighbors were not related.

In general, neighbors were those whose houses were nearby; spatial contiguity of land did not alone determine who counted as neighbor. In Lapos, where for the most part houses were regularly spaced in rows on the streets, people often had second or third neighbors—the occupants of homes two and three houses away in both directions. A house opposite one's own was also a neighbor, as were houses situated diagonally across the street. There were also *kert* neighbors, people whose kert-s (small plots of land or gardens, usually next to or behind houses, used for raising fruits, vegetables, and grapes for home consumption) bordered one another.

To a great degree, the remarks here apply to direct (contiguous) neighbors, although who actually was considered a neighbor depended much on the relationships that developed. Often the very nearness of neighbors determined their usefulness. For the borrowing of different types of farming implements or tools, the exchanges of small favors, and the reciprocal exchanges of work it was often simpler to go to a neighbor than to go across the village to a relative. For a small emergency like the birth of a calf, when several people would help pull the calf out to ease the cow's burden, neighbors were available on shorter notice. Because of this, much of the work exchanged, the borrowing carried on, and the favors done among neighbors closely resembled those practiced by relatives.

In general, reciprocity was expected in Kislapos, although it is unclear that over the short run favors, tools borrowed, and labor offered were expected to balance out exactly, as Fél and Hofer report about Átány (1969: 174–176). In some areas more exact exchange was awaited. For example, one prosperous middle peasant often offered or was asked for the use of a team for carting and plowing by his poor teamless small-holder neighbor. He would ask the smallholder for manual labor in return when he needed it, in accordance with the accounting that his wife had done.

For various kinds of borrowing and very short-term help, a principle of rough reciprocity seemed to hold, with the assumption that if A helped B, A could count on B's help in the same way or on B's loan of implements or tools, or on B helping out in some other way when A needed it. It is certain that mutual aid could have gone on for quite a while in Kislapos without an exact balance or a quick evening out of exchanges.[14]

Fél and Hofer (1969: 281) and Jávor (1978: 356) point out that poor villagers were more dependent upon the neighborhood borrowing net-work than their wealthier fellow villagers because they owned fewer implements, and those were often in poorer condition. The fact that their reckoning and cultivation of relatives was narrower probably also played a part in this dependency.

Neighbors were usually part of the kaláka for threshing, as well as part of the larger group for putting up the walls and roof of a new house. In the former case, they could count on reciprocation in kind. In the latter case, reciprocation might be much slower in coming.

At weddings, neighbors, who were invited to the wedding feast, often loaned dishes and chairs, gave lodging to relatives of the bride and groom, and made their homes available for other purposes. At the death of a neighbor, when the body of the deceased was kept in his family's home until the funeral, neighbors offered space in their homes for the occasional overflow of condoling visitors and helped out in other ways at the funeral. Although they were not usually invited to the pig-killing feast, they were sent samples of the meat prepared and reciprocated in kind.

In general, neighbors could be counted on for small favors like caring for children, and tending smaller animals, when the parents were away; they took part in several other neighborhood group-work tasks and paid each other frequent short visits (particularly women). All in all, though relatives came first, in a pinch neighbors could be depended upon to substitute for them; in a more limited fashion, neighbors served many of the same economic and social functions as relatives.

---

14. I have little data on past reciprocation of help or borrowed objects. Presently in Kislapos, less thought is given to precise reciprocation of such borrowed ob-jects, although longer work is paid or reciprocated. But objects loaned today are not usually as valuable as farming implements were in the past. It is possible that in Lapos as well as Átány there may have been more exact reciprocity in the past for implements, tools or even labor.

KOMA-S

The godfather of a villager's child, or a male for whose children one is a godparent, is one's koma. Such individuals reciprocally refer to each other as koma-s. Until recent outmigration from Lapos they maintained a close relationship with one another and with their godchildren. Although more limited in scope than the relationship between relatives, the koma tie was often very strong and more emotionally intense than many nonimmediate kin ties. In some ways koma relationships combined the tone of friendship and kinship. This was a function partly of the koma role itself and partly of the fact that koma-s generally were chosen from among close friends and often from among relatives.

Unlike Átány (Fél and Hofer 1969: 166), where there was a single baptismal koma, in Kislapos each child had baptismal and confirmational godparents. Occasionally the baptismal godparents were also chosen to be confirmational godparents. The difference in practice may have been a product of the religious differences between the two villages: Kislapos is Roman Catholic, Átány Calvinist.

The distinction between baptismal and confirmational koma-s led to differences between Átány and Kislapos in the roles of koma-s before World War II. Baptismal koma-s in both villages helped out at funerals. As good friends they participated in kaláka-s for their koma-s' threshing and house-building and helped out at other times. But in Kislapos they were not the *násznagy*-s (the best man and witness, the honored guest, the master of ceremonies, and in some ways the host at the reception) at weddings of their godchildren as were their counterparts in Átány. Nor did their wives serve as gazdasszony at the reception in charge of preparations. In Lapos it was generally the confirmational koma who filled the honored role of násznagy. He had the responsibility of making a large contribution to the cost of the reception and of providing a sizable gift for the newlyweds. Of course, the baptismal koma maintained a good relationship with child and parents, buying gifts for the child, visiting and being visited by him. Both koma relationships had a great purely social component.

This does not minimize the economic aid sometimes extended by godparents to their godchildren. When János Vas married in 1946, his prosperous middle peasant confirmational godparents gave the young, virtually landless couple a good strong blind horse, some money, a piglet to be raised for pork, employment as harvesters on their land, and some land for sharecropping.

The baptismal koma chosen by a husband or a couple had once usually been one of the best friends of the husband, most often from childhood or bachelorhood. Indeed, "koma" often means just that—a good male friend of the same age group or bachelor band of one's youth. Among newcomers like the cseléd-s and recent landless settlers it was common to pick the wealthy peasant for whom one worked as godparent, perhaps hoping to establish a fruitful relationship with him. For example, the confirmational godfather of the youth János Kis and his younger brother, who then worked along with their father and brothers as cseléd-s for Béla Magyar, was the very same Béla Magyar—also a distant kinsman through the younger János Kis's maternal grandmother. The godfather for an older brother was Béla Magyar's father.

But increasingly over the past fifty years, villagers have followed the nationwide tendency (Fél and Hofer 1969: 164) of picking close relatives as godparents. For example, Márton Kelemen, whose godchildren were all born thirty-five to fifty years ago, was baptismal godfather to sons of two of his wife's patrilateral parallel male cousins and his mother's youngest sister's daughter. He was confirmational godfather to Zoltán Nagy, his second cousin through grandparent brothers, to Lajos Pető, to Mihály Gazsó, a distant relation, and to Julianna Sike, his mother's brother's daughter.

This tendency has resulted in several changes in the nature of the koma relationship. In the past, good male friends were chosen to be baptismal godfathers and koma-s. There was a formal or sometimes informal agreement that any forthcoming children of the godfather would have the original requester as baptismal godfather. All future children of each would also have the same godfather. But this was already changing by the 1930s in several ways. There was no longer solely exclusive reciprocation; the reciprocation that did exist was often of a different form.

Exclusive reciprocation was sometimes made difficult by circumstances. Fél and Hofer (1969: 163) describe a case in Átány in which two friends in their bachelor days had promised one another to be godparents of their children. When one of them was asked by a third to be his baptismal koma, he first wanted to refuse because of his earlier promise; his parents argued that it was improper not to accept such an honor and did not let him refuse. He then agreed to be godfather but promised his other friend that he would ask him to be his children's godfather. This compromise was opposed by the parents of the third individual because their son would not then be the honored guest at his koma's child's wedding (an event of great honor in a male's life), as was customary in Átány for a baptismal godparent. He would then not be the baptismal godparent and would not get full reciprocation.

Attention to this norm is seen even in the case of János Kis. When he and his younger brother were married at the same time with a single reception, János asked Béla Magyar to be the násznagy. Since by then the family was working for another peasant, Ferenc Kovács, the younger brother wanted to ask Ferenc to be his násznagy; Ferenc, however, said that he should first ask Béla Magyar, his confirmational godfather. He did so, and Béla replied that being násznagy just for János was honor enough. Only then did Ferenc agree.

Koma-s were often exclusively one another's children's baptismal godfathers even as relatives, as was the case with Tibor Kakas and his older sister's son-in-law István Varga, who were about the same age and each of whom had three children in the 1950s. However, this pattern became less frequent as parents increasingly sought to give more relatives the honor; many wanted, for example, to have children's godparents from both sides of the family. The unequal ages and statuses of such koma-s tended to lead to another kind of reciprocation pattern, discussed below, while the shouldering of godparenthood before marriage to a spouse with different godparental obligations made exclusive reciprocation less probable.[15]

The reciprocation pattern that occurred with increasing frequency was an alternating one of the following form: A being godparent for B's child led to B's child being godparent for A's child (or for a descendant of a succeeding generation if the ages were thus more compatible or other commitments had to be satisfied first). This could take place in more indirect form, as in the previously mentioned case of Márton Kelemen and Zoltán Nagy. Not only was Zoltán the younger second cousin of Márton, but Zoltán's mother was Márton's wife's confirmational godparent. More complex alternating arrangements will be examined in a later chapter.

As younger relatives began to be called upon as baptismal godparents, godparents who were not couples became more common. Brothers and sisters and far less related pairs have been godparents. After marriage, of course, it was only proper to ask the couple as a whole, but increasingly before marriage husband and wife became godparents of different children.

ADOLESCENT COMPANIONS AND FRIENDSHIP

After marriage, family and kin ties largely structured one's social links. Friendship as a relationship independent of kinship, koma, and neighborhood ties did not play as important a part in people's lives as it had before marriage.

Much as in neighboring Átány (Fél and Hofer 1969: 185–201) and in the rest of Hungary, Kislapos's youth were divided into age grades of adolescent boys and girls. From the end of formal schooling, which roughly

---

15. Though not impossible: Zoltán Nagy's wife as a child of fourteen was asked by her cousin to be her infant's godmother. She accepted and was godmother for the succeeding two children also; in turn, she asked her cousin to be godmother for her own child. Had she had another child, however, one of her brothers would probably have been godfather and his wife godmother.

coincided with the beginning of adolescence, boys spent much of their free time in bands with other boys their age. Except for marriages, deaths, and migration out of the village, the composition of these groups did not change over the years. Within the framework of these bands boys and young men courted, held parties, played pranks, joined in the Easter Monday sprinkling of eligible girls,[16] caroled at Christmas, took part in other celebrations, went to the *Levente* association together for premilitary training (between the world wars) and entertainment,[17] joined the army, and talked, often gathering in barns at night.

Marriage marked the end of this association. The assumption of family responsibilities and duties left little time for entertainment with bachelorhood friends. Most friendships of this period lapsed, though not completely. These were considered to be the real friendships of one's life, and they often continued, though in modified form. Most outstanding was the choice of one's koma (in the sense of childhood friend) as baptismal koma.

Friends also continued to meet under other circumstances. If a villager went to the local tavern for a drink, he would seek out bachelorhood friends for conversation. In the Peasants' Circle, which met several times a week, adult males came together to talk, play cards, discuss agricultural matters and politics, and occasionally to organize village recreation. Occasionally men gathered in barns at night for card playing and conversation; friends were likely guests, along with relatives and neighbors. Sometimes economic aid was extended, as when friends exchanged work or helped one another. An outstanding example is that of Béla Magyar and Mihály Juhász, childhood friends.

Béla Magyar, son of a wealthy peasant, himself became one, and with his influence, drive, and education became the village mayor and president of the Peasants' Circle. Through his influence, Mihály Juhász, a middle peasant, was able to take over the handling of the newly built milk depository in 1928 and in the 1930s became the local postmaster—positions which improved his economic and social

16. It was traditional in many parts of Hungary on the Monday following Easter for adolescent boys in bands to seek out adolescent girls. Sometimes the girls hid. Once discovered, they were led to a well and doused with buckets of water.

Today, even in urban areas, a milder form is prevalent. Small boys (as well as older boys and grown men) go to the homes of relatives, neighbors, and friends to sprinkle a little perfume on girls and women alike. They are received with refreshments, with additional small gifts for the boys.

17. The Levente Association was established in Hungary in 1928 as a youth organization of voluntary membership. It provided preliminary military training and served in part to counteract terms of the 1920 Treaty of Trianon, which limited Hungary's standing army to a small size. In the late 1930s, membership became compulsory for boys leaving school at the age of twelve or thirteen, until they were eighteen (Fél and Hofer 1969: 323).

standing. They continued to be good friends throughout and met frequently at home as well as in the capacity of fellow officers in the Peasants' Circle.

Newcomers to the village often found it difficult in the beginning because they had no real friends, although they may have had considerable affinal ties. Friendship among men, however, was not confined solely to bachelorhood companions, although friends were predominantly from that group.

Károly Kelemen's neighbor was a shoemaker who had married a woman in Kislapos and moved there. Lacking his own draft animals, he asked his neighbor Károly Kelemen for help. At first the two wives became acquainted as neighbors (for such family and neighbor ties were chiefly a woman's province), then the men. In time Károly Kelemen and his neighbor became good friends as well, and Károly often helped him out. Károly also became good friends with two earlier neighbors, and, even though he moved to another house after a few years, remaining kert neighbors with one of the two, he kept up friendships with both, exchanging visits and help.

Significantly, even in cases where friendships developed in later years, almost invariably the two men involved were close in age.

Girls also gathered in groups by age, going to church together on Sundays, attending dances, and playing games in groups. Occasionally they held parties, sometimes inviting boys. (In the more distant past, girls came together in evenings to spin yarn or to shuck corn.) They met less often, the scope of their activities was more circumscribed, and they did not have the freedom of their male counterparts. The friendships developed were also lifelong, but the greater restrictions put on meny-s and the fewer opportunities given women to meet (outside of neighbors and relatives) kept these friendships from assuming even the reduced significance of male friendships after marriage. The fact that a woman was more likely than a man to leave her childhood village at marriage exacerbated the situation.

Chapter *4*

Village Institutions and Power

Some of the major pre-World War II institutions and associations in Kislapos were the church, the corporate village government, the Peasants' Circle, the grazing association, and the consumers' cooperative. The stratum of nagygazda-s, who dominated much of village civic life, formed the leadership in all these bodies, providing a constant tension or conflict—and, in the figure of one individual, a source of dynamism and economic progress. Smallholders and the landless had little say in these or other village affairs.

Most of these institutions had only males as participants, and all were dominated by men, reflecting the almost exclusive participation of males in the public arena.[1] This does not mean that women did not actively participate, for example, in the church. They took part in the preparations before the mass, were the "singing women" at masses, and were probably the more devout Catholics. But their participation was subordinate to that of the men, particularly in the political sphere.

THE ROMAN CATHOLIC CHURCH

The membership of Hungary's Roman Catholic Church, a powerful institution in Kislapos, comprised about 70 percent of the nation's inhabitants. As Hungary's largest single landholder, the Church owned 6 percent of the land; its landholdings were dominant in some areas of the country. Its strength as a politically conservative (to many, reactionary) force, a defender of its own interests, and a Church with a loyal, faithful, and sometimes browbeaten following cannot be overestimated.

Kislapos was (and is) a Roman Catholic community. Its church, built

---

1. Women, of course, played important interpersonal roles, maintaining ties with relatives and neighbors—roles that were in some sense public but did not constitute the public life of the village as seen by villagers.

about 1790, stands in the central part of the old portion of the village. Until the 1950s all villagers had Church weddings; until the late 1960s all were baptized into the Church, and all still undergo a religious burial ceremony. It is fair to say that most attended the long masses on Sundays. In the 1930s, church attendance was compulsory for school children and for members of the male youth organization, the Levente. The Church and secular authority were closely associated.

The village's small size precluded its having a priest of its own; it shared one with its larger neighbor, Kistó, where there is a larger church, as well as the rectory. Mass was held once every two weeks in the local sanctuary; attendance overtaxed the capacity of the small building, requiring many churchgoers, particularly young unmarried males, to stand in the narthex and outside the doors.

Seating in the church, as in the Calvinist church in Átány (Fél and Hofer 1969: 68–75), reflected the broad structural divisions in rural Hungarian society of socioeconomic and marital status and age and sex. In the front of the nave was a pew reserved for the wives of about five of the wealthiest nagygazda-s. On the left side of the chancel, to the left of the door entering the sacristy sat the wife of the village notary. To the right of the door was a rented pew reserved for the family of a wealthy member of the gentry, who owned a five hundred-hold estate and mansion on a tanya just across the Kistó border (his two brothers had estates of comparable size and a still larger mansion in Kistó proper); his family came to mass in a four-wheeled carriage. Opposite them on the other side of the chancel sat the village school teachers. The mayor sat in a special seat in the front.

In the nave, males sat in the pews on the right, women on the left, although there was occasionally some mixing of the sexes among the smaller children. School children were placed in the front near the altar with older children behind them. Further back were the adolescent girls. Adolescent boys and young bachelors were usually in the back, under the loft, or outside the church. Behind the children were the married and widowed adults of both sexes. Younger married men usually preferred to stand under the loft, leaving the pews for older men; or they went upstairs in the gallery, on the right with other older men, while the older bachelors occupied the left side.

Newly married males usually remained in the rear balcony with their bachelor friends for some months before joining the older married men. Young brides on the first postwedding Sunday came in their white bridal dresses and white silk kerchiefs and took places toward the front, standing between the pews. Although they soon moved back and dressed like the rest of the married women, they remained standing in the aisle for as long as ten or fifteen years until they, too, could sit (and probably be considered fully mature women or gazdasszony-s in their own right).

PARISH ADMINISTRATION

The Kislapos church was responsible for educating the village children.[2] Funds to run the school were provided from much the same source
as church funds: the common village-church fiscal base. A portion of the
community common land was allocated to the church. The priest received the use of eight hold-s (along with sixty to eighty hold-s in Kistó),
the cantor-schoolmaster and the village notary two hold-s each. Part of the
rent received from the village's fifty hold-s of common land also went to
the church. In addition, each married couple was assessed a "couple
rent" of twenty-two or twenty-three kilograms of wheat each year to be
offered to the priest. If the church's expenses were not covered by these
funds, an extra tax was levied, based on the quantity and quality of the
villagers' land.

Although the priest and Church superiors directed local church affairs,
and the laity was not expected to take much initiative, in Kislapos the laity
did in fact have a voice in some nondoctrinal affairs. The local church
council was the forum for such participation. Respected members of the
community were chosen to be members of the council. Invariably several
of the nagygazda-s were selected; and one almost always filled the president's position.

A common factor in the politics of Hungarian villages was resistance to
the increasing power of national or other central authority over village
affairs. This extended to the religious sphere. In Átány the village administrative bodies steadfastly resisted the inroads of extravillage authority.
In Kislapos the church council resisted the power of the highly centralized Catholic Church. Unlike Átány, where the minister was elected by
locals (Fél and Hofer 1969: 306–308), the Catholic priest was chosen by
higher authorities. In general, the Catholic Church councils had less
voice in Church decisions than their Calvinist counterparts, but in
Kislapos there was some resistance.

There was conflict on two issues during this period between the priest
and the church council. In one case the council felt that some of the
teachers were too lenient with their pupils, giving them excessively long
recesses so as to have more free time for themselves. At first the local
priest backed up his teachers, but when the matter was taken to higher
Church authorities, the council's opinion was upheld. In another case
there was disagreement over the method of assessing the extra Church tax
levied on privately owned village land. The council objected to the

2. This was also the case nationally because there were few public schools in
Hungary. Most schools were run by religious denominations; others were provided by larger industrial and mining companies and by some of the larger estates.
In 1945, 60 percent of all schools in Hungary were Roman Catholic (Kovats 1977:
302).

method proposed by the priest, which, it seems, would have resulted in a larger levy, perhaps especially for the wealthier. Again their objection was sustained by higher Church authorities.

Both of the above objections were initiated by wealthier members of the council, in particular by one nagygazda, the mayor. Although it does seem that village interests were served by these arrangements, it is evident that the wealthier strata resisted any encroachment on their interests and power.

VILLAGE GOVERNMENT

The village administration was run by the body of representatives, a smaller board of aldermen, the mayor, and the notary.[3] The body of representatives had twelve members, half of whom were *virilista*-s, the wealthiest taxpayers (the largest landowners) in the village, who were entitled to their seats without election.[4] The remaining members were elected by open (later by secret) ballot of the taxpaying males living in the village for at least two years (Fél and Hofer 1969: 325). Although a few of the representatives were smallholders, the vast majority were middle and wealthy peasants.

The body of representatives was responsible for fiscal and policy matters in the village. It determined how village funds should be spent and set local taxes and rentals of village land. The village employed several people: a field watchman; a town crier (whose full-time job included announcing villagers' deaths and public statements, delivering public documents and messages, cleaning up the town hall, maintaining public order at given times, and keeping street lamps lit); a fire chief; a midwife; a meat inspector; a public trustee responsible mainly for village orphans

---

3. For a more extensive treatment of village government, see Fél and Hofer (1969: 324–341; 1973).

4. See Horváth (1965: 600–615) for a discussion of the reasons behind the 1871 law establishing compulsory membership of the virilista-s in the local body of representatives, as well as the 1886 law further limiting local self-government. Two themes stand out. After the Compromise of 1867 the central government sought to reduce the scope of county self-government. In turn, the counties saw the possibility of their own self-rule enhanced in the strengthening of local government against the forces of centrally maintained rule. Furthermore, conflicts that had arisen between the "black-coated" and the "szűr-coated" (referring to the long, coarse woolen garment, often embroidered, worn by shepherds and peasants), between the landed and the landless, that reflected the growing restlessness of the poor once they had seen the ideals of equality proclaimed by the Revolution of 1848–49 gradually stifled, were heightened by the opportunities of the poor to gain power through local self-government. Giving reign to the virilista-s served to quash the county's aims and to protect the aristocracy and nobility from possible consequences of a powerful poor like the Paris Commune.

and welfare cases; a coroner; a treasurer; a village magistrate, who settled smaller differences, including boundary disputes and suits brought for trespassing, theft, or verbal or physical assault; aldermen; the notary; and the village mayor. Most of these were part-time positions with only an honorarium (which was often refused by wealthier individuals) or a payment by each of the families served. Some, like the magistrate, went unpaid and were rewarded primarily in terms of honor (Fél and Hofer 1969: 327). Others, like the midwife and notary, who were outsiders, were entitled to housing provided by the village. In addition, the village owned a blacksmith shop and house, which it rented out. Besides these matters, the representatives acted on the repair and upkeep of village streets and the maintenance of fire-fighting facilities, planned the construction of public buildings, and supervised the village wells. The board also had the right to grant residence to newcomers, supervised local welfare operations, organized local elections, and overlooked the work of the smaller village board.

Playing more of an executive and less of a fiscal or policy-making role in village administration was the smaller board of aldermen, made up of the mayor, the magistrate, the public trustee, the treasurer, and several "sworn men" or elected aldermen. These men were responsible for the village registers; they, instead of the magistrate, sometimes measured land or settled inheritance divisions; they estimated damages reported in the fields by watchmen, led police investigators or bailiffs to homes if necessary, and made estimates of crop yields when bank credit was requested or property prepared for forced sale. Fél and Hofer (1969: 328) report that in Átány at least one of these positions was reserved for teamless peasants.

The village notary was elected by the community, but unlike most other elected officials he was nominated by the county authorities. A non-villager, he was usually the sole "trained, technically qualified official of the local administration" (Fél and Hofer 1969: 324) and was often better educated than all other villagers. Part of his pay was provided by the village, part by the state. He took minutes of board meetings and, along with the mayor, directed the village economy and the collection of taxes. As chief record-keeper, he handled the registers, deeds of title, livestock lists, and the rate book. As notary, he certified, authenticated, and recorded state-controlled labor contracts involving, for example, harvester bands and summás-s. Because of the steadily increasing complexity of the tasks facing public administration and its greater bureaucratic nature, the role of village notaries, especially because of their lifetime terms, assumed greater importance in villages throughout the first half of this century. The mayor was the honored figure in the Hungarian community, but greater authority often rested in the notary's hands, and his ties to higher administrative authority enhanced this (Fél and Hofer 1969: 325).

Lapos, however, was a small village in which the bureaucracy was not well developed. Power was concentrated in the person of the mayor; and a strong, active man could take the initiative in many areas. As chairman of both the body of representatives and the village board, and as a figure of considerable prestige, the stamp of his personality often appeared on village affairs. This was especially true in Kislapos of the last pre-World War II mayor.

Until 1930, the mayor's position frequently changed hands among the wealthier peasants. Because of the wealth needed simply for electioneering (for example, to buy many liters of brandy), the time and expense involved in carrying out one's duties in a position rewarded more by honor and an honorarium than by a salary, and the personal influence required both to win such an election[5] and to wield influence in office, the mayor's position was essentially open only to the village's nagygazda-s. They were the ones whose wealth and greater experience in public affairs and in dealing with extravillage authorities commanded the respect and honor required of such positions. This pattern continued until the war's end, although the rapid turnover of mayors did not. The last prewar mayor, one of the two wealthiest peasants in the village, assumed the mayoralty around 1930. He continued to exert great influence on village politics and economics until the postwar era through his personal wealth and forceful personality, his membership on the county municipal board, and his presidency of the Peasants' Circle, in which he was the major force. He even ran unsuccessfully for a seat in Parliament several times, once losing only narrowly, partly due to the opposition he had provoked among Church leaders by his stances mentioned earlier.

During the war, the village government assumed the tasks of deciding who was to contribute animals and implements for the war effort. A special committee, consisting mainly of aldermen and representatives, was formed to judge these matters and to supervise compulsory deliveries to the state. Some of the wealthier peasants among the representatives made examples of themselves by offering their own property before assessing others, but some more recalcitrant nagygazda-s would have preferred to assess the poorer, leaving their own self-termed "model" farms intact. They were not successful. The representatives and aldermen also helped select villagers for military service during the war. There were complaints by some villagers that personal vendettas by some wealthier peasants led to their more frequent callup or to their being branded untrustworthy and being put into work battalions near the war's end.

5. See Fél and Hofer (1973) for a discussion of the personal and political patronage in Átány. While the tanyázás typical of Átány was clearly absent in Lapos, and patron-client relationships were less clear-cut, wealth and personal influence based on wealth were just as necessary in the latter to command respect and a political following.

Village expenses were partially covered by the rental of village lands to smallholders. Increased village expenses were met by an increasingly high surtax set as a percentage of the national tax. Much of these taxes was based directly on the value of land owned and was roughly proportionate to wealth. Other parts of the tax, like those on houses and income, were regressive in nature. With all taxes included, the poor smallholder paid two to three times the rate of the wealthy peasant and five to six times as much per hold as the owner of an estate of several thousand hold-s (Varga 1965: 292–295).

THE PEASANTS' CIRCLE

During the early 1920s the Peasants' Circle met several nights a week in empty houses rented by the group. The meetings were highlighted by the amiable conversation, political and economic discussions and arguments, and card playing characteristic of the informal get-togethers in homes and barns of friends and neighbors in Lapos and of the nightly tanyázás in the barns of Átány's middle and wealthy peasants (Fél and Hofer 1969; 1973). At first only the middle and wealthy peasants attended, but when the new cultural house (Népház), constructed with state support in 1928, was finished membership was broadened; younger men were encouraged to attend by older peasants so that there would be "descendants" to take over the group, and even the landless could attend if they behaved properly. Annual dues of two pengő-s were used to buy books for the small library, a radio, magazines, and newspapers, and to heat and maintain the building.[6] In its prime years membership reached a level of 90 to 110, nearly half the adult males of the village.

The Peasants' Circle was open four times a week: Tuesday, Thursday, and Saturday nights and all day Sundays after mass. Evening sessions were devoted to conversation and discussions, particularly of agricultural matters; newspapers were read aloud. On Sundays card playing was permitted and the emphasis shifted to entertainment. Alcoholic beverages were allowed only on occasions such as dances, when drinks were sold by the local cooperative's barkeeper.

Members of the Peasants' Circle were proud of the workings and success of their organization. Besides being the sounding board from which several progressive agricultural measures arose, the group sponsored many events, some of them the envy of nearby villages. These included an agricultural fair, unusual for a community so small, entertainments for the young, theatrical productions by village youth under a hired director, lectures, and a married men's ball on New Year's Eve, which evoked

6. A day laborer's average wage was slightly less than a pengő. For some this would have represented several days' earnings.

particular pride among leaders and members alike. Such an occasion for married couples was relatively rare, and the organization and planning involved were apparently not as well managed in other villages.

Special emphasis was placed on good behavior at these and other occasions. Individuals caught cheating in cards were led aside and threatened with ejection. Fighting, common among youths at entertainments, was strongly dealt with. Young men from neighboring estates were warned about such scrapes, as were village youths; if the warnings went unheeded, the offenders were thrown out. In earlier years entertainments rarely proceeded without a fight, but greater vigilance and experience reduced these occurrences in later years so that mothers could send their sons off to such affairs with less anxiety.[7]

The Peasants' Circle was a popular place for villagers, and "serious" individuals were encouraged to attend. Those most welcome were self-effacing (although wealthier peasants could afford to be less so), dependable individuals who did not drink heavily or cheat in cards and who were not inclined to rant or to argue violently. Members of all strata attended, but the landless, though welcome, were relatively few in number. Cseléd-s were absent due to work commitments, lack of cash, and the distance to the village from the tanya of two of the largest landholders. Several tradesmen also attended, attracted by some of the same features as the peasants and by the small library from which they could borrow technical and trade books. There was no separate reading circle in the village, as there was in Átány and other villages, made up of poorer and more

---

7. Fights, sometimes with knives and sticks, were not uncommon among village bachelors and youths in the early part of the century. They involved conflicts among youths courting or desiring to court the same girls and invasions of a youth band's territory. Fél and Hofer (1969: 170, 194–197) relate that most brawls were between members of youth bands of Átány's upper and lower ends. Dances were common settings for scuffles. Cutting in on another's dance often provided the impetus. Youths caught "trespassing" in the other end, or worse yet, courting a girl from that end, were especially open to attack.

Kislapos did not have clearly discernible ends and separate bands of the same age. Fighting and even knifings were typically the results of two youths courting the same girl. Youths from outside the community courting or attending dances in Kislapos were often deemed unwelcome by their village counterparts, especially if they were from nearby estates or tanya-s, whose hired hands and their families were viewed as uncouth and uncivilized by village youths and parents alike. See, for example, Fél and Hofer (1969: 281).

Exacerbating this tendency was the concept of *virtus*, or manly prowess, most clearly manifested for a bachelor in fighting, especially in dealing strong blows and not being hit. While fights were frequent and often went unreported, they were still against the law. Offenders were liable to jail sentences, and some of the supervisors in the early years of the Peasants' Circle found it a common experience after an entertainment to relate the circumstances of a brawl to the gendarmes.

leftist-leaning individuals. People attended to play cards ("the room was always filled with smoke"), to talk with acquaintances, and to be entertained.

Many felt that there was much to be learned from the discussions and presentations. On discussion nights, small groups of individuals conversed. If someone felt he had something important to say, he asked permission of the president to propose a topic. The group decided whether the topic was good and should be discussed, tabled, or postponed to a later meeting. If more information about a matter was needed, one or two members were assigned to research the issue, even to travel to make inquiries (if need be, their expenses were covered by the organization). When discussions were held and action was to be decided upon, the issues were voted by hand and reasons asked for negative votes, lest some aspect be left unexamined.

Some, however, viewed discussions about agricultural and economic affairs and planning as one-sided. In their view, the few leaders talked over the things to be done among themselves, reached agreement, and then presented their conclusions to the membership. There would be some discussion, but most listened merely to find out what had been decided, what would be done. One former leader of the organization said, "There weren't many differences of opinion. If someone did disagree, he didn't dare say it because he wasn't right anyway."

Leadership in the Peasants' Circle was concentrated in the hands of its president, the mayor, who held the office from the late 1920s until the organization's demise after the war. There were also a treasurer, a secretary, a supervisor, and a small supervisory committee. While these were usually not nagygazda-s, they were middle peasants, some of whom were good friends of the mayor.

Although many disliked the concentration of leadership in a few hands, most felt that through the organization and the leadership of its president the community achieved a great deal economically and socially. Whatever doubts many had about the mayor's personality, politics, and treatment of others as a nagygazda, few doubted that through his position as mayor and as president of the Peasants' Circle he had imparted a new impulse into Kislapos's economic development. As a member of the County Board, he was the village's prime channel for new information about agriculture and administrative matters, and he undoubtedly derived some of his power from this position as "gatekeeper." He would come back from a journey to the county seat in Eger to tell the membership what he had learned and heard, and he used his offices to initiate various actions profitable to the community.

In the early 1920s, a milk cooperative was formed in Kislapos and a dairy set up for the collection of milk. Before that, families had had to dispose of their own production. Much as in Varsány (Sárkány 1978: 71), villagers had made cream cheese from the milk or let it sour to feed to piglets, as they did the remains of the cream cheese. The dairy skimmed the cream off surplus milk, converted it into curds and butter, and took these to nearby Pont, where several small shops handled its sales. When the cultural house was built, half of it was allocated to the dairy.

Probably the most important step the community took was to certify the villagers' cattle and to develop a breeding program. Although Kislapos had in recent years increased its stock of cattle and pigs, and at the turn of the century had a large horse breeder, this move further improved and enlarged its animal stock. By 1935, when the national agricultural census was taken, Lapos had more than twice as many cattle per inhabitant as Gödör, one and three-quarters as many as Kistó, and slightly more per capita than Barnaföld, the site of a large model farm with several hundred cows. Moreover, the large number of calves in comparison to cattle indicated a strong breeding program. It was during these years that many in Kislapos won prizes for their cattle, that a small annual fair was held, and that the village achieved a reputation in the area for its cattle, its Peasants' Circle, and its capable farming. During this time the villagers' pig herd reached close to a thousand head, a large number for a community its size. The sale of bran for cattle feed during these years by the milk cooperative helped to coordinate efforts.

Melon and vegetable growing, both requiring intensive cultivation, were encouraged during these years. Through the Peasants' Circle the mayor brought about uniform stamping of watermelons. Each grower was assigned a number, which, along with the name of the village, was stamped onto each melon. Thus, each grower bore the responsibility for his own harvest, but for his harvest only.

The cultivation of tomatoes, particularly for export, brought a sizable income during this period. The mayor, having seen the results elsewhere, introduced the idea, and soon other peasants, small, middle, and wealthy, planted tomato crops and reaped profits. Fractions of a hold were more than enough for one family to work; some of the wealthier peasants with fewer family members gave out tomato land for sharecropping, as they were unable to cultivate more than a small amount themselves.

Through these innovations Kislapos began to shift away from the extensive cultivation of grains like wheat and maize to the more intensive cultivation of vegetables, melons, and fruits and to animal breeding. These were better suited to its relatively high population density, to the preponderance of small- and medium-sized enterprises, and to the changed agricultural price structure of the 1930s.

THE GRAZING ASSOCIATION

In 1913 grazing associations all over the country were reorganized by a national act. These associations superseded earlier cooperative efforts. In Kislapos, 1867 had seen the allocation of pasture rights in the common grazing land according to land owned. Landless peasants were entitled to a small amount also; but, lacking plowland, they asked for that instead of pasture.[8] As pasture rights were sold and divided through inheritance, they were no longer necessarily proportional to land owned.

The grazing association formed in the village by the 1913 act, and accorded official status by the local government, set seven-eighths of a hold as the amount needed to pasture one large animal, for example, a cow or horse. The right to pasture one large animal or appropriate numbers of smaller ones became one pasture right. Since these could be bought and sold, as well as inherited, animal owners rarely had the same number of pasture rights as the number of animals they sent out to the common pasture. Some complicated transactions were called for. Those who owned more pasture rights than animals sent out received a payment from the grazing association, whereas those in the opposite situation paid. Those with no rights but with animals grazing on the common land were assessed at a higher rate than those with pasture rights. Thus, the ownership of minimal pasture rights was eagerly sought. Those with a set minimum number of rights were eligible to vote for officers. The limited land "reforms" of the early 1920s also provided a small amount of pasture land for poor recipients, which, added to Kislapos's common pasture, brought the total of common grazing land to 136 hold-s (out of Lapos's more than 1,800 hold-s).

Animals were driven to pasture by the village herdsmen, one for pigs, one for cattle. They were hired by the association and were paid mainly in kind by each family according to the number of animals sent out. Several stud animals were also maintained. In order to provide straw for these animals, the association auctioned off rights to scythe some of the pasture's grassland for a share.

In addition to controlling pasture rights, the association set aside a small portion of the common grazing land for the production of adobe bricks used in constructing most of the village's buildings. Its use was reserved for those with pasture rights, but after the land consolidation of

---

8. This did not mean, however, that they were totally without land to use for pasture. For example, when consolidation was discussed in the village before it was executed in 1912, some opposed it because they felt that only through the use of the fallow land and the postharvest stubble for pasture in the old three-field rotation were they able to keep enough animals so that it brought almost as much income as tilling the arable land. In another village the concern was voiced that such measures would similarly endanger the landless day laborers' grazing rights on the stubble. A general conservatism in some also held against consolidation despite the fact that landholdings of less than ten hold-s were divided into an average of ten plots. One twenty-four-hold property was divided into sixty-five parcels and several thirty- to fifty-hold properties into forty or fifty parcels each (Simonffy 1965: 214–215, 260).

1912 and the establishment of the new Grazing Association soon thereafter, the "brick land" was made more available to all.

Officers of the association included a president, treasurer, secretary, and a supervisory committee. Fél and Hofer (1969: 314) relate that they were generally "recruited from among the medium or smallholders . . . who were willing to undertake a lot of trouble for small recompense." Such troubles included the painstaking calculation of payments due from or to be credited to owners of fractional rights (measured in Átány even to one-thousandth of a right). However, in Kislapos some of the wealthy peasants used the positions "to show how wealthy . . . [they] were compared to others." A former association secretary, describing one less than fully qualified nagygazda who had been elected president "so that he, too, would get something," told how at the spring meeting of the association's supervisory committee he had had to slip pieces of paper to the president to remind him of the items on the agenda—a matter to which the office-seeking nagygazda had given no thought.

THE CONSUMERS' COOPERATIVE

Kislapos joined the National Hangya (Ant) Cooperative Society in the first decade of this century. Members bought shares in the cooperative entitling them to an annual dividend of goods. The organization ran a general store and from time to time two or three smaller branch shops in Kislapos. In addition, it owned a tavern, which shared the cooperative building with the main shop.

Shopkeepers and barkeepers employed by the cooperative received a salary as well as a share of their sales. In good times—for example, at the construction of dikes along the Farkas by hundreds of unskilled laborers before World War I, when demand for food and drink by the workers was high—a sizable profit could be realized. At that time one nearly landless villager who ran the store, whose wife baked bread to be sold to the workers and whose father was the cooperative's barkeeper, was able to buy ten hold-s of land (or at least to put down a large downpayment on it, since inflation after the war made full payment easy).

The cooperative had a president, a managing director, a treasurer, and supervisory and directing committees of eight members each. Here, too, the leadership consisted of wealthier peasants, as well as smaller landholders with appropriate talents, all elected to office. Fél and Hofer (1969: 323) point out that some considered posts in the cooperative lucrative. Officers received a salary, in addition to travel expenses when they went to buy goods. Some could not resist the opportunities for embezzlement and fraud. Experiences in many cooperatives across the country in the early years of the century (Gyimesi 1965: 629) and in Kislapos's own postwar consumers' cooperative, the Hangya's successor, testify to this.

Although the leadership of the cooperative was mixed, containing "smaller men" with three to five hold-s along with wealthier peasants, if there was a showdown, wealth was the key to power. One former storekeeper for the association described how in the mid-1930s, after thirteen years of work for the organization, he quit because of a disagreement with the president, a landowner with ninety hold-s.

He had been having constant problems with the nagygazda, who earlier had been treasurer of the cooperative. On one occasion a buyer for the association borrowed 50 pengő-s from him to procure wine for the tavern. The buyer brought the wine back and reported the purchase to the treasurer. When the storekeeper approached the officer about the matter, he was promised payment of his money. Later, this nagygazda claimed that he had already paid back the amount, so the storekeeper brought suit for the money and won. After this incident the treasurer, who had since taken over the presidency, began to bore in on the storekeeper, even pushing the association's leadership into ruling that the storekeeper should pay him 50 pengő-s, the equivalent of a month's pay. Because of the nagygazda's pressure, the supervisory and directing boards ruled against the storekeeper, an owner of but six hold-s. As he said: "[The nagygazda] had ninety hold-s; it was hard for the board to make a decision against him." So he quit, had his resignation refused, and quit again.

INTERLOCKING DIRECTORATES

The village's wealthier peasants not only played a leading role in all of the community's major institutions—they dominated them. In the village government, by virtue of their virilista status and because of the wealth requirements for both the prestige and the electioneering required to run for higher office, the nagygazda-s in Kislapos controlled the board of representatives and had exclusive hold on the mayoralty. It was suggested by many of the aristocracy in defending the virilista concept when it was first introduced that "those who have a greater stake in the village should have a greater say" (Horváth 1965: 601), a notion undoubtedly supported by the local nagygazda-s. This say was not completely matched, however, by their contributions to local and national taxes. Indeed, taxes and the loss of parity in Hungarian agriculture after World War I resulted in more frequent forced auctions of peasants' land and housing due to inability to meet the taxes and payments on agricultural machinery—conditions that sometimes benefited the wealthier peasants.[9]

9. Because of their wealth the nagygazda-s locally and the richer in general were beneficiaries of these auctions, as they were able to buy land and machinery at reduced cost. While agricultural prices had fluctuated in the past, the buying power of the peasantry was severely reduced in the 1920s and 1930s following the breakup of the Hapsburg Monarchy and Hungary's resulting truncation. No longer did the peasants have the "captive market" within the monarchy's trade union;

In Kislapos the political clout of the more prosperous was reinforced by several factors, many common to the rest of Hungary. Because of the wealth, associated prestige, election resources, available free time, and public experience of the nagygazda-s, they were frequent choices for leadership positions. This tendency was strengthened by the patron-client relations developed by each landowner in his hiring of cseléd-s, harvesters, and day laborers; the help given on occasion to poorer peasants; and the landowner's ability to influence the hiring of community employees. The latter extended even to the choice of the first village postmaster when a local post office was established in the early 1930s. That position was filled by the middle peasant childhood friend of the mayor at the latter's request.

This case exemplifies two other factors: the friendships and kinship relations respectively, that wove together the lives of the nagygazda-s and those members of lower strata who joined with them to form the leadership of the various village institutions. As observed earlier, almost all in the wealthiest stratum in Kislapos were related by collateral or affinal kin ties. Such ties, of course, strengthened their already common interests. Other relatives were likely to be middle peasants, who were also willing to support their kinsmen's positions. Moreover, the more prosperous peasants were able to maintain a wider circle of kin ties than their poorer counterparts.

Ties of friendship across strata also brought informal alliances, which served to reinforce the authority of the nagygazda-s. Several smallholders and middle peasants serving as representatives, aldermen, and leaders in other village organizations were childhood friends of nagygazda-s. The aforementioned postmaster benefited in other ways from his close ties with the mayor. Earlier, through the latter's influence, he had been appointed to run the dairy; and years later he was nominated by the mayor to be village magistrate and a representative. Because of these and other positions he held at times, like those of treasurer and secretary of the Peasants' Circle and other organizations, he was accused of "hoarding positions." Some of their fellow villagers thought such individuals toadied to the nagygazda-s, although few questioned their competence for the more demanding positions like treasurer and secretary.

The fact that the nagygazda-s controlled the leadership of *all* village institutions is both the prime manifestation of their domination of the village and one more buttress of the social structure. "Interlocking direc-

---

they became subject to the fluctuations and lower grain prices of the world market and had to pay higher prices for industrial goods when protectionist policies were invoked by the successor states of the monarchy, including Hungary, in order to establish fledgling independent industrial production (Gunst 1976: 284–286).

torates" were the norm for the various groups; these involved not only the nagygazda-s, but several of the middle peasants and smallholders who regularly were officers or directing members of local groups. The multiple officeholding of these two strata was a function of several factors: the greater interest in public affairs of these men, their association and friendship with the nagygazda-s, and their own reputations for being honest, cultured individuals with the requisite abilities to carry out their duties. This multiple officeholding clearly did not decrease the power of officeholders, particularly the wealthier, since they were the chief beneficiaries of interlocking directorates.

One factor favoring the participation of nagygazda-s in a multiplicity of leading roles deserves further attention: the importance of prestige associated with wealth. The wealthy received considerable honor and respect on the basis of their holdings, the ownership of which was associated with the values of independence and self-sufficiency. Status differences were expressed in conversational tones, as well as in the deference shown the wealthier in address forms—a cultural area particularly rich in expressing the myriad of distinctions of the highly stratified wider Hungarian society. Church seating was another and the area of public service a third. Besides the personal characteristics of honesty, morality, cultivation, and intellectual fitness for the tasks at hand, appropriate wealth and its prestige were considered important for the choice of leaders (and for the determination of overall worth). Wealth was usually the most important factor.

Another point should be mentioned that, while not necessarily contributing to the nagygazda-s' impact on some institutions, strengthened their power as a whole in the village. The nagygazda-s, like the owners and managers of large estates and factories (in general, the ruling classes), had (or were believed to have) the gendarmes in their pockets. One of the chief functions of the gendarmes, whose local station was in Zöldfa, was to maintain public order. What this frequently meant in the countryside was preventing or counteracting any agitation or strike movements among agricultural laborers at the large estates, thus protecting the interests of the wealthy. Although in terms of extravillage politics local nagygazda-s had little real power and may only have been interested in protecting their power in the village from higher authority, in the microcosm and the truncated society of Kislapos (because, for example, it had no large estates or large landholders and little real intelligentsia within its boundaries) they were, especially to the landless and the cseléd-s, the local representatives, the incarnation of the ruling strata.

Chapter 5

Postwar Developments

The history of the Hungarian countryside from the end of World War II to the completion of the second phase of agricultural collectivization in 1961 was exciting, turbulent, and revolutionary. The end of the war signaled a new era. Prewar large-scale inequities stemming from concentrations of wealth and privilege in the hands of a few to the detriment of millions had for many stood far too long. A wave of idealism and new hope in the wake of the war's devastation freed great energy for the elimination of these inequalities; the presence of the occupying Soviet armies made this elimination inevitable, indeed, mandatory.

Ultimately resting in the Soviet sphere of influence under communist rule, Hungary experienced not only the abolition of much of its past inequities and inequalities, but also the major recasting of its social order. For many reasons this did not go smoothly. Much of the social transformation in the Hungarian countryside and in the nation as a whole was carried out more quickly than originally conceived. Stalinist methods were used. These brought resentment and fear to many, put great material burdens on much of the peasantry, temporarily lowered the standard of living nationally, and eventually sparked the conflagration of 1956. As seems inevitable in revolutionary times, the worst as well as the best in men rose to meet both the challenges and the opportunities for personal gain. What many viewed as unfairness and injustice ruled for several years.

When this period was over, Hungarian society and village society within it had been radically restructured. Following early land reforms, early nationalization of most factories, and the two major phases of collectivization in the countryside, land and private wealth had lost their centrality; they were no longer the basis for power and rank. The postwar years have seen inequality vastly reduced and opportunities for greater personal dignity, educational advancement, and the achievement of a higher standard of living enhanced for the vast majority of the population. Many experienced these for the first time.

THE WAR'S END

On April 4, 1945, all of Hungarian territory was finally freed from Nazi influence by the advancing Soviet forces of the Eastern Front. For Kislapos the war, or at least the fighting, ended almost a half-year earlier on November 14, 1944, when Soviet forces attacked rear-guard troops there and soon afterward occupied the village.

Although destruction in the village was light compared to other areas of the countryside (and to the country as a whole, which lost about 40 percent of its national wealth), Lapos did not pass unscathed. Several houses were destroyed or severely damaged, and a few inhabitants were severely injured by the shells of the attacking Soviet forces. The German troops, on the other hand, continuing their practice of making pursuit by the Soviet army as difficult as possible, blew up the sole bridge spanning the Farkas. Rapid pursuit was desirable, but the water at this time was high; so village men were conscripted to build a new bridge, using the electricity poles for wood. As a result the village remained without electricity until eight years later. Soon after this incident, in December 1944, a battalion of Red Army reinforcements was stationed in Kislapos, remaining until March 1945.

The war in general and the passing of the fighting front across the village resulted in other losses as well. As many as thirty or forty men died serving in the army and an equal number of prisoners of war did not return home for months or years after the war's end. All three armies, Hungarian, German, and Soviet, helped deplete the village's animal stock, its supply of feed, and its store of grain. The compulsory deliveries of draft animals, cattle, pigs, and produce for the war effort in Hungary has already been mentioned. Retreating German troops attempted at the last minute to take several hundred head of cattle from the village, to "save" them from the Russians, but were thwarted. The Soviet forces requisitioned horses, cattle, and pigs for themselves and also made extensive use of the villagers' stores of feed, fodder, and grain. Other property and machinery, like the truck constructed by two mechanically minded villagers, were also taken over. During the village's occupation, several homes were requisitioned for the Red Army's use and the inhabitants temporarily moved in with relatives, friends, and neighbors. The occupying troops brought typical problems, including heavy drinking and reports of rape and theft.

With the arrival of spring and the new planting season, and the departure of the Russian troops, the villagers began to resume a more normal life. This was not easy. The inhabitants had lost more than half their horses and, like peasants across the country, carried out their spring plowing with oxen and cows. Fertilizer, both natural and chemical (the use of which was still light in underdeveloped Hungarian agriculture), was less available than usual due to the loss of animals and the damage suffered by the country's few fertilizer plants. Astronomical inflation disrupted trade and commerce, rendering pay received by city and factory workers almost worthless within days of its receipt.[1] Much of the commerce between city and country took place without money; there was a "barter world" until the introduction of a stable currency, the forint, in August 1946. The inflation made credit, so desperately needed by many peasants following the war's losses, impossible to secure. At the same time there was a temporary influx of villagers' relatives and former villagers—who returned to the countryside because of the destruction in the cities, the reduced food supply during the last years of the war, and the harsh conditions following the war.

LAND REFORM

The first major item on the postwar agenda was the long-awaited and, to many, long overdue farreaching land reform—a redistribution that ultimately saw 35 percent of Hungary's land change hands (Andorka 1979: 60). With a great deal of popular support, the reform was guaranteed life by the presence of the Red Army, which, along with many Hungarians, sought to destroy the influence of the landed ruling classes. The first meeting of the country's newly formed provisional government in the eastern city of Debrecen in late 1944 discussed the terms of the imminent reform well before the complete liberation of the country. The final terms were announced in March 1945, and nationally the redistribution began in earnest in the spring of that year, with completion due by October 1945.

1. This inflation was the greatest ever recorded in history. Within the span of the year preceding August 1946 the price index went up by a factor of 4 octillion (4×10^{27}). At the time of the introduction of the new currency in August 1946, one prewar pengö was worth 828 octillion (8.28×10^{29}) pengö-s. At the peak of the inflation, in July 1946, prices more than tripled daily (Griffiths 1976: 142)!

The inflation also saved a number of the poorer villagers in debt from probable seizure and public auction of their property because it rendered past debts minuscule. The son of one peasant with five hold-s recalls how his family benefited from this. The death of his father after a long illness and of his two older sisters from tuberculosis in 1943–44 left the family deep in debt because of the expensive medical care and hospitalization involved. Only the canceling of their debts by inflation saved them from penury.

On the other hand, one of the wealthiest villagers, József Kovács, with nearly one hundred hold-s, easily would have been able to finish his wartime purchase of well over a hundred additional hold-s in neighboring Gödör, which would have made him Lapos's largest landholder and strengthened his influence greatly. Only the land reform and the new political balance prevented this.

The reform called for the expropriation of all land exceeding one hundred hold-s in the estates of the gentry and the Church and complete expropriation of all non-Church estates of over a thousand hold-s. Wealthy peasants were to be allowed to retain up to two hundred hold-s.[2] Those found guilty of war crimes and crimes against the people, or found to be Nazi leaders, traitors, or members of the *Volksbund*, faced complete confiscation of their property.

Although land received through the reform was not meant to be free, repayment was not a great burden until the establishment of the first collective farms. Large estates were first expropriated by the state. Thus, payment was owed the state, not the past owners, many of whom left the country before the advancing Soviet troops or soon thereafter.[3] The cost of the land was set on average at only one-fourth its market value. Repayment was to be spread over ten years for smallholders and twenty years for workers. The landless were entitled to several years' postponement in beginning repayment (Donáth 1977: 85). Ultimately for many the land was nearly free, a far cry from the earlier so-called reforms.

Responsibility for distributing the land rested in the hands of local committees of land claimants elected by their fellow claimants. There was to be one committee member for every twenty claimants. In Lapos the local committee had six or seven members. Their work was accountable to the larger mass of claimants. If disputes could not be settled locally, they were taken to the county committee in Eger, the county seat.

Unfortunately, Kislapos, like many other villages, did not have enough land to distribute. Its largest landholder had only slightly more than one hundred hold-s, not all of it in the village. Finally, the local land distributing committee was able to obtain a 220-hold share of the large neighboring estate in Kistó mentioned earlier.

2. The actual terms of the land reform were more complex than this. They specified the eligible recipients, the cases in which landowners were to be compensated, the conditions under which smaller properties (e.g., vineyards, orchards, and forest lands exceeding smaller limits and land needed for village building sites or community use) could be taken over, and the limits to be placed on land rentals by wealthier peasants, among the more important realms. See Orbán (1972: 22–45) and Donáth (1977: 21–86) for a more thorough treatment of these terms; the background discussion and arguments among different political parties that led to them; and execution of the land reform across the country on the local level.

3. The past owners in turn were to be repaid through a fund established from the new owners' payments, subject to the ability of the state to bear this burden. Because of the state's problems with postwar inflation, rebuilding, and indemnification, even if the state had wanted to, it could hardly have done much to carry this out. Moreover, the costs of the technical assistance in the reform and of implements given land recipients were to receive priority in the fund's appropriation. In fact, only a few received a small downpayment because of age or destitution (Donáth 1977: 86).

Land was also distributed to the village poor for building sites in the New Settlement and on the edges of town (see Map 1.2); new houses rose on many of these in the following quarter-century. Persons whose land was appropriated for this purpose received land from the 220 hold-s in exchange: 1.4 hold-s for every hold taken.

There was not enough plowland left for the poorer villagers who put in claims for land. By the terms of the reform, the minimum amount of land to be allotted was three hold-s (the maximum was fifteen), but in Lapos the majority of recipients had to settle for less, and many eligible claimants received nothing.

The local reform in Lapos, as in other communities, provoked great controversy. Because of the shortage of land to be dealt out compared to the number of claimants, and the fact that the guidelines for distribution specified grounds for eligibility but did not set up priorities among claimants, the local committees were faced with difficult choices. They had to decide how much land (if any) to give each of the eligible claimants: cseléd-s; workers; smallholders wishing to supplement their holdings; and married sons of smallholders with large families, who could expect inheritances of less than five hold-s. Need, measured in terms of family size, received major attention; but other considerations not explicitly mentioned in the guidelines, such as character and farming ability, were also important. In Lapos, as elsewhere, the local committee was in a position to be able to make judgments about these factors. This led, on the one hand, to the possibility of making decisions on bases considered fair by local standards and, on the other, to great controversy, conflict, and the possibility of abuse.

Because of these problems, final settlement of the land reform in Lapos dragged out over two years, much longer than the lightning-fast completions reached elsewhere. The Claimants Committee was formed and re-formed six times! Only at the end of 1947 were the claims settled and the property rights registered.

In the meantime, considerations other than character, poverty, family size, and farming ability figured in the committee's rulings. Corruption and self-seeking were a major problem. Several of the elected committee members took advantage of their position to grant themselves parcels as large as 5 or 10 hold-s, leaving other claimants with little or nothing. Some of them, as well as others ineligible for land, occupied 5- or 10-hold plots of the 220 hold-s in 1945, before its acquisition for Lapos's poor was secure, and farmed on them for a year or two. Although the most glaring examples were eventually corrected, this disturbed many villagers, particularly since some of these individuals remained in the local leadership in other capacities for several years. Moreover, when property deeds and tax bills from Kistó for the years 1945–1947 were sent out in 1947, several claimants who had used their land only in that last year were left with tax bills for three years; others who had used the land for the first two years were charged nothing. For example, one early Communist Party leader, who owned 7.5 hold-s and was thus ineligible for land, at least by local standards, occupied 10 hold-s the first year and 5 the second. As a pillar of the local Communist Party, he ultimately received one hold anyway and paid no taxes on the first two years of the larger parcel's use.

The Claimants Committee's first president, Ferenc Barna, stepped down in December 1945 (as well as resigning his position as local magistrate, to which he had been elected by the newly formed body of representatives) because of minor corruption. His wife had been persuaded by the above party official to collect a liter of sunflower oil from each family who had received land as thanks for her husband's role in the reform. When the party official then asked for half the oil, she refused; he reported the matter, and the hapless committee president, then party secretary in Lapos, was forced out.

Partisan politics also influenced the distributions. Many villagers claim they did not receive land because they were not Communist Party members.[4] Although nonparty members also received land, it is clear that there was such discrimination. To some degree the disproportionate number of party members among the recipients can be explained by the fact that locally the majority of party members were recruited from the ranks of the poorest, who were sympathetic to the radical stance of the party. Both for this reason and because of the party's strong initiative in the land reform nationwide, the committees in Lapos and throughout the nation had a larger share of Communist Party members than of members of any other party (Orbán 1972: 33). It is clear that these factors and the incipient struggle for power among the various postwar parties, particularly on the part of the Communist Party locally, were important in this distribution.

Many cseléd-s suffered from the incipient class struggle—or from what they believed might be one—as well as the interparty struggles. Many of them had not left their positions at the nagygazda-s because they had nowhere to go and no other way of making a living. They were encouraged by some of the local land reform committee members to seize the land of the wealthiest nagygazda-s, which could then also be distributed, but which the committee itself, bound by the rules of the reform (and perhaps also lacking full confidence), did not dare to do.[5] An effort was

4. Similar beliefs apparently influenced many to join the party at the time of the land reform. Sárkány (1978: 146) reports that in Varsány, where rumors circulated (and were apparently even spread by the Claimants Committee) that party members would receive one or two hold-s more than others, many quit the party in 1946–47 when these beliefs proved to be false.

5. Although the rules exempted peasant holdings under 200 hold-s, in other villages with inadequate land to distribute exceptions had been made. Moreover, when the poor claimants took matters into their own hands elsewhere, little could be done. Some committees simply reported the events to higher property settlement authorities, as did the committee president in the village of Endrőd, quoted

made by some, especially in the local Communist Party, to have the former village mayor branded a war criminal so that his land could be expropriated, but this did not succeed in time for the land reform. The cseléd-s, however, feared that if the old social system were to return (as it had with the White Terror after the short-lived Károlyi republic and the Hungarian Soviet Republic of 1918–19), they would have compromised themselves.[6] With no unambiguously positive choice, they stayed on. As a result, despite protests to higher authorities, they were excluded from the land distribution; for the antiaristocratic, anticapitalistic, populist spirit that allowed landowners only as much land as they themselves could work also prohibited men who were working as cseléd-s after April 1, 1945, from receiving land. A few eventually were allotted land when they quit as cseléd-s, and their family sizes were considered by higher authorities, but several harvesters who continued to work for nagygazda-s were branded as reactionary and as kulak supporters and received none. This same fear of the return of the old society had been manifested earlier in the resignation of three members of the Claimants Committee immediately after it was first established in 1945 in Kislapos.

One case illustrates how a combination of these factors played a role in land distribution. It shows how one individual used the reform for his own personal gain through his position within the newly formed political structure, particularly in the soon-to-be dominant Communist Party (hereafter referred to as the party, although it was not the only party until 1948 and has been reformed and renamed several times since).

A party leader, Gyula Fekete, for unknown reasons reported to the police that István Kovács, who lived in the back part of the house Gyula Fekete lived in, had a quintal of tobacco hidden away. When the police found nothing, István Kovács took Gyula Fekete to court for slander. During a recess Gyula Fekete offered to arrange for István Kovács to receive a hold through the reform if he dropped the charges. Earlier, István Kovács had put in a claim but had received nothing due to his former large holdings, which he had dissipated. He agreed. Gyula Fekete, as member of the local Claimants Committee, asked Imre Vas, the president, for the book containing the committee's recommendations. He crossed out Béla Varga's name and wrote in István Kovács's for one hold. However, although the higher authorities had not yet sanctioned the recommendations, they had already been

---

in Orbán (1972: 36): "we couldn't take away the land from our people now even with machine guns. This role we gladly relinquish to the county or even the national committee."

6. Károlyi (1956: 329) in his memoirs nicely captures the feelings of these people, referring to the earlier brief attempts at land reform that he had initiated by distributing his own land in 1919: "they remembered the March [1919] distribution. They had never quite believed in it at the time, for their intuition was deeper than mine; they knew that their lords were invincible, even if their own crazy Count stood up on their behalf. Only the might of the Red Army had been able to defeat their lords."

made public, and the recipients had started their plowing. Both Béla Varga and István Kovács sowed and hoed the land. Finally, Béla Varga's wife, a party member, brought complaint; the matter ultimately rested in the hands of the local National Committee. The committee's party members voted to back István Kovács (and thus Gyula Fekete), but the other parties' delegates voted for Béla Varga's wife, resulting in her victory.

All in all, although the reform was of major import in changing the lives of the poor and landless, in giving them a small measure of independence, its effects in Lapos were limited by the lack of available land to distribute. As in many other parts of the country, the recipients, especially the former landless cseléd-s, had no easy time. They lacked draft animals, implements, and machines, and sometimes even seed grain, as well as experience in running an enterprise. Because of inflation they were without the credit so vital for building a small foundation for their farming. Despite the land reform, they faced great hardships.

At the same time the nagygazda-s were hurt by the loss of the cseléd-s and the reduction in the size of the pool of landless who were available as cheap labor. But real reduction in their power came in the face of a new political reality and accompanying administrative and political maneuvers.

POLITICS: 1945–1948

In the initial postwar years, there was a struggle for power among political parties, a struggle that ultimately became one of the Communists against all others and resulted in the victory of the former and the incorporation of other left-wing parties into a Communist-led front. Locally and nationally much of the strength of the Communist Party derived from its ultimate backing by the Red Army, and more directly, by its control of the police and state security organizations. Locally the emergence of nationally supported organizations largely under the control of the party, with broad administrative powers and a membership more sympathetic to the party's program, if not necessarily to some of its leaders, provided further avenues for control. The period began with a brief attempt by the prefront leadership to maintain its preeminence, but this was soon forestalled by the party, which quickly assumed control of Kislapos's political life and much of its economic life as well.

The entry of Russian troops into Kislapos brought an immediate, though not permanent, upheaval of the local power structure. Some of the nagygazda-s lay low; the mayor moved into town from his tanya and hardly left the house for days. Those less fearful or with a knowledge of the Russian language (obtained as prisoners of war in World War I) temporarily occupied leadership positions, or at least acted as intermediaries between the occupiers and the villagers. When it became clear that no immediate retributions were to be expected, that the Red Army locally was less worried about whom it associated with than with obtaining supplies and rest, the mayor came out of hiding and invited the Soviet commander to take up quarters in his comfortable house; the invitation was accepted. The mayor began to resume a normal life.

During the three-month occupation of Lapos by Soviet reinforcements, the provisional government in Debrecen decided which parties were to be established in Hungary. When word reached the village, five parties including the Communist Party were quietly founded with the Russians' encouragement one evening at the mayor's home. This was reported to the authorities in Boros, along with the names of the deputies of each party. A local National Committee was then established, consisting of three members of each party. This body was to have limited policy-making and administrative powers.

For a while, only friends of the leaders and those considered trustworthy by them were recruited into the parties. For example, the Communist Party secretary was the assistant village notary. Other members included the middle peasant brother of the postmaster friend of the mayor; a carpenter; a former smallholder who had invested in a wheat thresher in the late 1920s and lost his investment when the depression and low wheat prices hit; and the mechanically-minded smallholder who built himself a truck and later a sunflower oil press with the aid of the aforementioned smallholder's son. That the other parties were also "friendly" to the mayor is suggested by the circumstances of their leaders: the Smallholders' Party was led by András Magyar, a nagygazda and the mayor's first cousin once removed; the Citizens Democratic Party was headed by the mayor's nagygazda brother-in-law's future nász; the Peasant Party was chaired by a friend, the village magistrate, a middle peasant; and the Social Democrats were led by a distant affinal relation—the brother of the sister-in-law of the mayor's first cousin once removed (the cousin's brother was one of the mayor's best friends and a leader in the Peasants' Circle), who was suspected by some as once having been a tale-bearer for the mayor. But this attempt to maintain power was short-lived.

In the meantime, not knowing of the establishment of the earlier party, several harvesters, day laborers, cseléd-s, smallholders, and craftsmen established another Communist Party headed by Ferenc Barna, a former cseléd. This party was much less sympathetic toward the mayor. Soon several of its members, hoping to remove him from the village and to obtain his land for distribution to the village poor, began a campaign to have him branded a war criminal. Charges were raised that when running for Parliament he had appeared on the same platform as known Arrow Cross Party members and that he had supported the Germans. Undoubtedly he was also accused of acting against the interests of the Hungarian people, both in his official capacity and as a nagygazda—not uncommon charges where land to be distributed was in short supply (Donáth 1977: 61–62). Ultimately, a few years later, the effort was successful; he was interned for several years and at his release was banned from returning to the village and confined mainly to neighboring Kocka where his sister and daughter lived. The confiscation of his land (his children did retain some of it) occurred too late for distribution, however, and in 1949 it became part of the land base for the village's first collective farm.

The attempt to eliminate the mayor dragged on and was not immediately successful. Several times before his demise he was arrested and taken from the village. An early arrest resulted in the discovery of the existence of the two Communist Parties. When he had been held in Boros for several days, the local National Committee voted unanimously to petition for his release. Soon after the mayor had been released, Ferenc Barna went to Boros to inquire about the release and other matters. He was asked who the three party members of the National Committee were who had signed the petition calling for the mayor's release as an honorable man. It was then that the existence of the two parties became known to Ferenc Barna and the authorities in Boros. Soon afterward the three "party" members of the National Committee, and not much later the former mayor as well, were ordered arrested by the district party authorities. The two parties were merged, and Ferenc Barna became secretary. Only three of the original party's charter members remained in the united party.

Political parties were not the only organizations set up in the village that influenced the villagers' lives, nor the only ones in which individuals could seek personal power and the party further bases for control. In 1946, for example, two mass organizations were established nationally as well as locally: FÉKOSZ (Földmunkások és Kisbirtokosok Országos Szövetsége, the National Association of Agricultural Workers and Smallholders) and ÚFOSZ (Újgazdák és Földhözjuttatottak Országos Szövetsége, the National Association of New Gazda-s and Land Recipients). FÉKOSZ was essentially an association of employees or agricultural workers trying to improve wages and working conditions for its members. Because it consisted mainly of the poorer strata and was headed by party members, it became one base from which the nagygazda-s were attacked locally. Closely associated with it was OTI (Országos Társadalombiztosító Intézet, the National Social Insurance Institute). FÉKOSZ kept track of who performed paid labor for others and who was available for such work; it represented the employees' interests and filled the role of an employment bureau. OTI dealt with the social insurance to which these workers were entitled. Because this was new and involved some expense for the employers, many of the latter at first did not buy the monthly stamps to insure their employees (a few cseléd-s, harvesters, and day laborers). These costs were greater than those of the earlier prefront registration of cseléd-s, which entitled them to some minimal benefits and which even then some nagygazda-s had tried to avoid. The registrar of OTI was advised by higher authorities to be patient at first, since the monthly payments would require some habituation on the part of the employers and, besides, the machinery to take offenders to justice did not yet exist. Later, however, local party leaders sought to use these measures to crack down on "blood-sucking," "sweat-extracting" nagygazda-s.

There was also a peasant counterpart to FÉKOSZ made up of small-holders. This had little of the political and administrative power and the connections of FÉKOSZ.

ÚFOSZ, of which Gyula Fekete was president, was formed nationally and locally in early 1946. Its purpose was to support the new land recipients, many of whom lacked experience as operators of independent enterprises and did not possess the necessary implements, draft animals, and usually even the seed grain for planting. In Kislapos, ÚFOSZ distributed most of the seed grain for the new landholders in 1946 and some of the seed stock used by others still suffering from wartime losses and the poor yields of the previous year.

The organization attracting the widest gathering and probably the most enthusiasm was the youth group. Actually, there were several such groups: MADISZ (Magyar Demokratikus Ifjúsági Szövetség, the Hungarian Democratic Youth Association), sponsored by the Communist Party, and KALOT (Katolikus Legények Országos Társasága, the National Young Men's Catholic Association) and KALÁSZ (Katolikus Lányok Szövetsége, the Catholic Girls' Association), supported by the less radical parties and by the Church. All the groups held dances, plays for which an outside director was hired, shows (for example, a small touring circus), and other entertainments similar to those of prefront days. There was a large ideological component as well. In MADISZ, for example, there were frequent denunciations of the nagygazda-s as exploiters. Fights among the young men of MADISZ and KALOT were also not unusual, and one group often chased the other out of the cultural house. While some of the youths were attracted by the politics, others found it too much and switched groups or quit. Communists all across the country paid considerable attention to the youth, who were regarded as the vanguard of the New Society. Most young people were attracted by the activities; some sought the leadership positions and the power and material benefits that could be derived from them. The strength of MADISZ was enhanced when the Catholic youth organizations were dismantled nationally in 1946.

While the leftist youth movement gathered steam, the Peasants' Circle expired; and with that, as one informant expressed it, "the life of the older men died." After the occupation by the Red Army the men had tried to start meeting again but were forestalled. MADISZ had taken over much of the cultural house for its own affairs; the leadership of the Peasants' Circle was prohibited by the party, which controlled the local police and the state security police, from entering the building to hold meetings. The Peasants' Circle had been a stronghold of the middle and wealthy peasants, and the local party was not eager to ease the organizing of its potential opponents. When they tried to hold meetings for a while, they were harassed; their meetings were interrupted, or it was announced that anyone could attend, not just the dues-paying members. The arrests and harassment of the former mayor, president of the Peasants' Circle, further limited the group's ability to reorganize. Later in 1946, when the cultural house was pressed into service to replace the old school, just torn down, the men were told that their smoking was bad for the village youth studying there.

That the police were largely controlled by the party was shown by other incidents as well. For example, from 1945 until the late 1960s marches were held in the village on such national holidays as May 1 and April 4 (the anniversary of the total liberation of the country from Nazi rule by Soviet troops). In the first few years of multiparty rule the Communists, Social Democrats, and members of FÉKOSZ were prominent participants. Several times, due to the influence of local officials, observers were held briefly or arrested by the local police for making disparaging remarks about the marches. At amusements it was customary for members of right- and left-wing parties to compete in singing against each other. On one occasion, several men, having drunken a lot, loudly criticized the Communist Party and the Russians. The matter was brought before the party, which decided that they should be confined in Boros, to be freed only after several weeks.

In July 1945 the board of representatives met for the first time. Its membership was very different from the prefront years; of its twenty-one members only two were former virilista-s, and only four had served in 1940. It decided on many of the same issues as the prefront board: setting pay for village employees; granting licenses to small businesses (for example, alcohol distilling, photography, movie projection); setting rents for village land; maintaining and building village structures; and contracting a village blacksmith, to name a few. With its strongly changed membership and the removal of the mayor from office, it was no longer an arena for instituting policies desired by the nagygazda-s.

In 1945, election reforms introduced universal suffrage and a secret ballot to Hungarian voters, but the results of the first elections did not manifest themselves in the political power relations of the postwar years. Local parliamentary election results in November 1945 did not differ substantially from nationwide totals, by which the Smallholders' Party gained 57 percent of the votes nationally, compared to the Communists' third place at 17 percent. Neither nationally nor locally, however, was this the major determinant of the power structure. The Communist Party nationally succeeded in discrediting and/or absorbing the other parties, while keeping control of the Ministry of the Interior, which controlled the police, security forces, and, in 1947, the lists of voters as well. By the spring of 1948 the Communist Party had "merged" with the Social Democratic Party and emerged with an iron grip on the reins of the government.

The strength of this hold was manifested most impressively to the villagers in 1948, when the local organizing session of DÉFOSZ (Dolgozók és Földművesek Országos Szövetsége, the National Association of Workers and Peasants) was held. Paralleling the merger of other political parties into the Communist Party, especially that of the Social Democrats in June 1948 with the Communists to form the Hungarian Workers' Party, FÉKOSZ and the peasants' association also merged. At this meeting many of the middle peasants and nagygazda-s, who had lost most of their local political influence, hoped through the election of new officers to regain some of their power, or at least to achieve policies less unfavorable to themselves. The meeting soon turned into an uproar; aroused former leaders and members of the community, dissatisfied with the changed political and economic climate of the village and particularly with what they felt to be discriminatory treatment against them by the new leadership, shouted and complained loudly. Police and security forces were called in from Boros. Sixteen of the men were questioned and beaten in the former room of the gendarmes and then taken to Miskolc, where they were kept and further mistreated until their release a week later. Two of them, the former mayor and his close friend, supporter, and first cousin once removed, were interned in a camp near Budapest; they were forbidden to return to the village after their release.

Many villagers were convinced that the action was planned by some of the party leaders. They had invited nagygazda-s, middle peasants, former gendarmes (highly suspect under the new conditions), and the supporters of the old leadership, although they had belonged neither to the peasants' association nor to FÉKOSZ. These were the ones most likely to cause a disturbance and to try to elect a leadership more sympathetic to their interests, and these were the ones taken away.

This action terrified both those involved and the rest of the villagers. Even years later, during the collectivization in 1959, when conditions and methods had eased greatly compared to earlier years, many villagers had these events on their minds when they signed the papers to become members and gave in their land.

THE LEAN YEARS: 1948–1956

By 1948 the consolidation of power was largely completed, and the nationalization and socialization of Hungarian industry and agriculture had begun.[7] In March 1948 companies and manufacturing concerns with more than one hundred employees, and larger banks, were nationalized. At the same time, small traders and shopkeepers were put under severe pressures to give up their businesses or to join small cooperatives. In Lapos these actions had but limited effects: one local carpenter who had a sideline of undertaking lost his horse-drawn hearse to a burial cooperative, while several villagers lost their oil presses and one a mill.

Of greater importance was the collectivization drive that began soon after the nationalizations. It was coupled with increases in the quotas of forced deliveries of produce to the government at unrealistically low prices; higher taxes; and an increasingly strong drive directed against the wealthy peasants or kulaks, who were said to be exploiting their workers and providing a base for capitalistic tendencies in the countryside.

As the national policy veered sharply toward the rapid socialization of agriculture and industry, the outlook for private farming changed. At first it was said that the socialist transformation was to be voluntary; private farming was to develop parallel to the cooperative sector and eventually dissolve into it. This view quickly gave way to an exaggerated fear of the capitalistic spirit of private farms, and particularly of the by then much reduced influence of the nagygazda-s. This reflected the suspicions regarding the peasantry and their great desire for land and independence, as well as the decidedly proindustry, proworker bias of party ideology. Combined, however, with the ideological blindness and fury of Stalinist measures, and the tendency to find fault not with mistaken agricultural and political policies, but with their incomplete administration or their sabotage, these attitudes led to a witch-hunt in the countryside against the so-called kulaks. They were assumed to be poisoning the rural atmosphere and were regarded as instigators of opposition to the socialization of agriculture who would have to be removed surgically from influencing their otherwise sympathetic middle peasant and smallholder neighbors or treated with strong medicine to eliminate their infectious capitalistic spirit. Thus, along with the planning and introduction of collectivization came stepped up efforts to weaken kulaks.

The term kulak, borrowed from the Russian—just as the policy pertaining to this stratum was derived from the Soviet policies of a quarter-century earlier—came to be defined officially as any landowner with over

---

7. Some, like Donáth (1977: 106–108), argue that the Cold War and the possibility of a new war led the party to try to drive into a few short years the development of heavy industry and the socialization of the countryside, originally viewed as more gradual processes. Others feel that this was part of the original hard-line view of those Hungarian leaders who had spent much of the interwar and world war years in the Soviet Union and saw Soviet history as a model for Hungary's development.

twenty-five hold-s, with land valued as producing 350 gold crowns of pure income, or with a combined land value and income exceeding the 350 gold crowns (translated into contemporary forint-s).[8] Gardens, orchards, and vineyards counted as five times their actual acreage.

Since only one of the above criteria had to be met, many landowners were included in this category who hardly fit the image of the exploitative nagygazda. Of the seventy thousand "kulaks" in 1948 only about one-half had thirty-five or more hold-s—a level viewed by many as more likely to qualify them as "real" kulaks, who employed full-time cseléd-s. Even contemporary reports stated that the limit was too low because it included many landholders with more than twenty-five hold-s of poor quality land; others with supposedly highly valued land (based, for example, on the by then irrelevant closeness to Viennese markets) but with low acreage; and still others who were primarily merchants, craftsmen, mill owners, or even doctors and lawyers, whose land plus income surpassed the 350-gold-crown value (Orbán 1972: 74–78).

Nor was this matter academic. The steps taken against those labeled as kulaks were strong. In many parts of the country they were under constant harassment by the police and administrative bodies for offenses, often trivial and sometimes imagined. They were subject to threats and in some areas were in fear of nighttime visits by the police, which might mean banishment from their communities (sometimes to concentration camps, more often to villages far away) and seizure of their property without compensation. These property limits were flexible, usually in the downward direction; this left open the possibility of local leaders settling personal scores against their enemies by the charge of kulakism (Moldova 1974: passim).

In Kislapos, only the two persons interned near Budapest after the local DÉFOSZ organizing session were forced to leave the village; but villagers branded as kulaks were subject to other measures common to the countryside. For example,

Gyula Kalicz and his wife, owning twenty-four hold-s, had in their old age moved into a small house next to their larger house and barns, leaving the latter for their son and his family, who had taken over the enterprise. When the families of several former cseléd-s, who had joined one of the two cooperatives, moved into the village from the tanya where they had worked earlier, Gyula Kalicz and his wife were forced to move back into their old house to make way for the family occupying the small house.

8. These ratings were based largely on surveys carried out during the Hapsburg Empire's rule for the purpose of establishing standards by which landowners could be taxed. The surveys took into account the quality of the soil, its uses, its nearness to the village and to markets—in short, its income-producing capability. Land in Kislapos averaged about 12.5 gold crowns per hold.

More typical was the discrimination faced not only by kulaks and other elements of the past society, like gendarmes, who were considered unreliable and threatening to the new order, but by their families and relatives as well. This was partly due to quotas encouraging the education of traditionally less-schooled children of industrial workers and the agricultural landless, but it also served to punish individuals whose past was considered less favorably.

Gyula Kalicz's son was dismissed from the police force in an industrial city when his father's kulak background was first taken into account in the late 1940s.

Gyula Kalicz's grandson was unable to go to the secondary school for which he was qualified and which he desired to attend because Gyula Kalicz's son was also branded a kulak.

János Pető went to work in Budapest as a young man in the early 1950s because the forced deliveries left little material incentive to work on his middle peasant father's enterprise. He was also tired of poverty and poor clothes, and, seeking work more suited to his limp, he found an industrial job. He advanced quickly, clothed himself better, and was soon asked if he would like to go to the party school. He replied that he would prefer to wait until his consciousness had developed further and soon afterward found that his supervisors and fellow workers were less friendly and helpful and were mocking his bad leg. Tiring of this, he quit after another year. He later found out that his personal information form indicated that he was "of wealthy origin," referring to the thirty-three hold-s owned by his maternal aunt's husband. The combination of his refusal and his background had caused him his troubles.

In 1954 Gábor Nagy was not accepted into secondary school because of his father's prefront gendarme status (his father did not return to Lapos until 1953; he was a Russian prisoner of war for several years after the war's end and was also interned in Hungary for a few years).

As difficult as these conditions were, they were not as economically crippling for wealthier landholders as were the forced deliveries and other administrative measures of these years. In autumn 1948 a governmental regulation set forty hold-s as the maximum total amount of land to be owned or rented by a peasant. Land exceeding this amount was expropriated by the government for the establishment of farming cooperatives (Orbán 1972: 79). These measures affected five or six landholders in Lapos. Their lands were used to form Lapos's first two collective farms in the following year.

Of greater significance to the nagygazda-s, as well as to most peasants both nationally and in Kislapos, were the financially crippling forced deliveries of quotas of agricultural goods at low prices to the government-run purchasing agencies.

These compulsory deliveries were not new. Soon after the end of the war they were imposed in order to insure a supply of relatively low-priced food to the urban populations, who had suffered greatly and who, because of the incredible postwar inflation and the breakdown of transportation and commerce, were greatly dependent on and at the mercy of the peasantry. At first the quotas were not as high as they were after 1949, but they still proved a hardship because of the additional burdens of feeding the Red Army, of paying reparations, and of poor harvests in the dry years of 1945 and 1946. Initially, aside from the first few months after the end of the war, surplus produce (wheat, rye, barley, oats, corn, beans, peas, lentils, millet, and potatoes) over amounts needed for household consumption and agriculture were to be sold at state-controlled prices to buyers. This, particularly for wealthier peasants, meant the greater part of production. After July 1945 the sale of animals at state-established prices was also mandated by law (Donáth 1976: 435–436).

When the forint was introduced in 1946, a relatively stable price structure was temporarily established. By this time the compulsory deliveries covered a smaller portion of production, with the government offering to buy up other surplus produce at the same low price while putting a higher limit on free market prices. Because of both the loss of farmers' parity and the poor harvests of these years, shortages developed in some of the crops, and black market prices were soon several times the official limits. This forced the government to allow prices to rise. As crops improved in the following years the amount required for compulsory deliveries dropped; by 1949 it was only 9 percent of the total produce sold for cash. From 1946 to 1949 a three-level price system was in effect: a low price for produce to fill the government's compulsory delivery quota; prices about half again as high offered by the government for produce surpassing the quota; and free market prices averaging two to three times the quota prices (Donáth 1976: 437–440).

In the summer of 1945 the quotas established for wheat were proportionate to acreage, but in the years following the quotas were made more progressive in relation to acreage planted. For example, in 1946–47 those with twenty to fifty hold-s of plowland gave 33 to 66 percent more, and those with more than fifty hold-s 100 percent more, of basic crops per hold than owners of five hold-s; in 1948 grain quotas were raised sharply for owners of more than fifteen hold-s, foreshadowing the years to come (Orbán 1972: 56).

In 1948–49 the per-hold quotas of produce for enterprises of more than twenty-five and fifty hold-s were set at respectively three and four times the quotas of five-hold farms, and in 1949–50 these were raised to four and five times as much and extended to lard, wine, and even straw besides the already mandated grains, poultry, and meat. It should be made clear that even if a peasant did not produce anything in a particular category he was required to fill that quota or face penalties. Thus in Lapos neighbors and relatives banded together to insure each the necessary amounts of every product specified in the quotas. One family might slaughter a cow and barter the meat in excess of the quota with a neighbor for other products required but not raised, so that each could fulfill quotas in areas in which they did not produce enough. Sometimes families even bought produce at market prices only to sell it at much lower prices to meet their quotas.[9]

For the wealthier peasants in particular, the higher quotas meant that little or no produce was left for sale at the higher market prices. Not only were they unable to capitalize, but they also slid into debt. Because progressive taxes (both in kind and in cash) on land were sharply increased in these years, they were increasingly unable to meet the quotas; this in turn subjected them to further financial penalties. In 1952–53, for example, only 46 percent of the "kulaks" nationally were able to meet their quotas in pork and 73.4 percent in wheat (Orbán 1972: 90–93). To reach a lower bracket, nagygazda-s tried desperately to give up the land they had so eagerly sought in the past, but freezes put on the sale of their land made it impossible to recoup their losses. Instead they had to offer their land free (or occasionally at far below market prices) to the government or face confiscation. By the mid-1950s the largest landholder had but twenty-six hold-s, and all the nagygazda-s were left with but a fraction of their original holdings. Nationally between 1949 and 1953, the number of landowners with more than twenty-five hold-s fell from 47,000 to little more than 10,000, and, due as much to the often forced nature of collectivization, the number of holdings of between twenty and twenty-five hold-s was more than halved (Orbán 1972: 91).

Despite initial efforts of the party to restrict these hardships largely to the kulaks, while trying to win over the other rural strata to collectivization and support of the government, the forced delivery quotas and raised tax rates also caused severe hardships for smaller landholders. Many in Lapos found that enforcement of the quotas saw their "attics swept bare of grain," leaving them little surplus for sale or sometimes even for sowing.

Increasingly, villagers both in Lapos and across the country began to view land with a different eye and to look for other possibilities than private agriculture to make better use of their labor. They could join the collective farm, but the two cooperatives established in Lapos had with few exceptions only the poorest as members and held little attraction for

---

9. As Sárkány (1978: 97–100) points out, peasants sometimes had to go to a neighboring village or even further to acquire the items specified by the quotas. Sometimes there was simply no tradition in a village of producing a specified crop. Although the intent of the quotas in these cases may partly have been to stimulate the introduction of new crops, these measures were often misguided and the workings of overzealous officials. They occasionally produced spectacular failures.

peasants. They could seek employment near Budapest and the manufacturing centers to the north in the rapidly expanding industrial and mining
sectors. Frequently (as with János Pető above) one member left to earn a
cash income for the family while those remaining maintained the shaky
family farming enterprise, to which one more farmhand could have lent
little aid. Many husbands worked for the railroad and in distant factories
while their wives and parents worked the land at home. They helped out
on weekends and took several weeks off from work in the summer to help
out with the harvest or, if they lacked land, to increase their earnings by
harvesting for others or even for a small nearby state farm. Others left
agriculture permanently, either moving to the cities or continuing often
exhausting daily (but more often weekly and biweekly) commuting patterns for years to come. Donáth (1977: 139–141) reports that between
1949 and 1953 the number of active agricultural earners dropped by a
quarter of a million (in a nation of less than ten million): almost all were
males in good working condition and experienced in farming.

Others tried to reduce their quotas. Some rented out their land; this
reduced the amounts of produce required, but the rents had to be very
low because the renter took over partial responsibility for the tax and
produce quotas and was not willing to pay much. Sharecropping was
more desirable for the cultivator because the forced deliveries and taxes
were payable entirely by the owner. Families with a small labor force
were in particularly bad straits because the quotas were established irre-
spective of this, and hired labor had to be paid in scarce cash.

Various ploys to reduce these quotas were attempted, the success of
which often depended on one's status and relation with village leaders.
Thus Gyula Kalicz tried to give half his land to his son at home, retaining
rights of usufruct; this would have put the land into lower tax and compulsory delivery brackets. But the move was disallowed because the son
did not set up a separate household. Others tried to parcel out their land
among family members for the same reason and succeeded. Károly Kelemen had nearly twenty hold-s and a brother who was vice-president of the
village council with considerable voice in local tax and delivery assess-
ments. Károly Kelemen was able to avoid compulsory deliveries on the
land left him by his father; he did not work it, but cultivated only his own
land while still managing ultimately to retain ownership of both.

As the collectivization drive intensified, these measures were directed
less exclusively toward the nagygazda-s and more generally toward the
private farming population as a whole. They were used to discourage
people from private agriculture and to encourage them to join cooperatives. Funds siphoned from the agricultural sector were plowed into
rapidly expanding industry, whose newly created jobs in manufacturing
and construction promised more than the now unprofitable rural life
could and further dulled the attraction of private farming.

There were other ways as well of pushing the rural population into joining the collective farms. One chief method was land consolidation. In order to insure large unbroken tracts of land appropriate for large-scale farming, it was necessary to consolidate the land of members. Nonmembers whose land rested within these proposed blocks were assigned equal amounts of land elsewhere as compensation for their holdings. However, these often were outlying parcels of poorer quality. Particularly in villages where consolidation occurred several times because of increasing membership in, or the establishment of, new farms, many villagers were convinced that it would be better to join the cooperatives than to suffer continuing losses.

Another tactic was to demand payments from those who had received land through the 1945 reforms. Because of their lack of implements, agricultural capital, and animals, many recipients were ill-prepared to begin paying and saw an easier road in joining collectives.

These payments, or the threat of them, were especially effective among the newly landed in Lapos, whose parcels were essentially all in one block and whose financial condition was weak. They were hard put to meet the demands of land payments, taxes, and forced deliveries. Those who remained landless after the reform, finding steadily fewer opportunities for agricultural work, were also attracted to the collective farms and to industry.

Few smallholders and no middle peasants could be persuaded to join the collectives in Lapos. Compared to circumstances in other areas, consolidation did not much affect them, and, more important, they were not subject to the threats and heavy-handed methods used elsewhere (Moldova 1974). Aside from the poorer strata, only those believing strongly in the rightness and ultimate success of the cooperative movement, those seeking leadership positions, and those seeking to reinforce their already strong positions joined willingly.

In Lapos some members were persuaded to join by other arguments. For example, Ferenc Jászi, a smallholder with five hold-s, was told that his son, a former gendarme then in a concentration camp, would be freed and allowed to come home if Ferenc joined one of the early cooperatives. He did so, and his son received a special dispensation, came home, and also joined.

THE EARLY COLLECTIVE FARMS

Two collective farms were established in Kislapos before 1959: the Petőfi cooperative in October 1949 and the May 1 cooperative in April 1950. Both were formed primarily on the basis of land given up by or confiscated from nagygazda-s, and each used the expropriated residence and farm buildings of one of the village's wealthiest peasants for its head-quarters and barns. The Petőfi took over the half of the tanya outside Lapos owned by the mayor; the May 1 occupied the residence and barns of the mayor's brother-in-law, the village's wealthiest landholder, in the center of the village. Both initially had as members ten or twelve families consisting mainly of former cseléd-s, harvesters, and landless. Several party and village leaders also joined, mainly as titular members who occasionally put in some work in support of the cooperatives but also as officers and even presidents of the groups.

Both groups, especially the Petőfi, grew over time, both in size, as more land was given up by wealthier peasants, and in numbers. Neither became very strong, however. The May 1 seems to have led a continuous hand-to-mouth existence. A number of its members were brought in from Zöldfa and put up for several years in rooms of the expropriated house used as headquarters. Because of the poverty of most members, the lack of agricultural training of its leaders, the lack of machinery, and its humble beginnings, the May 1 concentrated for a long time merely on trying to feed and clothe its members. Little attention and funds were available for development, and its membership grew very little despite its continuing land acquisitions from overburdened peasants eager to free themselves from the yoke of their land.

The Petőfi started off with somewhat more experienced leadership and entrepreneurial talent, as well as land more consolidated and closer to its headquarters. It gained more in numbers than its poorer counterpart and ultimately absorbed the few members of the May 1 cooperative who desired to remain in a collective when it chose to break up during the uprising of 1956.

In terms of their socialistic character, the collectives were of the "advanced" form: member families gave in their land to the collective farm, and all such land, as well as the land given up by peasants who did not join, was the property of the cooperative. Members were paid at the end of the year according to the number of work units they had accumulated over the course of the year. Different numbers of work units were assigned for different kinds and amounts of work. The value of work units was computed at the year's end and depended on the final surplus. Thus, the value was not fixed beforehand: a member's income was dependent on both the amount and type of labor done and on the size of the harvest. Most of the earnings were paid in kind. Advances were often given over the course of the year to tide members over until the final reckoning. Each member who worked more than a minimum number of units was entitled to a maximum plot of one hold for private use. This houseplot (*háztáji*) was usually planted with vegetables for the family's consumption if they did not already have a garden of their own, and with corn and turnips for the animals raised by individual member families.

It was customary for one member of each family, usually the family head, to take up full membership in the cooperative. Wives and children often joined in the work as supporting members and had their work units credited to the family head. Typically, much of the work, like harvesting corn and grains or hoeing, was done by members and their families separately. Small plots or rows of vegetables requiring careful attention (singling and hoeing) over a period of time were assigned to member families for several months, or sometimes just for one task, and the corresponding number of work units was credited to the family. At other times the membership worked together in larger bands, for example, picking fruit. These policies varied according to the desires of the members.

Specialization remained at a low level. Although there were a president and a bookkeeper for each cooperative, they often worked alongside other workers at collective tasks, and many of their work units were derived from work similar to that of other members. Neither of the collectives ever achieved a large stock of collectively owned animals. Thus, animal care was not usually a full-time job. Although the Petőfi had some horses and a teamster, the May 1 often depended on nonmembers for carting in exchange for manual labor or produce. Much of the plowing and preparation of the fields was carried out by the government-run tractor stations in Kistó and Boros.[10] The farms therefore had no tractors or tractor drivers of their own.

Considering their acreage (for example, in the mid-1950s the Petőfi reached a size of four or five hundred hold-s, a considerable size for its fifty full and supporting members), the cooperatives were relatively unsuccessful. It should be made clear, however, that they, too, suffered from problems beyond their control.[11]

One difficulty shared by these cooperatives and others across the country was the tempo of socialist transformation in the countryside. Though the government had campaigned to eliminate the influence of the wealthy peasants and had similarly "encouraged" rural inhabitants to join the collective farms, its measures were too extreme. Peasants left private

10. These tractor stations were established in the late 1940s and the 1950s to provide machinery for the collective farms established in their vicinity, machinery which for small farms would otherwise be very expensive, difficult to maintain, and uneconomical for limited use. Because of the low level of technical knowledge about agriculture among collective farm leaders, they were also to dispense advice and technical aid. Although use of the stations' machines was extended to the plowing of private land, this was last in priority for the machinery. The tractor stations also served to extend still further the government's centralized hold on the leadership and production of the nation's collective farms (Donáth 1977: 129–130).

11. See Donáth (1977: 144–156) and Orbán (1972: 111–125) for a more detailed discussion of these problems. The material in the following paragraphs is largely dependent on these sources.

agriculture at such a rapid pace that the collectives were unable to make up for their lost production. Moreover, since many peasants were giving up their land without joining the collectives, the cooperatives were left with an embarrassment of land that they, because of their limited membership and lack of machinery, were unable to absorb and cultivate properly.[12]

This situation was exacerbated by the lack of investment in agriculture by the government, which financed the rapid development of heavy industry at the expense of agriculture. The government did not even meet its own goals for agricultural investment, and much of the money went not into the new capital expansion so necessary for the introduction of large-scale agriculture (new barns, storage facilities, machinery to take advantage of economies of scale), but into the day-to-day support of the very existence of these fledgling enterprises.[13]

Farming collectives were also included under the provisions of the forced deliveries regulations. Because of the rapid reduction in size of the private sector, this burden soon became very heavy and severely limited the ability of the farms to market profitably their harvests and the animals they raised. Indeed, Orbán (1972: 124–125) points out that, as for individuals, meeting the quotas sometimes meant that the collective farms were left without seed grain for next year's planting or fodder for the animals. As many as half the cooperatives were unable to meet their quotas in various foodstuffs. Many were fined for their failure to fulfill the quotas, but local authorities were usually more lenient in dealing with the collectives than with individuals.

Thus, Kislapos's two cooperative farms had more land than they could fully use. The Petőfi, for example, attempted to raise vegetables like tomatoes and paprika, the production of which was being encouraged by the government and which fetched a good price. Because of the labor-intensive nature of these crops and the farms' relatively low membership in relation to land, however, they simply could not produce much without

12. Those who gave up land to the cooperatives often kept their valuable equipment for their remaining land or sold it.

13. Lack of organizational ability in the local collectives' leadership, especially in light of the wholesale reorganization necessary when hundreds of small units had to be fashioned into a much larger enterprise, also made this more difficult nationally. Of particular significance in many communities was the tendency of many new but unwilling members to concentrate their efforts and interest on their houseplot enterprises; while working the bare minimum of hours necessary to earn a plot, they often neglected the collective work for their own intensive horticulture. Collective farms with apparently adequate work forces frequently found themselves short of labor just when they needed it most—at the harvest. Leaders were chosen in many villages not for their ability to advance the collective interests but for their willingness to allow the members to pursue their individual interests.

neglecting a good portion of their land—something neither public opinion nor the government would have allowed. They did not have the use of such machinery as combines to ease the production of extensive crops like grains, so they could not concentrate more on intensive crops.

Neither farm had much available for investment. The May 1 collective often used the funds made available to it to buy necessities for its members or to extend personal credit to them. Both farms experienced difficulty in selling their production (or at least in selling it for what they considered a reasonable price) and therefore dealt out large stocks of grain and fodder to their members, who used them to raise their own animals. Because of this, the collectives, in turn, were sometimes forced to ask for seed grains and other aid from higher authorities.

In some ways, each cooperative constituted a small community separate from the village population. Outside of various village administrators and party leaders, who were mainly titular members, almost all of the Petőfi's members lived on the tanya outside of town where the collective's headquarters and barns were. They lived in the cseléd houses of the former mayor and his nagygazda brother-in-law (the latter continued to inhabit the tanya until 1955), as well as in the mayor's former residence. Several member families of the May 1 lived in the headquarters, while others occupied houses scattered throughout Lapos, mostly residences assigned in the past to cseléd-s.

Beyond this spatial factor, members spent most of their time together at work, at play, or in conversation. Having been cseléd-s, summás-s, or herders in the past, or even more recent newcomers to the village, most members had few kinsmen there; most of their close relatives in the village were also members of the farm.

As a result of all these factors, views of the collective farm members held by most of the other villagers were not very favorable. They were regarded first and foremost as outsiders, strangers, and "nomads" (*vándornép*) by the villagers. Because of the nature of their work and the conditions with which they met, they often changed positions after a few years; and moving was not unusual. Thus, they were not really seen as full inhabitants of Kislapos. Moreover, both their past and present status as tanya folk reinforced the negative aspects of this image. Families living on the tanya-s, particularly poorer ones, or on the estates outside town, had long been considered less civilized than their village counterparts. They appeared infrequently in the village and were seen as lacking fundamental social skills, as generally uncouth. Attempts by tanya laborers to send their children to the village schools, to gain village friends and to learn to behave properly, were regarded as hopeless (Fél and Hofer 1969: 281).

Because they were former cseléd-s and landless laborers (or, as some villagers claimed, those who "liked to be cseléd-s"), not peasant entrepreneurs, the villagers viewed their farming efforts with great skepticism; unfortunately, the performance of the collectives did little to dispel these impressions. The village peasants saw the aid granted to the collectives by the government, the large amounts of land they had, the priority they received over the local gazda-s in plowing by the tractor stations, and other seeming advantages and were both envious and contemptuous of farm members.

It was felt that the collective farm members did not adequately marshal their resources. Smallholders and middle peasants considered such collective farm practices as distributing the stock of grain to be squandering resources and failing to think ahead. Probably more sympathy was felt for the members when an illegal slaughter of a calf was reported on the Petőfi farm and several leaders were imprisoned for a few months; but this simply reinforced the peasants' views. While they, too, bridled at the restrictions on slaughtering animals and left some pig-killings unreported so as to escape some of the forced delivery requirements, the killing of a calf was seen as living today off tomorrow's produce.

Reports of thefts by members from common stores, of parties, and of drunkenness on the part of leaders of the weaker May 1 collective only strengthened further the peasants' convictions about the farms. In short, they saw the farm members as lacking the basic characteristics of the successful peasant and the good farmer. They squandered what they had instead of practicing self-denial, saving, and investing. They were said to carouse instead of working diligently. A former wealthy peasant's wife remarked, only half-jokingly, that she could get more women together to help her work than the collectives could! An inspector had once mistaken a group of women helping her as the cooperative's work brigade. Former farm members of the May 1 say that of the dozen member families only three or four consistently worked in the fields. In both farms the president, whose status was less differentiated from other members than it is today, was unable to order members to work but had to ask them to come.

Indeed, the president of neither farm had been a cseléd or identified by the villagers as a good farmer in the past. The president of the May 1 was a villager who had invested in a threshing machine in the late 1920s and lost it because of his inability to pay off debts when wheat prices plunged. In later years he was primarily a harvester and day laborer, sometimes selling candy and other small goods as a sideline. He was well known for his blustery temperament and his drinking.

The president of the Petőfi (until his removal for butchering a calf) was the son of the charter member of the Communist Party mentioned earlier who had similarly invested in a thresher and failed. Some say this was due to both parents' high living, as well as the changed agricultural prices. The son was better known for his mechanical skills than his farming talent. All of these individuals emerged as important local party leaders after World War II.

Whereas the Petőfi collective farm lasted through the second phase of collectivization in 1959 until the merger of Kislapos's collectives in 1961, the May 1 broke up during the 1956 uprising. Both faced pressures from nonmember villagers to disband at this time of revolt against policies of the recent past. The May 1, which had never been very strong, did so at the advice of its leaders. Those members who had given their land to the cooperative got it back; all members not joining the Petőfi were assessed an amount to cover some of the cooperative's debts. The remaining land and equipment went to the Petőfi.

LOCAL POLITICS: 1949–1956

By the end of 1949 the real major struggle for power by the Communist Party in Hungary had come to an end. Although the major political trials, like those of Rajk and Mindszenty, may have given or been designed to give the impression that the struggle against revisionism, the forces of capitalism, and the Church was very much alive, and that constant vigilance against these enemies was necessary, the trials were prime evidence that the new government was definitely in command.

In fact, there was little as yet to fear from "revisionism," except from desires for reform raised by the extremes of party policies. Capitalism in the countryside was strongly in check and could gain only through force of sympathy and empathy. The Roman Catholic Church, too, was largely under control. Although, near the end of the consolidation period, it had formed the sole organized opposition (Ignotus 1972: 203–204) and still had a powerful hold on its believers, its political power had been seriously undermined. Through the land reforms most of the huge estates owned by the wealthy Church had been seized, and in 1948 most schools were freed of Church supervision.

Thus, this period in Kislapos involved no abrupt departure from the power relations established after the war. It centered on the strengthening of the party's hold, the establishment of a socialist economy at the expense of the private sector and to some degree agriculture, and the implementation of party policies by an increasingly bureaucratic and more entrenched administrative and political structure whose chief positions were occupied by party members. A look at some of the institutions affected by this entrenchment and strengthening of party-influenced bases for local power and personal gain demonstrates and clarifies this process.

The Church

When the village schools were secularized, the organist-teachers were forced to choose between their secular and their church positions. The religious curriculum was severely cut. Those attending catechism had to have an average grade of C or above and had to have their parents' written approval; parents were often called to the school or town hall, where attempts were made to dissuade them. They were warned of the possible negative consequences for their children in seeking higher education or a job. Some villagers went to these meetings with their spouses so they could give each other moral support.

Reflecting these changes was the change in the daily greeting required of the children. Instead of "May Jesus Christ be praised," they were expected to say, in reference to the building of a socialist society, "Onward!" Students who forgot received a cuff from more determined teachers.

Of equal but more general significance was the overall antireligious attitude of the authorities at the time; religious activity and belief were held to be totally incompatible with party membership and with holding official positions. Locally, for example, one female party member teacher was roundly criticized at a party meeting for taking part in the Easter procession. Party officials visiting homes could often see the bare or lighter colored areas on walls from which religious pictures and crucifixes had been hastily removed by the nonparty inhabitants. From the late 1940s on, villagers seeking to avoid sanction for having their children baptized or confirmed went to more distant churches to have the rites performed. Not infrequently, grandparents had their grandchildren baptized without the knowledge of disapproving or fearful parents. In the late 1940s the village's first solely civil marriage ceremony took place, between a village woman and a member of the state security police, creating a stir.[14] A church ceremony was even cause for dismissal from police service for one villager.

The strong aversion of the party to the Church was demonstrated even to one of the village's early postwar mayors, an important local party member and wife of the village's party secretary. As Kislapos's first woman mayor, she had been approached by a member of the church council about having a fence placed around the old cemetery as a memorial to her mayoralty. All she had to do was speak to the priest—which, undoubtedly flattered, she did. When word leaked out to the Party Committee in neighboring Kistó, she was called there to explain how she as mayor and as a Communist could be negotiating with the priest. She was accused of being religious.

Although church attendance declined during these years, it did not fall as much as in later years.

The Village Administration

By the late 1940s the choice of the mayor, which in the past had largely been in the hands of the virilista-s on the board of representatives, had

14. Since the late nineteenth century a civil ceremony has been required in Hungary in addition to the usual religious rite.

passed into the hands of the party. Moreover, it was the higher party authorities who increasingly had a say in the selection of local officials. One year, when other local candidates were found wanting by the party or were undesirable to the villagers, the district party leadership in Boros picked the wife of the local party secretary to run, an unorthodox choice in light of the previous absolute male dominance in local politics. After 1951, when the board of representatives and mayor were replaced by a new administrative system with a council (soviet) and council president, the president was almost invariably selected by higher authorities outside the village. Since he ran unopposed in elections, his selection was tantamount to election, just as the choice of the previous woman mayor meant her election. Thus, local leaders' power came to rest to an even greater degree on their outside ties. It also rested on their ability to mediate policies established by higher party authorities.

During these years the village administration took on steadily greater power and an increasing number of functions. It played a particularly important role in the fixing and collection of forced delivery quotas, in the antikulak drives, and in the process of collectivization. The mayor and later the village council, largely in the person of its president, ultimately decided on the quotas to be assessed each village family through the compulsory delivery system. While village quotas as a whole were set by district officials, and clear guidelines existed for setting individual quotas on the basis of land owned, considerable discretion was left to the village council. The president or mayor could use a report of flooded farm land, illness, or poverty to postpone the collection of delivery quotas or to reduce them; he judged whether a family's land was to be considered as several small enterprises or one large one. The possibility was thus left open for the council to reduce some quotas while keeping others high, or even to increase the pressure on some. This allowed some relief from burdens for the hard-pressed, as well as the possibility of favoritism and patronage.

The penalties for nonpayment of taxes or nondelivery of low-priced produce were great. In the late 1940s there were even cases of villagers being locked up temporarily in the basement of the local consumers' cooperative as a result.

To encourage families to meet their quotas, contests were held and prizes of implements offered to families quickly reaching or surpassing their quotas. Whole villages were also involved in larger competitions. Lists displaying the names of villagers satisfying their quotas early in the year (and thus meriting praise), as well as those of delinquents, were posted in front of the town hall. One former gendarme, who had received a severe beating for his role in disrupting the local organizing session of DÉFOSZ, was always among the first to satisfy his quotas, but his name was finally stricken from the "praise" list by the mayor, who did not want to see a former gendarme leading the lists.

Similar discretion was left in dealing with kulaks. Although clear guidelines were set, zealous or vindictive local administrators raised quotas in many communities. Apparently in Lapos in the 1950s this was not common; but there it was the mayor and later the council president, along with the local tax collectors, who administered the tax and forced delivery systems to the wealthier peasants. They also directed outside officials to certain villagers, for example, when "peace loans" were collected to support the government.

Collectivization was another important area of activity for the administration. There was a great deal of cooperation between the mayor's office, and later the council, on one hand and the collective farm on the other. The former took part in land consolidations, the seizure of nagygazda-s' property for use by the farms, the setting of quotas for the farms, and other important matters. In fact, in Lapos the first president of the May 1 collective became the council president upon establishment of the council system and remained the party secretary for the collective, while a former village party secretary took over the collective farm's presidency and his wife, the former mayor, became its bookkeeper. Several members of the administration and the consumers' cooperative became supporting members of the collective. The council president played a central role in the establishment of later collective farms.

Finally, some informants also suggest that there were opportunities for personal financial gain in the village administration. For example, the village council president in the early 1950s is said to have received kickbacks of firewood for granting rental of state reserve land in the village to peasants, and to have pocketed loans approved for other villagers. Having established connections with district council officials, he was promoted to the district council before charges were brought against him for these offenses, charges that resulted in his being "demoted" as "punishment" to the council presidency of a nearby village. Returning to the council presidency of Kislapos after the events of 1956, he lost his position in 1969 when he was caught appropriating for his own use sixty quintals of cement earmarked for a new bridge across the Farkas. Even then he managed to retain a good position in the higher administrative circles of the consumers' cooperative.

The Consumers' Cooperative

In the late 1940s the Hangya Cooperative was reorganized. The new agricultural and marketing cooperative continued to maintain a general store and the village tavern, and also took over the purchasing of local agricultural production, including the forced deliveries. Members bought shares entitling them to vote for the leaders and to receive a fixed rate of interest on the shares they purchased.

Leadership in the local consumers' cooperative did not offer power, but it consistently did offer reasonable pay and opportunities for theft, embezzlement, and cheating. Several produce buyers in the 1950s and even the 1960s were dismissed from their positions or were sent to prison for shortweighing or for fraudulently reporting goods received in the village. Several naive village storekeepers and warehousemen for the local cooperative were victimized by embezzling directors. In the early years following 1948 the managing positions and that of the buyer were plums held by party members. Those found misusing their positions were at worst dismissed and often were simply transferred to a position elsewhere because of their party bureaucratic connections with higher ups. So well-known was the occasional thievery in these circles, the intriguing within the shifting higher-level leadership, and the associated patronage that one respectable smallholder was warned against continuing in the produce-buying position by knowledgeable acquaintances because he might well "pay" for having stayed on; a shift in leadership or the offering of patronage to someone else might lead others to pin some corruption on him in order to open his position for someone else or simply to get him out of the way.

OCTOBER–NOVEMBER 1956

The uprising of October and November 1956 passed in Kislapos without much violence, though with considerable upheaval. News of the events in Budapest and elsewhere reached the village over the radio, and soon nightly meetings were being held in the cultural house to discuss the day's events and to argue over what should be done. Much as in nearby villages and the larger Boros, where the district council and the district Party Committee had dissolved, the local council and the party also fell into disarray. A new temporary council was established and a president chosen, and a temporary police force came into being.

Although there was little violence in Kislapos, fear and threats were significant. On one occasion several men broke into the empty town hall and shot off several rounds; and shots were occasionally fired into the air by drunken villagers. The chief representatives and symbols of the previous years were put under pressure of threats and ill-feeling. Lists stating who should be "strung up" were circulated, but nothing came of them. The village council president, an outsider from a nearby village, fearing for his safety, fled to his home village. Many party members, similarly concerned for their well-being, burned or discarded their party membership booklets. During the two weeks of major upheaval, the local May 1 farming collective broke up because of its already weak condition, the uncertainty of the times, and the fears of its leadership in the face of the events. The leaders of the Petőfi resisted threats of harm and did not dissolve.

The sympathy of many in Lapos and in the countryside in general rested with those seeking reforms and with those who resisted the Soviet tanks that put down the uprising. Like many villagers nationwide they sent foodstuffs to the cities, especially Budapest, the scene of severe fighting and hardship during those days. The collective farms also joined in, though the Petőfi's president resisted efforts of outsiders to take even more than the considerable amounts volunteered.

The newly chosen leaders stayed in office for a while after it became clear that the uprising was crushed, but when it was obvious that they would not be recognized or paid by the reorganized district bodies, they left the village council chambers. Some weeks afterward, the new council president (actually the original one, who had for the last year or two served in a nearby village) took office, and the local party, by then disintegrated, began to reorganize. Calls were put out to old members, but many did not rejoin. In time, especially after 1959, the membership of the party took on a complexion very different from its earlier years.

In the aftermath two villagers were imprisoned, one for as long as six months, for their activities in Lapos in 1956. The more severely sentenced individual was alleged to have written and circulated a list of demands similar to those of the short-lived provisional government in Budapest. These included calls for the end of forced deliveries, for the departure of Soviet troops from Hungary, and for the punishment of compromised leaders. He also put up placards demanding the Russians to go home and repeating Smallholders' Party slogans. Because several others had engaged in similar activities, some feel that his jailing was partly a result of his having earned the enmity of the town council president several years earlier by reporting the president's illegal activities. After serving his time, he was allowed to go home.

BRIEF YEARS OF PROSPERITY: 1957–1959

In Kislapos the years 1957–1959 brought a great relaxation of the agricultural policies directed at the private farmer. Though most direct goals of the uprising remained unfulfilled, 1956 did see the end of the forced deliveries. Whereas in the past few years most peasants had at best just managed to break even, now many were able to reap good profits, particularly through intensive cultivation of vegetables.

Part of this was due to the higher prices producers were receiving, part due to their willingness to invest in new wells, pumps, implements, and small greenhouses, and part due to the success of the new vegetable growers' cooperative, which grew considerably in numbers during this period. All of these were strongly interrelated, and they will not be discussed independently, but in the context of the cooperative.

The vegetable growers' cooperative was established in Kislapos in 1955 through the backing of the local consumers' cooperative and its national organization and the often closely allied agency that bought up much of the country's agricultural output. Those joining paid a small membership fee and were promised slightly higher than standard prices for vegetables like tomatoes and paprika, as well as the chance to buy otherwise scarce wood frames and glass. These could be used to construct crates and small greenhouses (or warm beds) especially useful for the early cultivation of seedlings. They were also able to buy fertilizer and the seed for varieties of tomatoes and paprika especially desired on the market and otherwise difficult to obtain. These they began receiving in 1956. At that time members were also given the use of a large drill for a relatively low fee to bore wells used to irrigate the vegetable crops. (With the intervention of higher authorities, the members had resisted the efforts of two enterprising, mechanically inclined villagers, who had been delegated to go and observe a similar drilling machine, to maintain control over the drill they built on the basis of their trip and to charge large fees for its use.) Several bought gasoline motors from the state agency to work the pumps for these wells; others rented them.

Membership originally stood at 20–30 but rose in several years to 120. This was a "less advanced" form of cooperative than the two established earlier. It involved no surrender of private land to the collective. It did include the use of cooperatively owned machines, the cooperative buying of seed and other materials (though for private use and ownership), and the sale of produce at a contracted price to the same state-owned buying agency. The latter contract was quite important, along with the crates, because in past years tons of tomatoes had rotted in the fields due to lack of crates or the refusal of canners to buy the production.

In addition to these benefits, through the village council members could rent land given up by peasants who were unable or unwilling to continue meeting earlier forced deliveries and taxes or who had left the village for industry—land that the collective farms were unable to cultivate.

Those joining were mainly members of the smallholders' stratum and the lower ranges of the middle peasantry. Most had neither enough land to be self-sufficient in cultivating the more traditional grains nor the capital to pursue profitable animal breeding. However, even if, or especially if, they had large families, they were well-suited to cultivate vegetables intensively. In fact, most families were capable of handling at most a couple of hold-s by themselves.

Many of the wealthier peasants who did not join viewed the cooperative's members as of a "trading bent," being too commercially oriented. This phrase had a slightly pejorative connotation, associated as it was with horse and cattle traders and with the occasional underhanded dealings of the employees of the Hangya and the new consumers' cooperative. It also referred to the fact that these individuals had smaller landholdings and had to be more concerned with small price differences than did their wealthier counterparts.[15]

However, even some of the middle peasants did join and sowed at least a small portion of their holdings in these profitable crops. Many smallholders were able to acquire additional land with their profits during these years. Although they were unhappy to lose their land at the time of collectivization in 1959, especially since they had invested large sums in pumps, motors, and implements and had begun to improve their situations and prosper, some felt that even the year or two of using newly bought land in intensive farming had paid for the land. Many inhabitants of Lapos even today hark back to these times with great pride, remembering the quality and quantity of vegetables and fruits they produced, the profits they earned, and the improvements they made in their farming. They think back on the lines of heavily burdened wagons strung for several hundred meters on the village streets waiting to leave their produce at the local buyer's collection point. When collectivization seemed inevitable in 1959, some of the peasants offered the village council president thousands of forint-s for the opportunity to continue cultivating their own land for just one more year.

Those who did not focus on intensive production of vegetables also found their living standards rising due to the higher prices they received for their crops and the easing of restrictions on the sale and slaughter of animals, an area in which Kislapos's inhabitants had excelled.

THE BIG WAVE OF COLLECTIVIZATION

After two years of relative prosperity in private agriculture, the tidal wave of full collectivization struck Kislapos in 1959. It did not come completely as a surprise, for many had viewed the vegetable growers'

---

15. Sárkány (1978: 78–88) reports similar conditions and attitudes in Varsány. There the wealthy peasants, the smallholders, and the landless were most sensitive to the market conditions—the former group because they were most familiar with the profits to be derived and the latter two because they were the most dependent on slight changes in market conditions. "However ... [the middle peasants], although they too were in constant touch with the market, viewed market production and the use of money as a necessary evil, and if they could they avoided it" (87).

cooperative as a precursor to later collectivization. Moreover, reports of rapid collectivization in the nearby countries of Romania, Bulgaria, East Germany, and Czechoslovakia had reached Hungary from 1958 on. In 1958 the prices offered for agricultural products had slipped 13 percent compared to industrial prices, and taxes on agricultural land were increased, though not to the levels reached before 1956. Beyond that, discussion was taking place within the national party leadership (Donáth 1977: 167–170), rumors of which had reached the very interested peasants.

The big push to collectivize the greater part of Hungarian agriculture began in January 1959 and ended in the spring of 1961. During this period more than 95 percent of agricultural land came to belong to the socialist sector. The economic and social stratification based on landed wealth largely disappeared, for by 1961 almost 94 percent of agricultural workers labored in the socialist sector. This does not mean that past status immediately lost all significance. However, other ties and factors rapidly assumed greater importance.

Generally, the organizing activity took place during the winter months (ibid.: 171). Under the direction of the district council, all of Homok District was marked for organizing in the winter of 1958–1959. Thus the agitators so common during the organizing period in many villages appeared in Kislapos in January 1959. Mainly teachers and factory workers, usually from the cities, they came to the village for several days at a time to convince the peasants of the benefits of collective farming. In Kislapos as elsewhere the local council led the drive to organize the villagers into collective farms and directed the agitators to the homes of various villagers.

For the first several weeks these efforts were entirely fruitless. No one joined. The peasants, having seen the performance of the May 1 and the Petőfi collectives, and familiar with conditions elsewhere, were very skeptical of the claims and predictions made by people far less familiar with agriculture than they. Many household heads hid or left home for days at a time to avoid the constant pressure of argument and persuasion. Later even this tactic was unsuccessful, as their wives often caved in under the stress and joined in their stead.

Nonetheless, when it became clear that these initial efforts to lure the villagers into the already existing Petőfi farm would fail, the village council leaders adopted a different tack. Realizing that the peasantry did not want to place themselves under the leadership of the formerly landless leaders of the deprecated Petőfi, and that the success of collectivization in the village depended on getting the middle peasants to join, they adopted new techniques to establish a solid foundation on which the villagers would be more "willing" to build.

This description by the then council president of the further organizing offers a feeling for his problems, the peasants' mood, and the local solution.

There was a cooperative operating here, a vegetable producers' cooperative. Its leaders were István Fekete and Péter Kalicz, and Bálint Molnár was the president. Péter Kalicz was the treasurer of the cooperative. Well, anyway, they came out from the county party organization; they were really forcing the pace. It didn't go; it didn't go! This was a wealthy community. There was money in the cooperative; the cooperative really developed the paprika production in the village and things like that. It didn't go.

By the beginning of March I didn't know what to do. I thought it over. Let me speak openly, because the party organization wasn't so strong here. It wasn't so strong that it would have stirred things because, say, Mátyás Kollár [the party secretary]—he was also a party member—he didn't join the collective either. In short, the party members themselves didn't join the collective. This was my problem. No matter how much I kept pushing other mass organizations like the Patriotic People's Front[16] and the council members, it didn't go.

So I worked out a little program for myself as council president. I called a council meeting together . . . The council made the members pass the resolution calling for the community of Kislapos's agricultural reorganization. I declared it to the members. I mean it wasn't a dictatorial vote, but obviously the council members accepted it, adopted it, because it had to be. So they adopted it. This way I could make better propaganda. "Attention! The council's decision declared the agricultural reorganization of Kislapos, that Kislapos will be a socialist community, an agricultural community." It made it stronger.

That night I went to the cooperative. They were also deliberating. Before this I had listened and talked at these meetings, and I thought it was good politics that the cooperative granted various discounts, that they also got benefits from the state, or so I explained to them. "And that's right. When we produce then we're socialists; we have a socialist character. When we sell then we're capitalists, and this is the way it is, right. The production was of a socialist nature because through the state we all avail ourselves of benefits. When the goods reach market, then the law of supply and demand determines the price." I tried like this. "It can't go on like this. It can't go on that I accept everything from the state and the state takes nothing from me." They listened and listened. It didn't go. Everyone nicely straggled on home. Only two or three of us remained. We talked, not in anger but as friends. "Jancsi" [a familiar form of the council president's name], and they said it, "horse cock [bullshit]!" these peasants said; but, believe me, who else could I count on? So we talked together on a friendly basis.

The next day was Sunday. I'll never forget it. I called together Péter Kalicz and two or three others Sunday night. I talked with Péter Kalicz. "I mean it sincerely,

16. This organization was founded nationally and locally in 1948 with the merger of the political parties. Among other functions, it selected candidates for office and had limited influence on local policy.

because you, Péter Kalicz, will be the collective's president. I say it now that you'll be the collective farm president. Let's organize it." Bálint Molnár—I didn't tell him that he'd be the president because I knew that he didn't have the kind of kinship connections (because I built on the relatives in Lapos, on those masses, on those men who had lots of relatives and good middle peasant relatives) that the old Péter Kalicz did—this is the truth—and also István Fekete, who had a lot of cheek: I built on these; he'll be the head bookkeeper. And that's the way it turned out. It's another question of how long it would continue this way.

So I told Péter Kalicz to call a meeting of the cooperative on Monday night. Okay. And they also came from the county to help out . . . That night we called a meeting of the cooperative; I got Péter Kalicz to call a meeting. I didn't do it because, if it had been me, then they wouldn't have come. It's the truth. If they knew that "Jancsi wants that again, surely he wants that. . . !" Well, they were really afraid.

So they gathered together. "Damn it," says Pista Burom . . . He was the buyer for the cooperative . . . He says, "Let's drink one!"

What the hell; I never liked wine and I hardly drank it. But then I acted. "What the hell; let's drink one." They put together about 200 forint-s. "Bring the wine!" I resigned myself. What do I care; bring it on. And they got two drums of wine. But there was no real reason for the wine; he just concocted it. Okay, we talked, but I didn't mention the collective then. So we drank away. I didn't drink wine. I like cherry brandy. That's what I drink. Pista got hold of everything, but he didn't know either what I was leading to because I drank, too. We talked. It was already half past ten. "Well, men, I wouldn't mind if we stopped now."

"We have time, Jancsi," they said.

"But I want to report something," I said. "I brought the enrollment forms." I had it in my inner pocket. "I brought the enrollment forms. Let's try to found"—I had already hit upon it— "the Gold Spike [of corn] collective farm." They took a good look at me! They were surprised, although maybe not particularly so, since they knew anyway that I had something up my sleeve because of the county leaders being there.

So then Béla Nagy said, "Let's turn out the lights. Let's pass out the enrollment forms and turn the lights out. Let's not have the problem of who signs it first, who's the first to enroll. Let's put out the lights." Okay, I agreed. "But let there be no one else in the room besides us. Let the county people go outside." They had to leave.

For more than thirty minutes they wouldn't allow the lights to be put on. A little light shone in from outside . . . I also waited there. Every once in a while someone cracked a joke. Because my voice held sway I said, "Well, for Christ's sake, I'm going to turn this light on. Don't waste my time here now!"

"We're not wasting time."

"Then what's this? Come on, turn it on." Well, imagine—no one had signed. No one had signed the enrollment form, no one. Only Bálint Molnár had signed it, and he didn't show that he had signed. Bálint Molnár didn't show it.

The next day in the afternoon everyone in the group signed. They came into my office. I didn't go to houses. They came to my office in the council chambers and signed. There were eleven then.

This is how the organizing began, and by March 11, Imre Pető, who lives next to Miklós Magyar, in Imre Pető's barn, István Szegedi, Sándor Kalicz . . . gathered together. They said to me—Sándor Kalicz came in to get me— "Jancsi, come on out to the barn." Well, I went. They were all there. They asked me to take out the bylaws. Imagine that. I had to read out the bylaws, explaining them. So we had an understanding. This was at night.

Then the next morning about ten o'clock I had to go out to Gábor Pető's. I had to take out the bylaws to old Gábor Pető and explain them to his family, what's in them. I took them out to him, and I had to take them out alone to countless homes. Imagine, the next evening—that's not right, because on the eleventh the two collectives' preliminary committees reached their final form. So the next night I picked up my jacket—I had a leather jacket. I was standing at the door of the council president's office, thinking, what the hell, I'll go out again to find out what they're doing. When I had put on my coat, there they were, eleven or twelve of them. So Sándor Kalicz and István Szegedi say—but good and tipsy— "Jancsi, the preliminary committee's been formed with the name of Kossuth."

"Good. Who'll be the president?" I said it this way, word for word.

"István Szegedi."

"I'm glad," I said. "I'm glad." So, it was formed. Then I sat down and wrote out the enrollment forms. They signed them like the devil.

What is noteworthy about this solution is the deliberate and ultimately successful attempt to persuade and seduce the middle peasants to join, to establish a solid nucleus around which a cooperative farm could develop. This explains the council president's relative willingness to sanction the independent establishment of a second new cooperative, the Kossuth, by another group of middle peasants. This stratum came to occupy the important positions of leadership in the newly formed collectives, which formed the basis for a new shift in composition of the village leadership, from the formerly landless poor to the middle peasantry.

Interestingly, István Szegedi did not become president of the Kossuth collective. The next morning, when the organization was to be made formal, Miklós Magyar, a neighbor of Imre Pető, who had listened in on the planning, stepped forward when the name of the preliminary committee's president was asked and simply announced himself as head. When, despite misgivings and opposition, no one in the group actively opposed him, and István Szegedi withdrew, Miklós Magyar assumed the position, a post he held for seventeen years.

Some other villagers proposed to organize still a fourth collective farm in the wake of these developments, but the council president ruled that this would be too many for such a small village and that the resulting farms would not be viable. The rapid organization of the three new farms was followed by an equally swift enrollment of most of the agriculturally employed villagers.

Although this last phase of the reorganization went quickly, it was not an easy period for the villagers joining, nor did it involve simple decisions. The villagers did not really want to join the farms. They deeply felt the loss of their land, into which enormous effort, money, and emotional investment had gone. Moreover, land had meant financial self-sufficiency and, for the formerly landless, freedom from having to kowtow to others and take their abuse. For many, joining the collective farm was akin to returning to a cseléd position because it involved taking orders. In addition, the collective farm of the future was an uncertainty, whereas the prosperity of the past few years had been a fact.

In the meantime, psychological pressure continued to be applied. Agitators visited families for hours on end, not leaving until an application form was filled out. Whenever a new family signed up, that fact was announced over the loudspeakers spread out over the village. Once or twice outings were organized for villagers to visit nearby successful collective and state farms. Many villagers, remembering the beating of a decade earlier and unsure of the purpose of these bus trips, went with great trepidation. Finally, it must be remembered that with the whole district under the same organizing campaign, reports frequently came from nearby villages of organizing success; for Lapos's inhabitants this increased the feeling of inevitability of the collectivization.

When the enrollments began to mount, villagers became increasingly concerned lest they be left out. They were aware of the effect of consolidations on those whose land had been within the areas blocked out in earlier consolidations of collective farm land. Moreover, many were jockeying for leadership positions in the new farms; early action was vital for such consideration. Under these additional pressures the enrollments picked up still greater speed. Within days the vast majority of village farmland had been registered in the books of the three collective farms.

The grounds for the villagers' decisions of which collective farm to join were varied. In general, they were based on many of the same connections as were their social ties. They tended to enroll in the same cooperative farms as did their relatives and neighbors. Stem families joined as single units, and in-laws and other close relatives tended to join the same farm. Many informants reported that they had joined the same farm as their neighbors and people living in their section of the village, reminiscent of the kaláka.

As mentioned by the former council president, economic status was also a determinant in the establishment of the new cooperatives. To quote him further:

The reason I was able to bring this wealthy community into unity after a long drought was that I depended on those men above all. I didn't depend—I say it seriously—on the landless proletariat then because a good portion of them were already in the Petőfi collective. Márton Kelemen was the council vice-president. I immediately picked him out. "Come on, Uncle [a respectful, somewhat familiar way of addressing an older male] Márton," because from 1950 on he was the vice-president of the council. In short, in the movement I depended on all these men who, all in all, weren't our enemies, but rather they helped build up socialism. As long as they produced. That's another question, whether they were capitalists or whatever. But it was to my advantage. It was my goal to get hold of these people. Because I wouldn't have gotten anywhere with peasants having two or three hold-s . . . In their lives they got one or two hold-s of land at the land reform, right. They clung so tightly to the land, to the ownership, that they were happy if they drove one little horse or two cows because they used to be wretched proletarians, they were day laborers. But the middle peasant, he didn't feel it so much because from childhood on he always did that. With these land recipients I couldn't have formed a collective farm.

As it was, many in the Gold Spike, having been members of the vegetable growers' cooperative, were smallholders and middle peasants, whereas the membership of the Kossuth consisted of middle peasants and even some former wealthy peasants. Unlike the earlier phase of collectivization, in the early 1950s, when kulaks were often excluded from collective farm membership (in communities where a far larger portion of the population joined than in Kislapos), they were, if found acceptable to the other members, allowed to become members (Donáth 1977: 170), and in Kislapos they were even encouraged to. Many of the smallest landholders joined the Petőfi. As many said, they joined the collectives whose members were "their kind of people."

Of course, membership in these collectives was not totally along the lines of economic strata. Exceptions abounded. Kin, neighbor, and kinship connections often cut across stratum boundaries. Many joined the collective in which they could obtain the best positions. György Molnár, a middle peasant and one of the louder voices calling for the breakup of the Petőfi collective in 1956, took over the presidency of that cooperative in 1959 when its previous president, feeling that his limited education was inadequate for the position, left for training as a tractor driver. János Kis, a smallholder and the first president of the vegetable producers' cooperative, quit the Gold Spike after several months and joined the Petőfi when his older brother did not receive the brigade leader's position he had expected. On the other hand, Kálmán Kecskés changed his mind after accepting a position as brigade leader from his friend György Molnár in the Petőfi. He elected to join the Kossuth so that he would not have to part completely with his vineyards, which had been assigned to the Kossuth through the consolidation of village land into three large parcels, one for each collective.

Not all villagers joined. Some of the older males, uncertain about retirement benefits deriving from the few years they might work in the collective, went to work in factories and construction in the cities to qualify for a pension after a minimum ten years of employment. Others simply did not want to join but, mindful of the location and quality of the land they might receive as their own through the consolidations, also sought employment elsewhere. Many young men in particular, doubtful of the future in the collective farm and attracted to the glitter, entertainment, and higher wages of the city, sought jobs there. Almost all commuted, coming home every weekend or two, a life style· that those with families of their own found especially difficult. As there were few work opportunities nearby, most ultimately returned to take up a position in the collective farm or moved to the city.

Perhaps a half-dozen attempted to continue to farm privately on their own land.[17] Only three or four chose this route for more than two or three years. Through land consolidation, their holdings were exchanged for outlying land of poorer quality often subject to high groundwater. Two nonmembers who joined under the pressures of the organizing reconsidered within a few days and tried to step out; but they found their land could not come with them. They continued to farm privately on the small holdings they had held back and on plots still owned by relatives who had left the village. They are now in their seventies, widowers, and living alone, and are considered by villagers to be just hanging on; they are more objects of pity than of admiration. There were a couple of younger private farmers, men now in their fifties and early sixties, but they have since taken up other employment.

THE COLLECTIVES SINCE 1959

In the first growing season following the organizing the villagers continued to work their own lands; but after the harvest, the first collective sowing of winter wheat took place in the two new cooperatives. At the same time these enterprises acquired animals and implements from their members. Those whose implements were acquired were paid four-fifths of the assessed value of their property (the other fifth going to capital funds), which in turn was often lower than what they could have received on the free market had they been allowed to sell.

The Petőfi collective continued to use the barns on the tanya of two of Lapos's wealthiest nagygazda-s. The Kossuth quickly put in a request for the use of another nagygazda's large barns, which the May 1 collective had

17. Even collective farm members were allowed to keep up to one hold of land as a garden next to their houses. Because taxes on land increased sharply for land beyond one hold, those who did not join also found it convenient to keep just that much. Virtually all who worked this one hold did so only in conjunction with other employment, either on the collective farm or elsewhere. Houseplot enterprises were also, of course, subsidiary to collective farm work in Kislapos, although in some collective farms, particularly those near large cities, intensive houseplot production of vegetables and fruit for market assumed primary importance. Thus, "farming privately" here means as a nonmember of the collective, on one's own land as the major source of one's income.

used until its demise. The Gold Spike, on the other hand, lacking such large barns, was forced to embark on a crash construction program in its first year in order to achieve the efficiency of having the animals tended and milked together. That first year the animals of the Gold Spike were, thus, still kept in individual barns. Those of the Kossuth that did not fit into the central barns were kept in the larger barns of its former wealthier members.

The first year brought great group spirit on the part of many members of the three farms. Although there was uncertainty and skepticism about the future, and although some put in few hours that year, others were convinced that the farms were inevitable and that their future depended on their own efforts. A healthy competition soon sprung up between the two new farms; there was a race to see which would be the first to finish the spring plowing, sowing, harvesting, and other tasks. The Kossuth won almost all of these due to its greater resources and its united farming experience, but the competition and the relatively small size of the farms also succeeded in bringing a measure of group or "family" spirit to their members.

However, after only one year of independent operation the collectives were directed by district officials to merge for the sake of efficiency. In 1961, therefore, Kislapos had only one collective farm, with Miklós Magyar of the Kossuth as president and the presidents of the Petőfi and Gold Spike as vice-president and treasurer respectively. The collective remained on this scale until 1973, when a nationwide wave of farm mergers designed to achieve greater economies of scale hit Kislapos. A merger was pressed by the leadership upon the members, who did not want it but were resigned to what they considered inevitable. At that time Kislapos's collective united with the collectives of Kistó and Gödör; in the following year, these in turn were joined by the collectives of Barnaföld, Szikes, and the nearby settlement Sonka to form a cooperative of over ten thousand hectares. Lapos's president became leader of this much larger farm.

The newest mergers were not welcomed by Kislapos's inhabitants, for its collective farm had been quite successful alone. Before the first merger, over 5 million forint-s had gathered in its coffers, almost enough to pay the members their usual wages and pensions for a year even if nothing were produced. However, high government taxes on wage increases beyond a certain level made it prohibitive to distribute any of this to members. This amount compared favorably to the equal-sized Kistó surplus and the much smaller surplus in Gödör—and to the debts and shortages discovered in two of the other three collectives. For much of 1975, speculation centered on whether the new united collective would be fully able to meet its wage obligations at the end of the year (until 1976, the remaining 30 percent of the members' monthly pay was given in one lump sum when the books were closed at the end of the financial year) due to the poorer financial condition of some of the member farms.[18] There were additional capital expenditures involved in such projects as construction of the new central administrative building in Barnaföld— dubbed the White House by skeptical villagers who doubted the need for such an imposing new structure for their leaders.

Moreover, because Kislapos's wages had previously been higher than those of other farms, the first year or two saw little rise in local wage scales as the other members' earnings were brought into parity with Lapos's levels.

OTHER RECENT DEVELOPMENTS

In the years since 1959 there have been other developments in Kislapos: a decline in the population; development of the village and a rise in the standard of living; and secularization.

Population Decline

One of the most striking post-World War II trends in Kislapos has been the decline in population. From a high of 1,179 counted in the censuses of 1941 and 1949, the population fell to 1,145 in 1960, 950 in 1970, and about 890 in late 1975 (including about 90 Gypsies, who moved into the village in late 1974). The number of people living in the village declined by 17 percent from 1960 to 1970 and, not counting the arrival of the Gypsies, by another 16 percent in the next five years.

Several interdependent factors were involved in this rapid decline: the antipeasantry policies of the late 1950s and the collectivization of 1958– 1961, which caused many persons locally and hundreds of thousands nationally to leave agriculture and encourage their children to do so; the rapid industrialization that simultaneously attracted many to jobs in manufacturing, construction, and mining; the decline in the birthrate following the relaxation of restrictions on abortions after 1956[19] and the rapid outmigration of people of child-producing age; the increase in educational opportunities and desire for education (partly a result of the desire

18. Sárkány (1978: 106) reports exactly the same merger pattern in Varsány: pressure by leaders to merge, unwillingness of members to go along, followed by resignation and acceptance, then fear of the merger's effects on earnings because of amalgamation with a poorer farm.

19. Because of a decrease in the annual birthrate in the early 1950s in Hungary, strong measures were taken to reduce the number of abortions performed. Although the birthrate soon climbed to its highest level in twenty years, the measures were unpopular because of the depressed economic levels of the 1950s and the lack of economic and social-welfare policies designed to lighten the burden of raising children. Children born in these years were sometimes called "Ratkó

for a career outside agricultural labor), taking youth outside of Kislapos for schooling and introducing them to cultural, social, and recreational opportunities and a standard of living and employment opportunities unavailable in a small village like Lapos, which lacks many facilities and is poorly integrated into the nation's transportation network; and the collective farm's very success, enabling villagers to save money and facilitate their children's assimilation into urban life.

The decline in population, in turn, has led to changes almost guaranteed to produce further population decline. In 1969 the village lost its standing as an administrative entity with its own council president. Although it still has a village council, and a council secretary who handles many of the functions of the former president, this reduced status also means that the village will lose some of its functions to larger rural centers and that infrastructural investments will go to larger, more promising and better placed rural villages and towns.

Indeed, because of sharply lower enrollment in the village's eight-grade elementary school, declining from a high of 175 in 1962–63 to a low of 75 in 1971–72 (see Table 5.1), in 1974 the upper four grades were moved to the district seat in Boros. There the children live in dormitories, commuting home only on weekends—a state bemoaned by loving parents (who also acknowledge the higher quality of education there). Because of the same low birthrate, the nursery school, opened in the mid-1960s for the children of collective farm workers, was closed in 1972 because of low enrollment. Both these closings have caused the remaining young adults with children to reconsider staying in Lapos.

Although a small snack bar finally opened in 1977, the village lacks many social and cultural amenities that appeal to the young (for example, a jukebox, a real social center, a good store) and even their elders, and it is now even less likely to obtain them. The continuing lack of a village doctor and nurse, along with other factors, leads many of the elderly to have second thoughts as well.

One of the most outstanding results of this sharp decline in numbers has been the inflow of Gypsies. When high groundwater and potential flooding of the Farkas after heavy rains in the fall of 1974 threatened to

children," after an official closely associated with these measures. In June 1956 abortion restrictions were relaxed, and soon the incidence of induced abortion surpassed the birthrate. Since 1974, when concern about the low birthrate brought about newer social welfare measures, including economic incentives and somewhat more restrictive abortion requirements (though these were coupled with the greater availability of modern contraceptives), the birthrate has risen to past the replacement level, and the number of abortions has dropped sharply. See Szabady (1974) for a thorough but concise presentation of recent Hungarian fertility patterns and population policy.

Parents leading their school-age children to the bus stop on a Monday morning. The children attend the regional school in Boros, where they live in dormitories, and come home on weekends.

undermine the buildings and shanties in the low-lying Gypsy quarter of neighboring Gödör, local authorities seized upon the opportunity to do away with the squalor of that ghetto and to reduce its own "Gypsy problem" by having the settlement bulldozed flat, citing the present conditions as unsafe and unsanitary (which they may well have been). Kislapos, possessing empty houses left by outmigrating families and the elderly dying out, was earmarked by the district to receive about a dozen of the displaced households since demand for the houses was low and so were their prices.

This caused a great stir in Kislapos, for Gypsies were hardly a welcome sight there. Looked upon as lazy, conniving, and promiscuous, Gypsies in the village and in the country as a whole met with considerable discrimination. None had been allowed to settle into the village before the war, and many villagers still speak with pride of the old days, when "there were no Gypsies, beggars or Jews." Of the five Gypsy households established in Lapos between the war and these more recent developments, none had evoked full approval from the villagers for their life styles, although one or two had been viewed as relatively hardworking and honest; so the villagers were skeptical and unhappy about the new arrivals.

A significant result of the rapid population decline is the feeling of many inhabitants that the village may die out or become primarily a Gypsy community. In fifteen or twenty years, they argue, the elderly will have died and the young will have continued to migrate, leaving only those people now in their thirties to fifties. Others who continue to stay will be primarily those who lack the education and skills needed to obtain jobs elsewhere.

These views mesh well with what Szelényi (1977: 126–127) has characterized as the "partial societies" and "village slums" resulting from the centralized, rationally based regional management planning in Hungary and Eastern Europe as a whole. This planning tries to make optimal use of scarce investment resources for infrastructural development, encouraging a concentration of such investment in larger cities and county, district, and regional centers at the expense of smaller villages deemed by planners as least suited for development. An unintended result is a growing difference between rural and urban areas, a difference characterized by class and status distinctions and less so by the agricultural-industrial dimension. Although the declining villages remain more agricultural in character than other settlements, they are increasingly the home of working class families. While the old and the poor may be unable or unwilling to leave, these primarily unskilled workers, often with large families, either remain in the village because they cannot compete for housing in developing areas or move there in search of housing they can afford. Gypsies and other lumpen proletariat join them in a similar search. On the other hand, as these villages lose institutions and functions, their more professional inhabitants, like doctors, teachers, and local government and collective farm officials, who could best represent and articulate the interests of the villagers, move to larger centers to which their workplaces have been relocated and where people of similar interests and status live. Szelényi argues that this leads to local "part societies," in contrast to the formerly "total societies" of even the smallest communities.

These trends and recent developments in Lapos suggest that such a course is a strong possibility for the future.

Village Development and a Higher Standard of Living

Collectivization, of course, was not meant to be solely a way of eliminating capitalism and exploitation. One of its major aims, along with socialism as a whole, was to raise the standard of living of the poor and

Table 5.1 School Registration, Kislapos

Grade	1942-43	1943-44	1944-45	1945-46	1946-47	1947-48	1948-49	1949-50	1950-51	1951-52	1952-53	1953-54
1	25	35	33	43	39	23	24	17	—	—	22	19
2	25	22	25	27	25	26	26	23	—	—	15	20
3	19	23	21	22	23	27	28	31	—	—	16	17
4	25	25	20	23	20	25	26	21	—	—	19	20
5	19	26	21	24	34	22	25	31	—	—	15	20
6	16	11	22	9	1	20	23	18	—	—	26	15
7	19	12	9	8	1	4	16	16	—	—	21	24
8	7	12	6	2	1	0	0	12	—	—	12	19
Total	155	166	157	158	144	147	168	169			146	154

Grade	1954-55	1955-56	1956-57	1957-58	1958-59	1959-60	1960-61	1961-62	1962-63	1963-64	1964-65	1965-66
1	28	25	31	26	23	26	29	26	27	13	6	10
2	16	22	20	28	25	21	23	25	24	25	13	7
3	19	17	20	17	27	23	23	22	24	22	23	11
4	16	15	19	24	18	27	24	23	22	25	23	21
5	19	17	16	12	20	15	23	21	21	19	24	22
6	18	18	20	14	11	19	15	23	21	20	21	23
7	15	11	11	17	15	11	18	14	22	19	19	19
8	14	8	10	7	12	11	9	19	14	21	19	17
Total	146	133	147	145	151	153	164	173	175	164	148	130

Grade	1966-67	1967-68	1968-69	1969-70	1970-71	1971-72	1972-73	1973-74	1974-75	1975-76
1	16	14	11	10	13	10	4	11	5	13
2	8	15	11	10	11	13	14	7	12	6
3	7	7	12	10	10	10	14	13	12	14
4	11	10	8	13	10	8	8	12	11	12
5	22	8	8	7	12	10	8	7		
6	22	23	6	8	6	12	11	7		
7	22	22	22	6	8	4	13	11		
8	20	21	22	22	6	8	4	12		
Total	128	120	100	86	76	75	76	80	40	45

NOTE: For the years 1942–1950 figures were taken from the *felvételi napló*. For later years they are from the *anyakönyv*. The diagonals separate the following four groups: prewar babies, war babies, postwar babies, and post-1956 babies. The figures reflect the lower birthrates of the war years and of the years after 1956. Low figures for the upper grades, 1943–1949, are partly explicable by the need for workers due to the absence or death of adult males. Higher figures for 1975–76 include Gypsy children who moved into the village in 1974–75.

ultimately, through greater efficiency and economies of scale, to improve the living conditions of all, presumably at a faster rate than with the continuation of private enterprise. Indeed, the standard of living has risen substantially in the countryside, although it did not move very quickly in the first years of collectivization. Much of the 1960s saw a continued stagnation in Hungarian agricultural production. Investment was still relatively light, much of the machinery required to achieve greater efficiency and economies of scale was still lacking, and the initial conversion of many small farms into one large one with its attendant needs for investment (for example, the building of large barns and storage and maintenance buildings) and organizational problems burdened the new enterprises. In the late 1960s and the 1970s, after the introduction of the New Economic Mechanism in 1968 (which gave profit and incentives a higher priority in production and encouraged local initiative) and after investment in the agricultural sector had risen, agricultural production and collective farm members' earnings rose steadily, as did the standard of living of the farm members—at a pace faster than in the nation as a whole.

In the past decade numerous appliances have become common even in village homes: small refrigerators, washing machines, bottled-gas stoves, and the now ubiquitous television, which in the brief span of ten years went from being a rarity to a fixture in nearly nine-tenths of Lapos's households and considerably altered the patterns of evening visiting. Portable milling and milking machines have been bought by many villagers to ease their houseplot work, even though they only have two or three cows and could take their grain to the nearby mill of the collective farm. About forty-five private cars are registered in the village, roughly comparable to the national per capita figures, and both numbers are rising rapidly.

Of course, not all improvements are exclusive to the past decade. A great deal of house-building, renovating, and adding on occurred after World War II and especially from the late 1950s on. The brief prosperity of those years and the increased cash earnings from collective farm work and the private plot, no longer reinvested in family enterprises, put large amounts of money into savings, home improvement, and personal consumption. In the past three or four years, now that a number of expensive larger, more modern homes have been built by younger couples occupying managerial or administrative posts in the village (undoubtedly with help from their successful parents), construction of new homes has come to a halt. Villagers have come to question not only Lapos's viability and the likelihood of their remaining there but also, should they leave, the possibility of obtaining a reasonable price for their homes. In the meantime, by 1970 10–12 percent of the houses had acquired flush toilets and a much larger percentage had water piped into them. With a half-dozen exceptions, all the older houses that originally had thatched roofs now have tile.

*One of the larger, newer houses built in Lapos in the early
1970s (at the left). Though square and "tent-roofed," its
large foundation and basement, size, and fancy fence point
up the cost paid by the agronomist husband, chief-
bookkeeper wife, and well-to-do parents.*

The young who have remained in the village have acquired modern furniture, put in parquet flooring, and generally sought greater comfort within the home.

Through the village council, more general improvements have followed. Water lines have been extended throughout the village, and water is now pumped from a central well several hundred meters deep instead of from the frequently contaminated household wells. Electricity has been extended to all the houses in the village, unlike the prefront years when only the wealthy could afford it. Several of the village's streets have been paved, as have the roads leading to collective farm buildings on the former Gold Spike and Petőfi holdings. Sidewalks have been laid next to all the village streets so villagers can avoid the sea of mud so common on some streets in the winter.

In addition, the school was rebuilt in the 1950s and expanded in the 1960s, if only to be partially closed several years later. Bus routes, though still infrequent, were introduced in the 1950s and 1960s and brought a great improvement over walking along the Farkas River to Pont.

People's lives have improved not only in these obvious physical ways. Besides being better housed and better clothed, they also enjoy a better diet. So far this has been manifested primarily in a greater calorie intake and a not altogether healthy rise in the amounts of fat and starches consumed. However, fruits and vegetables are being eaten in greater amounts, and villagers are buying more expensive citrus fruits in the winter for their children and grandchildren.

In the last few years, "free" medical care (paid for by a small progressive tax on earnings and by state subsidies) has been made available to all Hungarian citizens, and medicine is sold at low prices.

One of the major advantages of the collective farms cited by many members is the farm's participation since 1967 in the national pension plan. Pensions are based on the number of years of employment and the average of the three highest years of income in the final five years of employment. Members who have worked a minimum of ten years are eligible for a pension of 33 percent of this average with corresponding increases up to a maximum of 75 percent for longer employment. Those who retired before 1967 also receive a small allowance. Moreover, from January 1976 until 1980 the retirement ages are being reduced annually by one year from sixty-five to sixty for men and from sixty to fifty-five for women. Changes in the rules for membership eligibility in the late 1960s saw many more women join as full members so that they too could acquire a pension.

In the early years of the collective farm, most elderly members did not qualify for pensions because they had not been employed for ten years. Retiring members received minimal benefits. Many peasants in their fifties and sixties went to work elsewhere to achieve the minimum ten years. Now, however, those who receive a pension from the collective regard it as of major importance. They remark that their land would have been little good to them anyway since their children would not have stayed to work it (forgetting that one reason many children left is the impossibility of maintaining private agriculture under the state's policies). Now they have an assured income.[20]

Finally, one of the most important dimensions of the postwar years has been the vast improvement of the educational system throughout the

20. In general, the pensions and allowances received now by those who retired in the early years are small. Incomes on which they were initially fixed were low, and most peasants had few years of employment. Although such allowances and pensions have been raised almost annually to keep pace with the cost of living, the aged both in the countryside and in the city constitute the largest segment of Hungary's poor. In 1979 the government introduced more drastic pension increases for the smallest pensions to help correct this situation.

country. In Lapos this means that most village youth now complete some sort of secondary schooling, whether academic or vocational, and many go on to the university. In prefront years a sizable number did not complete even the sixth grade; going beyond the eighth was a rarity.

Some of this improvement results from parents' increased desire for their children to enjoy a life free of agricultural labor—a wish stemming from its traditionally low status, as well as from the tribulations of the 1950s and the loss of independence under collectivization. But the state has made substantial efforts to open educational opportunity to the poor. Great value has been placed on education, both for the purpose of providing the trained population needed for industrial and agricultural development and to produce a more forward-looking, ideologically and technically trained youth. All this is not meant, however, to underestimate the considerable emphasis placed on cultural appreciation, on trying to raise standards of literacy and artistic performance and discrimination. For example, the publication of many books receives a state subsidy, and it is not unusual to see a considerable number of books on the shelves of younger villagers and even on the shelves of their parents (though many belonging to the latter may be of the almanac variety or the works of popular authors). Many watch the literary and cultural shows on television (though they find them less appealing than crime shows) and borrow from the village's small library in the council building.

This brief discussion of material and cultural progress would not be complete without mentioning a negative aspect that affects Hungarians both locally and nationally. Because of the lack of attention paid to consumer goods and services, especially during the early 1950s, because of the mistakes made in centralized economic planning, and because of the "growth pains" associated with rapid economic development, there has been considerable scarcity in many goods and services. This has encouraged the practice of tipping. In some areas giving a tip (*borravaló*) resembles practices familiar to Americans. One tips waiters, barbers, and beauticians. It is not uncommon to give postal letter carriers a few forint-s for bringing monthly pension payments (as many tip in the United States for safe delivery of their social security checks) or to give them a small gift at the end of the year.

Tips are also given when services are free or already paid for. Many repairmen are given tips equivalent to or even greater than the cost of the service they have performed, as are doctors and nurses. Patients try to ensure the "best" of care from doctors and nurses. Such tips given for home visits or to nurses and doctors for hospital care usually amount to a half or a full day's wages for an average worker and in more extreme cases to several times as much. In general, tips are given to ensure better service now or prompt and quality service in the future in areas where a shortage is assumed. For certain scarce products (for example, salami or good quality imported furniture) it is not unusual for a store customer to offer a tip so that he will be notified upon the arrival of such goods or so they will be put away for him.

This is so common in many service areas that even gas station attendants are given a tip of 1 or 2 percent for dispensing gas despite the fact that they perform no other services on the car. Most Hungarians themselves cannot explain this, but it is widely accepted that gas station attendants have very high incomes due to this practice and receive their positions due to patronage.

Tips often substitute for a personal relationship. Indeed, when giving a tip would be crass or considered bribery, as in relationships with bureaucrats, it is not uncommon to offer gifts of flowers, brandy, or chocolates on occasion—or to use friendships and personal connections—to smooth such a relationship so as to obtain favors, or even proper service, more easily.

There are differences in the ways in which tips are to be offered. Most frequently, additional money is simply offered verbally or pressed in cash upon the recipient. With doctors, however, tips are usually given in envelopes without comment, so as not to call attention to them, so as not to demean the relationship. The local doctor attending Lapos, an avid collector of folk art and old peasant objects, often feels free to ask for such materials that he sees around the houses instead of accepting tips.

Where friendships and personal connections are used to acquire scarce goods, services, favors, and positions or, for example, to attain a place in the university's entering class for one's child, the notion of tipping finds its counterpart in *protekció*: patronage or personal influence. Protekció (and variations of the term) is, and was even before the war, common in all of Eastern Europe. As Neuberg (1973: 156) points out, even now "the overwhelming majority of those young East Europeans who resented *proteksio* resented the fact that in some particular case they had been unable to secure enough of it." Protekció is an important factor in the distribution of benefits among Kislapos's collective farm members.

Secularization

The Church has lost much of its hold on the population but continues to be important in some areas of their lives. This loss of strength is most obvious in sharply reduced church attendance. A typical Sunday mass draws only forty or fifty, half to two-thirds of whom are elderly women dressed in their Sunday dark blue or black. The rest consist of several younger women, a handful of old men, and about a dozen children. The latter attend catechism afterward, and some serve as altar boys. On Church holidays, however, like Christmas, Easter, Ascension Day, and the day of Saint Stephen, the local patron saint, the church is packed, and many are forced to stand in the aisles and in the entrance.

Ironically, it has been during the 1960s and 1970s, when government and party policies directed against the Church were relaxed, that the most sizable erosion in beliefs and particularly church attendance has occurred. While the Church lost much of its power in the years immediately following the war, it maintained a considerable allegiance among the villagers. Attendance continued high, and non-Church weddings and unbaptized infants were a rarity. The Church remained a symbol of resistance against a communism that was unpopular with large segments of the population. This and the solace value of the Church was demonstrated in the 1956 uprising when, for example, prayers and crucifixes were reintroduced into the school. On November 4, the day the Russians intervened to crush the uprising, at the request of the villagers the school director's wife led the children into the church and the director played the organ. As one woman then in her thirties remembers it, "They sang 'I enter the Holy Temple.' Everyone was crying and it was very beautiful."

Since then far fewer attend. Villagers offer several explanations for their own and others' nonattendance. Some attribute it to the collective farm. They say that collective farm work, by occupying most of their working time, especially during the growing and harvesting seasons, leaves only the weekends for work on the all-important income-producing houseplots. Moreover, at the height of the season many work for the collective even on Sundays. Because of their irregular work, women are especially anxious to put in more hours to reach the minimum number of work hours needed to qualify for a houseplot. Associated with this is the view held by many that, due to the effects of the collective farm and its workings, the villagers are now more materialistically oriented, that the urge to get ahead and buy more is stronger, that people are "more envious" of one another. The Sunday work, however, is not as preponderant as some would have it. Nor does it explain the equally low attendance in winter—although the unheated church interior may.

The forty-five-year-old wife of a brigade leader says that she too went to mass in the past. Her father was the church treasurer, a position later assumed by her older half-brother. She attended with her mother, who lived next door; all the women from her neighborhood used to walk together. But now, ever since her mother died, "out of neglect" she no longer goes, although she does teach her grandson how to pray and to make the sign of the cross and expects to send him to catechism when he is old enough.

The comments of sixty-seven-year-old János Kis offer the same sort of nonexplanatory explanation. He points to the influence of the collective farm but also cites the fact that church attendance is no longer required (for example, for young men and girls). Unlike the past, when it was occasionally difficult to find employment if a man was not baptized or confirmed, Church affiliation now does little material good for anyone and, in fact, is negatively viewed by some authorities. Thus, he says, people view attendance as "superfluous," although at the appearance of great problems or crises "they invoke everything, even God."

Some complain that the local priest is too strict with the children and compare him unfavorably to past priests, who would go to the wedding receptions and sing and drink along with everyone else. Other informants cite him as not being punctual, as not being soldierly enough.

An excuse given less often but clearly a factor for many is the tendency of out-of-town siblings and children to visit on the weekend. Because most depend on public transportation, which limits arrival and departure possibilities, many families try to maximize the amount of time spent together and skip mass. The last outbound bus on Sundays leaves shortly after noon, pushing the large Sunday dinner into the late morning hours, the time of the mass. A similar attitude is reflected in the remark of one father, angry at the priest for refusing to confirm his daughter because of infrequent attendance at catechism: "Now, she comes home [from school in Boros] on Saturday [afternoon]. And that should be paramount that she go to mass or go to catechism?"

The same individual's further remarks are instructive about the degree to which villagers cling to Church rites. Although he claims he is not a "believer," he ultimately took his daughter to a priest in a nearby town to be confirmed. When asked why, he explained that it was traditional in Lapos and that people talked if the child was not baptized or confirmed or if there were no Church marriage. He did not want this for his daughters.

Thus, although civil name-giving ceremonies have been introduced to take the place of baptisms, and non-Church weddings have also occurred in Lapos, they are still not very popular. No civil funeral has ever been held in Lapos, although efforts are being made to "popularize" them. As János Kis says,

The parents raise the child to be religious. Later he considers it superfluous but still clings to it. Even the greatest Communist when he dies, or before death, calls for the priest to give last rites. Or for the burial there isn't one whose family doesn't call the priest and the cantor or doesn't have the ceremony. They don't just leave the deceased to be put in the ground without any rites.

Not only do many villagers keep up these rites, but they still do so often in the face of some official resistance. Local party members are strongly discouraged from having their children baptized or confirmed, fearing party sanctions if they do. For example, one new member in Lapos was

*On All Souls' Day, mourning relatives wait for the priest to
come and bless the bedecked graves of their recently
deceased family members.*

asked not to have his daughter take first communion the following year. It
is still not unusual for party members to take their children to more
distant larger towns for such rites in order to preserve their own ano-
nymity. Grandparents still have their grandchildren baptized without
their party member children's knowledge in order to thwart the resistance to such rites inspired by conviction or anxiety. This anxiety extends even to more mundane spheres, as when a young couple from
Lapos moved to a flat in a nearby city. When a priest kinsman came to bless
the new home, the husband, a party member, quickly shut the curtains.

This kind of discouragement is not limited solely to the party. It continues in schools, though in a more discreet manner than before. Teachers are chided by administrators for having so many students taking
catechism and are asked to explain this. They are expected to discourage
their students from attending.

However, even the authorities are often diplomatic in these matters.
For example, when there is a civil name-giving ceremony there is not
supposed to be a baptism; frequently officials simply do not ask if there
has already been a baptism.

In general, several elements stand out. First, the old cling much more strongly to the Church than the young. Their rate of church attendance and participation is much higher and they are often important activists in the baptism and ritual participation of their grandchildren. This is not uncommon wherever secularization has occurred, nor should it be surprising, considering the active role that the government and party have taken in trying to lead youth to a nonreligious, materialist world view.

Second, despite decreased interest and belief, participation in important religious rituals and festivals remains high. Few are willing to forsake all ties with the Church, whether due to social values placed on Church traditions or to doubts about ultimate questions of life and death.

Third, the collective farm may have usurped one of the functions of the Sunday mass. Jávor (1978: 336) suggests that, in Varsány, most individuals do not completely remove themselves from the practice of religion because that would mean to some degree excluding themselves from the community. There "the mass has remained the sole regular gathering occasion for different ages, sexes, and occupational groups." In Lapos the collective farm seems to have taken over this role, a function that may be somewhat reduced by today's increased "familism." This gathering in the collective may have been especially strong in its earlier years, when there was less specialization of labor. A far higher percentage of the village population is employed in Lapos's agricultural cooperative than in Varsány's, which may account for some of the difference. Clearly, the Church still assumes some of this function at funerals and church holidays, when attendance rises dramatically.

Last, a growing satisfaction with the fruits of communism and the compromises reached between Church and state in Hungary[21] have reduced the potency of the Church as a symbol and rallying point of the community in the face of "godless" and repressive communism. Whereas in the past many of its members resisted participating in the system, today most are endeavoring to obtain as many benefits as possible from it.

21. The state provides a portion of the clergy's salaries as well as part of Church operating funds and permits the publication of Church materials, textbooks, and Bibles in small numbers. It maintains a department in the Ministry of Culture to handle religious affairs and no longer actively works against the Church, although it does not at all encourage religious activity and faith. In return for this modicum of religious freedom the Church does not actively oppose state policies. In short, there is some greater effort at mutual accommodation.

Chapter 6

The Collective Farm

Relations within the collective farm are basic to the organization of power and status within the Hungarian village. In Lapos, as elsewhere, the collective provides a framework within which family and kinship continue to flourish as central organizing principles in village social and economic spheres. It is therefore important to understand the workings of this economic and social unit: the organization and fundamental principles of the farm, the comparative desirability of positions within it, its relationship with the community and with village organizations, and the more recent organizational changes within it, especially its growing rationalization.

BASIC PRINCIPLES

A collective farm is a large agricultural enterprise, owned, worked, and managed by its members. The capital of the farm—its land, machines, implements, buildings, animals and produce, fertilizer, and assorted materials—is owned collectively by its members. Their individual incomes derive from the following: 1) the amount and type of work they have performed for the farm, payment for which is based on the fiscal performance of the collective as a whole; 2) the small household plots granted them by the farm for private cultivation; and 3) small annual payments proportionate to the amount of land they contributed to the farm at joining. The collective is required to employ its members. The leaders of the collective are elected by its members, who at periodic meetings have final say in decisions of policy and administration.

Before considering the conditions of ownership, work and income, and management in detail, a comparison of the collective farm as treated here to the state farm and to "lower levels" of agricultural cooperative enterprises is in order, to clarify the larger Hungarian picture. Later, in discussing the actual workings of the farm, it will be seen that some of the distinctions are or have at times been more formal than real.

Collective farms are not state farms. State farms are owned by the state.

Their workers are employees of the farms and, like factory workers, are paid fixed wages determined in advance, independent of the performance of the farm that year. Usually the workers do not receive houseplots. As employees, not members, they have no more say in the operation of the farm or in the choice of its leaders than do employees of an industrial enterprise, for example, an American factory. Thus, collective farm members have a more direct interest in their enterprise's production growth than do their counterparts in the state sector. The Hungarian forms of the collective farm (*termelőszövetkezet*) and the state farm (*állami gazdaság*) are based largely on the Soviet *kolkhoz* and *sovkhoz,* respectively; the differences between them are basically the same as between their Soviet models.

The organizational form of Kislapos's collective farm is not the only form. There are less "advanced" forms—in the degree to which they exhibit collective work and collective ownership of land and implements. As Donáth (1977: 125–126) points out, since even the most advanced form with its multitude of individual houseplot enterprises is a compromise between collective and private enterprise, it should not be surprising that other forms of this compromise exist. They were devised with the hope of luring many into the collective sphere who would otherwise have been reluctant to part so suddenly and so totally from their traditional private agriculture.

In one simpler form, the members would keep their lands, animals, and implements under private ownership while combining their plowland into larger blocks to realize the advantages of mechanized cultivation of grains. The farming operations on this land were carried out by the owners working in concert according to a common plan. The allotment of grain at the end of the harvest was based on the amount of land included in the common plan and on the share of the common work done. These cooperatives never reached a large number. As time passed they were viewed by the government largely as ways of avoiding both collectivization and the measures of the 1950s dealing with individual enterprises; thus pressure was exerted to convert to a "higher level."

More common and longer lasting, though insignificant in terms of land involved compared to the above collective farms, were the producers' cooperatives (*szakszövetkezet*), dealing in more specialized labor-intensive crops like grapes, other fruits, and vegetables. An example was Kislapos's vegetable producers' cooperative. In these cooperatives, private land remained in individuals' hands, and cultivation was carried on in the traditional family units, not collectively. However, the members were obliged to contribute a portion of their incomes to maintain a fund for the acquisition of common capital goods like tools and machinery, fertilizer, and even land and plants. In this way, the collective sphere was to assume an ever greater importance in the cooperative.

These cooperatives are still common in the south-central portion of the country, where the prevalence of scattered farms makes it difficult to consolidate privately owned land into larger blocks. In general, less pressure was exerted on these farms to convert into more advanced forms because of the highly labor-intensive nature of the crops. Consolidation in many cases would have required clearing and replanting thousands of acres of orchards and vineyards, while further collectivization might have left the crops without an adequate work force. Not wishing to risk a large drop in production (and having learned from previous efforts), the government left the cooperatives alone.

Ownership

The collective farm's property—its land, buildings, machines and implements, materials, seed and fertilizer, animals, and produce—are owned collectively by the members of the farm, as are shops and other enterprises it may operate. Individual members are part owners of the land they gave to the collective farm at joining, but they are not allowed to withdraw their land if they quit. As part owners they are entitled to an annual payment for the use of their land by the collective. In recent years this payment has declined in importance, and for the average family it constitutes less than 5 percent of the income derived from farm wages. Because the land is often in the name of the elderly, whose pensions are low due to their short-term employment in the cooperative from 1959 until retirement, this land "rental" assumes greater significance for some.

When a member dies, his shares are inherited much like other property. However, only cooperative members are eligible to inherit such land shares and to receive this payment. If there is no such family member to inherit, the shares revert to full cooperative ownership.

This has not always been the case. Until 1967 nonmembers giving up their land to the collective were also eligible for such payments. In that year, new regulations were instituted nationally requiring the owners either to sell their land to the collective or to become members within a year. The vast majority sold their land.

Work and Income

Collective farm members receive two primary forms of income based on their labor for the farm: wages and the use of a plot of land (háztáji—houseplot) for private cultivation.

Wages are based on the amount and type of work performed by the member. In Kislapos and in most collective farms through the early 1970s, such wages were calculated on the basis of work units. Each labor operation (for example, plowing a hold of land with a tractor or milking twenty-five cows) was convertible into fixed numbers of work units, the value of which was not established until the end of the year, when the farm books were closed and the financial surplus ascertained. Thus, wages were (and still are) based not only on the quantity, sometimes quality, and type of work done, but also on the performance of the collective as a whole.[1] Many members, of course depended on some form of payment before the final reckoning to help them through the year. These payments were subtracted from the value assigned their amassed work units.

In the early collective farms of the 1950s and throughout the early 1960s, a sizable portion of these wages was paid in kind, not in cash. This was only a minor problem, as members would either market the goods themselves or use them for their household needs or, more likely, for feeding their animals, whose milk, eggs, and meat they would consume or sell.

In most collective farms, including Kislapos's, the system of work units was eventually replaced by one of cash wages, in which specific types and amounts of work were accorded a cash equivalent. Theoretically, this, too, was not totally fixed but at the end of the year was subject to modification depending on the farm's fiscal performance. In the early 1970s in Kislapos, 70 percent of the monthly earnings (other farms had varying though similar percentages) were distributed to members at the end of each month, constituting a guaranteed cash income; the remaining 30 percent was passed out at the year's end, subject again to adjustments of several percent. Finally, in 1976, after a year of operation of the merged local collective farm—a year in which there was considerable doubt by Kislapos's members and some doubt even on the part of leaders (despite their voiced optimism) about the ability of the collective to meet its 30 percent obligation (it did), a decision was made to increase the monthly payments to 100 percent of the established wage guidelines.

Beyond these earnings, members of the collective deemed praiseworthy by a farm committee have received bonus payments at the year's end sometimes amounting to 5 or 10 percent of their annual wages. In the case

---

1. Members of poorly performing farms, particularly in regions less suited for agriculture, continue to receive lower wages than their counterparts in more successful farms despite state subsidies partially designed to alleviate this discrepancy. One factor that exacerbates the situation and promises to make total equalization unlikely for the foreseeable future is the fact that investment in more productive enterprises has been shown to increase total national output more than investment in more poorly performing farms. Faced with limited investment capital, planners have chosen to concentrate investment in these more successful farms while keeping income differences relatively small through subsidies (Donáth 1977: 261–269).

of higher leadership, these bonuses have reached much higher levels,[2] as high, for example, as 70 percent for the collective's president in 1974.

The other major source of income for members is the háztáji. All members working over a set minimum of hours during the previous year are eligible to receive a plot of land from the collective, ranging from a half to a full hold, that can be used for private cultivation. The precise amount of land assigned a member depends on the number of hours worked. Women are eligible for half a hold if they worked the equivalent of 120 or more 10-hour days and a full hold after slightly over 2,000 hours; men are required to work about 1,600 and 2,500 hours for these respective amounts. Requirements for women are lower partly because they are less likely to be assigned regular year-round work and thus find it more difficult to accumulate hours. Formally retired members, even if they do not work for the farm any more (many work part-time to supplement their incomes) receive half a hold each.

Many members have retained garden plots next to their houses. Because the háztáji-s are assigned in the early spring of each year by lottery or other arbitrary method, and invariably in a different place from the last year, the quality of the plot usually varies from year to year, and there is little reason for members to try to improve the quality of its soil. Members, thus, prefer to work as large a home garden as possible because they can count on the constant quality of their own land, can benefit from efforts to fertilize and otherwise improve it, and, of course, find its closeness more convenient. These gardens also allow members to keep fruit and walnut trees, as well as grapevines (mainly for domestic wine consumption). In figuring the size of houseplots, the acreage of any such gardens or privately owned plots is subtracted from the amounts earned through previous work hours.

For most members the háztáji-s are in two or even three separate parts: corn land, potato land, and sometimes turnip land. Most of the harvest of the first two and all of the third are fed to the poultry, cattle, and pigs kept by most members for personal consumption and for their sale of the eggs, milk, and meat. Most income from the houseplots is derived from the sale of these animal products. The collective distributes these plots in different blocks of land; because, for example, the collective farm plows, fertilizes, harrows, and sows the corn land, this task is eased if all the corn land

---

2. Since 1968 the New Economic Mechanism has placed greater emphasis on the importance of cash incentives in increasing production in agricultural, industrial, service, and transport enterprises alike. Because of the greater responsibility of higher management in improving an enterprise's performance, a greater range of incentives has been introduced for them. Higher bonuses can be awarded them than to workers in the case of particularly good results, whereas in a bad year a high managerial official can take a cut in pay.

is together and separate from the potato land. Potatoes and turnips are sown by individual members, as are home garden plots. Arrangements can also be made for the collective to plow or harrow larger garden plots with a tractor or, as is usually necessary, with horses. A fee is charged, just as it is for the preparation and sowing of allotted plots.

In 1975, members were given the option of taking a houseplot in kind or cash. Instead of land, they could choose the collective's average barley or corn production for the acreage involved or a cash payment proportionate to the size of their plot. Within two years these options became immensely popular; in 1976, of the 350 hold-s to be distributed to Lapos's members as houseplots, over 50 percent was taken in cash and another 15 percent in kind. The first year a payment of 4,800 forint-s was offered per hold for the cash option and the second year 5,600. Besides this, the recipient was spared the 1,000 forint-s per hold to be paid the collective farm for plowing, harrowing, and seeding, potential additional costs for machine cultivation, a small tax levied on such land, and considerable labor. Instead of 5,600 forint-s, the total monetary benefits involved were about 7,000 forint-s per hold, equal to two months' wages for a collective farm worker paid better than average.[3]

Although their importance in Hungarian agriculture continues to decline, collective farm houseplot enterprises in 1975 still produced nearly 40 percent of the total net production (figured at contemporary prices) of the collective farms (Fazekas 1976: 310) and provided nearly one-half an average member's income in the early 1970s (Donáth 1977: 120). This highly labor-intensive production pays poorly in terms of work input but provides an important source of work and income for retired and irregularly employed members of the farms. Because of this and the houseplots' importance in the total production, their significance promises to be great for years to come.[4]

3. Recently, however, new regulations were introduced nationally. It was felt in higher ideological circles that this payment was essentially income attained without working and thus contrary to the principle of payment for work done. To discourage this tendency, a ceiling was set of 4,800 forint-s per hold, less than the amounts already being offered in Lapos and elsewhere.

4. The importance of household production in general in Hungary becomes even clearer when one realizes that four-fifths of *all* Hungarian villagers live in households that cultivate at least one-quarter hold (0.36 acre or 0.14 hectare) of plowland (or one-eighth hold of vineyards, orchards, or gardens) or that hold at least one large animal or fifty chickens (Andorka 1979: 101–102). Several hundred thousand of these households include *no* collective farm members.

Although some parts of the household plots' production are not particularly capital-intensive, the state and cooperative sectors still do not have the financial resources to take over quickly the production of certain crops and animal products on a large scale. The steadily decreasing agricultural work force already requires high capital expenditures to increase worker productivity. Taking over the pro-

Thus far the terms of income for collective farm members have been discussed. But nonmembers working for the collectives have taken on increased importance. Permanent nonmember employees constituted nearly 20 percent of the collectives' active workers nationally in 1974 (Fazekas 1976: 307).

In the early years following 1959, nonmembers also played an important role, but the character of this role has radically changed. In the early years usually only the head of the household joined. It was expected that household units would continue to function integrally in the production of the collective farms. For several years they did. Plots of labor-intensive crops were allotted to members to hoe, thin out, and harvest. Wives and other family members joined in the work, and their labor was figured into the work units assigned to the family heads. After several years, however, women in particular were encouraged to join. Many were glad to do so since they would thus be entitled to retirement benefits, additional houseplots, and opportunities for greater earnings. Indeed, at joining they were given the chance to pay several years of retroactive pension fund payments so that their earlier work would be counted toward their ultimate pension benefits.

Today, however, most such permanent nonmember employees are not family members doing unskilled labor to supplement family income, but skilled or technically trained workers who draw wages and benefits higher than most members. Such wages and benefits have been necessary since the late 1960s to attract trained personnel to collective farm administrative posts and to the operation, maintenance, and repair of increasingly complex farm machinery. Many such personnel, either accustomed to or desirous of the shorter hours and better working conditions of industry, have been reluctant to subject themselves to some of the membership requirements. In addition, the establishment of profitable subsidiary enterprises (canning plants, butchering operations, furniture assembly, various kinds of manufacturing), sometimes totally unrelated to agriculture but providing year-round work for otherwise irregularly employed members and filling holes in the nation's service and manufacturing network, has also provided more jobs for nonmember employees.

---

duction of cattle, pigs, poultry, and dairy products now would require greater expenditures for an already strapped capital budget. Thus, a significant economic role for household plots is forecast for the next twenty-five years. Presently the government is offering price incentives to maintain household plot production and to keep families, especially the young, from giving up the plots. Similar policies have been adopted in other East European nations (e.g., Romania) as the government and party have come to realize the continuing importance of household production (Kideckel 1976: 273).

In Lapos, maintenance and repair jobs were occupied by members and subsidiary enterprises were nonexistent (with the exception of gravel mining operations, which employed very few workers) until 1974, when mergers opened up such positions in other communities to Lapos's inhabitants. Until then permanent nonmember employees were few and largely restricted to individuals whom the collective would not accept into full membership, for example, the Gypsy swineherd, who for years was an employee despite his repeated applications for membership, and who was finally accepted as a member only in 1975.

Such nonmembers now receive houseplots with a maximum size of one-half hold. Although now all members and employees receive 100 percent of their wages at each payday, in the past only nonmember employees were so entitled.

One other category of worker is the melon-grower. Heves County is well known in Hungary for its melon-growing. Traditionally, two small villages to the west of Kislapos, Hort and Csány, have been especially renowned. Because the crop requires considerable soil preparation in the early spring and constant care and vigilance throughout much of the growing cycle and harvest, it has been the practice of melon-growers to live for six months of the year in small earthen huts next to their fields. Inhabitants of the two villages have fanned out year after year to different sections of the country to take up such positions on others' fields.

Kislapos, too, has recently set aside fields for melon-growing, which can be very profitable. But with no recent history of growing melons, it lacks the personnel willing and able to take on such work. Because of the specialized knowledge, the long hours of work, the discomforts of the life in the fields, and the risks of melon-growing (for example, hail, drought, and heavy rains, which can put to naught extremely high expenditures), such personnel have been able to extract favorable contracts from the local collective farm. In good years a melon-grower's family is able to net 300,000–400,000 forint-s, several times the gross income of most families with several active earners.

Presently there are five such families in Kislapos from Hort; their heads have been formally accepted as collective farm members, although they reside outside the village for half the year. Each family is assigned 15–25 hold-s. Although they do not handle the plowing and initial preparation of the fields, they are responsible for the complete tending and harvesting of the crop. Since these crops also require intensive labor, they must hire and pay day laborers—usually retired men, Gypsies, and women—to help with the hoeing and harvesting. The collective farm provides the trucks and drivers to deliver the melons to market. For their efforts and expenses, the melon-growers in 1975 received a 40 percent share of the gross receipts of their melon sales.

Management and Central Planning

As owners of the enterprise, members are supposed to have an important voice in the management of farm affairs. They elect the president and ultimately set local farm policies. The farm is to be run democratically by its members, who are able to shape its actions through various formal channels, including general meetings in which they have the opportunity to voice and propagate their opinions and to vote on farm policies, measures, and actions, grievance committees, and elections.

During the 1950s and even much of the 1960s, however, the state made most of the important decisions of farm policy and planning. As Donáth (1977: 114–116, 120–121) has pointed out, due to the myriad of ways in which the state could intervene and limit the cooperatives' freedom of action, "this quasi cooperative ownership was a disguised state ownership" (115). The collective farms' control over their instruments of production (capital goods), over the allocation and sale of their production, indeed, over their own farming and investment plans was very limited. Until the 1960s large machines like combines and most tractors could only be in the hands of the state machine and tractor stations; this allowed the state considerable input in the farms' plans. Only when the tractor stations were dismantled could the farms, too, buy larger machinery.

Until 1965, centralized planning mediated by the district party and council organs sharply restricted the individual farms' latitude of action. While the plans were not designed directly for individual collective farms, these lower organs broke down the overall plans into detailed formulas for each cooperative. The formulas explicitly set down the composition of the farms' production, which crops to plant, the acreage of cultivation, and the types of livestock (Robinson 1973: 66), and determined every important aspect of investment, acquisition, and marketing policy. The district administrative and party organs also supervised the execution of their directives. Although both the leadership and, through general meetings, the membership had the right to accept or reject these plans, discussion was often limited, and the whole process resembled a "ratifying acknowledgement" of these plans. The plans were virtually compulsory. In the early years, the local village councils had exerted direct control over investment and material inputs, using this to keep the cooperatives "in line" (ibid.).

Moreover, the collectives did not have full control over the disposition of their produce. The system of compulsory deliveries until 1956 severely limited the farms' marketing of their production. They were compelled to sell a huge portion of their harvest and animal-based production to state procurement agencies at prices so low that they did not cover the full costs of production including investment. The little that could be brought to market at more reasonable prices was often bought by other state controlled agencies, which exerted a strong hold on the whole marketing apparatus and helped keep prices low. Until the new agricultural cooperative law of 1967, the cooperatives still held a very subordinate position to the state procurement agencies; they were not allowed "to sell directly to the consumer, but only to agencies designated by the state" (ibid.).

Finally, even in the selection of the leadership the voice of the membership was often little more than an affirmation of recommendations of the higher organs. When, as in many farms, the nominee was an outsider little known to the membership, there was scant basis for an educated vote. The lack of a secret ballot until 1967 and the continuing practice of having only one nominee did not alleviate outside control.

The New Economic Mechanism (NEM) of 1968, which encouraged decentralization of planning and a greater role for monetary incentives, as well as the associated new regulations pertaining to the collective farms, has done much to alter this situation, to realize the intent of the basic principles. Because of the continued faltering of the economy and agricultural production nationally it had become more widely accepted that extremes of centralized planning had not achieved the intended results. In response to this, the NEM encouraged greater local independence and initiative in a variety of ways. To spur production it 1) has given collective farms increased room for material incentives for both leadership and workers; 2) has allowed local leaders greater scope in planning local production and investment, including the establishment of subsidiary enterprises to make use of surplus labor and to allow vertical integration within the sphere of farm activities to encompass food processing and even marketing; 3) has increased the prices offered for agricultural produce; and 4) has tried to encourage greater membership input into the planning and policy-making process.

Of course, supervision and intervention by higher organs have not been eliminated, nor has the input of members into policy-making and administration implied by farm rules and cooperative principles been implemented as fully and as widely in the form of collective farm democracy as many desired and expected. Many decisions and policies passed on to the collectives from above are still based on the country's real or felt needs and not necessarily the needs of the local farm membership. For example, powerful state-owned corporations and banks are still capable of enforcing their terms—terms that reflect national better than local needs and policies—on dependent collective farms.

As production has risen and income and profits soared, limits have been placed on annual wage increases in order to encourage further capital investment instead of higher increases in pay. A highly progressive tax on pay increases has made larger increases more prohibitive than the allocation of surpluses to further investment.

Central plans still influence local production, although not in the extremely detailed compulsory manner of the past. When, for example, the world price of sugar rose drastically in the early 1970s, government policy was directed at making the country more self-sufficient in sugar production, and the combined collective was given a noncompulsory allotment of 250 hold-s of less profitable sugar beets. It complied. District party and administrative leaders often continue to offer guidelines for crop composition, but local agronomists have more freedom to work within, modify, or even reject them.

In some areas, however, the district party and council have retained more power. They have maintained strong connections with local collective leadership, and their directives often remain supreme despite differences of opinion among the membership. As Donáth (1977: 278–279) has pointed out, despite surface changes brought on by legal measures, in many collective farms old power structures remain, as nonfarm administrative organs continue to utilize their old powers. This manipulation of the membership and farm policy has often continued for several reasons: 1) frequently the membership does not know its own rights, and 2) even if it does, realizing the power of the leaders and higher organs, it may not consider them realistic despite the new regulations; 3) because of the greater size and complexity of today's collective farm operations, members may not be capable of overseeing the farms' affairs.

Formal Organization

The formal organization of Kislapos's farm as set forth in its basic statutes before 1974, the year of the first merger with neighboring villages' farms, was similar to that of most Hungarian collectives. However, there can be—and, in Lapos's case, there are—significant differences between the formal organization of the farm and the relations that actually exist among its various organs. Both the formal organization and the discrepancies between the ideal and the actual structure of the farm's management are necessary for an understanding of the farm's workings.

Varga (1965: 21–24) offers a description of the formal organization of a collective farm in southwest Hungary that reflects the basic tenets of Kislapos's farm statutes. The ultimate authority in matters of policy, investment, the setting of wage rates, and the acceptance of new members is the whole membership in the form of the general meeting convened several times a year. A majority vote decides in most cases, but a two-thirds majority is required in matters such as amendments to the statutes, mergers, and recalls of officers.

Of course, such a body is too unwieldy to handle the day-to-day affairs of the farm and the detailed planning of crop structure, investment, and wage-scale setting; authority to plan and execute decisions and policies is delegated to the leadership. An administrative board, selected from among members and elected by them, "is responsible for implementing the resolutions of the general assembly [meeting], and for the general management of the cooperative between general assemblies" (ibid.: 21). It meets every few weeks with the president and technical experts of the farm.

Heading the collective is the president, elected every four years by the membership. He is the legal representative of the farm in dealings with outsiders, and he manages the farm on behalf of the administrative board. His main task is "to prepare, and enforce, the resolutions of the general assembly" (ibid.: 22) and to act on behalf of the administrative board.

Various committees of farm members elected at the general meetings oversee the farm's functions. The Control Committee reviews the farm's economic activities; the Disciplinary Committee investigates cases of alleged irregular behavior and advises what, if any, disciplinary action should be taken. The Unified Cooperative Law of 1971 required all cooperatives to establish grievance and complaint committees, composed only of nonmanagement members (Robinson 1973: 267), to settle disputes between management and membership on a daily basis. Other committees are concerned with the farm's wider social functions and the cultural and material needs of its members and of the community at large. These committees form a branch of leadership independent of the executive line.

In Kislapos, however, the president has been much more powerful than the above sketch would suggest. For reasons discussed in Chapter 8 he has been able to dominate the Administrative Board instead of executing at its behest and has been able to channel most farm policies and actions from above, not from below as would follow from the above description. Of course, this often happens when leadership is formalized. Here this is also manifested in the president's partial control over committee activities and ultimately over the selection of both committee and Administrative Board members. Although nominations for these positions can be taken from the floor at general meetings, usually they are prepared by an appropriate committee and voted upon by the membership. Since the nominating process is influenced by the president and the usual procedure is for but one candidate or slate of candidates to be presented for a vote, the influence of the president can be strong. This can be amplified by the form of the balloting (which is technically secret): assent requires absolutely no action, whereas a dissenting ballot must be marked.

Under the direction of the president are the vice-president and, more important, the agronomist, the head accountant, and the heads of any subsidiary operations (in Kislapos, for example, construction crews and gravel and sand pit crews). In charge of agricultural operations is the agronomist, who, within the scope allowed him by outside agencies and party and government policy, prepares the overall annual farming plan and coordinates day-to-day operations. The chief accountant is in charge of accounting, bookkeeping, and pay disbursement and also oversees farm warehouse, storage, and milling operations. The office workers under the accountant also handle the dispatching of the farm's trucks.

Farming operations in the collective are divided into three broad areas: animal-raising, horticulture and agricultural crops, and team and machine handling and maintenance. These in turn are split into several brigades of workers, most of whom work regularly in one area of activity.

Within the animal sector there are two brigades, each with a brigade leader roughly equivalent to a foreman. One brigade tends the animals on the old Gold Spike farmstead (cows, calves, and pigs); the other handles the heifers and steers raised for meat on the old Petőfi, as well as the baby chick raising program based there.

The horticultural and agricultural crop division has three brigade leaders but only two main brigades. Two of the leaders have as their main tasks directing groups of workers in the fields, calculating their pay on the basis of hours worked or daily production achieved, and calling the members to work in late evenings or early mornings. The third directs those workers in and around the greenhouse, seedling beds, and the pavilion where harvested vegetables are sorted and crated according to size and quality. Whereas in the animal-tending brigades workers usually labor in the same barns for months and even years on end, the horticultural and agricultural workers are frequently shifted from one setting to another, from one brigade to another. Few work steadily in one place or with one brigade leader.

The final brigade consists of the tractor drivers, the teamsters, and the workshop members, all largely under the direction of one brigade leader. The tractor drivers also handle the combines, attachments to the tractors, and the dredger used to load manure from the members' farmyards and the farm's barns onto wagons for distribution in the fields. The teamsters load, deliver, and unload produce, hay, corn stalks, manure, and other items within the confines of the farm. The workshop contains blacksmiths, carpenters, woodworkers, and some machinists and repairmen; they produce horseshoes and spare parts, make implements, crates, and frames for the greenhouses, and maintain and repair the tractors, trucks, and other machinery as best they can.

There is a great deal of interaction between this brigade and the other brigades and operations of the farm. Its actions are coordinated to meet the needs of the other brigades (to transport harvested produce or manure, for example, to pull workers behind a tractor on the equipment that plants seedlings they feed into it, or to dig turnips to be cleaned by fieldworkers). The grain and corn crops of the collective farm (though not the corn crop of land assigned to houseplots) are handled completely by these workers, as manual labor in this sector has been supplanted in all respects by machines.

The work force of the collective farm has not always been so thoroughly organized into brigades, nor has the work been as mechanized.[5]

Although after 1959 there were regular teamsters and animal-tenders, and the harvesting of the grain crops was done in large groups, the notion of brigades was still not well established. As noted earlier, for the first ten or twelve years individual households were accorded an important status in the nonhouseplot, collective production of the farm. They were often assigned plots of vegetables requiring intensive labor to hoe, single, and harvest. Work units were credited to the family head; occasionally bonuses were even given to individuals or families whose plots of collective produce were particularly productive. In the 1960s, even after farm membership was extended to other family members and the household unit's importance in production decreased, individuals often still volunteered to take on the hoeing of plots for a given number of work units.

Recent years have witnessed an increasingly collective character in the farm work. Except for sprinkling, which two men can handle by themselves, almost all manual field labor is now done in larger groups. Brigades are often split into groups of four or six, but these groups usually do the same kind of work side by side. For hourly work field hands are paid identical wages; but even when work is paid by the piece or according to output (for example, quantity of tomatoes or paprika picked), each member of the group doing the same kind of work is paid according to the group's production as a whole.

Heavier machinery was originally almost wholly in the hands of the machine and tractor stations. In the early 1960s this policy was changed, and collective farms were allowed and encouraged to buy and maintain their own machinery. In the first year or two of operation after 1959,

---

5. Mechanization still has quite a way to go to reach the level of Western nations. There are plans to continue increasing the degree of mechanization to augment production and to balance the loss of manpower in the agricultural sector. Interestingly, in some areas this decrease in the labor force has apparently come to an end. However, the composition of the resulting work force differs considerably from that of earlier times. It is on the whole younger and more technically trained. As conditions have improved in rural communities less isolated than Lapos, and the demand for skilled and technically trained workers has grown because of the mechanization and modernization of Hungarian agriculture, more young people have elected to stay in these communities; some outsiders have even moved in. These younger workers often have a different outlook from their elders. Many prefer not to join the farm as members, but work instead as employees. These workers and others who are members often prefer shorter hours and conditions comparable to industry. Thus, they often forsake the houseplot enterprise (sometimes completely, not even raising pigs or chickens), electing cash instead of a houseplot.

Kislapos's collectives had few, if any, tractors. Plowing, sowing, and other such operations were done with the machines of the local tractor station, often by workers from Lapos. As Lapos acquired more machinery of its own, more of its drivers were farm members. After a couple of years it also acquired a share of the tractor station's machinery; the station's employees from Lapos then became farm members.

Mechanization has been manifested in other ways, too. For the first few years after 1959 grains were harvested in traditional fashion: they were cut by bands of workers with scythes, tied in bundles, stacked, and carted off to be fed into large threshing machines by hand. In the late 1960s the local farm acquired its first combines, and grains and nonhouseplot corn were harvested mechanically. At the same time milking machines were introduced to the cow barns and trucks were bought for use within the farm and to transport goods to market. A steam shovel now excavates the sand and gravel used locally and sold by the farm to outsiders, and other construction machinery loads it onto trucks. Conveyor belts are used to lift grain and hay into storage facilities, and motors pump groundwater out to sprinkle onto vegetable crops. Numerous other machines are also used, and plans for the future following the mergers call for more modern and efficient machinery in greater numbers.

POSITIONS IN THE COLLECTIVE: MEMBERS' PERSPECTIVES

All positions in the collective farm are not equal in the eyes of its members. There is considerable agreement about the comparative desirability of various kinds of work, of their advantages and disadvantages, and about those who are fortunate enough to obtain the better positions.

Leaders versus Nonleaders

One primary distinction for members is that between leaders (*vezető-s*), generally viewed as those who direct others, and the rest of the farm's workers. As some put it, this includes everyone from the brigade leaders up: the president and vice-president; the agronomist and chief accountant; some of the office staff serving under the accountant, like the payroll clerk and the treasurer; and the brigade leaders. Occasionally included are the workshop foremen, although they are below the rank of brigade leaders. In general, those who are seen to influence the decisions concerning the work done and pay received by workers are grouped in this category.

Several tenets and attitudes are widely held about the leaders: in sum, they receive inordinately high pay considering that they do not work hard and are not especially qualified for their jobs.

Most vezető-s are among the higher paid workers in the farm; all but one or two earn 3,500 forint-s or more a month, twelve months of the year, whereas an average full-time Hungarian worker's monthly earnings are about 2,700–2,800 forint-s. The highest paid, such as the president, agronomist, and chief accountant, earn at least 5,000 forint-s monthly. As several members commented, these men earn enough so that their wives do not have to work. (A few of them *are* wives, but their husbands do work.)

More important, from the other workers' point of view most vezető-s do not do any hard work. As one woman stated, "Oh, they don't work; they're just this sort of brigade leaders." Referring to the form of their earnings and the lack of a concrete work output, the same woman added, "They don't work; their [salary] is already established." Clarifying this is the remark of another, similarly aged woman (late thirties) referring to the advantages enjoyed by those with official duties (*tisztbeosztás*) in the farm: "They don't have to work" (*nem kell melózni*). Noteworthy is the double meaning of the word "to work" (melózni). It refers on the one hand to hard work and on the other to physical labor, reflecting most villagers' feelings that the only true work is physical labor. Of course, villagers do accept other forms of work as legitimate; many have schooled their children so that they will be able to avoid the manual labor of the collective farm, so that they will have easier work than their parents, preferably a white-collar job. They do not feel that their children are not working, but they do believe that the work is easier.

Bearing on this is the explicit comparison villagers make of the brigade leaders in particular and the leadership in general to the nagygazda-s, the kulaks of the past. Some refer explicitly to the brigade leaders as like kulaks in that "they don't do any work; they just order people around." The image of the leaders' wives not working matches the findings of Sárkány (1978: 74, 90) that in precollective times the wives of the nagygazda-s in a hillier region northwest of Kislapos (and undoubtedly in the village, too) rarely worked in the fields. The feeling of many that some brigade leaders are rude and sometimes vulgar and drive the workers too hard contributes to this image, as does the fact that two of the six leaders were indeed labeled as kulaks before 1956. Given the scope of many villagers' relations with work leaders, limited in many cases to the nagygazda-s and estate foremen of the past, these views are not surprising. In the past the labor of wealthier nagygazda-s was not considered "real" work, either. Nor then is it surprising that many of the office staff, despite their more lowly positions, are also regarded as being in the leadership because they, too, do not do real work. Some people even say that the office staff "live off the rest of the workers."

All this is exacerbated by the view that the brigade and other leaders are not perceived as especially qualified for their jobs. With the exception of the young agronomist, an outsider with a university education (about whom none complain with respect either to lack of training or to income), and one or two others, none among the leadership has received any special training to particularly qualify him or her for the position. Many have received their positions through local patronage and friendship, or in a few cases due to some perceived talent or knowledge gained in the days of private agriculture. Many have since taken courses in agricultural and administrative affairs, but villagers still consider them no more qualified for their positions than other villagers with similar knowledge and perhaps greater talent.

High-Paying versus Low-Paying Positions and Steady versus Irregular Work

These two distinctions are highly interrelated, though not identical, and will be discussed together. High pay, of course, is considered desirable by all villagers, although for some it is not the only consideration in work choice. Most higher-paying jobs (averaging 3,500 forint-s or more per month) are available mainly to men; many of them require a limited skill. These jobs include tractor and truck driving, tending animals, leadership and administrative positions including brigade leaders, loaders (working with truck drivers), stonemasons, and several other positions. Of these only administrative and calf-tending positions are occupied by women. Women in general do the low-paying and seasonal work in the fields.

Seasonableness and irregularity of work distinguish many high-paying jobs from much less remunerative ones, although not from jobs of the middle range (for example, night watchmen, teamsters). Year-round jobs like tending animals, tractor driving, truck driving and loading, and administrative positions are desired for their generally higher pay. Thus, working women in the collective farm have annual earnings averaging 15,000–20,000 forint-s a year, less than half that of most men. Most of these women are able to work only eight or nine months a year, and not constantly during those months because of the weather and the agricultural work cycle. Even regular but relatively low-paying (per hour) jobs like those of night watchmen and chicken-tenders (in the past the farm had a hen house and raised chicks to maturity) produce far greater annual earnings than field work. The few women who have had some agricultural training and who work regularly around the greenhouse during the winter, and those working in the storage areas, are envied by many others, not so much for their pay scale (which is not very high—moreover, stacking grain and moving fifty- and seventy-five-kilo bags is no easy chore) but for their year-round work.

Regular work is also important in other ways. Because both houseplot allotment and vacation days are keyed to total hours worked, and because both have a fairly high minimum number of hours required for eligibility,

*Women, who do most of the manual labor in the fields,
hoeing weeds in the paprika fields. Though not always
spaced so closely, their work together offers considerable
opportunity for conversation and gossip.*

steady work makes it much easier to achieve the necessary hours. Moreover, in 1975 bonus payments for selected workers at the year's end were
set as a percentage of the year's income—a percentage increasing according to the number of hours worked.

Not surprisingly, these are the chief factors influencing women's
choice of work in agriculture. Women often have a choice between hoeing or picking vegetables or tobacco in the fields in one of two large bands
and staying near the greenhouse and horticultural headquarters to work
under the pavilion in jobs like sorting vegetables. The former is more
strenuous and pays better; younger women who can keep up the fast pace
volunteer for it. The latter is less physically demanding, can be done at a
more leisurely pace, and pays less; thus older women predominate, and
the group is often referred to as the "old band."[6] But it also provides

6. In Varsány, a similar distinction is made. A separate "old brigade" was established for women who work more slowly but steadily and who cannot keep the fast
pace of the younger (Jávor 1978: 329).

steadier work, since it is less dependent on the weather; thus some younger women in greater need of hours than high pay also choose such work. Since many women do not reach the minimum number of hours for the houseplot, or just barely do so, this consideration is important.

High pay is not dependent solely on regular work, however. For some jobs the wage scale is relatively high. Good stonemasons, despite their lack of winter work, earn well. Though tending animals is a year-round job, most feel that the hours are not really that long, even though it is a seven-day-a-week job. Milkers and cattle-tenders go to the barns twice a day, in the early morning and late afternoon, working a total of five or six hours (many villagers estimate four) daily. Although they each also have to spend eight or nine hours watching the animals between shifts once every six or eight days, and are "tied down" by their work, most villagers feel they are well paid for their efforts. On the other hand, truck drivers and loaders receive a moderate wage but work very long hours, especially during the summer and at harvest, and thus earn larger incomes.

Other Considerations

Some jobs, of course, are more physically arduous than others. Loading and unloading heavy bags of grain or fertilizer is difficult, and most men cannot continue it through retirement. Older, poorer quality tractors shake their drivers, and their effects on the stomach have caused several men to give up these fairly well-paying jobs. Milkers' work, with its short hours and the use of milking machines, is considered relatively easy. The high-paying positions of tending calves, with work sufficiently light so that women occupy two of the three slots, are considered plums. Other jobs (of night watchmen, for example) are less physically demanding and are open to retired, disabled, and generally older and weaker men. One forty-two-year-old with a bad back, who previously handled heavy machinery and trucks, remarked that he was afraid to take on such a position because he would be kidded for doing "old men's work." Older women often either work under the pavilion or quit the farm when they feel they can no longer keep up with the group.

Several other considerations enter into members' thoughts about these positions. For example, animal-tending jobs have the advantage of leaving the major part of the day open for other work, especially work in the houseplot enterprise. Moreover, such workers can occasionally skip a shift by making reciprocal arrangements with fellow workers. But the work literally "stinks" because one labors with animals and their defecation.

Minor and sometimes major "benefits" are associated with jobs. Loaders of trucks and wagons often receive tips from farm members when they deliver grain to members' houses. These tips (borravaló—literally, "for wine") take the form of a glass of wine or a shot of brandy and during the course of a day mount up. One wife, for example, persuaded her husband to change jobs because he was increasingly often coming home from work intoxicated.

Members holding the positions of cashier at the farm's gravel pit, materials procurer, and miller, all handling large quantities of cash, materials, or grain with relatively little supervision, are thought to have excellent possibilities for acquiring money or goods illegally. Villagers point to the modern homes built in cities by some for their children as evidence for such tendencies. Indeed, some of the leaders are suspected of similar actions.

Allocation of Positions

Ideally, individuals are chosen for jobs on the basis of the maxim, "From each according to his ability—to each according to his need." However, it also seems clear that favoritism based on personal connections (kin and nonkin) enters into such decisions.

In the very beginning, in 1959, the few jobs requiring special skills, like tractor driving, went to those few individuals who already had the training from army experience or work at tractor stations, or to members who volunteered for the requisite instruction. In cases of office work and bookkeeping individuals were chosen who had had appropriate schooling or previous experience elsewhere. Sometimes votes were taken among the membership to determine which of two persons with apparently equal qualifications was to get an administrative job or go for further schooling. A number of brigade leaders were chosen supposedly on the basis of their ability as manifested by their farming success in precollective times.

Other jobs were distributed on the basis of personal preference. For example, many of the teamsters chose their positions and have remained in them to the present because they "like cattle" or are "crazy about horses" (in early years there were two or three times as many teamsters as now, following mechanization). They have done so despite the decreased status and pay of carting relative to other positions in today's more highly automated and mechanized agriculture. Several, at least in the initial years, took such positions because they did not want to lose their prized teams of horses.[7]

---

7. Kunszabó (1970: 65–66) offers complementary data concerning the present status of members of different precollective economic strata within the collective farm at Heréd, west of Kislapos. He points out that most of the teamsters in the early years had already been team owners with six or more hold-s of land. Such positions then gave high and constant incomes and were relatively prestigious. This corresponds to Fél and Hofer's observations (1969: 275) that, before collectivization, team ownership was not only economically advantageous but also carried with it considerable status, since "the most conspicuous sign of the quality of

Of course, as noted earlier, there was considerable jockeying for leadership positions at the start; many brigade leaders and other high officials won their jobs as much on the strength of personal connections as on the basis of superior knowledge or talent. Although there was some evidence for early dissatisfaction with leadership choices, such feelings were less intense than they are today. The lack of automation and technological complexity at the time demanded a less specialized and skilled labor force; this and the early family-oriented work organization resulted in a less stratified worker hierarchy. Some of the best paid workers in the cooperative were field workers who had accumulated hundreds of work units through intense labor.

As the years passed and the work and pay hierarchy became more stratified, dissatisfaction increased. Many members, raised in an era when landed wealth largely determined status and economic opportunity, now saw little distinguishing those who were placed in higher-paying positions, not always requiring special skills (training in which was often suggested and subsidized by the cooperative), from those who remained in less remunerative jobs. Some of this distrust stems, of course, from an insensitivity to skills and talents only recently made salient by the need for greater organizational and technological skills; but there is considerable evidence that advancement in the collective is highly dependent on personal connections (including nepotism) and party membership, or, as villagers say, "standing close to the fire [leadership]."

Finally, assignment of work also depends on personal need. Since the cooperative is not to be solely an economic unit, but also an ongoing social group concerned with the material and social needs of its members, this should not be surprising. It is apparent, in both the functions of the committee dealing with the members' social and cultural needs and in the variety of relations maintained by the collective with its members and the village as a whole.

Decisions over the assignment of workers to higher-paying jobs are sometimes based on the relative financial positions of the workers; those, for example, with more children or still lacking a house of their own may receive higher priority. Similarly, members have often gone to their brigade leaders or to the president to request regular, higher-paying work because of such needs, and their requests have been met. Taking such considerations into account can lead to more flexible, often more humane

---

the *gazda* and of his farm are [were] the team and its equipment, the harness and the carriage." On the basis of their past ownership and greater knowledge of their animals, team owners in Heréd and Kislapos, generally possessing more than five hold-s of land, were able to carry over some of their prestige and economic advantage into the early years of collectivization. In Heréd some of them were the first to take up tractor driving.

decisions; they also reinforce particularistic tendencies in the collective (for example, favoritism), which may result in less rational decision-making and in heightened social tensions.

THE COLLECTIVE AND THE COMMUNITY

The cooperative farm is far more than just an employer and work-giver to its members. It plays an integral role in and supports its members' houseplot enterprises, provides monetary and material support for members at family crises, celebrations, and times of need, and maintains strong ties with other village institutions.

Houseplot Support

The collective does much to support the houseplot enterprises. For example, at corn harvesting time the collective allows tractor drivers and teamsters to go into the houseplot fields and bring in the corn picked by the harvesting groups. Families pay the drivers for their time.

Much of the cooperative's support is mutually beneficial for the member and the collective. For example, the farm buys newly hatched chicks and raises them to a hardier age. It sells them to members for a profit, while sparing members the need to provide warm quarters for these delicate and demanding birds. It also sells members different kinds of feed and grain (sometimes hard to get), as well as straw, usually at a slight discount, though providing itself a profit, and for a 5-percent share grinds this grain and the houseplot corn and grain for those lacking their own grinders. On the other hand, the farm buys the manure of the cattle on houseplots for about 5 forint-s per quintal and removes it from the farm-yards to spread onto its own fields. More important, since the establishment of its own meat-processing plant, the farm has contracted with its members to buy the pigs they raise when they are full-grown, saving members the cost and problems of transporting the animals to the pick-up points of meat-processing plants, while insuring a steady supply of meat for the farm. Milk produced by both the collective's and the members' own cows is purchased by the local creamery; eggs and produce sold by the villagers locally are bought by the consumer cooperative's buyer in the village.

In addition, the collective farm employs herders to take the villagers' privately owned cows and pigs out to pasture each day. In the late 1940s, the Grazing Association's land was nationalized, but its functioning continued largely unchanged. After the second wave of collectivization the association's land and functions were taken over by the collective, which in recent years has charged farm members 550 forint-s annually per cow

*The village herder, employed by the collective farm, driving
villagers' individually owned cows through the village streets
out to pasture with the aid of his puli herd dog. The Roman
Catholic Church is in the background.*

and nonmembers 800 forint-s. Smaller fees are paid for inseminations and
for grazing pigs.

Many of these services have mixed blessings. For several months in
1975 the capacity of the meat-processing plant was severely reduced because of reconstruction and repair. Many pigs for which the farm had
contracted were bought by the collective only after several months' delay
had put them into less profitable, higher weight ranges.

In general, the houseplot services enjoy low priority in collective farm
objectives. For example, in the spring of 1975 many villagers felt the
machine cultivation of their seeded corn plots was late, allowing considerable grass to grow. The farm had not made horses and men available
until its own needs were met. Members have sometimes complained that
the pigs are given poor-quality, muddy grazing land. Sometimes feed to
which their animals have grown accustomed is unavailable, leading to
rejection of other feed and resultant weight loss.

Monetary and Material Support

At important times in the lives of its members, the collective farm has provided material and financial aid for members and even for their non-member offspring. For years, members' children were given a sizable gift by the farm on their weddings and provided with interest-free loans to buy local housing. For children who were members, the farm would buy a house and have its building crew renovate it, then sell it to the member, offering a low-interest loan to be paid off by deductions from monthly earnings. Similar terms were worked out for new houses and for additions to older ones built by the construction brigade for farm members.

By the same token, if members elected to shoulder most of their building by themselves with the traditional help of relatives, neighbors, and friends, the collective farm often arranged to cart materials to the building site and provided bricks and cement at low cost. Low-cost loans were also offered to these members, as well as to members needing money for furniture and other large expenses. The farm even provides certain burial expenses for members.

Besides these more direct aids, the farm built a nursery school for the young children of its members, freeing them to continue to work. The school operated under the management of the farm for several years in the late 1960s and early 1970s until the declining birthrate forced it to close.

Ties with the Community

The collective also maintains important ties with nonmember villagers and with village institutions. Nonmembers' cattle may graze on collective farm land for a slightly higher fee than members'. Similarly, for a fee the collective farm has plowed the lands of the few villagers who remained in private, essentially full-time agriculture after 1959, as well as the smaller fields and gardens of villagers for whom agriculture provides a secondary (though significant) income in addition to nonagricultural jobs.

Most significant is the farm's tie with the local consumers' cooperative, which runs the general store and the tavern (and since 1977 the snack bar), buys up local produce and eggs, and sells heating oil and bottled gas locally. This has sometimes involved simple cooperation between the two. During the harvest season the farm has provided fresh fruits and vegetables to be sold in the cooperative's general store. At other times the collective has loaned its trucks to the cooperative to transport goods.

On another level, as observed earlier, in the early 1950s the officers of the consumers' cooperative were charter members of the early collective farms and to varying degrees took part in its work. During those years the loans given out by the consumers' coop were made available only to collective farm members. Some sharing of workers has also been evident recently. Several workers have moved back and forth between jobs in the two organizations with relative ease, indeed with the sanction and suggestion of the leaders. Suggestive of the continuing closeness is the fact that, until the most recent set of collective farm mergers locally, the tavern-keeper, a former employee of the farm and earlier the produce buyer of the cooperative, still received a household plot from the farm. Indeed, through common subordination to the same district and party officials and ultimately to national policy; through common party membership of the leaders of both organizations; through some degree of interlocking directorates; and, finally, through some mutual collusive support, the official and unofficial interests and policies of the two overlap strongly.

The collective has also maintained important ties with the village council. The council, through its president, was largely responsible for the organization of the farms in 1959 and maintained close ties with the earliest ones. The same common subordination to higher officials and policies and occasional mutual support among leaders that characterizes relations between the farm and the coop is reflected in the council-farm relations. The interests and policies of the council and the farm have meshed. As with the farm and the coop, this has sometimes been to the political and material benefit of the leaders—though because of personality and power conflicts among them the mutually beneficial peace has been tenuous.

On a more mundane level, the farm provides houseplots for the teachers employed by the local school, much as the church and village governments did in the past.

RECENT DEVELOPMENTS

The mergers that took effect in January 1974 and January 1975, resulting in the unification of three and six earlier separate cooperative farms, respectively, have already brought profound changes in the collective farm and promise still more farreaching developments. These mergers, part of the wave of mergers sweeping the nation in the early and mid-1970s, were intended to make greater use of economies of scale and to rationalize farm operations.[8] So quickly did this proceed in some areas of the country, and occasionally with so little regard to important local variation, that economists, government officials, and villagers feel the merging went too

8. These recent developments generally reflect the advent of the third important phase in the development of socialist agriculture. The first phase, common to all of Eastern Europe, was the wave(s) of collectivization in the countryside. The second, beginning in the late 1950s and continuing on through the 1960s and

far. There is some evidence that problems in coordinating numerous small diverse enterprises and in "too-bigness" may in some cases have offset the gains.

In Lapos the developments involve several processes often associated with modernization (Levy 1966): centralization and greater coordination in the collective farm; rationalization of planning with new, less traditional ideas; greater emphasis on universalistic criteria in the selection of leaders and in the assignment of jobs (versus favoritism and ties with leadership); and the development of greater work discipline, less oriented toward traditional peasant values. Accompanying these changes in size and organizational complexity was the growing inability of the individual to oversee and influence personally the operations of the farm.

Not all these changes were immediately evident; some speedup seems to have occurred with the appointment of a new president, an outsider with university training, considerable experience with large-scale modern agriculture, and a reputation for tight discipline, and a person with greater vision or at least more tolerant of other's visions than his predecessor.[9] After his assumption of office, the collective experienced far more change than it had previously; some of this, of course, may have been the result of previous plans only now taking effect.

From the start there was a centralizing tendency, typified by construction of the large, forty-room complex in Barnaföld, the "White House," for the farm's new central administrative building. With its completion, many administrative workers from each farm unit were moved to there. Of greater import, however, was the fact that the coordination of the six original enterprises was tightening and becoming more centrally controlled. Trucks were now to be dispatched centrally, although they still remained on the local farm enterprise. Much of the pay and social security calculations was transferred to central bookkeeping.

A good deal of the maintenance work was taken over by central maintenance in Kistó (which sometimes led to long delays in simple repairs for Lapos's machinery). Local workshop and administrative staffs were sharply reduced. Whereas Lapos's unit kept its older tractors and trucks "at home," other of its machinery was used all over the larger farm; a new

---

early 1970s, saw the development, solidification, and technical advancement of socialist large-scale farming. The third phase, which has begun only recently and is far from finished, involves the radical organizational restructuring of agriculture and the introduction and spread of agroindustrial complexes (Enyedi 1978: 157).

9. Formally, a selection committee of five members, one from each of the five merged farm units (the sixth original farm in Sonka had been appended to Kistó's unit), was chosen to select a new president. However, the district party had already selected a candidate, who was then unanimously approved by all the farm units except Lapos, where one or two ballots were cast for the resigning president and another member.

The "White House," as villagers christened it, the forty-room administrative headquarters of the newly merged 10,000 hectare collective farm encompassing five villages and six farms, including Kislapos. Under construction in 1975–76.

line of powerful Western tractors and combines, capable of far greater output than older machines, was bought by the merged collective and, while used in all the farm's land, was stored centrally.

Following the assumption of office by the new president, new buses were bought by the farm to transport workers of one unit daily to another unit where work demanded extra laborers. This occurred particularly often for the women field workers. Recently, men have experienced analogous, though different, mobility due to the machinations of the larger farm. Several milkers were given different work for months when the cow barns were partially emptied to make room for still growing, new, and better milk-producing calves. Such a large exchange of cows in the past, so drastically affecting one unit, was unheard of. Similarly, because of the power and productivity of the new tractors and their more efficient and less redundant use, only one-third to one-half of the former tractor drivers retained their old jobs. Thus the labor force of the farm was better coordinated and utilized according to the needs of the farm as a whole.

This reflects the general rationalization of management and planning of the new farm. The coordination of work forces at the "expense" of the local units typifies the trend toward elimination of the local enterprises as self-contained units in the farm, each continuing to maintain a full range of agricultural operations. There is considerable speculation that branches of several local operations will be eliminated and that there will be increased specialization of production in the former local units, one concentrating more on cattle, another, for example, on horticulture.

Characteristic of this grander scale of planning and greater utilization of available resources is the regional water management plan in which the collective farm will participate. The plan calls for the fashioning of large reservoirs at points scattered throughout the area, to be filled by ground and river water. The readily available water would help make possible large-scale intensive, presumably mechanized, cultivation of vegetables and fruit. Lapos's land is scheduled to be the site of a 250-hectare reservoir near the Farkas. Though the plan is obviously not the farm's own, it is significant that it comes at this time. Different national plans are being coordinated to increase the use of available resources. Large-scale rationalization of agricultural practices is rapidly taking place.

Although initial stages of the merger increased the size of the farm's administrative apparatus by adding another layer at the top, within two years higher party officials had determined and decreed that the hierarchy needed pruning. It is rumored that this was one of the issues around which the earlier president's resignation revolved. He apparently had been asked to relocate twenty administrative workers in the farm, to put them into literally productive work, and had not been willing to assume the responsibility.

However, it is also apparent that higher officials and leaders within the farm desired as president someone with greater education and experience in modern agriculture. The resigning president, who had assumed office in 1959, was a smallholder's son who had been a policeman and had later worked as vő on his father-in-law's land, until collectivization. Although he had handled the smaller collectives adequately, greater technical and practical knowledge was deemed necessary for modernizing such a large enterprise.

The new president undoubtedly was not without his own district and county political connections, having been the director of a nearby state farm and having later assumed a position in the county administration, but his appointment seemed to represent a move toward appointment of farm leaders on the basis of more universalistic criteria. In any case, in Kislapos it was clear that the old guard, the leadership under the former president, went through a great upheaval. There were large numbers of job transfers, many of them demotions from favored positions. Though in the past many people had assumed that there was significant theft, embezzlement, and personal "use" of farm resources by the leadership and those close to them, little had been done about it; now it was coming to light.

In general, people seem more convinced now that members are chosen for positions on the basis of their qualifications, rather than through favoritism and personal connections. They are satisfied that there is less personal misuse of the farm's property.

The stricter accounting of farm resources has also been extended to all members—one of the new president's priorities has been the protection of state property. Traditionally, most members have not been above taking fruit and vegetables for themselves from the fields, sometimes in large quantities, with the justification that it is all their own property (in common) anyway. Nicely characterizing the attitude are the telling comments of a sixty-one-year-old retired woman member describing a fellow worker's theft of a watermelon from the farm for lunch: "Well, somehow the woman obtained—in the collective farm they don't steal, they obtain [*szerezni*]—she obtained a melon."[10] Opportunities for such obtaining are apparently more limited as efforts have been made to restrict the practice. Workers traveling by bus from one village to another are less able to sneak home a basketful of paprika. Similarly, teamsters may no longer contract directly with individual families at corn harvesting time to go into the fields with the farm's teams to haul home privately owned corn. Such dealings must now be handled through the collective.

At first, villagers complained about these limitations and expressed concern over rumors that the farm was trying to raise 20 million forint-s of needed capital at the expense of the workers. But as pay for many women in the fields went up and the capital was raised elsewhere, these fears subsided. Interestingly, though, this does represent a shift in members' attitudes; there is now a greater willingness to give up more traditional benefits, such as "use" of common produce and even the much desired houseplot in exchange for cash payment and shorter hours.

Of course, this tendency is much stronger among the young than among their elders, but even with the latter there are signs of a shift in traditional attitudes. One example is the change in feelings toward the lunch program instituted by the farm in 1976. Field workers can now buy a substantial warm lunch brought to them in the fields by the farm for 10 forint-s, a price partially subsidized by the collective. Such a lunch is made necessary by the busing, which prevents their going home to eat. Now that it is clear that members do not have to pay for the meals in advance a week at a time but pay only for what they receive, they are more enthusiastic than in the past. (The busing does cause difficulties for women who used to go home for lunch and feed their animals, but many have made accommodations for this.)

10. Jávor (1978: 303, 335) reports the same attitude, only with a different term: bringing (*hozás*).

This is a far cry from the past, when for many collectivization conjured up the specter of a complete communal existence. When members discussed this image they often referred to communal kitchens and communal meals, an offshoot possibly of living "on one bread" and a concept very undesirable to most. Yet it is something of this very nature that many are now welcoming.

On the other hand, the mergers, by producing an enterprise of great size and complexity, have reduced the ability of the typical member to overview and influence the operations of the farm. Except the higher levels of leadership, which have as their specific task the overseeing and coordination of the farm's diverse operations, few members can now even see most operations outside their own work sphere and especially outside their own village; there is certainly little opportunity to understand the full complexity of choices in modern farming decisions, the economics of complex loan and financing arrangements, or the role of the state and political factors.

Thus, except in matters directly affecting their own livelihood (of which they are aware), such as changed pay scales for work norms, the introduction of lunches, changes concerning feed and grazing land for privately owned cattle, and the like, there is relatively little that most members feel they can do. In recent years some of their suggestions based on traditional farming methods have met only with scorn. For example, following heavy autumn rains in 1974 several members in their fifties suggested planting some winter wheat by hand in those fields left unsown by the tractors because of the soft, muddy earth. Their suggestions were laughed off as being "small peasant" methods, though to these members they still seemed superior to planting nothing.

Even if members do raise suggestions at general meetings, it is difficult to make much headway with them, for only a small portion of the farm's membership will hear them. The size of the membership and the distances involved now preclude general meetings of the farm's whole membership. Instead, "part" meetings are held periodically in each of the local enterprises. Although these meetings are open to suggestions, questions, criticisms, and motions for action, they are used more generally to report the leadership's plans and the state of the farm's operations.[11] Though the various committees, including the administrative board, still exist, each farm now contributes just a few representatives to each. As a result, the scope of direct democracy has been reduced. This, of course, is the almost inevitable result of such changes in size and range of operation.

---

11. Because of this transmission function, the members' decreased input, and some discouragement of criticism at these meetings (aside from some complaints and suggestions about minor issues like the availability of feed or the quality of

Naturally, not all the above developments have happened within the past few years only. But the mergers, and the radical changes in leadership following little more than a year later, have accelerated these developments; the rapid acceptance of the changes by the membership indicates just how far traditional values have changed over the past thirty years. They show the degree to which such values have been superseded by attitudes more characteristic of urban dwellers and factory workers, attitudes embracing developments the villagers feared, ridiculed and/or rejected twenty years ago and even more recently.

In general, members are satisfied now with many of the more recent changes. These developments and their reception by the farm members indicate that the collective farm in the future will increasingly resemble other large institutions like modern factories in its leadership hierarchy, its decision-making processes, and its organization and rationalization of operations. Efficiency, profit, and managerial authority and separateness will play larger roles. Members, too, will look increasingly like factory workers in their attitudes toward work and home, payoffs from work, and degree of input expected in farm operations. Indeed, as the offspring of earlier members leave farming and others take their places either as members or employees—further decreasing the amount of collective farm land that is partially owned by individual members—the cooperative character itself will in time disappear.

---

community pasture available for members' animals), segments of these meetings reserved for members' comments and questions are sometimes filled by almost embarrassing silence. Although, as Gyenes (1975: 106) has noted, this " 'silence' of the general meetings" may sometimes indicate that premeeting informal dialogues between management and members already may have occurred, here it seems to indicate Gyenes's other possibility, "an absence of democracy."

In Romania, Sampson (1976: 338) has noted similar silence at poorly attended meetings of village people's councils. These are ostensibly "intended to provide an opportunity for people to debate the directives of the executive council of the commune, but in reality they are used to propagandize and approve the party/state directives for the village." This similar lack of interest and input has moved the cooperative farm in Lapos to pay 50 forint-s to members to attend; the local consumers' cooperative sometimes holds raffles at its meetings, perhaps for similar reasons.

Chapter 7

Contemporary Family and Kinship

Events in Hungary since World War II have had far-reaching and sometimes revolutionary consequences for Hungarian society. Local representations and translations of these events have strongly influenced people's lives in the countryside and have introduced a radically different socioeconomic base—the collective farm—to village society. This has meant the end of private landownership as a major determinant of wealth, status, and power and, indeed, as the basis of village economic and social life.

Agriculture has declined in importance in the face of fast-growing industrial and service sectors, although it still plays a decisive role in most villages and is an important factor in the lives of most rural families. Other political, social, and economic policies have also had strong effects on the daily lives of villagers. In many cases the peasant family has been replaced by mixed occupational households, becoming the peasant-worker or even worker-peasant family (compare Sozan 1976; Jávor 1978; Sárkány 1978).

Given the past centrality of private landownership and the family as a combined economic and social unit, what has happened to the rural family under the onslaught of these changes? Does it have as great a role in the organization of daily activities and social relations as in the past, or have its scope and strength been reduced? How has the organization of the family itself changed?

The family has changed in many ways; its internal power structure has been significantly altered. Yet, the family and its kin and affinal extensions continue to play a central role in village social organization. Many of the social organizational principles characteristic of the family and kinsmen and, in general, of village social relations in the past are as primary today as they were in the past. Although it has lost some functions, the family has taken on significant new provinces.

In this chapter, the contemporary family and the important social relations of life in Kislapos today are examined. The goals and aspirations of

186

today's villagers and their children, the villagers' social and economic setting, and the constraints that impinge upon them are very different from the past, so the discussion will not be a strict comparison of past and present. It will explicate the present social order and discuss how principles of the past have survived or been modified under today's changed conditions, which will be discussed in detail.

DIVISION OF LABOR

The division of labor and of spheres of interest and responsibility by age and sex in Lapos have not changed greatly despite the introduction of a vastly different socioeconomic base resulting from the collectivization of most privately owned farm land. Much of the cultural basis for the past division of labor and the spheres of interest and responsibility has found full expression in contemporary socioeconomic forms of the collective farm and the smaller scale household enterprise. Since agriculture has continued to be the dominant element in the economic and social life of the village, this should not be surprising; indeed, the collective farm, though to a great degree modelled after the Soviet kolkhoz, was built on the work organization of the past. Some of its forms, like the household plot, which is even now an economic necessity for the production of certain labor-intensive products and a partial palliative for peasants losing their intensely desired land, were intended to give the family unit a continuing productive role.

Broadly speaking, men still do the heavier work in the family and in agriculture in general. However, whereas in the past this meant the tending and handling of larger animals, heavy work within the scope of the household enterprise is now more restricted. This is due mainly to the transfer of agricultural labor formerly in the family sphere to the collective farm, as well as to the many constraints put on the division of labor in the family by the outside work commitments of both spouses and by the household composition. Within the collective farm, men still do the heavier and more prestigious work of tending the cattle, horses, and pigs, carting and occasional small plowing with draft animals, and the loading and unloading of wagons and trucks. They handle most of the heavier machinery now performing tasks done previously by males in heavy manual labor. They drive the tractors, trucks, and combines, repair and maintain machines, and handle irrigation pumps, sprayers, and pipes.

Women perform most of the "lighter," less desirable field work within the scope of the collective farm. They prepare warm beds and seedlings; plant, hoe, thin, harvest, and sort fruits and vegetables; care for poultry and small chicks; and tend the calves. Office work, accounting, and administrative tasks are about evenly divided between the sexes, whereas positions like brigade leaders, agronomists, and presidents are almost all in the hands of males.

In the household, a more limited set of activities now forms the men's domain; again, men normally do the heavier work demanding greater strength and/or skills with tools. They almost exclusively prepare hay and fodder for larger animals, shovel manure, do heavy carrying and loading, dig in the garden and household plot, shell corn, prune and spray the vines, take care of heavier tasks around the house, and handle the major household repairs and construction. Scything grass, either at home or for the flood control and dike maintenance agency along the banks of the Farkas for a share, is also a male task.

Women continue to handle domestic chores—cooking, washing, minor sewing, and cleaning—as well as the lighter agricultural labor: caring for poultry and hoeing, singling, and harvesting the household garden. The delegation of much of the remaining household work (feeding and milking cows and much of the work in the garden and household plot, for example) depends on household composition and outside work commitments.

Today the nuclear family is both the statistical norm and the household arrangement preferred by increasing numbers of both younger and older generations. The stem family is no longer preponderant (see Table 7.1). Slightly more than half of all households in Lapos consist of couples living alone or with their unmarried children; slightly more than half of the village's inhabitants live in such households. Less than one-quarter of the households are of the stem variety, and only a little more than a third of the population reside in them. The remaining one-eighth of the villagers live in the quarter of the households classified as fragmentary (those consisting of widowed or divorced individuals, bachelors or spinsters, or widowed or divorced villagers living with a parent or unmarried children). There are no joint families (excluding Gypsies).

A primary decision to be made by nuclear families is whether both spouses should be employed outside the home. Unlike the stem family, in which an older parent can stay home and tend to household and garden tasks, a nuclear household has no such labor cushion. This limits the household's work arrangements. Wives in nuclear households are therefore far more likely to remain at home, much like the traditional arrangement, instead of working on the collective farm.

Mothers with small children often stay home for several years. The nursery school maintained by the collective in the late 1960s and early 1970s limited this tendency for a while. Though some mothers can depend upon their parents living nearby in the village to care for small children and to help out with work at home, for many families this is no solution. Recent government acts aimed partly at raising the sagging national birthrate have entitled mothers to three years of subsidized leave of absence (including six months of full pay) following the birth of a child without losing jobs or even pay increases. This has further encouraged village mothers to stay at home.

Later in the family cycle, however, the decisive factor in the wife's situation is the decision to maintain a household agricultural enterprise. The keeping of cows and more than a couple of pigs along with the cultivation of one or two hold-s of land is usually felt to necessitate the presence of an adult family member at home. Hence the wife stays home and the traditional household arrangement remains. Because women's work in the collective is usually neither full-time nor well paid, for the wife to remain at home is often justified as equally financially remunerative as working on the collective, despite the relatively low return per work hour of the household enterprise. Thus, women are customarily responsible for the garden and houseplot and the midday feeding of the animals; they often share in milking the cows and feeding the cattle if the men's time before and after work is limited. Men help out in all these tasks on weekends and take a sizable part of their vacations for digging, hoeing, and harvesting the household crops.

There are families in which both spouses work on the farm and keep up the household plot, but it is difficult to do this in a nuclear household without help from nearby parents. The situation of one couple in their late thirties illustrates these problems.

The couple married in 1960 and lived at first with the husband's parents. In a few years they moved to a rented house when the young meny tired of her mother-in-law finding fault in everything; soon they built their own home. Now with two daughters, eight and twelve years old, a constant theme of argument for the couple is the wife's employment. The husband works full-time as a milker, while his wife works as much as she can in the collective farm's fields to get the hours necessary to merit houseplot land in addition to her husband's. The corn raised is needed for feeding their cows and pigs, the sale of whose milk and meat provides added income. Although each recognizes the advantages of the extra income, the husband wants his wife to quit, as he is tired of dinner not being ready when he comes home, of constantly rushing to get work done, of having still more work to do after finishing with his job, of his wife's complaints about being tired. She does not yet want to quit, eyeing the extra income and probably the pension to which she would eventually be entitled.

In stem families an older parent stays at home. Where one or both parents are retired or partially disabled, the choice is obvious; otherwise the wife is the usual choice, maintaining the traditional household arrangement. Depending on her age and health, she handles most of the household chores, feeds the animals, and does much of the lighter garden

Table 7.1 Forms of Family Units, Kislapos, 1976

Household Types	NUMBER OF HOUSEHOLDS *Younger Couple Aged:* <40		40+		NUMBER OF PEOPLE *Younger Couple Aged:* <40		40+	
Fragments								
Divorced/widows								
Children in Lapos	.00%	0	15	5.56%	.00%	0	15	1.97%
Children gone	.00	0	25	9.26	.00	0	25	3.28
No children	.00	0	5	1.85	.00	0	5	.66
Children at home	4.81	13	7	2.59	4.33	33	14	1.84
Bachelors/spinsters	.74	2	0	0	.26	2	0	.00
	5.55%	15	52	19.26%	4.59%	35	59	7.74%
		67				94		
Total Fragments		24.81%				12.34%		
Nuclear								
Couples alone								
Children in Lapos	.00%	0	12	4.44%	.00%	0	24	3.15%
Children gone	.37	1	47	17.41	.26	2	94	12.34
No children	.37	1	7	2.59	.26	2	14	1.84
	.74%	2	66	24.44%	.52%	4	132	17.32%
		68				136		
		25.19%				17.85%		
Children at home								
Living at home	13.33%	36	27	10.00%	18.24%	139	90	11.81%
Children commuting from home	.74	2	7	2.59	.79	6	22	2.89
	14.07%	38	34	12.59%	19.03%	145	112	14.70%
		72				257		
		26.67%				33.73%		
		140				393		
Total Nuclear		51.86%				51.58%		
Stem								
Incomplete								
Children at home	4.81%	13	13	4.81%	8.14%	62	59	7.74%
Children commuting from home	.37	1	5	1.85	.52	4	21	2.76
Children in Lapos	.37	1	2	.74	.52	4	8	1.05
Children gone	.00	0	10	3.70	.00	0	30	3.94
No children	.37	1	2	.74	.52	4	6	.79
	5.93%	16	32	11.85%	9.71%	74	124	16.27%
		48				198		
		17.78%				25.98%		

Table 7.1   Forms of Family Units, Kislapos, 1976 (cont.)

Household Types	NUMBER OF HOUSEHOLDS Younger Couple Aged:				NUMBER OF PEOPLE Younger Couple Aged:			
	<40			40+	<40			40+
Stem								
Complete								
Children at home	2.22%	6	3	1.11%	4.20%	32	18	2.36%
Children commuting from home	.00	0	2	.74	.00	0	11	1.44
Children in Lapos	.00	0	1	.37	.00	0	4	.52
Children gone	.00	0	1	.37	.00	0	4	.52
No children	.37	1	1	.37	.52	4	4	.52
	2.59%	7	8	2.96	4.72%	36	41	5.38%
		15				77		
		5.56%				10.10%		
		63				275		
Total Stem		23.34%				36.08%		
	270 = 100%				762 = 100%			

NOTE: These figures are derived from my own household survey and represent the total non-Gypsy population.

work that the wife in the nuclear family carried out. Older women might restrict their work to cooking, light chores, and helping the younger wife. Infirm parents leave the younger couple in roughly the same position as in the nuclear family. An older retired couple living on one bread with the younger couple is likely to handle most work around the home and garden, including the care of the animals (except, perhaps, the heaviest work), leaving the houseplot work mainly in the hands of the younger couple. The elders' good health and the absence of small children allow both younger spouses to be employed outside the home.

Other important factors include the work schedule of family members, especially the males. Milkers and cattle-tenders leaving for the barns early in the morning for a half-shift and finishing their day's work in the late afternoon at the second feeding and milking have far more time during the day to help out at home and in the houseplot. However, with the exception of preparing hay and fodder, they cannot help much with the actual feeding and milking of the animals because of the time conflict. Most of this work is delegated to their wives or even parents or parents-in-law. During the summer months teamsters, truck and tractor drivers, and loaders work long hours; they, too, often have little time to help their families even with the animals. Their greatest contribution to the houseplot work comes with vacations. Much the same is true for those house-holds in which husbands work outside the village and come home only on weekends while their parents or wives work on the farm.

Finally, personal preferences and skills also play a role; some indi-viduals feel their spouses do a better job than they milking the cows by hand, or prefer to use a milking machine. Mutual agreement on some middle-range tasks is also a factor, as is health and physical ability.

Most interesting about all this is that the division of labor by age and sex among adults has essentially been preserved among those primarily engaged in agricultural work. But other things have changed.

The most striking change is the children's vastly decreased role in family labor. Contrary to past expectations of youth continuing in the parents' footsteps, and socialization directed toward this end, parents have been actively leading their children away from agriculture in the past fifteen years. The peasantry in the past had been looked down upon by urban dwellers and the educated but, while to some degree accepting this status distinction, had held its head high through the pride of indepen-dence and self-sufficiency that its own land gave it. Collectivization re-moved the basis for this traditional pride, leaving the peasant-worker with the negative self-image of doing long, hard, dirty work subject to others' orders. Collectivization in combination with the agricultural policies of the early 1950s and the realistic, higher-status alternative to agriculture provided by rapid industrialization and the attraction of the cities proved a crushing blow.

The 1960s and 1970s have witnessed efforts of collective farm members to ensure their children a better life than their own—a life outside agri-culture, often ideally a white-collar job.[1] A chief avenue has been educa-tion, a possibility opened to the nation's poor by the postwar government. Increasingly, parents not only put their children through the newly estab-lished minimum of eight grades, but also enroll them in commercial and technical schools, as well as *gimnázium*-s (secondary schools), leading to teacher training or the university for some. All this has prepared youth for a life outside the village. Indeed, education beyond the eighth grade, insofar as it involves attending a school outside the village, usually in a larger city, and almost always living there as well, provides a preliminary assimilation into a nonvillage environment. So frequently has education been a ticket out of Kislapos that villagers often say any youth staying in the collective farm "couldn't learn" or "did not come up to the mark in school."

1. This is also true of other areas in Eastern Europe where agricultural develop-ment for a long time was subordinated to industrial expansion. However, unlike Hungary, in many of these countries (e.g., Romania) the low status of working in agriculture and the tendency of youths to find work outside agriculture are exacer-bated by the continued low wages of the agricultural sphere compared to other areas (Sampson 1976: 332, 333, 340).

Thus, as Andorka (1979: 86–87) has noted, the pattern of movement away from agriculture has changed considerably since the late 1950s and early 1960s. Until then youths of peasant households became for the most part unskilled laborers, whereas today they are increasingly learning a trade or skill. The form of mobility has fundamentally changed: whereas earlier it was for the most part adult working peasants becoming unskilled industrial and other nonagricultural workers, in recent years the sons (and daughters) of peasants have learned a trade before the start of their working lives and have entered the work world as skilled tradesmen.

In encouraging their children to study further, parents now consciously spare them from much of the household labor and agricultural work still engaged in by the family. This is not to say that small children do not help with household chores and that children even in secondary schools and universities do not work in the houseplot. They do. However, there is such a difference between this and the near adult work expected of children in the past that the child's present work status in the family is much more comparable to an urban child's position.[2] Some of this reduced workload can be attributed to the reduced load of the family enterprise now that the collective farm has taken over much of its work. But there is considerable evidence that parents' attitudes toward their children have changed and that this has been a major factor in the reduced workloads.

This trend is reflected in many ways. Sárkány (1978: 120), for example, reports that teachers in Varsány feel that parents often spoil their children, giving them large amounts of spending money and expending too much for their clothing. Jávor (1978: 308, 353) comes to a similar conclusion and suggests that, whereas in the past the esteem by which children were held in the community was based on the standing of their parents, today parents' worth is measured in terms of the size of their material sacrifices for their children. Parents expect nothing from their children except that they accept the parents' material sacrifices; thus, they "use their children as a signboard of the family's financial situation" in the local competition for prestige (ibid.: 350). The prestige competition is not so severe in Lapos, but families do expect a great deal less today from their offspring in childhood.

The mere fact that the child is away from home from the eighth grade on, as much as or more than he is present there, removes him from much of the family work cycle—a development that recent events in Kislapos have further exacerbated. The transfer of grades five through eight in the

2. The amount of work children do at home also seems to vary from village to village. Erdei (1971: 80–81) describes how, in some villages surrounding Szeged, children, in addition to attending school, are expected to spend a substantial part of their free time working in the garden or houseplot: "At daybreak and in the evening they water, weed, hoe and tie, and afterwards go to school or prepare for the next day."

village school to Boros, nineteen kilometers away by bus, has taken children out of the work cycle at an even earlier age than before. Living in dormitories, children attending this school come home only on weekends; parents, happy to see them, are now more inclined to spare their children from work.

Though characteristic of most of Lapos's households, the two tendencies of the continuing age- and sex-based division of labor and the reduced work role of children in the family are not uniform across all occupational and income groups. The willingness to keep up a household enterprise, a prime determinant of the household division of labor, is much lower among the very old, the young, and those with the highest incomes (the higher administrative and leadership positions in the collective farm). These groups increasingly elect to take their plot in kind or money. The elderly, for whom cultivation is now too demanding but the grain desirable for raising poultry and a couple of pigs, prefer the former; the younger generation often choose the latter, preferring a more comfortable life with less physical labor. Members of the new managerial stratum, some of whom are young and well educated, and most of whom enjoy higher than average earnings, prefer greater free time, have grown unaccustomed to physical labor, and, outside of raising some pigs and poultry, have little need for the extra income of a full houseplot enterprise.

In the context of a full stem family, these differences are not so significant. Due to the work-intensive nature of the household enterprise, it is rare for households to work much more than two full plots (two hold-s of land). Thus, even if the younger or older couple (retired or active) does not take the land to which it is entitled, the household will still have one or two hold-s of land in addition to a garden to cultivate, as well as the money or grain received in lieu of land. László Vas's family illustrates how even in a nuclear household with sufficient active labor this can be true:

> László Vas is a brigade leader. His sons, twenty and twenty-three years old, are both metalworkers in the collective farm; the former works in an auxiliary plant in Gödör and the latter in the maintenance shop in Kistó. The younger son is an employee of the farm and is entitled to a one-half hold houseplot; his older brother is a member and, like his father, receives a full hold. The family cultivates the one and a half hold-s of the father and younger son and takes the remaining hold in cash. The housewife mother is principally responsible for the houseplot enterprise and receives weekend and occasional evening help from the male family members.

The managerial class requires less work at home or on the land from children (partly because their wives work less often for the farm, which leaves them more time to work the plot, and partly because they more often take the plot in kind or cash), but differences among strata are small.

The allocation of spheres of responsibility within the family by sex has not changed appreciably. Women are still the mainstay of domestic life. They are closer to their children than are their husbands and have greater concern for and understanding of their feelings, desires, and problems. Mothers still feel largely responsible for the school results of their offspring and often spend time going over their homework with them. As one forty-eight-year-old mother of three expressed it:

[Their father] . . . doesn't much want to accept what the youngsters say . . . Generally men are like this . . . In every family the woman sustains [the family]. She gives the entertainment, she sets the mood entirely in the family. Consider how that child is; if they come home and I also set myself against them, the child longs to go away. But this way he wants to come home.

The men, more distant, are more interested in good behavior and achievement.

Some signs of change are evident. The younger generation is more concerned with sharing family responsibilities. Educated young fathers have become more interested in the care and teaching of their children and in developing a closer emotional attachment to them. This is especially true of youth who ultimately leave the village for urban areas and of the more skilled, technically trained young men who work in less traditional agricultural occupations (tractor drivers, agronomists, maintenance men, administrators).

Even among older families there is evidence of changed expectations, though male behavior may not correspond to them. In several families women in their late thirties and early forties complain about their husbands' inadequate interest in the children and their unwillingness to go over schoolwork with them. Even those generations whom the school and youth organizations have had little chance to influence watch television, listen to the radio, and read newspapers and magazines aiming to educate the populace in new ways. In general, though, it continues to be the woman's role to provide the social glue of emotional closeness in the family.

The care of the family's purse remains, at least formally, in the hands of the wife, but changes have occurred. Young spouses usually emphasize that decisions concerning expenditures are made jointly, although it is the woman who handles the money. Others, including the children, may have access to it.

Overall, much of the division of labor is still traditionally defined, and spheres of responsibility have not changed significantly. But there is a greater tendency for mutuality of interests to be considered, and some blurring of sex roles is occurring, especially among younger couples.

DISTRIBUTION OF POWER

It is in this area that the family has most significantly changed. The agricultural policies of the 1950s undermined the viability of family farms and led young and old alike to question the desirability of staying on the family farm. This led many youth to seek work outside the family and village and the control of parents. Collectivization removed the material basis for parental power in families where children remained home. With the loss of control over his land, the gazda lost much of his dominance in the family. He was no longer the leader of an enterprise, but at best the family's representative in the collective farm (and later not even solely that). He no longer really had the authority or the arena in which to direct his grown children living at home. Aside from the land rent paid by the collective annually for use of his land, an amount that was soon small in relation to income from work for the collective, the former gazda's income was likely to be small compared to that of his grown son and perhaps even his meny. Less able to bear heavy physical labor than younger men and untrained in skills commanding higher pay, like tractor driving, older members often earned less than their sons; retirement in the early years of the collective guaranteed the magnification of this discrepancy, as pensions were based on income during the previous few years and the number of years employed and thus were very small for the earliest farm pensioners. As a result, instead of being able to provide through land the means of support both for himself and his children, the aged head of the stem family was reduced to near financial dependence on his own progeny.

These statements are true of older parents and their children currently in their thirties and forties, but the situation is somewhat different for children now in their teens, twenties, and thirties, who reached a responsible age under collectivization, and more of whom leave Kislapos than before. Their parents never really experienced the taste of power based on land. Although these parents now possess much greater financial resources than do their elders, they use them in a way that lends a far different quality to the parent-child relation than that of the past, or of the eldest generation with its children.

The gazdasszony of the now eldest generation also lost influence, but to a lesser extent, as her authority rested less on economic power. However, when her meny and son were able to enjoy an independent income of their own, her power waned as well. It is apparent that this was a slower change. Disagreements between the older woman and her meny, particularly where the mother-in-law seeks to assert her authority and her meny feels that she "butts into everything," were characteristic of many households and exist even today. These continue to be a frequent cause of the stem family's breakup.

Initially the work organization of the collective farm helped to retard these developments, but this proved only temporary. As noted previously, early conceptions, including the retention of the family as a productive unit within the collective, allowed one member of each family, the head, to join the farm, although considerable work for the farm was done by other family members. The fact that work units were credited to the family head no matter who actually did the work allowed the older couple to retain some control over resources.

The initial private plot arrangement entitling each member family to a maximum of one hold made it more fruitful for the young couple to form a "separate" family.[3] They, too, could have a plot. Later rule changes allowing all adult family members to join further decreased the older couple's hold.

The growing frequency of nuclear families has also decreased the influence of the older generation. Young couples now more often set up nuclear households after marriage, immediately removing themselves from their parents' daily control. In fact, most now leave the village altogether after marriage. Those who do not are more able and willing than young couples of the past to leave their parents' households should disagreements develop. Even when they do remain home, fewer are on one bread with their parents than in the past. They are more likely to keep their money separate, live in a different part of the house, and even eat separately. Young couples staying in the village are more willing to live with the wife's parents than before; vő-s are no longer as ill-treated or stigmatized as their predecessors were, and older couples who wish their children to live with them have to concede more to them because of the very real possibility of their moving in with the nász-s or leaving home altogether.

All this has led to parents giving far more help, particularly monetary, to young couples, both those staying home and those leaving. Much greater attention is given to the young couple's needs and desires, and correspondingly more attention is granted children and their goals, than was true in the past.

Illustrating these trends are the three areas of money handling, choice of the child's spouse, and choice of occupation. Money is treated more

3. Of course, this separateness, similar to the tactics used by villagers in the 1950s to reduce compulsory delivery quotas, may have been more apparent than real. This seems to be the case today in rural Romania, where "tax laws make it advantageous for a household to appear nuclear," so that it is misleading to draw conclusions about village household structures on the basis of statistics derived from village registers (Sampson 1976: 331).

openly nowadays. It is neither hidden from children, nor kept for disbursement by parents to the near exclusion of the younger couple. There is greater emphasis on mutual interests of the old and the young in deciding about expenditures. Most older couples spend more on their children than on themselves.

The choice of marital partners is now almost exclusively that of the potential spouses. Although parents can and do object to some of their children's choices, they make relatively little active effort to point their children in the direction of a certain someone and do not try to choose. Pressure exerted against a potential spouse is primarily emotional, not material. Land is now irrelevant, although parents do offer considerable material aid to their married offspring; they do not seem to use such potential aid as a weapon of pressure in this decision-making. Most children now choose a spouse from outside Kislapos, marrying someone met in the course of schooling, work, or recreation elsewhere. Thus, parents have even less control. While there are some widely known cases of villagers pressured into marriages by parents as recently as the late 1950s—marriages ending in a quick divorce or annulment—no such cases have been noted in the period since.

Once the choice has been made, some parents negotiate with their prospective nász-s about who is to give what and how much to the engaged pair. It is rumored that one engagement of a young couple in Kislapos fell through several years ago at this stage. The moderately prosperous parents of the groom offered to buy a house for the couple and suggested that the other parents buy a car and the furniture, so that, as one sixty-year-old informant put it, the gifts "would be in proportion." The other couple lacked the money, and the negotiations broke down. The informant justified such agreements by reasoning that if, for example, without such an agreement the young husband were to die, the property would be in both their names and the wife would receive it all. But had the families split the expenses in this way, then the husband's parents would also receive a share in the house they had given (presumably the agreement would allow them to retain some legal right in the house; rough equality of gifts would then leave the widow with other property of her own).

This example and the analysis of Jávor (1978: 350–351) in the village of Varsány suggest that in some cases and in some places parental influence may be greater than described above. She emphasizes the importance of parental financial support, especially when both spouses are from the same village, in establishing a household and notes that few couples are willing to incur the wrath of their parents (and the financial loss and hardships that might accompany it) at the time of their marriage or afterward by not following parental wishes.

Parents take a greater part in their children's occupational choices than they do in their marital selections, but compared to the past there is far less pressure toward any particular area. Occasionally parents push children into fields they dislike; in the late 1960s a grandfather even prevailed over the desires of both his granddaughter and her parents and sent her to an agricultural technical school (which, however, she did not finish). There is virtually no parental pressure now to stay in agriculture and even relatively little to stay at home. As late as the 1950s some youngest sons remained with their parents in agriculture only because of their parents' pleas. Today parents claim, and most youths agree, that what he does in the future is essentially the child's choice.

Male dominance within the family has decreased significantly. Few decisions are now unilateral. Those factors that once reinforced the ideal of male authority—ownership of land, unequal inheritance, and patrilocal residence—have decreased in importance and frequency. The increased economic importance of women, made possible by the existence of independent earnings outside the home, has also undermined this cultural ideal. Finally, as Sas (1973: 194) and Jávor (1978: 332, 338) have pointed out, the week-long absences of men commuting to industrial jobs in the cities have left many wives of peasant-worker families at the helm of the houseplot enterprise and the household. They make the daily decisions in the family and have developed an independent existence of their own. Although in Lapos the number of such peasant-worker families with commuters is relatively small because of the poor local public transportation, this is an important factor elsewhere, and the village is not left untouched by nationwide trends.

INHERITANCE AND THE HOUSEHOLD CYCLE

Inheritance of family property no longer occupies the preeminent position it held in the days of independent peasant enterprises. Two major factors are responsible: 1) the loss of privately owned land through collectivization and the ensuing loss of value assigned to land; and 2) the increased tendency of parents to transfer their assets during their own lifetimes to their children.

Today, inheritance primarily involves the division among survivors of the house, garden, and personal possessions. With the exception of those who have kept more than one hold of land and not joined the collective farm, there is little land of importance to be inherited. Land shares in the collective (the land given in by members, on which they receive rental payments from the collective) are inheritable, but they can be passed on only to descendants who are members. As children increasingly leave the village behind, more land reverts to collective ownership. Moreover, the value of the rental payment in proportion to earned income is steadily dropping, making it still less important.

Ideally, the house and other possessions are divided equally among all children, male and female. As in the past, allowances are made for furniture and cash given at the time of marriage, especially to brides. Children caring for infirm parents are usually given a larger share. To gain a clearer perspective on these principles and to understand other possibilities, let us examine a few cases, the first a relatively simple one.

When the mother of Mrs. Ferenc Fehér, a widow with two married daughters, died in 1968 a year after her husband, the parents' house and garden were divided equally among Mrs. Fehér and her two younger brothers (one had died a year earlier, so his share went to his family) in Budapest. Mrs. Fehér's daughters, Mrs. György Burom and Mrs. Illés Szabó, both had their own homes, for they had married an only son and an only child, respectively; however, Mrs. Burom's home would be divided with her husband's two married sisters upon the death of her widowed mother-in-law. Desiring to build a new house of their own, Mrs. Burom and her husband bought out the two one-third shares of Mrs. Fehér's brothers and received the remaining share as a gift from Mrs. Fehér, who had a home of her own. They tore down the old house and moved out of their old home at the completion of the new building. György Burom's mother continues to live with them, while Mrs. Fehér lives alone. (She is still in good health, and both her daughters live with their mothers-in-law.) Mrs. Fehér, although not legally required to, felt obligated to treat her other daughter equally and gave her a one-third share of the old house in cash.

This example illustrates the equality of inherited shares and the frequency with which one sibling or relative buys out the share of another. Although this did happen in the past, it is more frequent and easier now. The increased tendency for people to migrate from Kislapos and the resulting lack of demand for houses has kept prices down, making it easier to buy and leaving fewer siblings who remain in the village interested in keeping them. The absence of land, formerly the most valuable part of one's holdings, and the increased incomes of villagers, particularly relative to the price of old housing in Lapos, have made buying the whole estate of the deceased easier.

This case also exemplifies the greater willingness, indeed desire, of parents to part with their property in their own lifetimes. Although it was not unheard of to present married children with a home, furniture, some animals, cash, or a bit of land in the past, with the exception of furnishings it was generally a prospect only for the well-to-do.

The share of a child caring for an aged parent is usually the largest. The size of the increment is dependent on a number of factors. For example:

Several years ago, László Vas and his two widowed sisters decided that the youngest sister should take care of their father, a widower then in his sixties. This sister and her two sons lived in the home earlier offered her husband and herself by her father-in-law. It was one of four facing onto a common yard. Tired of the crowding, she agreed to care for her father and moved with her children into his home. With houses of their own, her two siblings gave up all claims to their father's house in return for seeing their father cared for. (Their father's drinking problem probably played a part in their generosity.)

Infirmity and age also lead to generous settlements for caretaker children.

Ernő Harangi's four siblings, each with their own homes, decided that their young twenty-five-year-old brother and his wife should be the sole beneficiaries of their parents' house. The young couple live with Ernő Harangi's recently retired sixty-year-old widowed mother and his ninety-nine-year-old infirm grandmother.

Sometimes such agreements are changed through the years.

Margit Burom and her three sisters, all married, lived in Lapos (recently all three, one after the other, have moved away with their families). Their parents lived alone. About sixteen years before her death, Margit Burom's mother was crippled by arthritis. Margit Burom volunteered to care for her, taking food to her parents and doing their washing and cleaning. When her father died fifteen years later, she received half the house for her efforts (the sisters had given up their shares of that half to her) and her mother retained the rest. Margit Burom then told her sisters that she could no longer care for her mother, since she also had to care for her aged father-in-law and her own family at home. When the sisters met to negotiate the estate, Margit Burom, who with her husband already owned a house, agreed to give up her half of the house to another sister if she would take over the care of their mother. They agreed; when the mother died a year later, the sister received the lion's share of the house for the one year of care. The few hold-s of land were split evenly among the sisters, so that each received a little land rent from the collective farm. Margit Burom ultimately remained disappointed at her small share of the estate after her years of effort.

One extended history exemplifies several of the principles discussed here.

When Gizella Nagy died in the 1920s, her husband, István Harangi, married Klára Vernel, a widow whose first husband, Ferenc Urbán, had died in World War I, leaving a daughter, Vilma Urbán. István Harangi and Gizella Nagy had had one child, István Harangi, Jr., who married and had one son, István Harangi III, before his early death. The wife of István Harangi, Jr., inherited a house through him in which his maternal grandmother still lived; he left rights of usufruct to his grandmother, however. When the grandmother died, the wife had already remarried, so the son (István Harangi III) inherited the house. He had left the village, and he rented the house to the collective farm, which gave it out in 1959 or 1960 to a poor family that moved into the village from the tanya used by the Kossuth collective.

Ultimately, the youngest István Harangi sold the house to that family.

In the meantime, István Harangi and Klára Vernel had a son, Rudolf Harangi, and two daughters, Mária and Erzsébet Harangi. Rudolf, as the only son, stayed home; the two sisters left home at marriage. Erzsébet married a carpenter in Kistó but soon returned with him to Kislapos, where he had less competition and more work. He eventually set up a small undertaking business as well. Mária married a middle peasant in Lapos. Rudolf and his wife lived at home with his mother, Klára Vernel, after István Harangi died. After they had had two children, Rudolf and his wife moved in with his parents-in-law because his wife could not get along with his mother. When in the 1960s Klára Vernel became unable to care for herself, the children decided to split the house and garden. The house was divided among Klára Vernel's four children, as it was originally her father's house; this excluded István Harangi, Jr. It was divided five ways, however: each sibling received one share and Mária Harangi two, since the mother stayed with her. Klára Vernel had stayed with the others and with her daughter Vilma Urbán, who lived in Kistó, but felt best at Mária's. The extra share was also to cover the cost of burial. Klára Vernel lived with Mária and her husband until Mária herself became ill. Her sister Erzsébet offered to take care of their mother for a couple of months. During that time, in 1974, their mother died. In the meantime, Erzsébet had bought new furniture and had borrowed 5,000 forint-s from Mária. Erzsébet and Mária had married at the same time. At that time Erzsébet received money for furniture; Mária received money only later because at the time her mother was short of funds. However, Mária's gift was greater than her sister's, so when Mária bought out the other shares of the house and garden for 8,000 forint-s each, she paid 8,000 forint-s to Erzsébet and the debt was forgotten. Since then the house has been torn down and Mária works the enlarged garden. The land was split evenly among the four.

All of István Harangi's children except his step-daughter Vilma Urbán shared in the house in which he had lived with Gizella Nagy.

This case highlights several trends: the earlier and continued tendency to allot more to that child who cared for the parent; the frequency of usufruct rights distinguished from rights of ownership; and the degree to which inheritance is subject to negotiation among the beneficiaries, often together with the living parent. Some complex divisions are often involved. It is likely that earlier transfers of property in the above case involved divisions of the inheritance and subsequent buying out, but that the informant was not as aware of these transactions as of later ones.

What these and other cases show is that the basic principles of inheritance did not substantially change during the first decade or so following collectivization. The timing of these transfers of property, the amount of voice the children have in ultimate disposition, and the relative importance of inherited property have changed. Collectivization was largely responsible for the latter shift. The trend toward nuclear families and a variety of historical and social changes seem to have brought about the former two.

In more recent years, however, much of the transfer of property has occurred even earlier. Increased earnings and only smaller increases in personal consumption have allowed parents to give steadily greater gifts to newly married children, including houses in the city, automobiles, household appliances, and furniture. This has led in many ways to greater independence from village norms and parental domination for the younger couple. Zsigmond (1978: 157–163) and Jávor (1978: 337) note that in the village of Varsány gifts to newlyweds have increased so rapidly in value that children who married but a few years earlier have become jealous and even sought financial redress from parents.

One other important effect of the decreased value of land should be noted. With the drop in importance of inherited wealth and the greater degree of material equality in the village and in Hungarian society in general, marital choices are less governed by gross material considerations than in the past. Landed wealth obviously is of no import; neither is parents' past socioeconomic status accorded great consideration. Indirectly, however, past and present socioeconomic status do affect marital choice insofar as they influence the other characteristics thought important in a spouse. For example, children of middle peasants in Lapos and elsewhere (compare Sárkány 1978: 111; Jávor 1978: 324–325) are still better educated in general than those of former cseléd-s, although these differences are disappearing. The high degree of intra- and intergenerational social mobility in the decade following World War II has helped to mitigate these differences, although it has not eliminated them. Social stratification now has a different basis. However, Zsigmond (1978: 159–160) finds that in Varsány "the village's most prosperous families consciously intertwine their ties of marriage, friendship, and common schooling, so that from a certain standpoint the strengthening of their prestige and isolation can be noted"; by the same token, the descendants of the former smallholders and farmhands, who make up the majority of the village, maintain their own distinct marriage "system." In Lapos such divisions are much less salient.

Besides personal characteristics that are thought important in marriage, such as similar interests and tastes, dependability and sincerity, and love of children, such social characteristics as levels of education and job training now receive emphasis, with equality or near equality preferred.[4]

Regarding the trend toward nuclear households, over the past half-

4. See Szilágyi (1971: 100). It should be noted, however, that wealth, such as cars or flats, is also taken into consideration. Classified advertisements by those seeking marital partners, usually but not always widows, divorced individuals, bachelors, and spinsters, place great emphasis on the possession of these items. A topic of debate in Hungary is the alleged tendency for people to place too much emphasis on material goods in the search for a spouse. Zsigmond (1978: 159–

century family size has decreased. The drop in birthrate throughout this period has been partially responsible. Equally important has been the pre-World War II switch from the joint family to the stem family and the postwar trend toward the nuclear family. The latter, along with the drop in the birthrate, is not unique to Kislapos, having occurred nationwide.[5]

Lacking comparable earlier data about the frequencies of different forms of family units in Kislapos, it is difficult to make descriptive statements about the nature of the change there over time. Fortunately, data exist from the early 1940s for nearby Átány, drawn from the family files prepared by the village pastor to register social status and church-tax payments of his flock (Fél and Hofer 1969: 403–406). It is an almost total sample of the village population. Kislapos's figures are drawn from January 1976 for the total non-Gypsy population (see Tables 7.1 and 7.2). Clearly, conclusions drawn from such a comparison are questionable, but it is worth looking at some of the major differences, which are quite suggestive. Furthermore, other data indicate that differences in family form frequencies between wartime Átány and Lapos were relatively small. Átány's greater number of peasants with ten or more hold-s implies that it may have had a slightly higher percentage of stem and joint families than Kislapos, since both household size and percentage of stem and joint households increase with the size of landholdings in Átány (Fél and Hofer 1969: 403–406).

Thus, Kislapos's almost 52 percent of nuclear households in 1976 compared to Átány's almost 48 percent in the early 1940s suggests little change. On the other hand, if we 1) look at the respective numbers of family fragments and stem families, 2) compare the numbers of incomplete and complete stem families in each population, and 3) break down the nuclear families into those of married couples living alone and couples living with their unmarried children, more substantial differences emerge.

In contemporary Kislapos, almost one-quarter of the households are family fragments, compared to less than 9 percent in wartime Átány; stem

160), for example, points out that in Varsány "although both parents and youth testify that in the marriages of the generation being considered selection from a financial standpoint does not prevail, it can be shown that they see this for the most part in relation to earlier conditions and that they view the newer material considerations as different from, and not identical with, these. [The children] . . . do not consider the newly acquired goods, and, although every youth conclusively judges his own marriage as a 'love match,' it turns out that in every case finely shaded family consideration and negotiations preceded even those marriages concluded in the early 1970s."

5. For example, census figures show a drop in the average family size from 3.36 in 1960 to 3.09 in 1970 in Hungarian towns and villages, excluding Budapest and the larger cities (Hegedüs 1970: 113; Kulcsár 1976: 277).

Table 7.2   Forms of Family Units, Átány, 1942–1945

Household Types	Number of Households		Number of Persons	
Fragments				
Single widows or widowers	19	3.84%	19	.93%
Bachelors	3	.61	3	.15
Widowed with family members	21	4.24	63	3.10
	43	8.69%	85	4.18%
Nuclear				
Married couples	65	13.13%	131	6.44%
Married couples and children	169	34.14	691	33.99
	234	47.27%	822	40.43%
Stem				
Incomplete	95	19.19%	433	21.30%
Complete	116	23.43	642	31.58
	211	42.62%	1075	52.88%
Joint families	7	1.41%	52	2.56%
	495 = 100%		2,034 = 100%	

NOTE: Adapted from Fél and Hofer (1969: 405). Some percentages and totals have been corrected.

families in Lapos constitute only 23 percent of the households, compared to earlier Átány's 43 percent. These figures suggest several possibilities. Children are increasingly leaving their parents' households at marriage or soon thereafter. Thus, what were once stem families, particularly incomplete ones, are now family fragments and nuclear families. This view finds support in the large proportion (almost 60 percent) of these fragmentary households that are a result of all children leaving home. The sizable number (37 percent) of families in which all children have left the village points to another major trend. Of course, it could be argued that with a decreased birthrate and fewer children, for an aged parent to end up living alone fewer couples have to establish independent households than in the past. One could further argue that this great rise in the number of fragmentary units is a function of decreased birthrate. This is partly true, but it ignores the fact that children are more willing (and able) to leave parents home alone.

Looking at the stem families shows that, whereas in Átány in the early 1940s there were more complete families than incomplete, in Kislapos today incomplete stem families outnumber by three to one those with both parents present. This cannot be explained by a longer life span, for then the opposite should result. Rather, this is a result of children increasingly leaving home and then taking in, or moving in with, a widowed parent in later years. They may also be less likely to leave a widowed parent than to leave a living couple.

This idea finds some support in the almost equal number of nuclear couples without children as with children at home living in Lapos, whereas in wartime Átány nuclear families with unmarried children at home were more than two and a half times as common as their solitary couple counterparts. This points up the fact that more older nuclear couples live in Lapos now than younger ones. That younger nuclear couples are far more likely to leave the community is emphasized by the fact that the more than 70 percent of nuclear couples living alone have children who have all left the village.

The simple reason that nuclear couples in Kislapos today are not much more common than in yesterday's Átány is that the younger couples and the young in general leave the village completely. They are not counted in these statistics.

The overwhelming tendency for Kislapos's young to leave home and to establish nuclear households at marriage or within a few years is not limited to older children but extends to younger and only children who in years past would have remained with their parents. Increasingly, both parents and children feel that it is better to live separately, that there are far fewer problems this way, particularly for the young couple.

That the younger generation feels this way is not surprising; in fact, it may not be much of a change. In the past, aside from being the cultural norm, staying at home generally meant a more secure and materially easy life than starting out on one's own. There often was a price to be paid, of course—suffering the somewhat tyrannical authority of parents, and, for the meny, the mother-in-law. As one middle-aged informant described the pre-cooperative days, "the meny accommodated herself to her mother-in-law; they came to terms and things were fine. If they [the younger couple] couldn't take it, then they had to go separately. That was trouble. Then they moved away from there." He stated that this sometimes happened, but that it was better if they could come to an agreement and stay, since then "they made more headway." A few informants argued that a man was better off working for himself than for the common good due to be inherited partly by others; but this seems a matter of personal taste. Furthermore, the independence from parental authority in the past was often purchased by substitution of frequently tyrannical authority in harvesting, day labor, and even sharecropping. It was often desirable to get out from under the influence of the older generation and to be more independent, but the material and sometimes social costs were too high.

What caused this change? No one historical, social, or cultural factor alone sufficiently explains it. A combination of historical events, government policies, geographic factors, and social changes within the family has led to this, as observed earlier. Even before the major and final phase of collectivization occurred in the village in 1959, several nationwide developments had led to a changed environment and outlook for a large portion of the peasantry: large-scale government development of heavy industry at the expense of much-needed agricultural investment in the early 1950s; progressively scaled taxes and compulsory deliveries of agricultural produce designed to provide the population with low-cost food, but serving in the 1950s to deprive wealthy peasants particularly (but middle peasants and smallholders as well) of the motivation and sometimes means to continue private production; the antikulak drives and other measures, which also intimidated and affected a sizable portion of middle peasants; and the well-intended but often ill-conceived, poorly funded, and forced collectivization of the early 1950s following on the heels of the hopes for economic and social independence that had been raised among the former landless and smallholders by the popular and long overdue land reform of 1945. These all served to channel labor from agriculture to industry and the cities and to cause the peasantry to question the validity of continuing the peasant way of life, of the son following in the footsteps of the father, of the honor to be gained from one's own land. A common result of that period was a dramatic increase in the numbers commuting from the villages to industrial centers, a rise in peasant-worker families in which sons and fathers would come home on weekends or even less frequently to see their families and to help out with the agricultural work carried on by the rest of the family in their absence.

In Kislapos this meant that a large number of mainly younger men commuted to the mines, factories, and construction sites in the mountains, to the industrial centers to the north and in Budapest, and to the railroads connecting them. Frequently, youngest sons living at home with smallholder and even middle peasant parents left for these jobs. They and their families felt that it simply was not worthwhile for them to put their labor into the family farms. Given the restrictions on and difficulties in farming, such industrial work was viewed as a better way of earning a cash income, of supplementing the often meager leavings after compulsory deliveries. Many left agriculture and Lapos altogether.

Compared to many better situated rural communities, relatively few in Lapos remained commuters throughout the early 1950s. Most either came back to agriculture in the village or moved away completely. The lack of local industry and the village's poor standing in the transportation network made finding nonagricultural work locally and commuting daily very difficult. Thus, the peasant-worker family, in which part of the household income is derived from agriculture, but in which at least one member works outside the agricultural sphere, increased in numbers more slowly in Kislapos than elsewhere. This was especially true of households where the nonagricultural worker stayed home or commuted daily.

Collectivization brought a renewed surge in the numbers of migrants and commuters. Though many returned after a few years to the collective farm, they were often not as willing to return to a traditional family in which parents exercised authority.

Collectivization, along with changed attitudes toward agricultural labor, parents' new aspirations for their children, the poor position of Kislapos in the transportation network, the poorly developed infrastructure, and the lack of nearby industry have led to increased outmigration, especially of the young to the cities. This has affected the relationships of parents to their married children remaining in the village, as well as to those leaving. The empty housing left by this exodus and the depressed market value of these houses have made it much easier for younger couples to establish separate households. The removal by collectivization of much of the power over material resources from the hands of parents and the availability of income to the young, independent of their parents, have left young couples less willing to endure the continued attempts by some parents to exercise authority. This relative financial independence and the availability of housing have led to a situation in which considerably less provocation has been required by the younger couples in stem families to break away. Thus, not only couples leaving the village but couples staying are more likely to establish nuclear households, frequently even some years after marriage.

Situations abound in which couples lived for several months or even years with parents before disagreements led to a breakup. Typically, a young meny living with her husband's parents finds that her mother-in-law is "dissatisfied with everything" as she does it; there may be a struggle over who will be the gazdasszony in the household, or else everyone will find the situation is unendurable with "two gazdasszony-s in the house." In the past, young husbands sometimes stood by powerlessly, but today they usually side with their wives in these arguments; if the disagreements cannot be ironed out, the younger couple moves. In rare cases husbands have sided with their mothers. In one instance the husband remarked that he could replace his wife but not his mother, which led to a speedy divorce.

Other problems are also possible.

Three brothers, all of whom drink a great deal, got along very poorly with their respective parents-in-law.

 Zsigmond Heves and his wife lived for a year or two with her widowed mother.

With her high-strung and short-tempered nature, the mother-in-law had little patience with her vő's drinking; they argued constantly. The young couple then moved in with his widowed mother, but left after six months to buy a house of their own because Zsigmond Heves's wife did not get along with her mother-in-law.

Lajos Heves and his wife left her parents' home after a year because her father strongly disapproved of her husband's heavy drinking, and she did not want to see them arguing so frequently. They bought a house of their own with their savings and a loan from the collective farm.

János Heves and his wife still live at her mother's home after more than fifteen years, but disagreements between her mother and János Heves punctuate the relationship.

More common today are young couples living at home for several years with parents and working in jobs outside the village, usually non-agricultural, who elect to move to one of the larger towns and cities within a forty-kilometer radius of Kislapos. Today those who stay for a year or two have planned from the start to leave after this time, using the period at home to augment their savings or to wait until their house or flat in the city is completed. In years past, some such couples starting out at home planned to settle in the village, but after a few years they found the daily inconvenience of commuting and the village's shortage of cultural, recreational, social, and shopping facilities too trying to continue. The absence of child-care facilities, the move of the school's upper grades to Boros, and the unwelcome influx of Gypsies have exacerbated this tendency and led even established couples in their thirties to leave the village and their parents for new homes and jobs in the city.

Ernő Kis [the son of János Kis, mentioned in Chapter 3], a thirty-seven-year-old only son, and the latter's thirty-six-year-old wife, also from Kislapos, moved in with his parents after their marriage in 1961. At first a driver in the nearby state tractor station, Ernő Kis joined the cooperative as a tractor driver a few years later when maintenance facilities and tractors were transferred to the farm. Since 1959 his wife has worked in the fields for the collective; having some horticultural training, she has taken a greater role in the cultivation of seedlings and greenhouse work in the winter and works more hours annually, with greater resulting income, than most women doing essentially physical labor for the farm. They have an eleven-year-old daughter.

In the early 1960s the couple bought a motorcycle, which they used for frequent small outings. In 1971, with the help of parents, they bought a used car and two years later a new one, in which they often went on outings to nearby towns for shopping, and occasionally to the theater in Eger. During these years they went on tours arranged through the collective farm to Italy, Czechoslovakia, and Russia. In September 1976 they moved into a flat in Eger, which they had bought. Despite leaving home and a good relationship with parents, the probability of lower incomes, and the lack of a garden in Eger, they feel their move is justified. Their daughter, then entering the fifth grade, will not have to go away from home to school, their work hours will be shorter and less physically demanding, and their dissatisfaction over the collective farm's treatment of workers, over its leadership and favoritism, will no longer be a problem and cause tension for them. They bought the house for their daughter and think it will be hers when she marries. They would move back to Kislapos then or at retirement, since their parents' house will still be available then.

Similar reasons have motivated others to move.

Mihály Kalicz, thirty-eight, his thirty-year-old wife, and eleven-year-old daughter left Kislapos in 1976 for Eger. Mihály Kalicz had finished his military duty in 1960 and had gone to work for the railroad in Budapest, commuting every other day from Lapos. When his father died in an accident in 1964, his mother asked Mihály Kalicz, her only child, to stay at home. He did so, married a girl from Lapos soon after, and worked as a milker in the farm until his departure to Eger. His wife worked in the cooperative until illness three years ago left her too weak. They, too, wanted to avoid having their daughter go away to school and feel that now she will be able to stay at home with them through high school or technical school. In fact, they hope she will make her home with them when she marries. Mihály Kalicz feels that his new work as a truck driver will be lighter physically and, thus, easier to continue to retirement.

More frequent are couples who live in Lapos, work elsewhere, and then elect to move away after several years.

József Veres has worked for the land office in Boros for nine years but lives at home in Kislapos with his parents, wife, and small child. His wife, a native of Kistó, worked and lived in Eger until their marriage in 1972 and would have liked to stay there. However, they found rents too high and decided to live with his parents "until . . ." Before the birth of their son, now one, they both commuted daily by car to Boros, where the wife worked at City Hall. With parental aid they are having a house built now in Boros and will move in at completion. This way they will not have to commute the seventeen kilometers each way, which they find expensive and, in the winter on the poor roads, sometimes dangerous; more important, there is a preschool there, and, too, when the child reaches fifth grade he will not have to go away to school. Later the husband's parents, if they like, can come and join the couple. József Veres admits that if they did not have a child he would think twice about leaving the village, to which he has grown very accustomed. (His wife, however, may have fewer doubts.)

Gyula Berkes's daughter and son-in-law and their small son illustrate a similar situation.

They have lived with Gyula Berkes, his wife, and his aged mother since their marriage in 1970. At that time the house was enlarged to accommodate them. The young wife commutes three times a week to Boros, where she works in a pharmacy; she goes to school twice weekly in Eger to become a medical assistant. Gyula Berkes's vő, who was raised in a nearby settlement, works as a parquet buffer in construction in the northern industrial town of Salgótarján and commutes there weekly. Now that the daughter has finished her three years of maternity leave, she and her husband have decided to move to Eger, where they have put in a downpayment for a home of their own. The school situation, as well as the difficulties of commuting, were deciding factors for the young pair; the wife will no longer have to commute, and her husband will probably find a job in a local building cooperative.

Others have left the village for a combination of the reasons presented above. Gábor Molnár, his wife, and two children are a good example.

After their marriage in 1969 they rented a house in Zöldfa, the wife's home town, since the husband had younger brothers at home. The following year they returned to Lapos because his pay there as a truck driver for the collective farm was much higher than for similar work in Zöldfa's cooperative. They lived in the front part of the house with his parents and two brothers in back. When the brothers married, they left to live, respectively, in Zöldfa with the bride's widowed father and in Budapest, where the bride had been working while her fiance was in the service.

At times Gábor Molnár's wife did not get along very well with her interfering mother-in-law, but they stayed until 1976. Then they again left for Zöldfa, a move precipitated by a fierce argument between the wife and a neighbor. Soon afterward they settled in nearby Kistó, where there is a preschool for their children and a full grammar school. Public transportation is better there, and Kistó has places to which Gábor Molnár feels he can take his wife—a contrast to Kislapos and its bar. In addition, Gábor Molnár can continue to work for the same (now expanded) farm.

This example is instructive in its demonstration of the possibility now of moving and still remaining in the cooperative. It has become more popular to move to Kistó recently because of its greater size, its better facilities (school, preschool, snack bars, greater recreational possibilities) and public transportation, and its nearness to Kislapos.

The examples cited thus far have been ones in which parents have encouraged their children to stay in Lapos for at least a few years. But it is now more common for concerned parents to lead their children out of the village.

In the late 1960s, when Kristóf Pető was deciding to construct a large new house in Kislapos, his father recommended that he not build. With a good position then at the branch of a metals firm in nearby Pont, Kristóf Pető nonetheless decided in favor of construction. Now thirty-nine and managing director of the metal works branch, with a six-year-old son and a wife of eleven years, who works as fiscal secretary and tax collector for the village council, Kristóf Pető wants to move to

Budapest to take up a still better position. His parents and maternal grandmother, who have lived with the couple, will occupy the house, though it will be too big for them. If Kristóf Pető wanted to sell the house, he could not possibly recoup the money invested in it because of Lapos's depressed housing market.

Indeed, one of the most interesting and now increasingly common relations is that maintained between older parents and their married children, usually skilled laborers or white-collar workers, who live outside the village in nearby larger towns. Although many of these younger couples quite deliberately chose work outside the collective farm and agriculture, it is ironically the very success of the collective that has contributed to the ease of their relocation. Parents in the village who have maintained their relatively selfless standard of living (though often improving their housing) have sometimes made considerably more money than in the past.[6] To some degree they have kept up the consumption

6. There are some indications of conspicuous consumption among villagers, especially those thirty to forty-five years old who have high administrative positions in the collective farm or the local consumers' cooperative, and who have decided to stay and have recently built new homes in the village. As Hegedüs (1970: 52) and some villagers point out, these persons often receive higher incomes than their counterparts in industry and the city, and many may not have as much training. A number of them have built large houses that are more modern than most, the probable costs of which are clear to most villagers. Indeed, on my first appearance by myself in Kislapos, one who happened to give me a ride into the village, when he learned who I was, almost immediately told me that his new house had cost over a half-million forint-s. It is clear that these younger, better educated, somewhat more urban-oriented villagers have greater demands of comfort and convenience in a home, but it is also clear that they are proud of the amount spent. They too, along with other villagers, have taken part in rural Hungary's "fence culture," in which fences built around homes are an item of status. As if not knowing what else to do with their money, they have spent it on fences with high concrete- or even expensive stone-based, iron-slatted fencing.

Autos in the village and given to children living outside the village are also items of prestige, although as they become more common this is decreasing (as with television, now found in most homes). Although some have relatively little need of such cars, their use is increasing, and some villagers are beginning to enjoy the pleasures of easier outings, shopping, and visiting. Though other villagers are at once envious and contemptuous of fellow inhabitants who buy cars with little apparent need for them (at least to the individual voicing the opinion), this status-seeking does not begin to approach the proportions of a perhaps legendary case in another village. There a family, having recently bought a car that no member could drive, pushed it out in front of the house every Sunday, spent the day sitting in it, and pushed it back into the garage in the evening.

Nor does it approach the more typical level seen in Varsány (Jávor 1978: 308–309), where more emphasis is placed than in Lapos on iron fencing, height of houses, decorative mansard roofs (of which twenty were built even after a 5,000 forint fine—almost two months' wages—was levied locally on their construction), children's clothing, etc. It appears that this is somewhat less important in Lapos,

pattern of the past, which was adaptive to acquiring funds to buy more land. Parents now in their late forties, fifties, and even sixties (as opposed to the generation that was in their forties, fifties and sixties at collectivization and retired soon thereafter) have been able to save considerable money. This they have applied to the cost of buying houses, cars, and/or appliances for their children living in the city.[7] This is particularly true of administrative workers, skilled workers like stonemasons, and those with steady, high incomes like truck and tractor drivers and men who care for larger animals, as well as families with fewer children among whom to disperse savings.[8]

Children who do not live far from Kislapos also benefit from the private plots at home; they are often given a portion of the yield to help out with relatively high food costs. As young workers' pay is relatively low, and food and sometimes hard-to-obtain housing is expensive in relation to Hungarian earnings, all this is a tremendous help to a young couple. Though usually such help is not a sine qua non for youth or young married couples in the city, it does make all the difference in their material existence for perhaps the first twenty years of their city lives: the difference between living in an expensive crowded one-room sublet of a larger apartment while scraping together funds for a home or waiting for a public apartment to be made available and having such an apartment from the beginning, or between long hours of moonlighting and a normal work week, or between staying at home and being able to go out and enjoy some of the entertainment and culture of the city.

This aid stems from the earlier pattern of commuting family members who worked in the city taking produce, eggs, and meat to work and

---

where youngsters are more likely to leave the village at marriage. Although there is considerable pride and some boasting in Lapos about money spent on children's housing, automobiles, furnishings, and appliances, these are less visible and seem to have provoked less of a "prestige contest" than in Varsány.

7. Emphasis on increased expenditures on adult children and more modern housing for the younger generation is seen even when married children do not leave the village. Typically, when married children live with one set of parents and the house has been refurbished, the younger couple live in the modern portion of the house, while the elder couple are content with the often older, less comfortable kitchen, the back part of the house, or the separate "summer kitchen." This is a considerable shift from the subordinate position of the younger couple in the past and their often far less comfortable living conditions.

A similar pattern is evident in Hungary's tanya regions. In the past it was a goal of households living on scattered farms to build a house in the village core; the older "retired" peasants would move in, leaving the younger couple to live and work on the farm. Today it is more common for the young couple to move into the "more civilized" housing (Erdei 1971: 91).

8. See Erdei (1964: 36) and Hegedüs (1970: 62) for information on the effects of family size and increased numbers of dependents on per capita income.

bringing home their pay minus expenses. Similarly, students living away from home have traditionally brought food from home and, when resources were available, had their rooming and other costs largely paid by their parents. When entering the job market, unmarried after school, they, too, have shared and continue to share that commuter's pattern. Parents, with increasing resources and, as yet for this generation, relatively steady demands of consumption, have more available to give them now, and they sometimes purchase housing even for unmarried children.

Two examples of many illustrate this:

Béla Gazsó [of Chapter 3], a fifty-three-year-old milker in the cooperative, and his wife, forty-eight, bought a house in Eger for their twenty-six-year-old son, who works there as a turret-lathe operator. Their daughter, now twenty-three, working as a sales clerk in a store, lived there too until her marriage to an Eger man in late 1975. Both children have lived in Eger since they began their schooling there; the son went to an industrial trade school, subletting a room, served his two years in the army, and returned to work in Eger, moving into the new house at its completion.[9] The daughter attended commercial school and has since lived and worked there. The son continues to give his pay to his parents to save; they buy necessities for him, including clothing. The daughter (for whom the parents were uncertain there would be enough money for a house) decided eventually to keep her pay and buy her own clothing and whatever else she needed, such as a washing machine and a television. Until the daughter's marriage the children alternated coming home on weekends, each taking a supply of foodstuffs back to the city. On these weekend visits the children, especially the son, often helped out with work at home and in the houseplot.

Not all families are quite as well off, but the basic pattern still holds in poorer families.

Ferenc Kassa, the twenty-one-year-old son of Margit Burom, mentioned earlier, went to secondary school in Gyöngyös, where two of his mother's sisters had moved. He had wanted to be an auto mechanic, and he learned his trade there. Now living at his aunt's daughter's house, he repairs cars for a large auto repair concern, doing occasional private work in Gyöngyös and in Kislapos. He comes home weekly, giving all but 400 forint-s monthly (15–20 percent of his take-home pay) to his mother; he uses that small amount for transportation and miscellaneous expenses. He keeps the proceeds from his moonlighting in Gyöngyös for himself, covering basic costs of room, board, and entertainment, and gives much of what he earns in Kislapos to his mother. In turn, he is given money for

9. For village records, census purposes, and my village household size survey such individuals are considered to be living at home and commuting to the city. City administrative records and census surveys would show them as temporary residents. When they themselves make the administrative changes—which undoubtedly reflects a change in their felt residence status—community and census records would register this.

clothes and major expenses when he requests it and leaves with packages of food when he goes back to town. After he finishes his two years of military service, he intends to stay in Gyöngyös, where there are more opportunities for entertainment: jukeboxes, dance halls, bands, and snack bars. He says, "I come home just so that my parents can see me," but when at home he does the work "a son is responsible for": hoeing the houseplot ("I don't know how, but I do it as if I did know!"), digging, and carrying sand, gravel, and straw with his teamster father. When his mother works, he cleans and cooks what he can and also helps with the animals. Undoubtedly, his parents will help him acquire a house or flat later with his and their savings, though it is unlikely they could buy a whole house.

The parents' aid to their children does not go unreciprocated, but economically, at least, the return is small compared to the "investment." Nor is this help exclusively for the young. Children, even those well into their thirties and forties, continue to come "home" regularly to help with the work of the houseplot and other tasks. Many elderly parents also expect that when they are no longer able to care for themselves, room will be made available to them in the house or flat they bought or helped finance. However, most older parents now prefer to live alone in the village until that time despite the repeated calls of children to move in with them. For many, the change would be too great. Some feel, as does Pál Koczka, now on a disability pension though still working part-time, that they would find the life style in the city strange and would not want to impose their ways on their children. Others know of examples like the widowed Mrs. Miklós Király, who, despite misgivings about moving in with her son because of past problems with her meny, sold her house in Kislapos and went to live with them in Gyöngyös, only to have her son die of a heart attack two months later. Or of Sára Kelemen, who lived at the home of her daughter until the latter's death in childbirth, then moved in with her son's family; he ultimately sent her back to Kislapos with hardly any belongings to live with her other son. She died a pathetic figure a few months later.

Many of these parents have unspoken, though clear, expectations of being able to visit the city through their children's homes. They have easier access than before to the city's greater shopping possibilities.

More important, however, the gifts of housing, food, and cars serve to increase Hungarian family togetherness and reflect the growing importance of affective relations within the rural family. This is a common result of modernization, industrialization, and the usurpation of the economic functions from the family sphere. In the Hungarian case, all these gifts are at least to some degree based on affect and have the effect of bringing the children home more often. This is quite obvious regarding cars and food. A car is often explicitly presented in the hope that children will be able to come home more easily and often. And they do. Food, with the necessity of occasional transport and the implicit agreement to continue to help with the household plot, also serves to pull youth home. The acquisition of a home for one's children both increases the demands for affective reciprocation and frees the younger generation from the scrimping and extra work that could prevent them from visiting more often.

Close relationships with frequent personal interaction are encouraged by all these types of reciprocation. Although affection was obviously part of family life in the past, the psychological needs met through the family were subordinate to needs in the economic sphere. Recent trends have tended to increase this affective component of rural family life. With the vastly decreased economic role of the family due to farm collectivization, and the associated breakdown of the dominance order through the loss of economic and social importance of the older generation, a reversal of the parent- and older-generation-centered pattern has occurred. As less of the parents' self-esteem and personal satisfaction can be found in the role of independent leader and planner in a small private enterprise, parents are increasingly seeking such satisfaction through the lives and goals of their children. They have encouraged and helped their children to find a life outside agriculture with a higher status, and have found their children better prepared to adjust to and find their places in the changed economic and social order of modernizing Hungary.

On the other hand, starting a new life with low pay has put youth in a financial position at least temporarily lower than their parents. The latter, in turn, have used their savings and produce, not to try to maintain a superiority over their children (which might be untenable and disastrous), but rather to give their children a boost and in so doing to cement a relationship of affection and greater equality.

Of course, in its own way this aid can lead to a rigidly delimited, prescribed way of life. As Zsigmond (1978: 156–158, 163–164) points out, though all such aid promises complete material independence from the parental household, a good deal of the young couple's future life may be rigidly set.[10] In Lapos, perhaps because of the large-scale outmigration of

10. Zsigmond (1978: 156–158, 163–164) describes how in Varsány the two sets of parents frequently determine the material needs of a newly married couple, often establishing a standard of living exceeding that of both families. The couple has little say except in minor matters such as tile colors and door quality, while parents and kin select a house or choose a plot to build on and determine the house style. Because the families' desires are often beyond their means, the plans are at first only temporarily realized. In the years to come, therefore, the newly married couple of Varsány can be fixed in the pattern of completing the outline of their home, and even their lives, as set by parents. Even if they are fortunate enough to receive a completed house, there are often numerous commitments of help to kinsmen and other villagers in reciprocation for construction work; of debts to be repaid; and of aid to be given to even newer married couples. Such responsibilities, along with the birth of their own children, almost totally occupy the free time of a new couple, often forcing them to forsake activities and interests

youths and married couples, youths' lives are less enmeshed in the village pattern of commitments and parental choice.

While the loss of parental dominance is not accepted by all parents, there is increasingly a child-centeredness in the family. This can be seen in the efforts to spare children from much (but not all) of the weight of family economic chores, in the greater concern with their affairs and plans, and even in the steadily increasing use of the reciprocal *te* (you), as opposed to the more formal *maga*, between parents and children—a usage corresponding to the greater informality of intergenerational ties within the family.[11]

The village family in its adjustment to changing conditions—to urban migration, industrialization, and collectivization—has retained much of its importance in rural life with a considerable shift in its structure and scope and in the role it plays in both rural and urban lives.

SIGNIFICANT SOCIAL OTHERS

There were broad commonalities in precollective relations among kinsmen, neighbors, koma-s, and friends. These significant groups of social others often participated in identical activities and shared many of the same social responsibilities. The same is true today.

This does not mean that members of the same category or of all these categories are treated equally. They are not. A villager is more likely to have frequent interaction and maintain a more intense relationship and stronger emotional ties with a sibling than with a cousin or in-law. But not always. Ties with neighbors are not equivalent to ties with siblings, but they overlap considerably. Generally, there are culturally accepted preferences for activation of social ties in given situations; but because of various contingencies, one tie often substitutes for another. Such factors include the absence or nonexistence of particular relations (as with only

---

they had once thought desirable (reading, going to the movies, and so on). Jávor (1978: 350) indicates that the psychological debt to parents sometimes keeps married children in Varsány from furnishing or arranging their home to their own tastes and needs even later on if these differ from their parents'.

11. The more traditional usage is for the parents to *tegez* (use "te" and the second person singular verb forms, a mode of talking to familiars of the same or younger age) their children and for the children to *magáz* (use "maga" and the third person singular verb forms, used with less familiar people and older individuals—the constraints on the use of these and other pronouns and forms of address are, of course, more complex and interesting) their parents. In more recent years it has not been unusual for children to try to make inroads in address usage by trying to tegez their parents or, more slyly, to use other forms consistent with tegez-ing, although their parents are now more likely to accept their children's use of "te" to address them. In the city this tendency is less recent.

children, siblings who have left the village, and deceased parents), distance within the village, the exclusion of some people from helping due to sex, age, or poor health, idiosyncratically good or bad relations, and personal preferences (for example, involving the degree of kinship ties to be activated, or the degree of proximity to be considered a neighbor). Thus, one's field of choice in certain activities is quite open.

Because of these contingencies and scope for freedom of choice, and because activities and occasions like weddings and housebuilding can easily be considered and described as integrated wholes, these several categories of social ties will for the time being be lumped together while arenas such as the kaláka, common to them all, are discussed; later they will be considered individually.

Labor Exchange and Help

Collectivization has reduced the breadth of activities in which aid is offered in the economic sphere. Such tasks as threshing, plowing, and carting are outside the sphere of the houseplot and garden enterprise; but within this more limited domain, mutual aid and reciprocation, particularly among relatives, is as significant today as in precollective days.

Today the most common help given is reciprocal aid with shucking and harvesting maize on the collective farm members' houseplots. In the past this was often done individually by families, who each day brought in their own harvest by wagon. Lacking teams now and depending on the collective farm to cart home their harvest, villagers work together so that each can bring in his entire harvest in a single day with one trip (Jávor 1978: 355).

Eight people are needed for a typical plot of maize. A family often asks much the same group of individuals year after year to help out in return for similar help. Such "bands" consist (in order of preference) of close family members, relatives by blood and marriage, friends, koma-s, neighbors, and hired day laborers. These groups have much the same social and recreational functions as work groups of the past. They reduce the onerousness of the harvesting, provide occasion for socializing, and make some of the work more efficient. Typically, there are the parents and siblings of both spouses, sógors, sógornő-s (sisters-in-law and any female relative by marriage of the same generation, as with sógor-s), and, less often, cousins.

For a better idea of the composition of these groups, let us look at a number of examples.

To work on the plot of Márton Kelemen and his wife (until 1970, that is, when Márton, now seventy, had a stroke and gave his land out for sharecropping [one-third]—he now takes the share in grain), there were the Kelemens, helped by

*Relatives and friends helping each other out in work
exchanges. Here two* nász-s *(parents-in-law of each other's
children) and a male friend hoe one of the women's
mother's corn plot. Villagers working on other collective
farm houseplots can be seen scattered in the background.*

Márton's brother and sister and their spouses, his wife's male cousin, and the cousin's wife.

Lajos Lövei, a thirty-six-year-old stonemason in the cooperative, and his wife, also a member, had their plots worked by them and Lajos Lövei's sister and brother-in-law, his half-brother (by his father's deceased first wife) and his son, his parents, and his wife's parents, who live nearby.

Mihály Kalicz worked his plot with the help of his uncle (and godfather), two fellow milkers, his cousin, his mother-in-law, his wife's cousin's husband (his daughter's godfather), and his wife's uncle.

Simon Kis, fifty-six, and his wife worked their plot helped by Mrs. Kis's sister's daughter and son-in-law (for whose child they are godparents), Mrs. Kis's second cousin (Simon's good friend, once fellow teamster, and now the leader of the brigade) and his wife, and Mrs. Kis's first cousin and her husband.

Gyula Pári, thirty-four, and his wife work their plot with Gyula's widowed mother, Mrs. Pári's parents, their koma-s (for whose daughter Gyula and his wife are godparents—the young wife is Mrs. Pári's father's second cousin), and Mrs. István Barna (whose son is a friend of Gyula and had called him last year to help with his maize harvesting but had been unable to reciprocate; his mother is now reciprocating).

These examples have been placed in order of decreasing participation by close relatives. In each case, however, the principals have largely adhered to the same rule of preference for close relatives. In Márton Kelemen's case the only possible closer nonparticipant was his son, who with his wife lives with the older couple; but he was busy with his work as agronomist in a neighboring cooperative and did not have his own plot. Lajos Lövei exhausted his supply of close relatives with the exception of his wife's sister, whose husband had been ill for several months and has four siblings to work with anyway. Mihály Kalicz's widowed mother is old and unable to help. He is an only child. Only his wife's sole sibling, an eighteen-year-old working for the collective farm in Gödör who perhaps lacks a plot of his own, could also have helped. Simon Kis has no children, and both spouses' parents are deceased or infirm. Mrs. Kis's siblings could have joined them in the past, but in this particular year their plots were in the same section as Simon Kis's; they could not help because they had to harvest their own maize at the same time.[12] Mrs. Gyula Pári's siblings either live outside Kislapos or do not have plots of their own.

In general, because of such limitations, the whole range of close ties is utilized. Those whose circle of connections is circumscribed or, as is more often the case, who are unable to reciprocate due to age, health, or time limitations, hire day laborers or take their plots in cash or kind.[13]

The harvesting and pressing of grapes is run on a similar basis. Fewer people are needed, since grapes in Kislapos are mainly for home consumption of wine and are usually confined to the area around the house and in the garden. Mainly parents and children, siblings, nász-s, and sógor-s participate.

12. Corn land in the collective farm is assigned essentially by lot. At harvest time the collective requires all those in the same larger block of land to gather their corn at the same time, within a period of a week or two. In this way the collective can make more efficient use of large blocks of land for the preparation of the next year's crops; the possibility of corn theft is also minimized. Because those in the same block may not have time to help one another, occupied as they are with their own corn and other work, some members of one's harvesting group may vary from year to year.

13. Some older members, particularly if they live with their children, let them work the plot. The grain is useful for feeding animals.

Hoeing and harvesting of houseplot potatoes and turnips is often done by immediate family members alone, as the number of hands required is smaller. If help is given it is by the closer relations.

As noted earlier, children in the city often help out with these tasks, whether they are commuting or have long ago taken up permanent residence in the city. Occasionally it is the children's out-of-town parents-in-law and, more frequently, the nász-s living in Lapos who still help out.

Housebuilding continued well into the 1960s on much the same pattern as in the past. Parents, siblings, sógor-s, cousins, koma-s, nász-s, friends, and neighbors were called upon to help in raising the walls and roof of the house. Frequently the collective farm would provide cartage of materials. However, throughout the late 1950s and 1960s some of the more distant relatives took a lesser role, as builders-to-be would come to help in return for help with their own construction later. While stonemasons usually have played some role in putting up village houses, they have been utilized more extensively since 1959. Many farm members and even nonmembers, with greater cash incomes than in the past and less time to spare from work, are now more willing to pay for labor. Moreover, the collective farm's own building brigade, established to meet the cooperative's needs for construction of barns and maintenance and storage buildings, has increasingly taken over the construction of homes in Kislapos. As the number of houses built decreased in the 1970s, fewer potential home builders were available to help others; thus, housing construction became almost entirely a financial operation. Today in Lapos usually only minor repairs, remodeling, and construction of extra rooms, fences, pigpens, garages, and other outbuildings are carried out in such cooperative fashion.

As in the past, relatives, neighbors, and friends are sought when help is needed or an item is borrowed. Tasks for which they are called upon include feeding animals when family members are away from the village (shopping, visiting relatives, or in times of emergency, for example), helping at the birth of a calf, moving heavy objects, sewing clothing, and cutting down trees. Those shopping or visiting in the city are often asked to buy an item unavailable in the village or to take an item to relatives living there. Usually there is no question of strictly calculated reciprocation, just a general obligation to help out in the same range of tasks.

Borrowing fits into this same general scheme, with commodities and objects loaned ranging from a cup of sugar or eggs through a vermicelli maker to tools and implements, large wooden troughs, and barrels. There are expectations both of borrowing in return at a later date and of relatively prompt return of the borrowed object, but these expectations are sometimes not met. This fact, or misuse, may lead to bad feeling on the part of the lender (as when, for example, István Kelemen found that a wooden trough of his, usually used for preparing meat, loaned long ago and half forgotten, was being used as a drinking trough for ducks); but they are not supposed to lead to words. They have led to wariness about borrowing, in order to avoid having to lend. This seems little different from past problems of borrowing and lending (Fél and Hofer 1969: 175–176).

Although villagers borrow from relatives, neighbors, and friends alike (in fact, perhaps more often from neighbors because of the convenience), most prefer to borrow from relatives. A woman discussing the advantages of having her parents live a few houses down the street explained, "This way no matter what I can't get from the store, I don't have to go to the neighbors for anything."

Yet both neighbors and friends are approached, particularly if relations are good and reciprocity is maintained. To avoid arguments and feelings of exploitation, past customs of the "pricing" of certain help in relation to other kinds, or of bartering help, are kept up and extended to whole new ranges of work and aid.

István Kelemen's neighbor bought a large barrel for use in pressing grapes but had no room to store it. In return for keeping it in one of his outbuildings, István Kelemen may use it whenever he needs.

István Kelemen asked Antal Himer, who works in the collective farm's blacksmith and repair shop, to help plug a hole in his bathroom boiler. In exchange, Antal Himer requested István Kelemen to help dig in his garden along with several hired Gypsies.

Because of the infrequent bus service to Pont and Boros and the lack of direct service to other nearby villages, several auto owners are willing to take fellow villagers to or from Pont or other nearby villages for a standard price.

Of course, there are problems even when such agreements are made.

When Lajos Heves and his wife helped József Kis and his wife put a roof on their garage after the arrival of József Kis's new car, Lajos Heves and his wife accepted no money but asked in return that József Kis take them on occasion to visit their young son attending school in Boros, where József Kis's son of the same age also went to school. Later, the Kis family felt that the other couple were constantly stepping into their car.

These problems seem to arise most frequently when no exact recompense is established, particularly when the party helping out refuses to accept money, implicitly or explicitly setting up an obligation to help out later in return. Many villagers dislike this because they feel the recipro-cated work asked for later will be greater than that first given.[14]

István Kelemen occasionally asks Ferenc Kovács [of Chapter 2]—a seventy-seven-year-old former nagygazda, who after working ten years in the cooperative retired and bought a team of horses to do some carting—to haul corn from his small field or coal from a fuel dealer several kilometers away. He sometimes resents, how-ever, that the elderly man always refuses money, saying that he can help out later with something.

Other problems arise when individuals, asked how much they are owed for help, reply "nothing," with the expectation that the expected amount will then be pressed on them. Both helper and recipient face a dilemma: the helper, because in cases of friendship or distant kinship it is not correct to ask for money; the recipient, because outside of certain clear-cut day labor situations like digging in gardens, construction, and corn harvesting, labor rates are not established, and also because it is unclear whether this is a sincere refusal or a refusal given in hopes of having cash pressed upon oneself.

János Fekete and his wife were asked by one of the local school teachers, Mrs. István Fekete, to help put harvested corn into her loft. She had called only six people in day labor instead of the usual eight to harvest her one-hold corn plot, and the six, agreeing to work until 5:30 in the afternoon, had not had time to finish the job. (Neither did they have the motivation, since they were too few for the job and were to be paid only several days later, when Mrs. István Fekete received more cash.) When the couple were finished, Mrs. István Fekete asked how much she owed them. János Fekete, whose father's brother's son is Mrs. István Fekete's husband (now separated from her and living elsewhere), expecting 200 forint-s, replied, "Nothing." To this Mrs. István Fekete gave him a 100-forint bill, which János Fekete gave back, saying, "I don't need this," and stalked off angrily.

Some of these problems, including the lack of a well-established rate of exchange between tasks, may heighten the tendency to ask only closer relatives for help. Some families are more able to do this than others. There are several cases of sets of three or more siblings living in Lapos among whom there is a great deal of cooperation, involving virtually all the tasks mentioned above. In cases where sisters are involved, sógor-s are enlisted; and even sets of sisters marrying into the village have pro-duced a high intensity of cooperation among sógor-s.

14. Of course, as Foster (1961: 11) points out, such lack of exact reciprocation may ensure that these relationships continue.

Family Celebrations and Crises

The pattern of participation at important family events has not changed substantially. When a child is born, the mother's mother still provides a great deal of help in the weeks following. Frequently even if the young couple lives alone in the city, the mothers go to live with them for the first few weeks. Sisters and sógornő-s alternately provide meals for siblings and close relatives still living in Kislapos for several weeks after the mother and child have arrived home from the hospital. Different god-parents are now often chosen for each child. Those in Lapos are now almost invariably drawn from among relatives.

Marriages and funerals continue to be occasions at which the attendance of relatives near and far is expected. Less distant relatives along with neighbors and good friends supply chickens and other food and help in preparations for a wedding reception. The relatives who help include uncles, parents, siblings, cousins, and their spouses; when the relationship has been good, even a cousin's brother-in-law's family and a deceased cousin's wife (since remarried) have helped. All these, along with koma-s and friends, are invited. The godparents of the bride and groom serve as násznagy and *nyoszolyóasszony* (maid of honor), as well as host and hostess at the reception. Not only are they key figures in the wedding and the reception, but they are expected to give the largest gifts (outside of parents) to the newlyweds.

Although some parents now throw receptions in the restaurants of nearby towns, prewedding celebrations are still held locally, and in these friends, neighbors, and relatives help with preparations and with the pig-killing.

Funerals are attended by an even wider circle of relatives and friends. Neighbors, former neighbors, people living in the same street, friends, and relatives, both in and outside the village, try to attend, along with many other villagers. A close relative, friend, or neighbor makes arrangements for friends, neighbors, fellow workers, and more distant relations to be pallbearers and grave diggers. Mourning has not been quite as formalized since, several years ago, a little mortuary was built in the cemetery, to which the body is taken soon after death. Close relatives are nearest the coffin before burial and during funeral rites; they attend the funeral feast after the burial.

Pig-killing remains an important family celebration for a limited circle of relatives. Siblings, parents, and/or nász-s, and children and their spouses are usually invited for dinner after the butchering and preparation of meats is finished; not all families have a large feast afterward. In past years some of these feasts involved larger sets of relatives, often including friends, cousins, and even more distant relations. Today this is rare. Those joining in the work are a subset of the guests, with the possible

*Pre-wedding reception preparations. Friends, neighbors,
and relatives of the bride's family gather to prepare the feast,
bringing food, stoves, and other necessities. Here chickens
are cleaned and dressed.*

exception of the person who actually plunges the blade into the pig's
throat and does the butchering. He is often one of several villagers who
hire themselves out for such occasional service.

Most of the meat remains for the family doing the pig-killing. Occasionally a parent or grandparent will raise a pig, and part or all of the meat will
go to a son or grandson living in the city. Virtually all villagers send
"tastes" (a portion of meat and sausages) to close relatives and neighbors
within several days of the pig-killing and, in return, themselves receive
tastes. Some examples follow:

Péter Erdei, forty-nine, and his wife, forty-seven, send samples to fifteen places: to
his three siblings in Kislapos, her two siblings there, their two pairs of nász-s (one

for each married child), their five neighbors (two on one side, three on the other—across the street there are mainly Gypsies), her sister in Budapest, one of her nephews, and her cousin in Lapos.

András Kis, sixty-four, and his wife, sixty-one, send to seven places: their two married children living outside Lapos, their two sets of nász-s, and three neighbors.

Gyula Pári, thirty-four, and his wife, twenty-seven, send to nine places: his two brothers, his mother, her brother, her parents and brother still at home, their koma-s, and three neighbors (two on one side and one across the street).

Béla Burom, sixty-three, and his wife, fifty-four, send to ten places: his two siblings in Lapos, her four siblings, two neighbors (one on each side; one is the wife's sister), an old neighbor of theirs (the sister's husband's brother, whose family, until building a new house elsewhere in the village, also lived next door), their nász-s, and their daughter's family.

Tibor Kakas, fifty-five, and his wife, forty-eight, send to fourteen places: her three brothers and sisters elsewhere in Hungary, her husband's deceased sister's widower, her widowed mother, her husband's four nephews and nieces (one of whom is their baptismal koma), one neighbor, one kert neighbor, and three friends.

Almost invariably included among those sent tastes are siblings and parents of both spouses, children and nász-s, some neighbors, and some friends. In some of the above cases this is not obvious. Tibor Kakas's family has a separate pig-killing for their children—which their children and nász-s attend, removing the "necessity" of sending tastes. Similarly, Péter Erdei's children come home for the pig-killing.

More interesting has been the tendency to reduce the number of participants in the taste exchanges. At the time Mrs. Tibor Kakas joined the Kakas family at marriage, coming from Zöldfa in 1951, Tibor Kakas's parents had exchanged with twenty-three families. András Kis and his wife have reduced the number in recent years through mutual agreements with some neighbors, cousins, and even siblings who do not live in Lapos. Some villagers remember pig-killing feasts in their childhood with as many as twenty sitting around the table, compared to today's six or eight.

Part of this is cyclical fluctuation. When children marry, new relations are introduced while much of the full range of past relatives of the parents' generation as well as the children's is still alive. As these die off, the scope of relations is temporarily reduced until the marriage of the children, when new in-law and nász relations are established and two sets of relations exist: those primarily of the married children and those of the older couple, with some "shared." Gradually the children's relations begin to assume greater importance.

As parents age, their children assume greater significance in their lives, and relations established through children's marriages become primary. For example, regarding the tastes sent out from a pig-killing, Mrs. Tibor Kakas says:

We [once] sent to lots of places. But we gave up some because there are plenty [of people to send to] there as well [in those families] where the children have married; their families have expanded, and my family has expanded, hasn't it. My daughter has left [home]; we sent samples to her landlady . . . and to the other [daughter's] as well. So we broke off with this [family]; we send to this many. It was impossible [to continue]. We even stopped sending to our koma's children because they have their domestic circle, their own children, to whom they send, and I also send [to mine].

Over the past thirty years, the number of children and siblings has decreased, leading to a reduction in the circle of relatives. Further, there is greater emphasis on more limited family and sógor ties now than in the past. The greater emphasis on children's accomplishments and their advancement in a changed world, often outside the community, as well as the decreased importance of the stem and joint families and that of land in focusing the interests of more distant relatives, have resulted in a decrease in scope of kin relations and a tightening of focus onto the parent-child, sógor, sibling, and nász relations.

Visiting and Socializing

Socializing was and is an important part of many traditional activities. Some such activities are almost exclusively social events, such as the evening gatherings of neighbor women and friends to cut and shape noodles for soup, especially in the winter. Rotating among homes, these sessions are devoted to catching up on gossip and socializing. Much the same is true of knitting and embroidering sessions among women, sometimes accompanied by card playing among husbands. The introduction of television into the village in the mid-1960s reduced the frequency of some of these gatherings, though not for the first few years. In fact, the opposite may have happened then: relatives and friends dropped in several evenings a week to view the scarce television screens. There were frequently ten or fifteen people seated around the sets; because the parents conversed as in the past, had more difficulty following the new medium, and often asked for clarification, children often asked them to be quiet. As sets became more common the gatherings became smaller. Today visiting to watch television is more the exception than the rule, as most homes have a set. The increase in viewing has led to an overall decrease in evening visiting.

Most visits longer than a few minutes still do occur in the evenings, especially in winter, when working hours in both the collective farm and the houseplot and garden are shorter (or, for many women, nonexistent). Parents, children, siblings, and sógor-s, friends, and koma-s are occasional visitors for several hours at these times and on weekends. More frequent weekend visitors (some for a day or two, many for a Sunday or Sunday morning, since the last Sunday bus leaves Lapos at noon) are children, both those who commute and those permanently settled in other communities.

Shorter visits during the day are more common among neighboring women, parents and their children, and siblings, especially those retired or not working in the collective farm. Among neighbors visits are usually quite brief, frequently involving a request, advice, and the exchange of pleasantries, news, and gossip. Others stop in for a short stay on the way to the store, the milk collection depot, or another errand; relatives and friends sometimes come directly for a short visit. Gossip, goings-on in the collective, children, and advice on domestic work and problems are frequent conversational topics.

On Sunday afternoons, the elderly often sit in front of their houses by the sidewalk on benches to relax, to greet passers-by, and to discuss them and days past with friends and neighbors.

Kinsmen

Although close family ties have always been primary, in recent years there has been some tightening of the social focus among relatives to a smaller circle of parents, children, siblings and their spouses, nász-s, and parents-in-law. More distant relations, like cousins, other sógor-s, and often uncles and aunts, have begun to recede in importance. Aside from the traditionally more inclusive cases of marriage and death, occasions of visiting, celebrating, and seeking help have become more restricted to this smaller core of kinsmen. This has already been noted in terms of helping relations. Aid sought beyond this core is often viewed in terms of more direct and equal reciprocation or cash payment for service rendered. Cases of keeping up closer ties with more distant relations are often due to a lack of closer kin living in the community.

Similar reductions are seen in the numbers and scope of relations involved in pig-killing and the exchanges of meat samples, as well as in the more frequent interaction of visiting and socializing. It is the latter that will be examined more closely here.

It is first worth noting that distinguishing such long-term trends from cyclical fluctuations in family cycles is difficult. As parents age and their children at home assume greater authority in the household, the emphasis shifts from the older parents' ties to those of their children. Relationships with parents' siblings, nephews and nieces, and in-laws give way to those with the children's siblings and in-laws and the new násv-s. This on the face of it is what would be expected from a long-term trend as well, and we see it in Mrs. Tibor Kakas's comment above.

What is most significant recently is the degree to which the emphasis remains and the earlier age at which the shift occurs. Not only has the circle of kin become tighter, but even close ties with childhood friends and koma-s have been replaced to a greater degree than in the past by these relations. When visiting, József Veres's family, for example, goes to his parents-in-law, his wife's siblings, or his father's siblings. To visit more, he says, would require too much time and effort. Most of his childhood friends have moved from the village, and he sees them only rarely. Cousins are not even mentioned.

The same is true of many other young married couples and their parents. Affinal relations have assumed greater importance than in the past; more distant kin relations, childhood friendships, and koma relations have decreased relatively in significance.

What has caused this? Several of the reasons have been touched upon earlier. First, there is greater emphasis on good relations with one's children and on their accomplishments and status. Second, as the family loses its economic productive functions, particularly among the young, the conjugal relationship and affinal ties in general assume a different hue and significance. Third, because children leave home and even the village more often, they are less tied to their parents' authority, their parents' way of life, and, because of collectivization, their parents' land; they are tied less exclusively to the husband's household and relatives. Fourth, since all youth are leaving the village in greater numbers, and family size has decreased, there are fewer cousins, aunts, and more distant relatives settled in the village with whom ties can be easily maintained. Improvements in transportation help children keep the ties with parents and close kin strong but do not allow much time for other ties.

On occasions like weddings, funerals, and the day of the village patron saint, ties with more distant relatives and friends can be renewed, but these occasions are infrequent. Moreover, even on St. Stephen's Day, when relatives and friends come home to visit, feast, and go to the booths and rides set up in the celebrating village, people spend the most time with their parents and siblings.

Interestingly, when several siblings live in the same village and maintain strong ties of cooperation and visiting with one another and with their parents, spatial factors are still very important. If, for example, one sibling lives on the way to the village center and its post office, bus stop, butcher shop, milk depot, and administration building, then that sibling is much more likely to be visited than another in a house less conveniently on the way. Reciprocation may not be equal, however, for the same reason. In any case, such sibling relationships and parent-child ties, especially between mother and daughter, are usually far more intense in terms of frequency of contact and mutual aid than all other nonnuclear family ties.

Neighbors

Relationships with neighbors have changed relatively little. They are still usually the province of women. Ties with neighbors have a greater instrumental component than other relationships considered here; one of the most important attributes of a neighbor is "the readiness to help."

On the other hand, if there is compatibility of age and interests between neighbors, friendship often develops. Many even consider this the norm, as the following case illustrates.

One early spring day, an older woman came out on her bicycle to the horticultural division of the collective farm, seeking her younger neighbor woman. The other women speculated on the reason for her trip. One suggested that maybe guests had arrived, but others discounted that possibility since there was only a half-hour until the women were to finish work anyway. It must be something urgent, they concluded, for the two women were "only on speaking terms." This meant that "they were not on such good terms with each other; they just say 'hello' to each other," whereas neighbors usually make friends with one another—"they tell each other all sorts of confidential matters." It turned out that the younger woman's mother had become ill.

Although cultural expectations are for good ties, there is ample opportunity for conflict. Since women are the primary participants in neighborly relations, and some of the chief activities are gossiping and, when the relationship warms up, exchanging confidential information, clashes between women are frequent results. Men are rarely involved directly. As one informant expressed it,

A person has a circle of friends . . . and a person has a neighbor. A neighbor is just considered a neighbor, but if a proper circle of friends develops . . . that's entirely different . . . But visiting neighbors is such that one who likes a neighbor frequently comes to grief. Two neighbors get together, then one tells a third; it goes [gets passed on] this way word for word. Then they clash and you have a grudge out of it.

Other sources of conflict include one's poultry being found in a neighbor's brood, children stepping on flowers planted in front of a house, and pigs feeding and excreting in front of a neighbor's fence. Large age differences usually preclude both very cold and very warm relationships.

When neighbors are close, it is common for women to go together to work in the fields of the collective farm and even to work side by side. In these cases there is often less time spent visiting one another at home. In general, those who work in the collective farm have less time for neighbors and perhaps less need—they can catch up on village news and gossip at work and are less isolated than those remaining at home.

Koma-s

Baptismal and confirmational koma-s are chosen almost exclusively today from among relatives. This has been a tendency throughout Hungary. Other trends have continued, including that of choosing different godparents for each child and that of trying to have both sides of the family represented among koma-s, as well as the cross-generational reciprocation pattern mentioned earlier.

A look at Mrs. András Zöldi's two daughters illustrates the first two:

The eldest's baptismal godmother is András Zöldi's eldest sister, and the confirmational godmother is the baptismal godmother's married daughter (the godfathers are the spouses). The youngest's baptismal and confirmational godmothers are Mrs. Zöldi's older brother's wife and her younger sister, respectively. As Mrs. Zöldi explained, "This way each branch would be represented, and no stranger" [non-relative] would be called on, nor just the same one constantly. The children would be in greater contact with their relatives and "honor" them more. Mrs. Zöldi has eight godchildren, some baptismal, some confirmational. They are her mother's siblings' children and her husband's sister's daughter (who is her daughter's confirmational godmother).

Mrs. Zöldi's case also provides an example of the type of reciprocation going on. To show just how complex the reciprocity can be and the mix of relations involved, the following story is presented, of how a child born to Irén Németh late in 1975 ended up with her brother's wife as baptismal godmother.

István Lengyel's baptismal godmother sixteen years ago was Irén Németh (then unmarried), since Irén's father and István's mother were second cousins and the Lengyels and Némeths were neighbors. Later, Katalin, István's older sister, chose Irén and her husband as confirmational godparents (her baptismal godmother was one of her mother's sisters). When István was approaching confirmation, he asked Irén's husband to be his godfather; the latter consented and even gave István a pocket radio, though he ultimately never was confirmed since he had not attended catechism enough. When Irén's elder daughter Judit (whose baptismal godparents are one of her father's siblings and his wife) was to be confirmed, she wanted Katalin to be her godmother. Irén Németh, however, had planned to have her sister-in-law (for whose daughter she was confirmational godmother) to be her daughter Judit's confirmational godmother and Katalin to be her newborn child's baptismal godmother. Her daughter argued fiercely for her own choice; and, more important, Katalin was to be married soon, but not in a church wedding. This would disqualify her from being the newborn's godmother. Thus, Katalin became Judit's confirmational godmother before she married, and Irén Németh's sister-in-law became the newborn child's godmother.

In this manner, both the prior generation's godparents (that is, with Katalin Lengyel's parents and Irén Németh as koma-s) and the present's (since Irén Németh is her sister-in-law's daughter's confirmational godmother) were reciprocated, and members of both Irén Németh's and her husband's families are now godparents for Irén's children.

Godfathers continue to play the primary role of násznagy at weddings. Customarily, the confirmational godfather is chosen for this role and his wife is the nyoszolyóasszony; sometimes one is chosen from each pair of godparents. The násznagy might be the confirmational godfather, the nyoszolyóasszony the baptismal godmother.

Godchildren usually pay occasional visits to their godparents (often in the context of visiting relatives), while godparents play an important role in celebrations of important events in the lives of their young godchildren, including marriage and graduation. Outside of parents, their gifts are still the largest. These relationships are usually warm and affectionate.

Adolescent Companions and Friendship

The importance of adolescent friendships later in life has been greatly reduced in recent years. This can be seen in two areas: the transformation of the koma relationship into a primarily kin-based one, often involving individuals of different ages, and the now greater importance of friendships established in ways and times other than adolescence. The former has been treated in Chapter 3 and earlier in this chapter; the latter will be discussed here.

For virtually all villagers, friendship implies that two people "understand each other," that they "can talk in confidence." Men in particular subsume that via this "understanding" they "can crack jokes with one another" and "pull each other's leg" without fear of insult. They should greet, speak to, and like one another and not harbor resentment. For some it also means that they can borrow money; and for most it implies willingness to help and give advice when asked and, in general, spending much time with one another.

For men there is an additional category of *haver*, which approximates the adolescent *cimbora*, or chum, pal, and even friend. It especially connotes a companion with whom one drinks and has a good time in recreation, joking, and talking. Such friends are often, though not always, distinguished from more serious friends with whom one can be more confidential and speak of matters of greater personal concern. There are times when the word for "friend" (barát) is also used as a cover term for the wider category of haver and cimbora of which the class of close friends is a subset.

Until recently, one's only real friends in the eyes of villagers were the companions of adolescence, one's koma-s or the feminine counterpart for women. These friendships remained alive after marriage, although much of the activity that gave them content subsided with the change in status and role. Of course, the few men and the greater number of women who moved or married into the village, particularly before World War II, developed some such ties (as among meny-s who moved into the village at the same time), but for the most part such friendships were left behind and few took their place quickly.

Today, both for men and for women, friendship, based on or bolstered by a common work place or position in the cooperative, has largely supplanted adolescent ties. Teamsters' friends are other teamsters, milkers' friends other milkers, and so on. For men these are the individuals with whom they spend a large part of the day, with whom they have drinks in the local bar, and whom they occasionally invite home for a drink after work or for other visits. Women spend much of their time chatting and joking with fellow workers, exchanging gossip, advice, and personal concerns.

For many these are the best friends; most of their adolescent chums have left the village. While the latter ties are often renewed at St. Stephen's Day, when people from all over come to visit their relatives and celebrate, they no longer constitute viable on-going relationships. Ties with one's age-group friends may slacken for other reasons if the common workplace does not help to reinforce them. The greater emphasis on the nuclear family and children's affines have weakened some earlier friendship ties. As one fifty-year-old male says of his adolescent friend, whom he visited for years after their respective marriages, "Now the kinship has changed as well since his son also married, and he's gotten closer relatives. Now he's more occupied."

For those working in the collective farm the ties of fellow workers constitute the bulk of friendship ties. Those women who spend several years at home after the birth of a child or leave the collective farm to stay at home often lose these ties and feel quite alone.

All this does not mean that the bases for friendship have changed entirely. Not all fellow workers are friends. Friendship still involves the same sex almost exclusively, and there are strong age preferences. Although among men it is no longer rare for friendships to involve age differences as great as ten years, most ties involve differences of less than

Villagers and visiting friends and relatives crowding around carnival booths set up for Kislapos's local Saint Day. The old collective farm headquarters, once the home of the village's wealthiest nagygazda, is in the background.

five years and often little or no difference.[15] The same is true for women. For example, women harvesting vegetables or hoeing are often organized into two crews, one generally older and one younger. The older tend to go more slowly and do more careful work, whereas the younger prefer fast-paced work, trying to increase their earnings on quantity of work done. Younger women generally prefer work companions of the same age; they prefer talking about fashions, gossip, and contemporary affairs, not days long past. When they are given the chance to choose their fellow workers, they try to pick friends with similar interests and work and conversational styles, people who are usually of the same age.

Even outside the collective farm, friendships among women are based on similar factors. Many women whose children are friends and classmates in school become friends themselves, having met often at parent-teacher conferences or at the bus stop when their children leave for

15. Interestingly, one of the determinants of the use of more and less formal address forms and pronouns is age difference. Differences of about five years separate the more formal from the less formal usages.

school at Boros on Monday mornings and arrive home at the end of the week. Here, too, although the women may not have been childhood friends, their ages are usually similar even if their ties are based on similarity of circumstances.

Men's and women's friendships differ in important ways. Men are less open and confidential with one another: the stress is on joking, drinking together, and talking about less personal matters. Because women will discuss personal problems and exchange advice, their relationships are more frequently volatile; some women therefore have reservations about friendships, feeling that it is sometimes safer not to put much faith in them. Among women there may be misplaced confidences, or betrayals for personal gain.

Jávor (1978: 358–359) finds the same reservations in women about friendships. She points out that these relationships are mainly limited to common work and do not extend to the home. Home visits are still largely restricted to relatives and neighbors. Jávor ties these limitations to traditional views, which allow little scope for free time for women and suspect immorality in all such relations outside the family.

Adolescents still maintain close ties with their peers, but several factors militate against these ties being as close as in the past. Youth leave the village at an earlier age now, often for secondary schools and beyond, where few of their classmates are fellow villagers. Numerous ties are established with youths their own age outside the community. The ties of those who remain in Kislapos or who return for dances and to hop onto motorcycles together to seek entertainment and girls in neighboring villages are less exclusive. It is not unusual for both boys and girls to bring friends home from school. Nor is courting done largely within the structure of such age groups any more; and even the less formal parties arranged by girlfriends at the home of one of them, reminiscent of the corn shucking get-togethers of the past, have largely disappeared.[16] Indeed, while young male classmates may, for example, vow to attend one another's weddings, whenever and wherever they may be, and gather on Sunday afternoons to bowl and talk, bands as ongoing groups have disappeared.

The mere fact that simple friendships across sexes are not uncommon, even if they are less frequent than in urban areas, demonstrates the vast change from the past in this area as well.

16. This may be a simple function of the reduction in numbers of youth of similar age in Lapos and may not be characteristic of larger villages.

Chapter 8

Local Patronage, Kinship, and the New Leadership

After World War II, tremendous changes took place in the leadership of Kislapos. The land- and wealth-based stratificational system was replaced both nationally and locally by a materially far more egalitarian structure.[1] For the first few years, Lapos's former wealthier strata were almost completely shorn of power and kept out of village administrative functions. Positions of power were assumed by the poor and landless and by a few smallholders and middle peasants. This was done largely through their membership in the Communist Party, which took over the reins of power locally and nationally. Some, as we have seen, were more concerned with their own personal gain, with expanding personal power, and sometimes with pursuing vendettas than in building a new society. Many of the latter lost their positions in local power within a few years, although they often did not completely leave the various organs associated with the village administration (for example, the early collective farms, the consumers' cooperative, and the state produce purchasing agencies) or other politically oriented agencies.

Others of these less wealthy strata stayed on and put in varying degrees of devoted service in the village administration and in the other locally

1. Underlying this new stratification is a variety of factors: technical and special skills; education; personal connections; Party connections; managerial and bureaucratic power; and the readiness and opportunities to take advantage of shortages and demand partly created and unfulfilled by a strongly centralized and occasionally misdirected, but now increasingly less centralized economic planning. This work will deal only with those which are important in this village. For a treatment of factors and groups not covered here and for further information on the postwar transformation of the Hungarian countryside, see Andorka (1979), Bango (1976), Bodrogi (1978), Donáth (1977), Erdei (1971), Hegedüs (1970, 1971), Kulcsár (1976), Márkus (1971), Neuberg (1973), Orbán (1972), Szabady (1972), Volgyes (MS, 1973), and Zsarnóczai (1964).

See Chapters 5 and 6 for further information on postwar changes in leadership in Kislapos.

important political and economic institutions. Although few were fully accepted by villagers as worthy of leadership status, as were many of the more "puritan," less self-serving leaders of poor origin in other villages where patterns similar to the above emerged (Sárkány 1978: 102, 128, 146), some did obtain legitimacy as leaders and administrators in the eyes of large segments of the village population.

These developments marked changes in two important aspects of village leadership. The first is the obvious fact that the occupants of the leadership positions had changed drastically. No longer was wealth the important criterion for leadership. For a decade local power was largely in the hands of the formerly poor.

The second change was the increase in the importance of extra-village connections as prerequisites for holding local power. Connections with such supravillage organs as the district council and party, the police, state purchasing agencies, and upper levels of the consumers' cooperatives were very important in obtaining positions of power in the village. Village officials, including the mayor and council president, were often chosen by these organs, which in turn provided them with the power to act and to maintain their positions. This is most clear in the years from 1945 to 1956.

It is true that the power of both pre- and post-World War II officials depended upon the regulations and laws promulgated by national bodies and that both groups made use of state security (for example, gendarmes) to protect the interests of the state or the ruling classes and to enforce their own will, if need be. Moreover, as Szelényi (1977: 29–30) argues:

The new local government organization in Hungary and elsewhere in Eastern Europe followed the Russian pattern of local soviets, but since the inherited institutions were already shaped by highly centralized State bureaucracies to secure the obedient execution of central orders, rather than to represent local countervailing power, they could be taken over without significant structural changes, the town hall renamed city soviet, and the mayor renamed the president of the local council.

This sometimes did not involve much change in administrative personnel, although in Lapos it did. But it is equally clear that once they were in office prewar virilista-s were more independent of higher authorities because they depended much less on them for their own positions.

The importance of patron-client relations, however, shows less change. The personnel involved and the nature of the relationships changed, but the centrality of such relations did not diminish significantly in the early postwar years. Landed wealth was of far less import in controlling and distributing important resources like jobs, administrative posts, and lightened tax loads. Party ties, connections with members of supravillage organs, past economic status, and relations with a far different set of local leaders became salient. Some of the forums for meetings of patrons and clients, like the Peasants' Circle and the occasional get-togethers in barns, disappeared, and meetings in party headquarters and in cooperative farm offices took their place. Others, like the consumers' cooperative and the town hall, remained.

Later years brought further important changes. The extension of collectivization to the vast majority of the rural population, the introduction of the New Economic Mechanism in 1968, and the social, cultural, and political changes stemming from the latter have been the most important factors behind this. Locally one of the most significant changes has been the shift in the source of personnel occupying leadership positions in the village. The establishment of the new collective farms in 1959 and their continued viability, as noted earlier, depended on (and was perceived by both local and national leadership as depending on) the broad participation and eventual support of the strata of landowning peasants with farming experience. This group was actively recruited into the farms and into their leadership. Some of the first leaders were chosen precisely because of their broad circle of relatives within the middle peasant and smallholder strata. This has brought the increasing integration of these strata into wider Hungarian society; the rights and privileges (pensions, maternity leave, state supported medical care) enjoyed by most of the rest of the population have been extended to the peasantry. The years since 1959 have also seen the solidification of the position of these strata in the village leadership, particularly as the collective farms have strengthened and assumed a greater role, not only in the lives of their membership but in the community as a whole.

Neither the fact of outside influence nor that of patron-client ties in the village social structure has been eliminated. Both remain important elements of village power relations, although the personnel and even the nature of their interactions and the possibilities available to them have changed, as have many of the official "rules" regulating them. For example, the NEM and the far-reaching administrative changes reflecting its spirit eliminated the district councils but not the influence of outside political and administrative organs on village and farm affairs.

Before proceeding with the analysis in this chapter, which examines the new power structure that arose in Kislapos in the wake of collectivization, an important aspect of the data to be presented should be noted. Much of it is the product of "white room" ethnography: it has been obtained through informal and formal discussions and structured and unstructured interviews with scores of villagers and through some formal cognitive anthropological tasks with a smaller number of informants; much of the alleged behavior was not observed by me. Because of the nature of the information, it was often difficult to obtain corroborating "evidence" for some people's views (and occasionally the charges they were leveling). It is therefore difficult to judge just how well these views reflect reality.

Three matters are certain, however. One is that this presentation reflects a view shared in varying degrees by a large portion of the village and the collective farm population. It is an important part of their social reality.

Second, as Hungarians say, "The underbrush doesn't rustle without the wind blowing it." There is considerable favoritism and some corruption in the collective farm, some of which may well be tied to outside administrative and political organs. In many ways the reality clearly does not match the ideals of democracy, communism, and equality of opportunity that the villagers have come to expect and for which the government has striven so hard in the past two decades. Ideally, the collective farm should embody these values.[2]

This leads to the third point. Much of what the villagers feel must be understood within the context of the accomplishments (and, of course, the problems) of the past three decades. Within that time span Hungary has become one of the most materially egalitarian countries in the world: it has one of the world's most equal income distributions (Jain 1975). Indeed, such equality of income has come to be expected by many Hungarians. As a result, aspects of the NEM that proposed greater material incentives and thus a greater differentiation of pay scales have not been well received by a portion of the population and some elements of the party leadership. Particularly galling to many in the first few years of the NEM were the very high bonuses received by management for production performances achieved on paper only. Since then bonuses have been readjusted to more realistic and acceptable levels. Although many favor the rise in living standards brought by the NEM and approve of increased opportunities for a better living, they are anxious about the effects on themselves of the NEM and the possible upheaval it may bring; they resent others' receiving more, particularly on the basis of what they see as "money-grubbing" or petit bourgeois attitudes.[3]

By the same token, this heightened sensitivity to perceived inequality and inequity may result in a greater number of complaints than might otherwise seem justified in the eyes of outsiders. It may lead to seeing wealth as unfairly accumulated, when the results of new economic forces and often not so new collective farm rules are not fully understood.

Finally, an observation by Károlyi (1956: 329), though written about the Hungarian peasantry of the past from the perspective of a former count (albeit a very liberal and, indeed, for his station and time a radical one)

2. See, for example, Gyenes (1975).
3. See Robinson (1973: 331–345) for a more detailed explication of what I have greatly simplified.

with, perhaps, a slightly biased point of view, is relevant even today: "They were critical and discontented as peasants usually are; they grumbled on principle, for, if they did not, their masters would think them satisfied. Grumbling for them is a sort of self-protection, a warding-off of envy, for to be envied is dangerous." On the other hand, many villagers' perceptions are undoubtedly accurate.

These points should all be kept in mind in reading the following.

A BRIEF OVERVIEW

In 1959 two new collective farms came into being with memberships almost entirely made up of former landed peasants. The presidencies of the two new and the one old cooperatives were occupied by landowners, though none were members of the prefront village leadership. Because it was primarily the landed peasantry, especially the middle peasants, on whom the new collectives built, most of their leadership positions were occupied by pre-1959 smallholders, middle peasants, and even some former "kulaks."

Through kin connections, party membership, the control of resources and rewards in the collective, and the establishment of connections with higher administrative and political organs, some members of these strata were able to consolidate and increase their newly acquired power. Though in the early years improvements in the standard of living fostered by the economic success of collectivization rendered mild the discontent spawned by favoritism and by the lack of input into local decisions, further elements of favoritism and apparent corruption made more obvious the necessity of higher-level support for the farm's leadership. When that disappeared in 1975–76 (and more experienced and trained management was deemed a necessity), the leadership and much of its patronage network collapsed.

NEW PERSONNEL

The predominance of the middle peasantry in the leadership was facilitated by the deliberate efforts of the village council in organizing the farms. It was also aided by the greater farming experience and the prestige of the middle and wealthy peasants—by virtue of their land and their large base of local kin support (taken into consideration by the local council president) compared to the landless. Kin support was especially important in light of the pattern of relatives joining the same collective farms. Those with more relatives could count on greater support in their efforts to acquire leadership positions. The precollective stratification also affected the allocation of nonleadership posts, so that, for example, it was the middle and wealthy peasants who became (initially, at least) the higher paid teamsters.

Not all the landed peasants who assumed the more important positions in these years had had much land prior to 1945. In the intervening years a few virtually landless harvester/day laborers had acquired a little land through the 1945 reform and had managed to buy more to build up respectable family enterprises by 1959.

By the same token, most of the village's former wealthy peasants had less important roles in the leadership. Most had been reduced to the level of middle peasants and, some, as Sárkány points out, became "broken men, who lost the ground from under their feet."[4] Moreover, the middle peasants had been less affected than the wealthy ones by the policies of the earlier years and were generally more able to evoke sympathy for their problems from local council leaders. In some places they were able to evade regulations, which the wealthy peasants were not, and, unlike their poorer counterparts, were still able to maintain a many-sided agricultural operation. They emerged from the 1950s as the wealthiest group in the village (Sárkány: 99–100).

There was also some repetition in 1959 of the incidences in the early 1950s when some were "encouraged" to join a cooperative by the possibility of direct rewards and punishments. A few villagers with black marks from the past (for example, for having been pre-1945 policemen or gendarmes) were enlisted to join lest, for example, their children not be accepted in technical school. They were chosen to do some of the harder "dirty work," like going from house to house to determine which equipment and animals each household should contribute to the collective enterprise. As one so chosen put it, people like that could be depended on to make things come out all right because they themselves depended on just that: to produce. It is also likely that such people were expendable; if things did not go well, they were subject to scapegoating—the past could be blamed for the errors of the present.

The merger of the three collectives in 1961 further consolidated the position of the new leadership. Even fewer of the precollective leaders and of the poorer members remained in the leadership. The number of administrative officials was temporarily reduced, and the voice of earlier and poorer members was diluted in the merger with wealthier members. A still greater percentage of the reduced numbers in the leadership hierarchy now consisted of former smallholders and middle peasants.

4. However, as Sárkány (1978: 101; also 128–129) adds, many of the former wealthy and middle peasants put much greater emphasis than others did on the education of their children and grandchildren, thus ultimately affording them better positions outside the village in a different social setting. In general, these strata have emphasized the education and higher education of their children more than have the formerly landless.

Aside from this, the power of the middle peasantry also increased as some, especially the leaders of the collective, joined the party. Although one can only speculate on individual motivations, several points are clear. For one thing, unlike the later years of the NEM, there was a greater expectation that party members would be leaders and leaders would be party members. Several early leaders, including the president of the combined collective, joined the party in the first few years after 1959. The tendency of the leaders to join was undoubtedly heightened by the party's continued rebuilding and increase in membership following its collapse both nationally and locally in 1956. Many earlier members did not rejoin; though the party's policy was not to have as many members as possible, nor was it necessarily to reach the same number as in years past (for it has been publicly acknowledged several times in the past three decades that many members of a large party will be less than totally committed communists), it was clear that new members were welcome. They often replaced less wealthy members of the past.

The farm mergers were also accompanied by consolidation of local party groups. Before the merger, each individual cooperative had had its own separate party organization and secretary. The last party secretary of the Petőfi, a longtime member of that cooperative, became village party secretary, a post he has occupied since; nonetheless, the strong position of the former landless within the party became diluted over time as new party members began to assume important positions and develop contacts with higher party officials.

As had happened sometimes in the past, some of the new party members joined to advance their own careers, for party members are often preferred in job advancement. Some of the young villagers who left the community for administrative and professional positions elsewhere have joined; and for many, job advancement was one, if not necessarily the primary, reason for joining.[5]

5. It should be pointed out, though, that Hungary, perhaps more than any East European country, has encouraged and allowed talented and skilled nonmembers to assume positions of responsibility in cultural, economic, and to some degree even governmental and political spheres. The Communist Party has most certainly sought the advice of nonparty economic experts. This policy has been an important element of First Party Secretary Kádár's general dictum that "those who are not against us are with us." The importance of talent and expertise, whether in the hands of party members or others, has been further increased by the New Economic Mechanism.

There has also been a tendency to try to enlist managers and other talented and skilled individuals into the party, a policy often accompanied by some pressure. Thus, Sampson's observation (1976: 335) that in Romania, because "practically everyone in any high status position is a party member already, party membership as a social marker is superfluous," though perhaps exaggerated, bears considerable relevance to Hungarian circumstances. It must be tempered somewhat by the stereotypes below relating to party membership.

Two examples characterize many of the villagers' feelings about those who join. Many villagers state that all the brigade leaders are party members. In fact, in 1975 at least half were not. Compared to their share in the general population (5–10 percent) the party does hold a large number of these positions, but what the villagers say is not true. It is even unclear how firmly they believe their statements. But the statements do reflect their beliefs that the brigade leaders and other leaders are chosen less for their ability than for other characteristics, chief among these being party membership.

A related belief is typified by the expression "(self-)interest Communist" (*érdekkommunista*). Many feel that a large proportion of members are such self-interest Communists. Some individuals are unwilling to join lest they be identified as such.

Bearing on this also is the labeling of brigade leaders as kulaks. Although this has alleged behavioral referents on the part of brigade leaders and reflects the villagers' attitudes toward the work requirements and prerogatives of the brigade leaders, it also mirrors the villagers' perceptions that the wealthy and middle peasants have usurped the village leadership. This is particularly true of once poorer villagers. As a literal claim, this labeling has only limited basis. Two of the six brigade leaders were kulaks or sons of kulaks, and both their enterprises were at the lower end of the wealthy peasant category.

Earlier, one other former kulak had similar brigade leader status, but at that time neither of the two mentioned above occupied such positions. In addition, the prefront mayor's son was the agronomist of the Kossuth; after taking positions in other enterprises for many years, in 1974–75 he was briefly the chief agronomist for the large united collective encompassing Lapos, then downgraded to the agronomist of Lapos's subdivision. While nagygazda-s have occupied such positions in greater numbers than their share of the population due to their knowledge, prestige, and so on, their number has still been small.

In fact, a large set of beliefs and stereotypes concerning the brigade leaders and other administrators are reflected by this labeling. It was observed earlier that many of the brigade leaders are accused of being vulgar and verbally abusive, and that some are said to drive their workers too hard. Another stereotypical aspect of "kulak behavior" attributed to the leadership is "wanting everything only for themselves." This reflects the feeling that the leaders try to keep the workers from earning too much, at times even from receiving their just earnings. Stories abound that the one who sets work norms often assigns fewer work units or a lower rate of payment than what workers think right or appropriate, and of brigade leaders incorrectly writing down a worker's labor or miscalculating his pay. Some of the latter mistakes are viewed as incompetence; they serve to corroborate workers' attitudes concerning the presence or absence of special knowledge, ability, and training among brigade leaders. The occasional refusal of some brigade leaders to acknowledge such errors is sometimes taken for stubbornness and sometimes as a sign of desire for personal enrichment. Some are even convinced that the local doctor has connections with the farm leadership. They say he will often not give them sick leave, even when they are legitimately sick. They feel the farm and the leadership are trying to squeeze the most possible work out of them at the least cost.

The fact that brigade leaders earn more than the average worker (though many animal-tenders, milkers, and skilled workers earn more on average than some of the brigade leaders) and the highest leaders and administrative workers much more (two or three times as much) reinforces this view. Though many members acknowledge that some leaders keep the best interests of the farm in mind, even they feel that some want things only for themselves. In members' minds this takes the form of keeping workers' earnings down and receiving correspondingly higher wages or bonuses for bringing greater profits to the farm, or of corruption through graft and patronage—appropriating the farm's resources and best jobs for themselves and their close ties.

One other aspect of the kulak stereotype allegedly shared by the brigade leaders is that they take advantage of women. In the extreme, a few suggest that every brigade leader "has a woman" other than his wife. Some supposedly carry on affairs with those they supervise. Brigade leaders allegedly extend favors—higher pay and steadier and easier work—to these women or to their family members. Many villagers believe that some women play up to the brigade leaders in order to obtain more favors, since it is they who control the individual work assignments and calculate the pay. The strength of these beliefs is manifested in the willingness of some women to attribute such motives to fellow workers who have better pay or work.

It is noteworthy that, though such "kulak" behavior was sometimes attributed to wealthy peasants in the past, it was perhaps more common of foremen and overseers on large estates (Illyés 1967: 188–203). This suggests three possibilities, none of which necessarily excludes the others. First, lacking other role models for directing workers and filling leadership positions, many brigade leaders and other high administrators, particularly the older ones, may have copied the models of the past.

Second, many villagers, similarly steeped in such cultural expectations, are wont to interpret situations, behavior, and others' success or failure according to past patterns. These perceptions may be accurate at times, but often they may be an older interpretation of newer, incompletely understood demands and contingencies.

Finally, however true these hypotheses may be, the characteristics attributed to the leadership undoubtedly reflect an increasing gap between leaders and the led, a gap strongly felt by villagers. Even while complaining of corruption, patronage, and nepotism, inequities and injustices, and the occasional "selfishness" or intransigence of leaders, farm members are quick to point out that, more than ever before, a man earns what he works for, and that those willing to work will prosper. At the same time, it is clear that what started out (as many informants expressed it) as "one large family" in each of the early farms after 1959 has in the intervening years become more stratified and differentiated. Many feel that they have less control over their own work, the management of the farm, and the important decisions that influence their everyday lives as farm members than they did in earlier years. Although recent events have exacerbated this tendency, the feeling was widespread in Lapos even before 1974. The leadership, despite a lack of specialized training, has left the membership increasingly out of the decision-making process (though it is unclear at times how much the leadership itself has played an active role in these decisions)[6] and has grown apart from the rest of the membership.[7] For many villagers, this has been a disappointment and a strong bone of contention. For although they were skeptical about the collective to begin with, once they had accepted the inevitable they became eager to make the best of it, to cooperate as equals in a community enterprise.

PATRONAGE, NEPOTISM, AND CONTROL

According to a letter to *Szabad Föld* of September 20, 1970:

In our village things developed so that the head administrator is the president's daughter, and the second administrator is the daughter of the president's wife's cousin. The Control Committee's president is the husband of a cousin of the president's wife. The second agronomist is the husband of another cousin of the president's wife. The warehouse head is the cousin of the president, a brigade leader is also a relative of the president's wife, the truck driver as well, as is the chauffeur. The head bookkeeper is the vice-president's cousin, the first agrono-

6. A similar pattern of political alienation seems to exist in some Transylvanian Romanian villages, both in the cooperative farms (Kideckel 1976: 271, 272, 275) and in the village councils (Sampson 1976: 338). The apathy and feelings of futility of villagers in these cases seem to stem more from centralized party/state direction of local policies that leave villagers little real voice in local matters.

7. Sárkány (1978: 123) reports a different situation in Varsány: "family and kinship ties also bind the leaders of local origin to the rest of the inhabitants; thus we cannot speak of a sharp line of demarcation between 'leader' and 'led,' although undoubtedly the interweaving of higher technical training and the leadership sphere separates people of different work functions from each other, especially if the leaders are not locals." Similar ties exist across incipient strata boundaries in Lapos today; indeed, they also spanned pre-World War II strata boundaries, as did many other ties. Nonetheless, in Lapos, then as now, villagers perceived a strong distinction between "leader" and "led."

mist the husband of the vice-president's cousin. Most of the other relatives of the vice-president obtained the community's other posts—sometimes without qualifications. The kinship connections extend even to the management of the post office and the general store. Now and then inventory is taken in the general store, and the post office is inspected. But the two are never inspected at the same time. The manager of the general store sends the store's receipts to his wife at the post office [which has banking facilities]. If he notices a shortage, he fills out a check, and his wife stamps it. The post office is now short of the money, but only for a couple of days while the inventory is coming to completion in the general store. Then the store manager quickly replaces the shortage at the post office with his daily receipts and now there will be a shortage at the store until the next inventory. Thus, the post office can easily protect the store manager from a shortage at inventory, especially if the postmaster is the store manager's wife.

This letter, which appeared in a nationally distributed newspaper directed mainly toward rural readers, is a description of Kislapos. The charges about inventory shortages cannot be verified, but the letter is otherwise accurate, if somewhat incomplete. One or two aspects have become even more extreme. When the president of the local collective assumed the presidency of the united collective in 1974, his daughter became the enterprise head despite specific prohibitions against such arrangements in the bylaws. His son-in-law became head of the collective's meat-processing plant. The president's nepotism is widely believed to extend much further, and the facts seem to bear this out. Although the president has relatively few close blood relatives in Lapos—his father had no siblings there, his own siblings left Lapos, died early, or were widowed, and relatives on his mother's side have largely left the village—and his wife was an only child, he has a large group of relatives, including many sógor-s, through marriage by virtue of the seven siblings each of his parents-in-law. Moreover, almost all of them were from the group of precollective middle peasants who assumed greater importance in village leadership after 1959, and they have provided a local base of support for the president.

In the beginning, most of these relatives had positions little different from those of the rest of the membership. As the differentiation of the farm's job structure increased, as animal-tending and jobs dealing with machines came to be better paying and steadier, an increasing number of the leaders' relatives entered these positions. Young male relatives returning to work in the village from exhausting commuting to jobs in the city were offered similar posts. Today these relatives typically occupy positions like milkers, animal-tenders, truck drivers, that of the president's personal chauffeur, brigade leaders, and others considered desirable and higher paying.

Because more than half of the male-occupied positions are considered among the more desirable jobs, there are not enough relatives of the president and his wife to fill them. But, compared to everyone else, a disproportionate number of these relatives occupy desirable positions.

Most members have been pleased with the farm's performance, including the president's leadership, and with the considerable improvements in their life circumstances; however, the nepotism, patronage, and corruption of recent years have brought increased envy and, with that, dissatisfaction with the president in the eyes of the "have-nots." They feel that those close to the leadership can and do expect more for themselves (including the best jobs) and feel little sympathy for others. A truck driver's close relative complained that the president's wife's cousin's husband, also a truck driver, gets a newer truck earlier than his kinsman even though the latter has been a truck driver longer and has long driven the same old truck, while the leader's relative has several times received another truck. Another member attributes this partially to the selfishness of the president's relative.

As the above letter makes clear, villagers also believe that relatives of other leaders have greater opportunities. They cite examples: the school teacher son-in-law of the agronomist living in a distant town, who was hired to replace another tractor driver for the hard, demanding, but lucrative combine driving during the wheat harvest; the local postmaster, originally hired through the alleged influence of her brigade-leader, party-member father despite the apparently higher qualifications and greater need of two other candidates; the brother of the wife of the party secretary (who is also a brigade leader), displacing a longtime animal-tender and thus joining his two brothers in animal-tending positions.

Those closer to the leadership, both in reality and in the eyes of the villagers, include not only relatives of the leaders but the former middle peasantry. For example, before he himself had assumed the position of animal-tender, the party secretary's brother-in-law, son of a former cseléd, had complained that all who were good middle peasants in the past are now animal-tenders and milkers. Many people claim that those who "stand close to the fire [leadership]" receive more privileges and better positions, pay, and bonuses than others. Without patronage from above, one has a greatly reduced chance of achieving a good position or good pay. Those who hold this view cite scores of examples of their fellow workers getting better machinery, more regular work, and higher pay because they are friends of the brigade leader or of higher-level leaders.

The alleged favoritism is not restricted to jobs and pay. Villagers have complained that some receive greater disability pensions than others due to connections. Others have thankfully cited the president for helping them receive higher retirement pensions by allowing them to work longer hours in their final year, to achieve higher earnings and ultimately receive a higher pension. There have been both praise and complaints about the president's giving or refusing monetary or material aid for housebuilding or renovation, or loans for this and other large purchases.

Complaints abound about the allocation of houseplots, especially about receiving poor-quality land while others supposedly "closer to the fire" receive better land. One retired member remarked that the president sees to it that the aged receive good-quality plots close to the village only because his father-in-law is also old. There are occasional complaints about mismeasurement of plots and disputes about how much should be allotted. An older widow, a nonmember of the collective and thus ineligible for land rent from her member husband's former land, complained that after her husband's death she was not allowed to join the farm, allegedly due to her age (sixty); yet close relatives of the president in similar circumstances who were even older were supposedly allowed to join and benefit.

When the intake of the farm's meat-processing plant was severely reduced because of renovations, members who raised pigs and contracted with the farm desperately tried to sell their animals before they passed out of the weight range that draws the highest price. But the farm still bought a few pigs each week, and many claimed that the brigade leader in charge of procurement took delivery from the relatives and friends of the leadership. Some claimed, for example, that the party secretary's pigs were picked up twice, only to be returned both times for being underweight. At the same time, others' pigs were allowed to go overweight and unbought.

One pig-tender caught stealing from the farm was sentenced to six months in prison. Many claim that the president arranged matters so that he could serve the six months working for the collective farm instead. Others with no such patrons have been discharged from farm membership for lesser thefts.

Some allegations are even more serious. Numerous villagers believe that several of the most expensive new houses, built both in the village and outside it by some of the farm's leaders and administrators and by the local doctor, were constructed with material owned by and/or labor supplied by the farm without adequate compensation. In some cases outright theft is suspected. During my research period rumors circulated about police investigations into the matter.

It is difficult to say how much of this favoritism is just that. It is clear that the president and other leaders exercise considerable personal discretion in many such matters and may well grant favors to some and not to others on the basis of personal feelings and personal connections. However, it is also clear that the beliefs about favoritism are so deeply ingrained in some that almost any action or decision is interpreted in line with these beliefs. If one's own request is rejected, it is automatically unfair and is due to one's previously voiced complaints and to prejudice. Acceptance, though basically deserved anyway, is interpreted either as totally justified by the fact of one's rightness or, occasionally, as due to a leader's largesse. Others' success and failure are interpreted likewise, though sometimes conversely, depending on personal sympathies and antipathies.

It is obvious that, if houseplot land is randomly distributed, some will receive poorer quality land and others better. However, villagers often cite examples of some members' receiving better land as confirming evidence for their suspicions, while ignoring an equal number of countervailing examples. Many other cases are similarly interpreted. Members are often ignorant of some of the rules applying to their cases and are prone to see the application of universalistic rules in personalistic (or particularistic) terms.

On the other hand, the prevalence of the view that matters would change with new leadership and the perception that conditions differ elsewhere suggest strongly that all this is not groundless suspicion, that it has considerable basis in fact. This view is strongly reinforced by several elements. First, when in 1976 a new president was inducted who strongly emphasized the protection of collective property, within a year most of those suspected of larger thefts and private use of public property were demoted or placed where they had less access to collective holdings. Indeed, the whole local administration was strongly shaken up.

Second, since the merger of the farms in 1961, many villagers who voiced dissatisfaction with the leadership's policies or actively opposed some of its actions met with official or unofficial sanctions. One tractor driver who successfully spoke, at a General Assembly meeting, in opposition to the leadership's suggestion to dismiss a member from the farm, found that soon afterward his tractor went unrepaired for three months. The son and daughter-in-law of an older member who often spoke publicly against the leadership's decisions were told by their respective superiors that they would do better for themselves if the old man would not speak up. In general, members feel it is not worth speaking up, lest one receive poor or only sporadic work from disturbed leaders or face other repercussions.

More serious sanctions are also reputed to have been imposed. One woman is alleged to have been demoted to a lower position when it was reported to the president that she had been telling others that district and party officials had received gifts of fruits, vegetables, and poultry from the farm. Another member was dismissed when he led a campaign to unseat the president, accusing him of committing wartime atrocities as a policeman sent to patrol a Hungarian city in Slovakia that had been returned to Hungary by the Vienna award of 1938. Several others joining in the attempt were supposedly bought off by favors and promotions.

Some state that this has been the situation since Kislapos's three farms merged and local leaders consolidated their positions. A few suggest that the beatings of the early 1950s left their mark on locals and made them fearful about speaking up. This seems an unlikely explanation because most villagers perceive a vast difference between conditions of the past and present. In any case, many villagers feel that members of other collective farms speak up more and are more forceful in making their desires known to leaders and in attaining their goals. Harvesters from a neighboring farm who work alongside men from Lapos once successfully demanded beverages to keep from dehydrating in the sun before they would resume work on their machines. The men from Lapos were pleasantly surprised since they would not have dared to make such demands.

Several factors have strengthened the position of the leadership. First, by unreservedly supporting his brigade leaders when disputes with them have arisen, the president has built up considerable political credit and thus has been able to count on these men for support. As one former brigade leader related, if there was a dispute between ⌐ ' rigade leader and a worker, the president sided with the leader even if the worker was right "lest he discredit a leader." However, the control extended still further. As the same former leader put it (and as many others concurred), the complainant could always go to the Disciplinary Committee, but that was also influenced by the president. Many feel that he was equally capable of manipulating the Control Committee and that, though some members on it held a degree of antipathy for his decisions, he was able to have his policies accepted.

The same was said about the Disciplinary and the Complaint and Grievance committees. The former, some said, ignored lapses in the execution of duties by leaders (for example, allowing grass or alfalfa to be stacked and stored without proper drying, causing buildup of heat and sometimes fire in the stacks) but punished workers, especially those in disfavor with the leadership, for minor offenses like "obtaining" a few vegetables at work. Some felt that, while the leaders were privileged, they were not accountable—there was no real responsibility. As one member put it, the Disciplinary Committee is merely a "formality. They baptize it so it will have a name." The Complaint and Grievance committee (required in all farms by the Unified Coop Law of 1971), which was to settle disputes between management and the membership, similarly swallowed complaints without a trace despite the fact that it was appointed by and responsible to the General Assembly and was forbidden to include representatives of management (Robinson 1973: 267). Apparently the leadership was still able to control the nominating process. Some members claim, further, that those on the Control Committee who disagreed with the president were not reappointed. Indeed, supposedly the president several times overruled the committee that determined the distribution of bonuses; according to some, for years these were based on the personal preferences of the leadership.

A large portion of the membership thus believes that the present leadership (before the change in early 1976, that is) has been able to establish a local base of power through kinship and to build on it through credit gained via patronage and by the numerous rewards and punishments available to it.

OUTSIDE CONNECTIONS

For many villagers, the picture drawn thus far is incomplete. The ultimate power of the president of the collective farm, they claim, rests in the backing he receives from higher circles. Over the years he has established ties with members of the district and county councils[8] and (having joined the party soon after the establishment of the collective farms) with higher party officials. Since for a long time these three groups largely determined the year's agricultural plans and the farm's investment policies, pay scales, and even sales outlets for produce, ultimate power rested in their hands. One villager, speaking of the mergers in the 1970s (which, of course, most villagers did not want and which were pushed from above), reflecting the beliefs of many, said that if this president had not accepted the merger plans, a new president would have: the implication, of course, is that the choice of the president, while formally resting in the hands of the membership, is essentially determined by higher political circles. Thus, the president has had to make solid connections with higher organs. Many are convinced that he has done more than merely establish a strong working relationship with them. They claim that he has traded favors with them and that, with the credit he has built up, he has been able to increase his local power and save himself from severe threats to his power and position.

Much of this trading of favors has involved gifts of collective farm produce, poultry, and meat. Typical is the claim that higher party and administrative officials have often visited the farm and packed their car trunks with produce and poultry. This may have had the effect of creating good will toward the farm as well as its leaders, but many villagers resent it. They see this as one more example of the leaders wanting more for themselves and strengthening their own positions while trying to eliminate small-scale theft by the membership (of course, this small-scale

8. District councils were abolished in 1970 and their powers transferred to the county councils. This lessened the ability of such councils to dictate policy to local collectives, particularly since the majority of county council members must be elected by the relevant local councils from among their own members. But it also leaves some possibilities for domination by the district party committee, which can step into the vacuum created to take over some of the district council functions (Robinson 1973: 168, 249, 265–266).

"obtaining" can mount up to huge losses for the collective). Reflecting this is the reaction of one villager to the news that the local field watchman had hauled in the drivers of the postal truck for picking a few paprika from the fields. Instead of approval, the watchman was given a dressing down for the action, for creating a great fuss over a trivial infraction. The villager joked that the watchman's problem was that he did not yet know how to differentiate between those who are allowed to steal and those who are not.[9]

In the same way, villagers resent the leadership's wining and dining of visiting party, administrative, and "corporate" officials (for example, of the consumers' cooperative and produce-buying and distributing agencies with whom the farm does considerable business) on farm funds and produce.

Similar practices had served to strengthen ties with the local council and allegedly even the police in the past. For years, the council president received a cow from the farm; when this became known the practice ended, and he was forced to pay for past gifts. One villager charged that in the early 1960s he was sent a tax bill for land worked in a neighboring community, which in fact had been used by a policeman serving locally and had been awarded by the farm.

The president no doubt also built up a store of political credit by his willingness to carry out orders and policies handed down from above. This and other forms of credit have served him well. Members have mixed feelings about the president. They feel that during the seventeen years of his presidency he has pursued bold policies that have benefited the farm and its members. But it is felt that in later years he has increasingly grown "superior" and has come under more and more private (not public) criticism, and that he has used his connections and strong support from above to put down attempts to unseat him. Numerous villagers expressed the opinion that a police investigation clearing him of charges of wartime atrocities was merely a coverup and was stifled by his connections. Similar intervention mediated by the president is suspected in the case of the pig-tender who was able to work off his six-month jail sentence in the farm. A few even believe that some of the corruption they perceive in the collective is sanctioned by higher officials.

In general, villagers feel that farm leaders receive better treatment than other members from the law and in the justice of the collective. In 1975 a meek sixty-year-old worker, unhappy with the assignments he had been given, accused a brigade leader, the local party secretary, of giving good

9. The watchman was the same villager who in the 1950s, as a member of the Petőfi collective, reported the illegal slaughter of a pig by the farm's leadership. This did eventually lead to prosecution of the offenders, but it did not endear him to local and higher party leaders, who ultimately recommended that he quit the farm. This incident, too, played a role in the villager's remark.

work only to his supposed mistress. For this he received several sharp blows from the brigade leader, who several days later was persuaded to apologize formally. The worker, however, was sensitive to the teasing he received from his fellow workers and was despondent over the incident; a week later he hanged himself in his small stable. Many felt that the brigade leader was in some way responsible for his death and that his position as party secretary saved him from official sanction.

In another case, the father of a member was accidentally run over by a car. Some claim that a close relative of the president was really driving, but that he persuaded the chauffeur with him to shoulder the guilt in return for compensation. The member, who is supposed to have witnessed the incident, allegedly was promoted to brigade leader for remaining silent.

When the president of the farm eventually did step down in 1976, it was not because the local opposition had forced him out. Rather, it was because there was opposition to him in the other communities and because higher party organs had offered him the choice of effecting hard, perhaps unpopular, administrative measures or resigning. Clearly, he had lost the support of higher circles, and his local support was of little moment. Indeed, it was the individuals who had benefited most directly from his patronage and/or who were most suspect of corruption or theft who were most affected by the demotions and new job assignments ordered under his successor.

BEHAVIORAL ADAPTATIONS AND ATTITUDES

Not only do many villagers who were interviewed disapprove of the practices and the lack of local democracy in the collective farm—at the same time acknowledging its real material benefits for them—but they also deeply dislike the behavioral and attitudinal tendencies that the practices have encouraged. Many feel that their lack of voice in the farm operations and the fact that they are ordered about puts them in a very subordinate position. Extending the metaphor of prefront social relations, they claim they are like cseléd-s, like hired hands taking orders from the kulak leaders. Some of this is inevitable, considering the strong desire for independence from others' control that many have grown up valuing and the state of self-sufficiency that was a culturally defined goal for generations before collectivization. Many did not want to join for precisely these reasons.

Some resent the humiliation they have felt under the new order and the perceived need for self-abasement to reach a good position in the farm: the strategy for obtaining a good position, known as *cigánykodás*, involves worming oneself into the good graces of the leadership through ingratiation, two-facedness, betraying fellow workers, flattery, holding back complaints, granting sexual favors, or, expressed metaphorically, "licking upward and spitting (or kicking) downward." As one worker argues: "One can't be on good terms with both the workers and the leadership." Alleged examples of such behavior include the following: a would-be truck loader helping out a driver by cutting wood, assisting in the delivery of a calf, and doing other favors to win the position; women in the collective hoeing a brigade leader's houseplot so he would arrange to sell their pigs to the farm during the renovation of the meat-processing plant; the demotion of the woman worker who had reported gifts of produce and poultry to higher officials—a demotion allegedly caused by her brother-in-law's bearing of tales to the leadership; the general be-friending of brigade leaders by workers.

Two elements not seen as either necessary or sufficient determinants of good positions and good pay are ability and hard work. The first has been discussed. The ambivalence regarding the second is seen in the remarks of several members: *aki melózik az nem ér rá pénzt keresni* (he who works is too busy to make money). In the eyes of many members, those who have large salaries do not work much, while those who work long hours, particularly doing physical labor (*meló*), earn less. Reflected in this observation is the members' feeling that only physical labor is "real" work. It is, of course, irksome for many to see people they consider no more talented and little better educated than themselves receiving higher wages without doing any "real" work. Beliefs about party members, those "close to the fire," and alleged corruption often find expression in this observation.

Many perceive an increasing envy among villagers of the success of their fellow inhabitants. The lack of perceived "objective" justification (superior knowledge, talent, or education, for example) for other work-ers' advancement to better jobs or leadership positions and the belief in unfair behavior of fellow workers both serve to increase envy of those with superior rewards. The envy, in turn, strengthens such beliefs.

SOME CAUTIONS

Although it is uncertain how well these beliefs and envy reflect real events and motivations, it is clear that there is considerable truth to vil-lagers' allegations. The importance of this should not be minimized. It is likely that increased training and education of members, increased exer-cise of cooperative democratic principles, increased sensitivity among leaders, and significant reduction in favoritistic tendencies of the collec-tive farm will help weaken such beliefs and envy. The actions of the new president have been strong in these directions and foreshadow a reduc-tion in discontent. Nonetheless, given the persistence of some fundamental structural and attitudinal factors it is likely that many, though fewer, of these problems and complaints will persist into the future.

For one thing, it is ironic, though perhaps understandable, that such beliefs come in the face of far greater equality and personal opportunity than has ever been known. In fact, most villagers—and many of them are the same people who complain about and emphasize the importance of flattery, connections, and two-facedness—feel that those who work hard can create a decent life for themselves, that opportunities now are far better than in the past. In their own eyes, those less prosperous are those who cannot properly "steer" or "control themselves" (for example, who drink away their earnings, are lazy, or are not frugal). Some of the complaints may stem from the exaggerated perception of relatively small differences in wealth, income, and privilege. In the past, far greater differences existed on the basis of landed wealth and were accepted by many as natural (if not good) under a vastly different ideology and social structure. Today's egalitarianism focuses on the present relatively small differences, promoting discontent.

All this is further magnified by several closely related factors. First, such a large collective enterprise, no matter how egalitarian, has need of hierarchy and discipline. The local origin of the collective farm leadership can be an advantage; nevertheless, a native involved in the attempt to establish hierarchy and discipline risks making himself a pariah unless he is very sensitive to local feelings and individual needs. The lack of clear publicly accepted measures of ability makes the problem especially difficult and leads to some dissatisfaction no matter how great the talent of the leader. Often there is a need for outsiders to take leadership roles in order to avoid such problems and entanglements. This partially explains the relative satisfaction with the newly elected president.

Similarly, many villagers are in competition for higher-paying non-leadership positions, many of which as yet require little special ability or knowledge. Most villagers are still relatively uneducated anyway, so there are no objective grounds on which to distinguish among workers. Almost any choice is likely to lead to discontent on the part of those not chosen for the better jobs.

A second factor has been the nature of the position of the president. He is technically elected by the members of the collective farm, though it is clear that higher party and administrative organs also play an important part in his selection. At the same time he is the transmitter and often the administrator of policies generated outside the local farm by these higher authorities. Because of this, many policies and practices essentially dictated from above have been attributed to his personal desires. Members have recognized this when mergers were called for, whereas they probably have not when greater farm investment and economy were indicated, often at the expense of greater increases in wages and benefits. Some of the belief in the selfishness of the leadership may stem from this.

A third factor has been the generalized tendency to attribute personal intent to leaders when they have employed universalistic criteria in applying a policy or rule to a member's situation. This is sometimes due to members' imperfect understanding of the rules and sometimes to the pervasiveness of the application of particularistic criteria in the past and, in many cases, in the present. Many people assume that most decisions are still made on the basis of such criteria. Of course, many of the leadership have *not* always used universalistic criteria, and, as we have seen, there are glaring examples of their use of personalistic ones.

Finally, however, it is not always certain that those holding a grievance really want universalistic criteria applied, rather than just different, more favorable personalistic ones. They may decry the use by others of tactics involving personal connections, yet they themselves are not above using them. Indeed, Jávor (1978: 364) claims that in Varsány villagers often try to establish direct personal relationships with village officials, attempting to establish a basis for the village norm of reciprocity. Through this they seek to commit the officials and thus transform the relationships to unofficial personal ones. If they succeed, villagers feel that they can rightly await appropriate reciprocation.[10]

Jávor's observations characterize Lapos as well. Similar tactics have been observed in the villagers' use of protekció (though they themselves do not call it that) and of the ubiquitous tipping in its various forms to obtain favors or better services and goods, or even admission to better

---

10. A similar combination of the three factors above has been noted in the problems associated with the positions of collective farm leaders in other socialist countries. In Romania, in Transylvanian cooperative farms the brigade leader is an "information broker" between the farm administration and the workers, but he must also "fill a number of other roles in that he is himself a local producer and a kinsman or neighbor to other villagers. The demands of these roles frequently conflict, so that those who hold the position . . . are subjected to considerable stress." The brigade leader "is forced to mediate the conflicting demands of two systems . . . with which he is simultaneously involved and as a result, satisfies neither" (Kideckel 1976: 271). The president is the ultimate arbitor of members' complaints; this and his administrative duties keep him from showing up in the fields and participating directly in the production process. Because the president "is constantly put in the position of supporting national CAP [cooperative farm] policies, rather than the complaining workers, social distance between him and the workers is increasing." This and his rare appearance in the fields lead to unfavorable evaluations of the president (ibid.: 272). Such problems have led to "a persistent disenchantment with the organization's managerial class," and it is suggested that "structural discontinuities (between workers and managers) . . . play a major role in impeding the production goals of the CAP, and will be an impediment to the building of socialism in the Romanian countryside" (ibid.: 275).

schools for their children. Many villagers admit to willingness to use the oft criticized flattery if need be. One retired member related an argument she had had with her husband. He resented being ordered about, and if a brigade leader gave him orders, he refused to obey them. His wife, disagreeing, said that if she were put in such a desirable job as his, she "would even lick the brigade leader's ass." Many villagers practice such tactics in small ways, but they term this "accommodating" (*alkalmazkodás*), as Jávor (1978: 335) points out, often a euphemism for lying or hypocrisy.

This discussion points up the often critical difference between the language of claims villagers use—the principles they claim to adhere to (which in themselves can conflict)—on the one hand, and the various strategies they use to reach their ends, on the other. This language of claims, akin to the "myths" and "principles" that Bailey (1977) sees political actors using, implies the acceptance of universalistic norms. Villagers speak in terms of using less favoritistic criteria in distributing jobs and other rewards, decry the lack of knowledge, experience, cultivation, and education of the leaders, and generally criticize the unfairness they perceive in terms of violations of universalistic norms. Farm leaders, on the other hand, claim that the leadership is democratic, argue that many of those who complain are ignorant of the rules and do not speak up to complain when they feel something is wrong, and extoll the virtues of the universalistic norms applied in Lapos, especially when comparing the present to the past. Many related claims are made and similar norms appealed to.

This discussion, however, should not mislead one into assuming that villagers all accept and necessarily act by the principles behind the language of claims. These principles may be accepted as legitimate versions of what should be, but perhaps not when applied to the villagers' own particular cases in an imperfect world. As Bailey points out, they are idealized visions of reality, which have some legitimacy but which are often advanced in order to achieve particular ends.

In particular, the advancement of claims paying homage to universalistic norms should not blind the observer into thinking that there will not always be conflicting personal goals in the farm, and that villagers will not make frequent private use of strategies based on the more particularistic norms that characterize other relationships in Kislapos.

Chapter 9

Social Ranking and
Social Perception

In analyzing the events of the past thirty-five years, and of both the change and the stability seen in Kislapos's social structure, little attention has been given to villagers' views of their fellow men. This chapter deals with the cognitive categories used by Kislapos's inhabitants in talking about and considering their fellow villagers, pointing up areas of stability and change in social perception.

The degree of continuity between the past and present is significant. The past three and a half decades have seen enormous social and economic upheavals in this rural community. The socioeconomic basis of village life has been profoundly altered, yet in fundamental ways villagers think about their fellow men in much the same terms as their parents and grandparents did. Why is this so?

Much of it can be ascribed to the relative lack of change in significant areas of social interaction and to changes that have permitted aspects of past social interaction to continue. The "small world," small village nature of life in Kislapos, which provides considerable knowledge of neighbors and fellow workers and face-to-face interaction with them, also plays an important role in this continuity. Moreover, many of those who are now adults in Lapos matured in the period prior to the most significant of these changes: collectivization of agricultural production. Some of the views of these individuals may be relatively immutable over time. However, impressionistic evidence suggests that today's youth, growing up in changed circumstances, and increasingly carried away from the village by schooling, the search for nonagricultural work, and a different life style, may differ from their elders.

METHODS

Data concerning the cognitive categories used by the villagers were collected in several ways. Much was learned from structured and unstructured interviews. Villagers volunteered opinions and observations about others and were asked to comment on significant figures in their lives, ranging from family members to village and farm leaders in the past and the present. These interviews give an idea of the organization and the salience of attributes in people's thinking. Similar information was derived from numerous conversations with villagers and among villagers. The interviews and recorded conversations were also important for obtaining as wide as possible a range of relevant themes. Essentially, I was interested in what kinds of individuals villagers perceived, in how they categorized and distinguished among villagers—including personality attribution.

Several formal tasks were also given. A few informants were asked to describe in detail fellow villagers of both sexes, to talk about their interpersonal behavior (*viselkedés*), personality (*személyiség*), and nature or disposition (*természet*), among other characteristics. Beyond that they were encouraged to talk about whatever they thought important.

A larger number of villagers performed sorting tasks. Individuals were given a small pile of about thirty cards on which were typed the names of villagers, all of the same sex (usually the same as the informant). A few older, retired informants were given names of people of their own generation or older, many of whom had already died or left the village. Otherwise, the names were those of adults residing in Lapos, varying in age from the mid-twenties to the mid-seventies. After going through the cards once to make sure it was clear whose names were involved (some names are duplicated in the village, although they are distinguished by Jr. or Sr. or by nicknames and occupations), informants were instructed to sort the cards into piles on the basis of similarity. Those cards with individuals who were most similar were to be placed together; those different were to be placed in distinct piles. Many informants asked on what basis they should sort, or what was meant by similar; they were told to sort on whatever basis they thought was important or clear to them. These sortings were recorded, as were any comments made about individuals named during the physical sorting and examination of cards. After a complete sorting, informants were instructed to combine piles, two at a time, in order of greatest to least similarity and to indicate the reasons for combining those piles. They were then asked to repeat the task using a different dimension or criterion.[1]

Finally, a few informants, from whom a sufficiently large corpus of attributions was obtained, were asked to rate thirty villagers of their own sex on a representative sample of about sixty attributions culled from their own protocols in previous tasks and interviews. They were to indi-

---

1. Quite often, informants used multiple criteria in a single sorting, mixing dimensions; for repeat sortings informants were simply asked to sort the cards in a way different from the previous sorting(s).

cate whether each of these attributions was true or not for each of thirty fellow villagers. These data were then run through an implicational analysis, which uncovers the structure of logical implications among attributions.[2] This gives some further idea of the possible relationships in villagers' thinking among the different attributes, of the organization of their perceptual world, of the model(s) they use in understanding human behavior. Of course, it does not specify the beliefs (if any) underlying these logical relationships.

PRESTIGE AND AUTHORITY

In both the past and the present, much of a person's social ranking and personal characteristics could be summed up by the prestige and authority he commanded, in short, by his *tekintély*. This had both socioeconomic and personal components. Today these personal components are summarized more by the degree to which a person is "proper" (*rendes*) and "cultivated" (*müvelt*). These categories, significant to villagers in their own right, will be treated later; the present discussion will focus on the socioeconomic, social ranking components of tekintély.

Power and Income

In the past, the most important element of tekintély and, in general, the most outstanding distinction made was the joint one of wealth-occupation and social standing.[3] As we have seen, wealth, especially in the form of land, was preeminent in determining social status and work possibilities in Kislapos; it is not surprising, then, that a potentially three-dimensional scale of social ranking (wealth, occupation, and social status) was compressed into one dimension. In sorting tasks and conversa-

2. The mode of analysis was that developed by Roy G. D'Andrade as set forth in D'Andrade (1976). The computer program on which these data were analyzed was written by me in 1974. It exists in two versions: one in ALGOL, compatible with the Burroughs 7800 in operation at the University of California, San Diego; the other in SIMULA, running on the Control Data computer of the Computer Technology Center of the Hungarian Academy of Sciences in Budapest. Listings of the program are available from me.

3. It is clear that important distinctions were, and are still, based on age and sex, as has become clear in Chapters 2, 3, 4, 6, 7, and 8. Such distinctions are reinforced by the continued operation of the Hungarian system of address and greeting, within which these two dimensions are important, along with closeness of dyadic ties and relative tekintély. They also receive emphasis in youth age groups and in school classes, and in the past were reinforced by church seating patterns, military service, and so on. This work will not deal specifically with age distinctions and characteristics associated with age differentiation; it will cover differences in the types of attributes and stereotypes associated with men and women.

tions, aged informants almost invariably made use of these socioeconomic categories when distinguishing among pre-World War II adult inhabitants of the village.

At the top of the scale stood peasants (nagygazda-s) wealthy enough so that their families could not work their land by themselves; they were divisible into those who performed physical labor alongside their hired hands and those, usually with more land, who primarily directed work. Beneath them were the middle peasants (középparaszt-s) who owned enough land to be self-sufficient and to provide a living for their family members. Next in ranking were the smallholders (kisbirtokos-s or törpebirtokos-s) whose holdings were too small to support their families with farm work and who thus had to find other means to augment their income and use their labor; they rented or sharecropped land or hired themselves out for day labor and harvesting. Those with little or no land of their own, the landless proletariat (nincstelen-s), were divided into two main types: those who did harvesting and day labor for wealthier peasants and nearby estates to scrape together an existence (arató-napszámos-s) and those who hired themselves out to wealthier peasants and large estates as seasonal laborers or year-long hired hands (summás-s and cseléd-s respectively).

Some, like the local priest, the notary, the school administrator, and teachers did not fit neatly into these categories; nor did craftsmen and storekeepers. The greater education and cultivation of the former group gave them high status and great tekintély as the village intelligentsia. Craftsmen and storekeepers sometimes enjoyed a status equal to the middle peasantry.

There was considerable shading of one category into another, particularly at the lower end of the scale. Each stratum emphasized one distinction over another, generally to its own advantage. Poorer smallholders were often lumped together with the harvester/day laborers in the category of share-workers (részes-munkás-s). Although there was often little difference between the living standards of landless share-workers and hired hands, the former in their responses tended to highlight the line separating the two. They especially noted the lack of independence and supposed lack of motivation of the cseléd-s, factors that played an important role in the low societal status and prestige of cseléd-s. On the other hand, the smallholders tended to contrast their own existence as independent private farmers (*magángazdálkodó-s*) to that of both cseléd-s and landless share-workers. They classed themselves with those who had enough land of their own and thus either took no orders or gave orders themselves.[4]

4. Jávor (1978: 299) reports that in Varsány even today it is this stratum of former smallholders that most strongly emphasizes past differences between strata, both upward and downward.

The landed peasants, share-workers and cseléd types formed a continuum of categories combining the occupational, wealth, and status dimensions. This continuum was based largely on the important values of independence and power, won through land ownership. Power and independence, or rather powerlessness and dependence, went hand in hand. The total interdependence, the absolute correspondence of these economic, sociopolitical, and occupational dimensions reinforced the prestige and authority of those at the top of the scale.

There were several stereotypes associated with the highest and lowest statuses: the wealthy peasants in the village were reputed to be bloodthirsty, to drive their hired hands to do as much work as possible, to take advantage of them and even beat them; cseléd-s were viewed by the landed as lazy, as lacking motivation and initiative.

Despite great changes in the social system, today's ranking system, especially for males, resembles that of the past. Although land has lost its basic importance, some of the above dimensions are reflected in contemporary rankings. The fundamental division among men is between leaders—collective farm president, council secretary, brigade leaders, and so on—and everyone else. For example, when informants used several dimensions at once in card sortings, leaders were not initially distinguished by behavioral characteristics, whereas others, besides being sorted by wealth and occupation, were categorized by drinking, friendliness, and the like. Of course, villagers could describe leaders in these terms and did so in conversations and other tasks. Nonetheless, this aspect of sorting further emphasized the separateness of leaders. Even when a behavior like drinking was mentioned in sorting tasks, it referred to leaders drinking in separate groups in the village tavern.

A characteristic of this division seen in the past is the notion of leaders and followers, of those giving orders and those having to take them, discussed earlier. The lumping of administrative workers with leaders reflects the past distinction between those who directed work and those who did the work (with only physical labor deemed as real work). Related distinctions are seen in the representation of some leaders as kulaks and in the self-characterization of some workers as cseléd-s in relation to those giving orders, even though the life of today's collective farm member bears little resemblance to that of yesterday's cseléd. Earlier discussion has revealed parallels perceived between present leaders and the wealthy peasants of the past, parallels that bore witness to invidious distinction against the leadership. Power and subservience are still important themes underlying these broad divisions. Some feel that "only the leadership has tekintély, special tekintély." They tend to distinguish tekintély from any overall evaluation of a person, from general respect and honor (*becsület*). Others have a broader notion.

The other workers tended to be ranked along several dimensions. One, essentially an occupational-income dimension, was a continuation of the leadership scale. Leaders are considered to be at the top of this scale, although some informants recognized that the incomes of many are no better than those of better-paid workers. Those with steady working conditions and high income were rated at the top (or at the middle, behind the leaders); at the lower end of the scale were those with irregular and poorer-paying work. Ratings of accumulated wealth almost completely mirror this scale, though thriftiness and perceptions of hard work and precollective wealth also have some influence in ratings. Villagers who work outside the farm are ranked among these men. Their status depends on income, but is even more dependent upon personal characteristics than those within the farm.

Women's rankings are still based largely on their husbands' economic and social status. When they are ranked in terms of wealth or income, their ordering corresponds strongly to that of their husbands. Though women's economic contributions are highly valued, their income is still seen as supplementary. In general, their prestige is based more on their husbands' positions. Only a few women hold positions of high power and prestige in the collective farm. To the degree that it is dependent on their own work and power, women's prestige is mainly based on doing "mental" (*szellemi*) or white-collar work rather than physical labor.

Sortings based on work typically divide women into three major categories: 1) those "white-collar" office workers (*irodista*-s), whose work is more intellectual, or at least not directly agricultural—including those with leadership or higher administrative positions, as well as school teachers and sometimes even the postal delivery woman; 2) agricultural workers in the collective farm; and 3) housewives. Sometimes the high-status group is labeled the "leadership branch" (*vezetőkar*); such sortings often include most of the white-collar workers above and the wives of some of the leaders in the farm, even if they themselves do not work on the farm. This group corresponds more clearly to the group judged most prosperous. The rest of the women are sorted into housewives and agricultural workers or according to personal attributions involving behavior and refinement. Indeed, for women these attributions of behavior and "cultivation" may contribute more to their personal prestige than other measures of social status. Certainly they are more important than for men.

PERSONAL ATTRIBUTIONS

Categories dealing more directly with the personal qualities and behavior of individuals are divisible into three main types: 1) work and thriftiness, 2) sociability and interpersonal behavior, and 3) cultivation and self-presentation. These themes are not completely distinct; they are not orthogonal dimensions. There is some overlap, particularly between the latter two; and some combinations are more likely than others. But they are conceptually distinct and are treated as potentially independent by the villagers.

These categories, too, bear traces of past distinctions; the continued high rate of personal interaction characteristic of village life and the accompanying knowledge of others' lives and habits play important roles. The collective farm may actually have increased the frequency of interpersonal interaction, especially among women. The importance of these attributional factors has probably increased. As the unidimensionality of the economic and political areas presented above diminishes, as a factor like land loses value, such personal characteristics are correctly understood to play more important roles in individual success and life style. The language of claims also changes accordingly. As land-based socioeconomic roles give way, such personal characteristics assume greater importance in defining social roles and behavior.

Work and Thriftiness

Today the categories of hard work and thrift are still important measures of a man. Although positive instances of willingness to work hard or put in long hours (especially in one's houseplot enterprise) are not always noted, negative ones are usually pointed out. Laziness is rejected, and individuals who are considered "slackers" (*munkakerülő*-s) or those who "loiter about" (*elcsavarog*) receive little respect, either in their presence or absence. Positive judgments are expressed in terms of "liking to work" (*szeret dolgozni*) or being "industrious" or "diligent" (*iparkodó, dolgos, szorgalmas*). Older informants especially value the latter traits and like to characterize themselves as not knowing what to do with their free time; they keep busy with one task or another. Such industry is highly valued, though those under forty increasingly value leisure time.

For workers, liking to work and earning a living by one's labor stand in opposition to several different traits and strategies for advancement. Taking the latter first, a constant theme of the villagers is the distinction between those who earn a living by their hard work and those who advance on the basis of two-facedness or personal connections. In the sorting task, for example, one elderly male divided up his fellowmen into those who are "good workers" and those with "good connections." Another, in his early forties, distinguished between the "flatterer" (*behízelgő*) and the "tale-bearer" (*besugó*) on one hand and the "proper" or "decent" type doing his job on the other. Typical of the combination of dimensions exhibited in sorting protocols and of the views expressed about the leadership, work, earning of a living, and respect for those who work is the sorting of a former villager in his late thirties, who married out of the village but retains close ties with his family there. He divided the village males into the following categories: 1) those whom he did not like, primarily leaders, who treated people badly, cheated their spouses, and/or tried to get something for nothing, to get money on other people's work; 2) those "who got into positions in which they don't have to work"; 3) a "betrayer" (*áruló*) or "informer" (*spicli*); and 4) "decent workers, people, physical workers."

Here, too, the hard-working majority doing manual labor is distinguished from the leaders, who do not do physical labor, but "use their brains." The latter may have tekintély, but many do not respect them as individuals, nor do they see them as good workers. This view stems, of course, from the manner in which many leaders are perceived to have reached their positions and from their lack of greater education. But women engaged in white-collar work (irodista-s) are not viewed so negatively. Rarely is it said that they do not work or that they received their positions other than through ability or training. Their continued relatively small numbers in the leadership positions and the perceived necessity for special aptitude or training in the positions they occupy probably account for this. Moreover, the pay of many of them is not significantly higher than that of their counterparts doing physical labor. That these women are often seen as being more cultivated, a characteristic befitting leadership, reinforces this perception.

Those persons perceived to have sought to escape the drudgery of work in the fields have been negatively branded. Though factory workers may have been looked down on for their lack of land in the past and their inferior agricultural knowledge, their basic stand toward physical labor was not questioned. Those enlisting in the army for other than mandatory service and those who became gendarmes and policemen, figures often unpopular in the village, were considered lazy and were said to join because they "didn't like to work."[5]

Even among those who do physical labor or who work in the fields there are some who "do not like to work." There are differences along sex lines in how this is manifested. For men, drinking and working are often set in opposition, though neither totally precludes the other. Some men are said to drink instead of working. They are late for work because of drinking, or miss a day after a drinking bout; on the job their work often suffers from the effects of alcohol. More extreme examples of this relationship are dissipated villagers who cannot hold down a job because of their alcoholism; they often meet with ridicule.

For women, drinking is not such a problem. Though a few women are said to drink away their family's earnings and others are known for their proclivity toward alcohol, drinking is not an important consideration in

5. Policemen nationally are the butt of many jokes, which otherwise resemble American "Polish" jokes.

the thinking about women. Verbal behavior is an important dimension of perceived feminine behavior. In particular, women who talk a great deal or loudly are considered to work less. One woman in her fifties, describing some of her fellow workers in the collective farm, said, "There are plenty of coworkers who are very loud. They like to earn a lot with little work." Many women in characterizing the type of coworker they choose in the fields rule out those who are lazy or talk too much. They often explicitly equate the two. This shows some evidence of changing, for younger women seem less averse to conversation during work than their elders.

Less important than work but closely allied is thriftiness. Like work, thriftiness is noted more in its absence than in its presence. Nonetheless, how a person budgets his earnings and time greatly determines his standard of living. As many say, those "who work and value their earnings will get something out of life." Men are considered negligent if they drink away a large part of their earnings; women are criticized for carelessly spending money on luxuries. Spending funds on food that one could raise on one's houseplot and paying for services that could be handled oneself are considered by many as both lack of willingness to work and wastefulness. Since a family's cash is usually still in the hands of women, it is incumbent upon women to be thrifty.

Prior to collectivization, willingness to work and thriftiness were central in the estimation of a person by villagers, for these were prime factors in the success of one's agricultural endeavors. Excluding inheritance, hard work and thriftiness were the chief avenues of maintaining or increasing one's holdings and providing for one's family. Although intelligence and cleverness were prized, they were not valued in peasants as much as hard work and diligence. Several villagers were admired for their intelligence and their ability to work with, repair, and even construct machines, but living by one's wits in minor entrepreneurial activities was denigrated and distrusted. Such people were labeled *spekuláns*, speculators, commercial adventurers, or profiteers. Negative attitudes were often evident toward horse traders, who bought rundown animals, "spruced" them up, and sold them for profit. It is also seen in the attitude toward the pair who constructed a well-digger for the pre-1959 vegetable growers' cooperative and tried to rent it to members for a personal profit, and the similar view of a retired farm member reputed to employ Gypsies for drinks and low wages to work a small plot of land for sizable profit.

These views reflect the traditional peasant distrust of entrepreneurs (and of wealthy peasant employers), a view reinforced by postwar regulations and ideology condemning profiteering. They also indicate the feeling that hard work, not speculation, should underlie success. The ambivalence (or perhaps just the desire to avoid saying clearly bad things about others) concerning such intelligence and cunning is seen in the summary comments of two villagers: "quick-witted, more speculative men . . . [who] can squeeze more out of life"; "these aren't bad [men] . . . Through speculation they cheat many people." This ambivalence is clarified somewhat by Jávor's observation (1978: 365) that diligence is central to the scale of values in Varsány. It sometimes was a goal in itself, in which the result was unimportant. The person who gained income by numerous time-consuming, painstaking tasks was more highly valued than someone who by an innovation simplified work. On the other hand, Varsány's villagers also feel that "there's room for a little guile in honor," that it is impossible to advance without a little theft, a little lying; only the degree separates "resourcefulness" (*élelmesség*) from crime (ibid.: 304). Thus, as Fél and Hofer report (1969: 139–140), hard work, in the form of physical fitness, was the most important personal trait sought in a potential spouse.

Judgments about the work of the wealthiest villagers and of the poorest are not much different from the stereotypes of the past. Nor is the theme of two-facedness and betrayal of recent origin. Speaking of prewar events and personages, villagers remarked about the following: the leader of a harvest band who "rubbed up" (*dörzsölődött*) against, or ingratiated himself to, estate managers to secure and maintain his position; a local village officeholder who owed his positions to his mayor friend and was considered by some to be an "ass-licker" (*seggnyaló*); a hired hand who reportedly informed to his wealthy peasant employer about the activities and opinions of other cseléd-s. Even Gyula Illyés, in his sociographic, semi-autobiographical account of the cseléd-s' life on a large estate, comments (1967: 11–18) on the frequent attribution to the Hungarian poor of two-faced behavior.

Men's drinking and women's chattering set in opposition to hard work are not new themes. Older villagers often mention drink having led fellow villagers, even fathers and grandfathers, to neglect their work or dissipate their holdings. The norm of brief visits between neighboring women in Átány, mentioned by Fél and Hofer (1969: 173), also common in Kislapos, reflects the attitude expressed in the past and even today that longer visits and conversations are impediments to work and the carrying out of household chores. Women in Lapos who engage in longer visits were and are potentially regarded as lazy chatterboxes.

One of the most important factors in the continued centrality of work is the very size of the village. Everyone knows everyone, and it is known what kind of workers most people are, from either firsthand evidence or hearsay. If anything, the collective farm has helped to increase the salience of work. In the past, villagers occasionally joined in collective labor and ascertained how others worked; otherwise they might sometimes see villagers at work in the fields. Today they constantly work in groups. Women farm members spend far more time together in work than did their precollective counterparts. Since both men and women have often worked on different types of farm tasks for the collective, they have had a greater chance than in earlier years to familiarize themselves with others' work habits. Because their pay often depends on the efforts of all the members of a brigade or a work team, they are more concerned.[6]

Sociability

Kislapos's small size and its relative isolation in the transport network are important factors in the salience of interpersonal behavior as a dimension of social perception. In such a village everyone knows everyone else, relationships are multiplex, and social networks are dense. Boissevain (1974: 90–92, 123–124) has pointed out that this leads to considerable "sociability" in the social personality of the inhabitants of smaller communities, indeed, often an inability to handle single-stranded relations. Villagers meeting strangers tend to personalize these new relations. Taking this one step further, one predicts that they would have strong expectations for such sociability. This, of course, is reflected in the many types of reciprocity and exchanges expected in multistranded relations involving kinsmen, neighbors, and other villagers. In the thinking of Lapos's inhabitants it is seen in the salience of categories of interpersonal behavior and sociability; that is, in general, how well one gets along with others, how easy one is to get along with.

Villagers are frequently characterized in terms of being friendly (*barátságos*), convivial (*kedélyes*), and amiable, gracious, kind, and pleasant (*nyájas, kedves*). On the negative side are several traits that help to define further some of the dimensions important for villagers: impossible to get along with (*összeférhetetlen*) and quarrelsome and petulant (*veszekedős, kötekedő*). Social qualities are preferred and emphasized that smooth the way for pleasant, frequent, if often superficial interaction. Persons who often disturb the peaceful flow of interaction are especially marked, including individuals who "find fault in everything" and "butt into everything." Having a bad temper is not ill thought of, as long as it is not constant.

Several related dimensions also contribute to sociability, but their absence is less negatively viewed. For example, those who are bubbly, exuberant, and outgoing or like to chat (*társalgó*) are often liked; but

---

6. The importance of this collective work and judgment is seen in the reservations of some older women about evaluating nonmember women with whom they have not worked. See also Jávor (1978: 342–343) for a brief discussion of evaluative judgments stemming from collective work and accompanying talk among women.

being reticent (*zárkozott*) or quiet is usually not devalued. Those who like crowds or active interaction with people (*a tömeget szereti*) are positively viewed, but those who are more introverted and keep to themselves (*magánakvaló*) are judged according to the motivation or disposition seen as underlying their behavior. Set in opposition to "meddling in everything" (in other people's business—*mindenbe beleavatkozik*), keeping to oneself is positively viewed as an attribute of quiet unassumingness, as "minding one's own business" (*saját magával törődik*). It is negatively cast when seen as selfishness or unwillingness to help. On the other hand, quietness and keeping to oneself are more valued than the apparently ubiquitous gossipy (*pletykás*) individual, or "nest of gossip" (*pletykafészek*).

Another important area is that of paying people the proper amount of respect. This has several different aspects, ranging from properly greeting everyone (*mindenkit megköszön*) and addressing them in a manner appropriate to their statuses to more generally treating them with due respect (*megadja a tiszteletet*).[7] Many villagers complain that some of the farm leaders, particularly the brigade leaders, are vulgar in their treatment of workers and that they do not properly "honor" (*megtisztel*) or pay due respect to them. There is also the closely related theme of being arrogant (*pökhendi*) or supercilious and uppish (*fölényes, lenéző*), of thinking oneself important (*azt gondolja, hogy ő a valaki*), on the one hand, and of being modest (*szerény*), on the other.

Finally, sincerity and honesty are prized attributes. As has been seen, flattery and two-facedness (cigánykodás) are disdained by many, and cheating and deception, or even lying by omission in trade and speculation, are considered highly questionable. More positively viewed are those who "tell the truth" (*az igazat mondja*), especially if vociferously or publicly, who are sincere, trustworthy, steadfast, and can be counted on (*megbízható*), or who are fair and just (*igazságos*). Considering the prevailing view about many in the leadership and the perceived roads to success, as well as the considerable political jockeying and upheaval of the past, it should not be surprising that these are important themes.

Less desirable traits are the related ones of always speaking one's mind (*ami a szívén van, a száján van; megmondja a magáét*) and always saying what one wants (*mondogat amit ő akar*). Though these bespeak

---

7. Among other things, this involves a greeting appropriate to the relationship between the two people, to the status and gender of the one greeted, and to the difference in ages. Criteria are similar to those involved in the system of address and to that of using the informal and formal modes of "you" (including the specialized forms of *tetszik* and *ön*). Proper form involves using the correct greeting term, usually with the lower-status person (generally the younger) greeting the higher first, and responding appropriately (see Chapter 7, n. 11).

sincerity, they are also denigrated because they are seen to reflect un-
thinking outbursts and lack of foresight, circumspection, sophistication,
and wisdom. Often those who are viewed negatively as loudmouthed
(*nagyszájú*) or flippant and insolent (*nyelves*) are seen as being free in
their comments.[8]

Aside from these more general attributions, most people also have
considerable specific knowledge about how others get along with their
families, their parents, spouses, and children. Especially noteworthy are
marital infidelity, family conflicts (bad relations between mothers- and
daughters-in-law, unhappy marriages), and particularly good or bad upbringing of children. In sortings these considerations were usually secondary, but in personal descriptions, conversations, and gossip they
played prime roles.

Although tekintély is determined largely by one's status in the leadership hierarchy, the other basic measure of an individual, whether or not
he is decent or proper (*rendes*) or honorable (*becsületes*), is based
mainly on these interpersonal behavioral attributes and one's work, diligence, and thriftiness. Honesty and fairness, hard work and thriftiness,
respect for others, and respectable behavior (especially involving one's
parents, spouse, and children) are all necessary for one to be considered a
decent person. Those who possess these traits are positively evaluated. As
one male near fifty expressed it, "I respect those who don't disdain the
friendship of others, who if they see that one is poorer or more helpless,
don't look down on him."[9] Having prestige and authority is not equivalent to being decent or proper. Pointing up the difference between
them, another member in his mid-forties said that, although he is inclined
to place greater faith in what a "decent" person says, "still, what they say
from above, what they order, is the important thing; in vain do I believe
what he [a decent person] says—that's the important thing [what they
order from above]."

Some traits are sex-linked. Men are more often characterized in terms
of their ability to joke, to give and take in joking interactions, to understand and take a joke (*nem tud viccelődni*). As observed earlier, this is
one of the basic requirements of male friendship, or at least a minimal
one for many. Men are more likely than women to use this dimension in
their descriptions and sortings.

The other partly interpersonal behavior category used frequently with
men and hardly at all with women is that of drinking: the amount drunk

8. These paragraphs hardly comprise an exhaustive treatment, of course; there
are numerous other attributions, and many more complex ones. But the more
dominant themes are covered here.

9. Jávor (1978: 331) reports that in Varsány the most important criteria for honor
are quality of work done and respect for one's fellowman, with greater emphasis
on the latter.

and the degree to which this affects work and behavior. Several men and women actually did a whole sorting only on the basis of drinking, while many others combined drinking with occupational, work-related, and interpersonal behavior sortings, as well as those involving "cultivation." For example, one woman, sorting on the basis of work, classified a group as "simple workers, tending animals, calm . . . they drink their liquor." Another woman distinguished between those 1) who "lead a sober life," 2) the type who "likes alcohol, takes some drinks, but who meets his family and work responsibilities," and 3) those who are "alcoholics, who drink during work."

The first group does not necessarily consist of teetotalers (though a few hardly drink at all), nor do these men never enter the village tavern; rather, they are minimally under the influence of alcohol and are rarely, if ever, intoxicated. The second category consists of individuals who are often seen in the local tavern and are occasionally intoxicated in public but whose lives and work by village standards are relatively unaffected by their drinking—though these often are criticized by close family members for drinking, spending too much money in the tavern, and coming home after work intoxicated. Some of those considered near the bottom of this group, indeed, even some near the top, had been seen in a drunken state being fetched with great difficulty by their children or wives from the tavern or from other villagers' homes (for example, after participating in a pig-killing). The final group includes those whose drinking often affects their work or behavior, who are frequently intoxicated. Some of them are viewed as doing very precise work when sober or as being friendly; they become, respectively, sloppy workers and quarrelsome or even wife-beaters during their frequent drinking.

Most informants made finer gradations than these in the course of conversation and interviews, especially in the amounts of drinking involved, the degree to which men "like to drink," and the point(s) at which drinking was considered to be a problem. Drinking is salient in the social perception of Kislapos; in both the past and the present it has been culturally and socially important. The salience is reflected in the number and variety of terms and expressions referring to drinking, to levels of intoxication, and to drinkers.

Drinking has traditionally been closely associated with all levels of social occasions and with work itself. In the past, day workers, harvesters, and even cseléd-s laboring on the estates or for wealthy peasants received a ration of brandy and/or wine as part of their expected payment—often a shot of brandy to start the day and a glass or two of wine at midday. Drinking of wine, beer, and brandy played a part in the men's nightly gatherings in barns and in the get-togethers of youths, was widely used in soliciting votes in local elections, and was everpresent in large amounts at family and village celebrations.

Today it is no less important. A prime activity for male friends is drinking together.[10] Family plots of wine grapes often produce several hundred liters of wine.[11] Until recently, many in the collective farm still started their day with a shot of brandy in the local tavern.[12]

Total consumption of alcohol locally has probably increased in recent years. In Hungary as a whole, between 1950 and 1972 per capita annual consumption of wine increased from 33 to 40 liters, of beer from 8.3 to 59 liters, and of brandy from 1.5 to 6 liters (Mieczkowski 1975: 235). A rise in the standard of living has enabled inhabitants of Kislapos to purchase more than they had in the past while keeping up much of their own domestic consumption. Here, as in the rest of Hungary, there is a great alcoholism problem.[13]

Villagers tend to be unaware of this. While they see that many "like to drink" and occasionally drink too much, causing accidents and frequent absenteeism at work, while many wives and parents complain about men's drinking and women refuse to give their husbands more pocket money lest they spend it all on drink, there is ambivalence regarding drinking in general and an unwillingness to see it as a problem. This is reflected in the sample sorting presented above, as well as in the comment of one villager in her thirties about her husband: *Nagyon szereti egy kicsit az italt* (He really likes to drink a little). Drinking is an accepted, though occasionally problematic, behavior for men.

Women are distinguished on the basis of their verbal behavior. Even attributions that are not directly verbal are couched in verbal terms. Women are quiet (*csendes*), which includes being steady or serious (*szolid*), placid or meek (*szelid*), and modest (*szerény*); or else they are outspoken (*szókimondó*), cheeky or insolent (*szájas*) or flippant (*nyelves*), gossipy (*pletykás*), quarrelsome (*veszekedős*), talkative (*beszédes*), and loud-mouthed (*nagyszájú*), and they chatter (*csacsog*), offend everyone (*mindenkit megbánt*), and speak more than necessary (*feleslegesen beszél*). Although many women enjoy others who talk a lot

10. In fact, until the opening of the new snack bar in 1977, the tavern was the only real gathering place for adults (mostly males) in the village. But this has not changed much, for the former tavern was transformed into the snack bar, which still sells alcoholic drinks, and the room next door, with a separate entry, became the new tavern. Most patrons of the old tavern now go to the snack bar.

11. And they often produce more than is reported to local authorities. Many families underreport in order to reduce their taxes on such wine.

12. This is a common pattern, both in the cities and the countryside. Measures invoked nationally in Hungary in 1978 to reduce alcoholism and work accidents have closed taverns at early hours of the day to curb such drinking. Sales of bottled one-shot portions of brandy were ended.

13. In 1978 and 1979, in recognition of this problem, the price of alcoholic beverages was increased considerably and other measures were instituted and programs expanded to curb excessive consumption.

and have a good sense of humor (*jó dumája van*), individuals exhibiting talkativeness and loud behavior tend to be more negatively evaluated; this is seen in the opposition mentioned above between talk and work, and in the fact that such behavior is not attributed to those women in the positively evaluated, "more cultured" (*műveltebb*) category. These attributes are correlated with negatively valued traits; their entailment by deeper negatively evaluated dispositional traits (impossible to get along with, *összeférhetetlen*; cantankerous, quarrelsome, *házsártos*; selfish, *önző*) implies that they are surface traits for these dispositions.

Why women are so characterized is uncertain. A woman in her fifties said (and many others implied) that "women in general are more loud-mouthed than men." This seems to be accepted by most villagers; impressionistic data suggest that it may be true. Women workers talk back to their brigade leaders (all men) more often than do men. At work they keep up more animated and constant conversations than males. The cause of this is unclear. One possibility is that men's dominion in the family in the past left only this avenue open to women for attaining power within the family.

Equally relevant is the far more frequent couching of women's than of men's behavioral attributes in terms of verbal behaviors. This seems to mirror their functional role differences in the past. Although much of a family's prestige depended on the farming ability, wealth, and work of the male head of the family, it was the wife who maintained ties with neighbors and relatives. While it was as often men's as women's labor that was the medium of exchange in such relations, women through their daily interaction with neighbors, relatives, and family, and through their help at times of family crises and celebration, were the lubricant that kept social exchange running smoothly. Their ability or inability in this area and in providing warmth within and between households is reflected in this category structure.

Collectivization and its accompanying changes have not significantly altered this. Temporarily, at least, they may have reinforced it. Those women who stay at home and do not join the farm still fill much the same roles, though their power within the family has increased as land has been devalued. At the same time, though men's working patterns may bring them together in labor more frequently than in precollective days, this is even truer of women working together in large brigades that encourage intense social interaction and continuing attention to women's verbal interplay.

One other global judgment frequently made about individuals concerns their nature or disposition (*természet*), or "basic nature" (*alaptermészet*). Judgments concerning this involve the same behaviors as many of the above distinctions but are more abstract, sometimes involving the evaluative dimension of good- and bad-natured. The former tends to encompass friendliness, fairness, quietness, even-temperedness, and helpfulness; the latter turns especially on being quarrelsome, impossible to get along with, irritable, unfair, dishonest, selfish, or in general, as many put it, ill-intentioned (*rossz szándékú*). Questions about a person's nature often invoked a response of X-natured, where X is a marked characteristic of the individual (for example, talkative, quiet, good-humored, heavy-drinking).

The most frequent responses are "nervous" (*ideges*) and "calm" (*nyugodt*). To some degree these are culturally standard answers to this question, but it is also clear from conversations that this dimension of calmness-nervousness is a very salient, if not central, one.[14] Villagers especially use this dimension when they speak of "basic nature." Although entailment analyses do not clearly tie this dimension to many other attributions, several traits are seen as signifying nervousness. Having an explosive temper (*robbanékony*) or being subject to sudden mood changes (*hirtelen*), talking a great deal, moving quickly, or always doing something all indicate this disposition. Nervousness as a dispositional trait seems to cover a general reactivity or sometimes activity, a lack of complete control over some inner energy. Calmness is more positively valued than nervousness, but the latter is not strongly disapproved of. It is seen as more basic to a person's character than the other traits, as something over which he has little control.

Cultivation

Refinement and learnedness constitute the third important area of interpersonal perception. These two facets of cultivation, or *műveltség*, are highly correlated though conceptually distinct. Learnedness has traditionally been highly admired in the Hungarian village; but few, however, were able to acquire many years of schooling. Usually only children of the wealthier middle peasants and the nagygazda-s were able to attend school beyond the sixth grade. Those who obtained such schooling left the village, entering professions or finding secure positions in the civil bureaucracy. The few educated individuals in the village, the teachers, the priest, and the village notary—all outsiders—who constituted the village intelligentsia were accorded great prestige. Today an education is easier to acquire and is still valued. However, greater education is demanded today to qualify for "learnedness," or *műveltség*, the primary meaning of cultivation.

There are degrees of *műveltség*. Some in the past who could read better, had a broader vocabulary, knew another language, or were familiar

14. My impression is that it is also salient in urban areas, though I am not certain its underlying meaning is the same there.

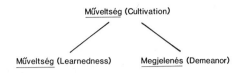

FIGURE 9.1 Forms of Cultivation

with a variety of subjects were also regarded as more cultured (művelt). Even today those who can speak intelligently about almost any topic are considered cultured. An extended notion includes refined behavior, calm speaking and even-temperedness. These shade over into the other area of műveltség: *megjelenés*, or demeanor (bearing, manner, mien)—not a physical or postural trait (though one or two villagers did sort on the basis of such physical measures), but a behavioral one. Thus, műveltség as cultivation serves both as a cover term for this dimension, encompassing learnedness and bearing, and as the term for the primary, more specific form—learnedness—in partial distinction to bearing or *megjelenés* (see Figure 9.1).

Several examples clarify this relationship and the different emphases. One informant, an articulate woman in her early fifties, was one of the few who stated the underlying dimension before beginning each sort (indeed, she would ask which dimension to do next: age, financial circumstance, status, cultivation?) and followed through without mixing dimensions. After sorting women by age, she followed with a sort on the basis of műveltség. This she divided into three major groups. The first was made up of those who had "completed [higher] schooling": a school teacher, a trained bookkeeper, several women who had gone to agricultural technical schools, and others who had completed gimnázium and had white-collar jobs. The second group was described as not having "completed [school], but better at expressing themselves" (*jobb kifejezésű*). One, for example, was said to have "improved her mind on her own" (*magániuton művelődött*). Of these two groups combined, she stated that they were "more at home in the world at large . . . When they meet, they have something to talk about or they're interested in various things that others aren't." The third group consisted of individuals who were "average . . . [with] little cultivation." About these she stated in interviews that they "didn't cultivate their knowledge." This sorting essentially involved the learnedness dimension with some extension of the meaning toward bearing.

A later sorting on the basis of a dimension she termed "status rank" (*ranglista*) involved many of the themes of sociability and interpersonal behavior. These were divided into five groups, the first consisting of one woman separated from the others more by age than character. She was "old, but can steer herself well . . . What she started, she did well. She's not selfish. With her speech she presents herself well." A second group, composed, with a couple of exceptions, of the first two groups of her earlier sorting (described above), was characterized by "serious thinking . . . One can't say that they look down on people." There were also remarks about specific individuals in the group: "She minds her own business; she lives her own life"; "they're fairly cultivated [refined? (művelt)] but haven't much schooling"; "she doesn't pass judgment on others, she doesn't run about [gossiping]." Of the third group, she said that they "sometimes like to gossip about one another." The fourth group was characterized as "nests of gossip. If something happened, you'll hear it from their mouths." They are also "quarrelsome types, big mouths. They're the ones you hear about in quarrels and fights." They are "selfish, impossible to get along with," and are the "louder ones." The final group was characterized by similar qualities, only "less so." Here the villagers were distinguished by their behavioral refinement, their demeanor. Those seen as more "serious," as better able to express themselves, who mind their own business, are more cultivated even without learnedness, and, in short, are művelt in the sense of having good demeanor, good manners or good breeding, were judged more favorably than the unrefined or boorish.

To make this clearer and to demonstrate further that these are two aspects of the same dimension, here is a comparison of the behavior of two village women by another woman in her mid-forties. Asked about the megjelenés of a similarly aged woman, she responded,

Well, her demeanor is a little boorish, sort of crude. In a word, you really can't compare her demeanor to [X's] . . . There's a big difference, so that if she's in a more dignified place, in good places, she's very . . . well, less refined, kind of crusty. [X] . . . is much more equal to the occasion; she can express herself in a more refined way . . . and she knows how to make an appearance. She behaves more properly in any situation, . . . she's more refined (műveltebb), although I think they're the same age; they both finished the eighth grade. But somehow she . . . can join in any discussion more easily than . . . [Y]. You see, she [Y] can't join in a conversation any time, she doesn't watch as much television, or I don't know . . . She doesn't improve herself as much.

Here, too, there are two different kinds of cultivation. One shades into the other, and there is the expectation that learnedness is somehow associated with, perhaps even causes, refinement of demeanor.

Men are similarly categorized, though, with the exception of the few men in the village who have had higher education and who for the most part work outside the village, demeanor, not learnedness, is the basis for distinction. For example, before sorting men on the basis of drinking and then financial condition, the older villager above divided the men into four groups: 1) one person who is "the most cantankerous, a drinker, hits his wife . . . whom you have to avoid . . . [who] on every ground is stupid— he even smashes windows"; 2) "average men, who are not completely uncultivated," but most either drink, are a little debauched (*kicsapongó*), "or like someone else's wife," and are "more laughable," doing things like "climbing out windows"; 3) those who "are also average, but their lifestyle is different, their bearing is different—[they] don't stand so stupidly, don't seem so good-for-nothing"— "at their level of cultivation, in their own way, they live a good life"; and 4) those who "make a better appearance," whose "degree of cultivation by village standards is better, for whom a book is more interesting." Further distinguishing between the last two groups, she added that the third "had just as much schooling, but they don't stand out. Their demeanor is all right, but they don't have the experience. They didn't develop themselves; they didn't reach that same level."

Speaking of a moderately cultivated man, the younger woman stated that his demeanor

was not so well polished . . . [but] like a peasant . . . He's not so refined, doesn't have much schooling. You can tell. But he's not stupid; he's more rustic . . . He's more rough-mannered because he's a peasant. You can see he's not a gentleman, he's not a schooled person . . . His speech gives him away. Not because he's vulgar, but it separates him from the more cultivated men. Otherwise, in his own way he puts in a decent appearance in his own group. Well, he's not an educated person. He's just a peasant type; that's the way he presents himself.

Only women have been quoted because, although men occasionally mentioned the categories of schooling and refinement, when they considered behavioral categories they were more likely to concentrate on sociability and conviviality than on cultivation. None of their sortings was as clearly based on cultivation or refinement. In general it appears that women, younger persons, and those who themselves are considered more cultivated are more likely to use this as an important criterion in distinguishing among villagers.

The shading of one type of category into another that we have seen, of one dimension into another, occurs frequently in the villagers' attribution and social perception processes. Many of the behavioral categories cited in the discussion of refinement are the same as those involved in sociability and interpersonal behavior, but they are nonetheless conceptually distinct in villagers' thinking. This is reflected in the types of questions that best elicited the respective types of responses.

Early in the study, questions about family members, friends, fellow workers and leaders tended to be restricted to the form of "What kind of (*milyen*) a person is X?" Some villagers did not know how to reply to these questions at first. All eventually began responding in terms of areas like viselkedés (behavior), természet (nature), megjelenés (demeanor), and *magatartás* (conduct, bearing—somewhere between behavior and demeanor). Besides using the categories appropriate to these areas, they specifically mentioned a person's viselkedés (especially with respect to others, their families, or the informant himself), their megjelenés, and természet. It soon became clear that to elicit salient perceptual attributions or descriptions of individuals in terms easy for them to deal with, it was useful to phrase questions using these terms. These organizing categories obtained in interviews match those of the sortings.

Much of the overlap in these dimensions and much of the mixing of dimensions derives from villagers' expectations of certain status positions. These expectations and stereotypes play an important role in the villagers' dissatisfaction with the local leadership. Leaders are expected to be cultivated, to be learned and to have a refined demeanor. Very often, the village and farm leadership are placed in one category, whereas other individuals are sorted on the basis of attributions of interpersonal behavior, some of which are related to cultivation, especially the lack of it. The implication is that this group is above such behavioral judgment, or that its members are more cultivated. When multiple sortings are made using different dimensions, most of those rated in one sorting as leaders are classified in others as more cultivated. If categories of sociability and interpersonal behavior are used, then, although the leaders may not be classified as friendly or modest (but, for example, as arrogant or disdainful), they are not for the most part seen as gossipy or quarrelsome, either. While some of the male leadership are viewed as vulgar and loud-mouthed, white-collar and leadership women are explicitly characterized as refined.

However, these are expectations that the leadership does not always meet, particularly the men. The expectations derive partly from the past, when the leading posts in the village were filled by individuals who were either more educated or refined. Those entering the village from the outside—the notary and the priest—were more educated than anyone else. The wealthiest peasants usually were able to obtain more schooling than their poorer neighbors. Those less wealthy who played leading roles in village associations often did so on the basis of some ability or talent that was widely acknowledged. One of the requirements for participation in the Peasants' Circle, especially important for leadership positions, seems to have been a minimum level of refined behavior.

There were also exceptions to this. Although an officeholder's ability might be acknowledged, officeholding might still be attributed to personal connections and patronage. Moreover, the behavior of some of the wealthiest peasants was considered much less than refined. Many villagers thought the less of them for this, but it is likely that the same type of reasoning underlay people's acceptance of the discrepancy, as mirrored by one villager who partially excused a very wealthy neighbor's arrogance: "He could afford to be arrogant." The extremely tight interdependence of economic, sociopolitical, and occupational dimensions and their reinforcement of the prestige and authority of the village's highest strata probably served to lessen discontent with the individual occupants of privileged statuses, or at least to hold up a definition of the situation as "natural." Today, no longer offset by wealth and its associated prestige, the occasional absence of these qualities in leaders is more negatively viewed than in the past.

Ironically, two other positive elements of the post-World War II transformation—the greater equality of wealth and opportunity and the vastly increased rate of social mobility—have helped increase discontent based on the lack of perceived cultivation among the leadership.[15] On the one hand, villagers are less willing to accept vulgar language and boorish treatment from leaders they consider little, if any, better than themselves. On the other hand, such mobility has elevated many of the former poor into higher positions (though the former middle peasantry still holds down most higher positions in Lapos). Both entailment analysis and inspection of sortings indicate a belief that those in the village of poor origin are less refined than those of wealthier origin. Those women considered quarrelsome, flippant, loud-mouthed and insensitive are also categorized as being of poor origin (though the reverse does not necessarily hold). To the degree that they have been able to take leadership positions through heightened social mobility, perceptions of decreasing leadership cultivation have also increased.

In particular, collectivization and the whole postwar transformation has broken down the old hierarchies and introduced newer ones.[16] Events have elevated new men from the ranks of the villagers into the leadership. These men and women have to meet many of the villagers' expectations regarding leaders, including learnedness and a more refined manner, as well as appropriate talent and skills. In addition, however, because of both the new egalitarianism and the leaders' rise from among equals, more is demanded of them. They are expected to be friendly to all, or at least to be gracious and not arrogant.

Thus, in the dimensions of cultivation and sociability, not only are leaders expected to be able to speak intelligently in any situation, they are also expected to adopt the proper tone in speaking to anyone. This is

15. Social mobility shows signs of slowing down as newer, privileged strata nationally are increasingly able to pass on greater wealth and particularly educational opportunities to their children.

16. Remnants of the old hierarchies still remain, especially in the differential in wealth between the former poor and the middle peasantry, and in the differences in emphasis placed on education, one of the keys to success and mobility, by the two groups.

exemplified by comments made about one of the local school teachers and the village's young agronomist. Of the former, one woman admirer in her fifties said that she

can interact with people in such a way that, let us say . . . if she speaks with a real peasant type, then she can turn that side [of herself] to provide a topic of conversation; on the other hand, if she meets with an intellectual, then she stands her ground there, too. She gives a good account of herself with every level.

A retired woman worker spoke equally positively about the young agronomist, who paid proper respect to her work and character and that of her constant work companion.

He always said that you don't have to give orders to the two old women; they know what to do . . . He's a very decent person . . . He judges the person by his work. We never argued with him. If he said . . . "[name of woman, using respectful address for older woman], this needs to be done. Would you do it?"

"We'll do it, [man's Christian name, using informal, friendly address for younger man, accented by diminutive]. Of course!"

"Then please do it."

Later he came back; he went around the fields once. "Did you take care of it, [respectful address for woman]?"

"Yes."

"Good. Thank you very much."

You see, he was a very decent person . . . Then there was a time when we were sitting when he came over. [The companion], having a very excitable disposition, jumped up. I said to him, "Now that you've come over, [informal address term], there's a free spot."

But he just replied, "Please sit down, [respectful address]. Just sit down. Let's talk a bit. Take a little rest."

Well, it really feels good for someone, right, when the employer says, "Just take a little rest." But he knew we'd do that quantity [of work].

Much of the appreciation of this superior stems from his ability and willingness to handle the idiom of respect, appreciation, and address appropriate to the villagers' age, sex, and work. This is an aspect of cultivation that shades into sociability.

On the other hand, others in high positions in the farm have been criticized for the lack of such behavior. One such official was said to

protect the collective farm's property, but is brusque with the members. She refuses [their requests]; she likes to reject them. If you go a little later than she thinks right, then she won't give out your pay. Or if you go early, she won't pay early . . . In a word, she's very haughty with the members. Where she feels that she is someone's subordinate, someone is her superior, there she's first class; there she can accommodate. With the members she's rough.

Another, the son of the former pre-front mayor, who for a while was the farm's agronomist, was the subject of complaint for similar reasons.

He doesn't have that graciousness . . . He isn't so friendly; he isn't so courteous to everyone. [In the barn] . . . he greeted everyone, but there was one person among the horses brushing . . . He didn't go over there [and shake hands with him]. To that person it was blatant. "God damn his kulak mother," he said. "He didn't even come over here, but he shook hands with you!"

The informant went on to say that despite his greater schooling, even technical school, this man was less able to deal with people than his former mayor father, who had only completed the sixth grade. He judged the man too laconic and said that, though he is not supercilious, he is comfortable only with his friends and childhood pals.

Thus, a combination of both sociability and cultivation is necessary, a graciousness, willingness, and ability to deal with all levels of people. It is significant, and probably no accident, that the first two individuals above, who received such favorable evaluations, were outsiders, while the other two grew up in the village. Although the latter two may simply be less socially skilled, there is also the possibility that at least one of them accepts the village view that those in the leading stratum "can afford to be proud." But when this status is not reinforced by wealth and its prestige and power, the superciliousness may be viewed as unjustified.

More significant, outsiders may benefit from lower expectations regarding themselves. Although as leaders they, too, are expected to be civil and cultivated, because they are not as deeply enmeshed in the village web of interrelationships, the gracious friendliness awaited from others might be expected from them in lesser degrees. To the degree that they fulfill or surpass minimal expectations, they meet with great approval.

Similarly, since they are not from the village originally, they have not "come up through the ranks" in the eyes of the villagers. When they entered the village they were not equals, but learned and trained individuals meriting respect by their status. Initially, at least, they were not so subject to the personal demands of sociability built up through years of interaction with fellow villagers. Locals, however, are subject to numerous expectations and in some sense will always be perceived as equals, especially if they lack superior training. For them the demands of sociability are greater; unfortunately, given the past models of leadership style (particularly employers') in the village, these expectations are more likely to go unmet.

Naturally it might be expected that such newcomers to the village would become increasingly embedded in village relations and subject to increased expectations. Both the outsiders discussed above, however, were able to do this and maintain their prestige and high rating. It may well be that the new collective farm president, possessing a university degree and continuing to maintain a home in Boros instead of moving to one of the villages, will benefit from the distance and from the lesser social demands he will be expected to meet.

It is perhaps no coincidence that the local leadership over the years has aroused the greatest dissatisfaction in Lapos. The great turmoil and local political conflict notwithstanding, it is significant that especially in the realm of leadership do we meet with high expectations concerning the separate but intertwined themes of rural Hungarian interpersonal perception, the dimensions of status and authority, work, sociability, and cultivation.

Chapter *10*

The "New Magyars"

      Gypsies constitute a rapidly increasing portion of the Hungarian population. A representative sample taken in 1971 showed that they number around 320,000, about 3 percent of the population. With a birthrate more than twice that of the rest of the population, it is expected that by 1990 they will account for 4–5 percent of the population (Kemény 1974: 64, 70–71). Other estimates place their present numbers even higher.

For several hundred years Gypsies have resisted assimilation and in turn have experienced discrimination in Hungary and in the rest of Europe. Their rapidly increasing numbers, the loss in the past half-century of their traditional economic roles in the face of technology and changed demand, and the increased attempts by the Hungarian government to bring them into mainstream society present interesting and thought-provoking problems for planners and social scientists.

Present-day efforts to integrate Hungarian Gypsies into the national society and to improve their living conditions are not the first such attempt. Following their appearance in Hungary and in Western Europe in the fifteenth century, their treatment in Austria-Hungary was generally less extreme than their persecution and banishment in England and France. But Gypsies in the Hapsburg Empire, too, were subject to occasional government attacks and popular persecution that led to excesses of punishment for alleged crimes such as cannibalism, rape, and abduction of children.

In the late eighteenth century, Maria Theresa and Joseph II attempted to settle them, though ultimately this proved unsuccessful. Further bad treatment and general stigmatization by the populace followed, no doubt stemming from beliefs and stereotypes connected with their nomadic way of life and their non-European customs. The most extreme persecution was the mass executions by the Nazis in World War II when 400,000 Gypsies, 50,000 of them from Hungary, were put to death along with millions of Jews as "impure" ethnic groups (Clébert 1967: 101–102, 251; Ortutay 1977, vol. II: 426).

Although Gypsies in Hungary have traditionally wandered less than their contemporaries in Western Europe, only after the end of World War II was their settlement completed. With the rapid development of heavy industry in the 1950s, large numbers of Gypsies were pulled into the mainstream of the economic system as unskilled laborers for the first time (Csalog 1976: 236).

The situation of the Gypsies in Hungary remains poor, however, both economically and socially. Most continue to occupy the lowest social rungs and the worst-paying positions in the work hierarchy (ibid.: 234; Kemény 1974). In 1971, two-thirds of them still lived in the Gypsy settlements into which they have been channeled since the eighteenth century (Kemény 1974: 66), amid great poverty, dirt, and unhygienic living conditions; these settlements provide little in the way of education, culture, or training for life in a modern society. Poverty is their hallmark (Csalog 1976: 234).

Such researchers as Csalog (1976: 236) feel that after the first large improvement in the conditions of Hungarian Gypsies deriving from their massive entry into the work force in the 1950s and 1960s, progress may have slowed. In fact, anti-Gypsy prejudice may be on the upswing as they leave their ghetto-like settlements and settle into other communities. They are still largely regarded as pariahs in Hungary.

In late 1974 and early 1975, when Kislapos experienced its sudden, massive influx of nearly a hundred Gypsies from Gödör and became somewhat of a microcosm of the national situation, many of the displaced were offered houses in Lapos that had become vacant in recent years. Villagers, traditionally Magyar (for our purposes, non-Gypsy), were very displeased about their new neighbors and anticipated the worst. Lapos had had few Gypsy inhabitants and prided itself for having "neither Gypsies, beggars, nor Jews."

Although the newcomers had lived together in a densely settled Gypsy quarter in Gödör, they are now spread out all over little Kislapos. Despite this, because of their earlier relationships in the previous village and their numerous kin connections, as well as the frequent lack of a welcome by the Magyars, Gypsies interact chiefly with Gypsies and Magyars with Magyars.

For an outsider it is not difficult to distinguish Gypsies from Magyars; they generally have darker skin and somewhat different facial features. Of course, some are barely, if at all, distinguishable—a circumstance that frequent intermingling of the two largely endogamous systems has heightened over the years. But, as Csalog (1976: 233) points out, even if their facial features are no different, many Gypsies even in the streets of Budapest can be identified by their gait, gestures, and general body movements. Most, but not all, Gypsies in the village can be distinguished by the tonal and dialectical difference of their speech and by their clothing, spotty wardrobes worn frequently.[1] In Lapos, flamboyance is not characteristic of their clothing.

EARLY GYPSY INHABITANTS

In spite of the villagers' claims concerning Lapos's past "purity," the 1900 national census reports that there were five people of Jewish faith in the village. At the end of World War II there was a Gypsy cowherd living there. Even before the recent influx, which extended over several months, five separate Gypsy households had been established.

In the early 1950s, two Gypsy families moved into the village. One came from neighboring Zöldfa to take over as swineherd, a position that has been held by that family for over twenty years now. The family, including the children and women, have shared the swineherd's duties and often the cowherd's as well. They have supplemented their income by washing and ironing clothes, cleaning, and day labor. The father and two sons are now employed by the collective farm. This family has maintained a reputation for willingness to work, although their house is sparsely and poorly furnished (for a time they lived in the village swineherd's quarters), the parents are known to enjoy drinking, and other doubts are sometimes expressed about their characters. The household has ten members: the two parents, the wife's mother (until recently living in Zöldfa), four sons still at home, of whom two have common-law wives, and one grandchild. A daughter, her husband (a worker in the collective farm), and their two children live elsewhere in the village, having recently split off from the main household.

The other family moved to Lapos shortly after the first. The situation of this household is much worse. For heating purposes they have stripped of wood both houses in which they have lived. The windows are gone and have been papered over, and there is no electricity. Typical of their home existence was one winter evening when they were huddled under blankets in darkness on a raised surface around an empty fire pit in the middle of the dirt floor. Their household contains twelve people: two brothers and a sister, their common-law spouses, their small children, and their aged widowed mother. The oldest brother's first common-law wife was described by one villager as half-Magyar and "modest" (not flamboyant, disrespectful, or promiscuous), doing considerable day labor like hoeing; but after fifteen years of childless cohabitation, he drove her off and took up with another woman. She bore him several children but, according to villagers, is "dirty." The younger brother lives with a Magyar, the granddaughter of a former villager. The adults are unemployed, scraping together an existence by occasional day labor and reputedly by minor theft.

1. Like most (71.0 percent) Gypsies in Hungary, the mother tongue of these newcomers to the village is Hungarian; they do not know how to speak the Gypsy language, Romany. A little more than a fifth (21.2 percent) of Hungarian Gypsies speak Romany as their mother tongue, 7.6 percent Romanian, and 0.2 percent other languages (Kemény 1974: 65).

The third family, a couple, moved into the village in the late 1950s. The wife, then a girl, came with her widowed mother, younger sister, and older brother and his wife. The mother did day labor for local families. The brother, a miner who had been an industrial apprentice before going to work in the mines, commuted to work, coming home every few weeks. Eventually he left his wife for another woman. His wife and children left the village to live with her parents, leaving the widowed mother and two daughters. The mother eventually died and the younger daughter, a very good student who finished commercial school, married and left Lapos, leaving her older sister, who had by then married. The latter's husband occasionally makes baskets and does day labor, though he has also been in and out of jail several times, most recently for minor theft (of which he is often suspected). They live in a small, relatively neat house and have no children.

A fourth family moved into Lapos in the early 1970s. The husband, now in his late twenties, works on maintaining and inspecting the earthen dikes of the Farkas. They have four children. The wife's younger sister lived with them for several years when her mother died, but in her mid-teens she moved in with one of the sons of the swineherd and a year later had a child. The dike inspector's family is considered relatively respectable and clean.

A fifth family moved in from Gödör about a year before the flooding: a man in his sixties, his wife in her fifties, and the wife's eleven-year-old daughter by her first marriage. Several months after their move, the man's twenty-year-old son from an earlier marriage, having finished his military service, moved in with them along with his fifteen-year-old common-law wife; she had just finished the eighth grade. The son works in construction in the mountains to the north, commuting weekly. The older man is called irregularly to work in the collective farm, does some day labor, and occasionally tries to earn some pocket money by playing his violin in the tavern. Though he is considered lazy and is the butt of some joking, villagers count the family among the more acceptable Gypsies. Both older spouses have close relatives among the newly arrived families. The husband has two daughters and another son living in Lapos with their own families, and the older woman has an older brother (with whose son one of her husband's daughters lives) and a niece (her husband's son's wife) living locally.

BELIEFS ABOUT THE NEWCOMERS

Members of the community complained long and loudly about the newcomers; they felt that the Gypsies, whose arrival coincided with the continuing departure of village youth to the cities and nonfarming jobs and the resulting decreases in population, spelled the death knell for the village as they knew it. Some are familiar with news stories of abandoned villages in other parts of the country that have become Gypsy communities, and a few claim to know of similar "plans" for this village.[2]

Even if this is not the case, villagers disapprove strongly of the Gypsies because of the various undesirable behaviors, desires, and physical and

---

2. It is unlikely that there is such a plan, although it may well be, as Szelényi (1977: 126) points out, that such Gypsy or "lumpenproletariat" villages are one unintended result of Hungarian regional planning.

psychological traits they associate with Gypsies. Many of these views are held in Hungary at all levels of society, in nearby Romania (Sampson 1976: 334; Beck 1976: 366), and, indeed, in countries and by people far removed from Hungary, such as Andalusian Spain (Brandes 1977) and much of the rest of Europe (Barth 1969: 31, 38). Such stereotypes attribute to the Gypsies laziness, begging, stealing, spending and consuming in the present without regard to future needs, dirtiness, promiscuity, prolific reproduction, eating rotten meat, and two-facedness (to name the most salient traits).

These characteristics are highly interrelated. Laziness, begging, and stealing hang together as a cluster in informants' minds. Gypsies are viewed as disliking work. They are believed to "live on what others earn" rather than by their own work; they beg and steal and are content to live off the largesse of others, including the government. In support of the ideas of laziness and distaste for work, villagers cite how rarely they see Gypsy men at work. Gypsies doing day labor or odd jobs are felt to be far more concerned about payment than work, constantly asking about their wages even before they begin. The Magyars note that the Gypsies neglect the gardens next to their newly acquired houses. In general, according to the Magyars, Gypsies "would rather dance than work." Commenting on the poor position of the village in the local transportation network and on the Gypsies' alleged desires for mobility, as opposed to settling down and working steadily, some villagers predict that the Gypsies will come to dislike their new home because "they like to go on trains but not to work."

Begging and stealing, in contrast with work, are said to typify Gypsies. In the past Gypsies came to Lapos from nearby villages and went from house to house begging for food or clothing. Villagers even now give old clothing to Gypsies, especially for their children, but sometimes try to avoid putting themselves in positions where they would be subject to minor but often forceful begging. For example, one family began harvesting grapes very early one September morning so they would finish working next to the fence separating their property from that of the Gypsies next door before the Gypsies were up and would have a chance to ask for some. Gypsy children are often implicated, though not caught, in thefts of items such as fruit, flowers, and chickens. Their elders have supposedly stolen sausages from homes and corn from collective and private plots and are thought to be responsible for much more, especially thefts of bicycles. Many villagers now lock their gates at night.[3]

3. Ironically, Sampson (1976: 339) reports that in one larger, developing Romanian village (in Transylvania) the same beliefs concerning theft and the need to lock front gates are held by "native" Saxons and Romanians about poor migrant Romanians, Gypsies, *and* Magyars who have moved in from outlying underdeveloped areas.

The villagers' envy has been aroused by the feeling that the Gypsies' laziness is rewarded by government aid. Because of their large families the Gypsies receive greater amounts of family aid, and the villagers perceive them as misusing it. Due to the loss of their homes in Gödör, the newcomers have received interest-free government loans to buy houses; many villagers feel these loans will never be repaid, or that before they are the Gypsies will have let their houses deteriorate. The same disdain is aroused by the feeling that Gypsies crowd the doctor's office on consulting days to obtain free care (available to all) for imaginary illnesses and to be excused from work.

Closely associated with these beliefs is the image of the Gypsy as short-sighted in budgeting his meager resources. One Gypsy family is the prototype for villagers' views. Having occupied a house in the center of the village across from the town hall, which they allowed to deteriorate, they were offered another house at the edge of the village several years ago. They have used the wood from the porch, doors, and window frames as fuel to heat the house in winter, permitted the children to defecate all around the house, and generally let the house disintegrate. Villagers expect this to happen with other Gypsy houses. They blame the Gypsies for not keeping up the gardens sold them with the houses and thus being forced to buy or beg vegetables from other, self-sufficient villagers. They see all of this as typical short-sightedness.

Some used similar beliefs to justify not accepting another longtime Gypsy inhabitant as a member of the collective farm, although for twenty years he had been the village's swineherd and for much of this time a farm employee. They argued that the farm's method of payment would not have been suitable to Gypsies because they quickly spend their pay on food and drink and would be short of funds for most of each month and most of the year.

Villagers feel that Gypsies are unable to accumulate money and thus are always buying small quantities of vegetables and eggs from their fellow villagers, not larger amounts as Magyars would do. If they work, they are reputed to spend much of their pay in the tavern on the first of the month. They are seen as typically working to acquire a little money and then quitting. "If their stomachs are full, they don't worry about tomorrow."

A Magyar exaggeratedly washing a glass two or three times after a Gypsy had drunk from it typifies the feeling that Gypsies are thought of as dirty and unhygienic. The villagers view squalor as a natural state for Gypsies, and for this and aforementioned reasons they fear the deterioration of the newly bought homes and the village as a whole. The finding that all but one of the Gypsy children, but none of the Magyars, attending the local four-grade school had fleas in their scalps simply reinforced these views. Some express disgust at the idea of entering a Gypsy house, claiming they would be unable to bear the smell.

A few of the Gypsy children whose families moved into the village recently, to the displeasure of most village residents.

Gypsies are thought to be endowed with greater sexual appetites and sometimes greater sexual organs than others, or at least to be less in control of their sexual desires. Villagers view the often young age of motherhood of Gypsy girls, the high illegitimacy rate, and the frequent perceived absence of male providers, as well as the low ages of first cohabitation, as reflective of their promiscuity. Couples who marry only to be eligible for loans and other state aid, or to have children baptized, do little to dispel this image.

The large family sizes of Gypsies are frequently noted and prove dismaying to locals (and Hungarians in general), who fear the village will be inundated and taken over by them. Magyars feel that this too is a sign of irresponsibility and lack of foresight, since the Gypsies do not think of the consequences of their sexual practices or the care and money that will be needed by their children. The anecdote related by one villager about a Gypsy child of eight or nine aptly illustrates the views of the Magyars. When asked how many were in his family, he had to stop to think, finally answering eleven: some were from his first father, now in prison, some from his second. This for the Magyars illustrates the prolificacy of the Gypsies, the lack of stability in their relationships, and their general lack of trustworthiness.

Putting the Gypsies even more strongly into a distinct realm are the beliefs about their penchant for carrion. Most villagers can cite stories of such Gypsy predilections. Typical is the description of a Gypsy walking into a yard and asking for some meat. (Villagers mention how in the past Gypsies visiting the village would ask for bread, but now with bread available at government-subsidized low prices, they ask for bacon.) He was refused. But when he saw the leg of a buried dead chicken that had turned green, he eagerly dug it up. The narrative about a stolen hen being eaten by a Gypsy family despite the supposed "fever"-like quality of its meat (induced by its laying) illustrates both the beliefs about thievery and those of the Gypsies' taste for spoiled meat. A similar combination of attitudes is seen in the remarks of two villagers as they watched a pair of Gypsies walking on a dirt track through the fields toward a neighboring village. One suggested that they might be trying to steal some corn; the other speculated that they were on their way to the ditch where diseased cattle were buried.

Last but hardly least is the attribution of two-facedness, of simulation or flattery, to the Gypsies. Indeed, one of the verb forms in Hungarian for flattering, for such simulation, cigánykodni, is derived from the word for Gypsy: *cigány*. The stereotype undoubtedly is related to the often subservient forms of begging Gypsies use, theft that occurs in conjunction with this, and the general feeling that mobile Gypsy traders and bands in the past (though now virtually all Gypsies live in permanent settlements) were out to take advantage of people while attempting to win their confidence.

All in all, the stereotypes of Gypsy behavior are totally the opposite of what has been expected in the past of "proper peasants" and now of the collective farm members. The valued traits of hard work, thriftiness, honesty, faithfulness to and providing for the family, and maintaining a certain dignity are seen as absent in Gypsies, as is cultivation. Their sociability is viewed with suspicion. When a wholesale judgment is rendered, the Gypsy is not regarded as being "proper" (rendes). He is outside the bounds of the "moral community" (Bailey 1971: 7, 16–18). Although his behavior is not approved, it is not judged as harshly as another villager's would be. Thus, when two villagers discussed a Gypsy who worked occasionally on the collective farm, one remarked that he was a "good hard-working field laborer; he works." When the other sarcastically replied, "In the summer," the former amended his statement by saying, "Well, [he works hard] for a Gypsy." Gypsies' faults are expected, for Gypsies are seen as lacking self-control.

Indeed, to Hungarians they are not fully people and are not to be considered as such. For example, an underlying dimension of Hungarian personal attribution, that of calmness-nervousness, is excluded from attributions of Gypsy behavior. Although Gypsies are thought to be volatile and explosive, characteristics reflective of the nervousness end of the dimension—for example, they supposedly get into fights frequently,[4] and in fact it is often said that one moment they may be fighting with fists or knives and the next be the best of friends—unlike Magyars they are not referred to as having the dispositional traits of nervousness or calmness.

BELIEFS AND REALITY

To what degree are these stereotypes accurate? If they are not, why do they persist?

It seems that they are only partly accurate. A majority of the males are in fact employed, but farming is not their preferred work. Because other job opportunities are largely unavailable locally, most Gypsy workers commute weekly to jobs elsewhere, especially in unskilled construction work, coming home only on weekends. Thus, few residents actually see them working, as they would see their fellow collective farm members, though many villagers have a dim awareness that, beyond the few Gypsies with part-time jobs or performing day labor in the village, there are full-time workers with jobs elsewhere.

Relatively few Gypsies now in the village beg for food or other goods; lacking their own gardens and animals, they do go from house to house trying to buy poultry and vegetables, which are unavailable in local shops. This is clearly not begging; but many villagers prefer not to sell their produce and poultry on a regular basis, especially in small quantities. When some Gypsies are thus forced into pity-provoking, persuasive, or badgering modes of discourse to try to buy something, in the eyes of many they exhibit beggar-like behavior.

Promiscuity is difficult to measure, but the young age of many Gypsies when they begin to cohabit without sanction of marriage contributes to this image, as does the number of technically illegitimate children. The absence of many males during the week helps reinforce the image of women as unattached but maintaining sexual relations and producing children.

Prolific reproduction assumes exaggerated dimensions in the eyes of villagers. It should be made clear that Gypsies, in fact, do have a higher birthrate presently than do Magyars, though it is no higher than that of Magyars one or two generations ago. It is also probably not significantly

4. Magyars have an idealized vision of their own fighting, often ignoring its past, and even present, frequency.

higher than that of the poorest Magyars, whose socioeconomic status is only a little better than that of the Gypsies.[5] (Gypsy culture may, however, place more emphasis on male demonstrations of potency or fertility through the siring of children.) However high the birthrate, villagers' perceptions of it are heightened by the Gypsies' poverty, which often forces them into crowded housing. Several brothers and sisters living together in one house in unwed unions, sometimes together with parents, produce the illusion of very large "families." Villagers point out these households of fourteen or fifteen members, which often contain two or three child-producing couples.

This brief discussion does not completely discredit the stereotypes held by villagers, but it does suggest that their views are significantly unsubstantiated as generalizations about a whole population. Why then do Magyars continue to hold them?

BELIEFS AND PERSISTENCE

It seems clear that there are several reasons for the persistence of villagers' beliefs about the Gypsies—and I am not even considering deeper psychological explanations. First, at least a number of the stereotypes are partly true. The Gypsies do have a higher birthrate; their children do have fleas. Some aspects of other stereotypes may be more characteristic of Gypsies than of Magyars (for example, living in more rundown houses; having a larger percentage of people on state aid).[6] This, of course, strengthens the credibility of the remaining stereotypes.

Moreover, to the degree that some of the attributes described above may be proportionally more characteristic of Gypsies than of Magyars (for example, there are more unemployed among the former than the latter, though hardly a majority even among the Gypsies), villagers see them as being characteristic of Gypsies in general. Part of this may be due to what Shweder (1977) characterizes as human inability in intuitional thinking to deal with correlational data; part to what D'Andrade (1974) has shown is a strong tendency to lump together attributions of behavior on the basis of semantic or conceptual similarity, not on the basis of co-occurence; and part to an implicit belief in a threshold effect (for example, see Hull

5. Indeed, Kemény (1974: 69–71), comparing Gypsies nationally to the poorest strata of Hungarian families having at least one active wage-earner, shows that differences between the two groups in size of family and number of children are quite slim.

6. All Hungarians with children are eligible for maternity benefits and child support, however. Having more children, Gypsies receive larger amounts of this type of state aid. On the other hand, they benefit far less from state-supported educational opportunities, state-subsidized housing, etc.

1943). Thus, a given attribute is manifested only if its strength surpasses a certain threshold or if inhibitions are weakened, lowering the effective threshold. For example, after the influx of Gypsies, the behavior of several Gypsies who had lived in the village for a longer time was said to have changed for the worse. Whereas they had been perceived as relatively proper and hard-working, now they were said to have started drinking more and missing work more frequently. Villagers attributed this to the influence of the newer Gypsies and to the underlying Gypsy nature of these individuals, which was brought out by their association with the newcomers. Such a notion of threshold and underlying, latent dispositions would allow villagers to assume wider distribution of stereotypic characteristics than the limited manifestation of these characteristics might warrant.

Second, the villagers only partly perceive and sometimes misperceive relevant behaviors. Magyars frequently do not possess the information to be able to evaluate accurately the truth of their beliefs. They do not see Gypsies working because most Gypsies are employed elsewhere. Similarly, households and sometimes even several partially independent families living in the same house are taken as individual families. Villagers often do not recognize the relative permanence of the relationships between Gypsy couples and mistake them for temporary liaisons because of the absence of official or Church sanction.

Third, like many people, the villagers are prone to jump to dispositional conclusions in their interpretations of Gypsy behavior and living conditions rather than attributing causal significance to situational and contextual factors (Jones and Nisbett 1971). Thus, the poverty so central in Gypsies' lives is not seen as causing many of their problems but is viewed as the result of their lack of effort and self-denial. The lack of schooling of many working-age Gypsies, the paucity of skills that results, the squalor of their living conditions, and the filth they endured in the old Gypsy quarters are viewed as the results of their own personal weaknesses rather than as a function of their initial poverty. Similarly, the personal and material discrimination faced by Gypsies is justified in terms of the same stereotypes by the villagers, who do not realize that just this discrimination makes mobility and finding good work all the more difficult. Thus, while arguing that Gypsies would not be able to accustom themselves to the pay schedules and work schedules of the farm, villagers have forestalled efforts by some Gypsies who have sought steady work through the collective and have even tried to join. The work they have been given is not high-paying. In fact, some villagers acknowledge that their neighbors who hire Gypsies for day labor pay them very low wages.

Fourth, the Gypsies are not farmers and do not have a strong tradition of agricultural labor, particularly not of maintaining a small agricultural enterprise. However, as we have seen, Gypsies are in many ways judged (though not closely) against peasant ideals.[7] They are considered lazy because they are not often seen doing agricultural labor or keeping up gardens. (Those who do are in a sense discounted.)

The fifth and perhaps the most important reason for the persistence of these stereotypes is the nature of the term cigány, Gypsy, itself. I will argue that the term is as much a behavioral descriptor as it is an ethnic or racial category. Villagers continue to believe in many of their assertions about Gypsies because the assertions are true by definition. They are not necessarily true in general about this particular ethnic group. But because of the nature of the term the two meanings are intertwined.

We have already had an example of the use of the term cigány independent of its ethnic meaning in cigánykodni, a term used quite generally in the village to refer to two-faced behavior or insincere flattery used for personal gain. This dimension of behavior is important in the thinking of many villagers, for it infuses a major concern of theirs. It has been seen, for example, that many villagers feel that much of one's success in the collective farm depends on one's personal connections or one's protekció (a term more often used by urban Hungarians than by villagers). Many believe that kinship ties play an important role in the assigning of better-paying positions in the collective farm. In general, they feel that those "who are close to the fire" do best. Both protekció and the chain of patron-client relations important locally and nationally in the past (Neuberg 1973: 155–156, 250–251, 254; Fél and Hofer 1973) still play a major role in Hungarian institutions and daily life in both the village and the rest of the country, despite the introduction of a more egalitarian social order based, not on wealth and birth, but on more universalistic norms.

Villagers perceive a large gap between "them" [the leadership or management] and themselves in the collective farm, a gap felt also in factories (Haraszti 1978) and other social and economic institutions in the country. One perceived road to personal success is cigánykodni, working oneself into the good graces of superiors. But this is often despised by those who choose not to follow that path and even by some who do.

Some villagers, describing their perception of increased envy and desire for better jobs, and the tactics used to achieve them in recent years, state that now "the people are cigány." Though it involves an ethnic slur built into the language, this is not an ethnic judgment.

Similarly, cigány has come to mean the lumpen type for the villagers. One day in the horse barns, a Magyar considered by most to be very lazy, a heavy drinker, and generally irresponsible was seen talking with a some-

---

7. Thus, though they may work in construction, they can be judged for agricultural knowledge and ability. A similar note was struck in the past in Varsány, where if one was a factory worker he was still judged on the basis of his land and farming ability and thus was lumped with the agricultural proletariat (Sárkány 1978: 91).

what more accepted (if not respected) Gypsy, who worked on occasion for the collective farm. Another worker observing them said, "You see, the two cigány-s came to terms," and then indicated that they were drinking. Cigány thus has the general meaning of irresponsible and not to be counted on—all in all, not a proper person.

This becomes especially clear when villagers speak of a Gypsy who in fact does work, who does meet general expectations for propriety. For example, one man discussing a young Gypsy who worked regularly for the collective farm said, "I can't say he's a Gypsy, because he works; he provides for his family." In discussing a Gypsy family, villagers noted, "They're not Gypsies—well, they're proper Gypsies. They don't go begging and asking for things." Talking more generally, many have uttered comments like the following: "He's no Gypsy if he's proper."[8]

What occurs is an intertwining of the separate meanings of cigány, a confusion, as it were. Those who are Gypsies and meet the standards of the community are in a sense no longer Gypsies in the minds of the villagers. They are not taken into account when stereotypical statements are uttered, for they are not Gypsies! Those who do not meet the villagers' standards are Gypsies by definition.

COMMUNITIES APART

Given these beliefs, how then have the Magyars and Gypsies gotten along? What types of relationships have developed between the two groups?

Two moral communities have developed that at least from the point of view of the Magyars and from the perspective of social, economic, and political status, can easily be hierarchically arranged. An important element of this has been the high degree of intragroup kin ties, which strongly channel social interaction. This has been noted among the Magyars; it is true also of the Gypsies. The examples above note several close kinship relations between separate households; the same is true for many of the other Gypsy families. This reinforces the pattern of more frequent interaction within group boundaries than across them, despite the relative dispersion of Gypsies throughout the village. Previous nonkin village ties also reinforce these ethnic groupings.

The boundaries, however, are permeable. If they meet the expectations of the Magyars regarding work and materially responsible and other "morally" relevant behavior, Gypsies can throw off their second-class status. What happens in the interactions between the two groups, therefore, is that those Gypsies who meet the standards are allowed and en-

---

8. The same distinction seems to be made more generally in Hungary as a whole. Csalog (1976: 228) mentions a piano teacher whom, "because she is a Gypsy, *but* a proper person, we must not insult by saying *cigány* in her presence."

couraged by the Magyars to interact more frequently; as neighbors they keep up the mutual visiting, borrowing, and helping characteristic of Magyar neighbors. Friendships typical of Magyars have developed at work between some Gypsies and Magyars.

Those who do not meet these expectations are treated with derisive behavior or occasional joking or are even ignored, befitting those who are not to be taken seriously. Some, making an effort but still not meeting the whole set of expectations, lacking cows and poultry of their own, regularly buy milk and eggs from their neighbors; but within their joking interactions, the superior-inferior, skeptic-flatterer, and exploiter-exploited themes persist. These themes, the lack of appropriate local work opportunities, the maintenance of disapproved life styles by some Gypsies, and the semantics of the term Gypsy serve to maintain separate moral communities.

Overview

Sweeping economic and political changes have passed over the Hungarian countryside since the end of World War II. The old political order based on personal wealth has passed away. Private land ownership, the cornerstone of wealth, has been largely eliminated as an important factor in everyday life. Traditional peasant agriculture, the mainstay and ideal of rural life, has given way to large-scale modern collective enterprises, which increasingly resemble industrial concerns in their size, organization of management, division of labor, payment of workers, rationalization of administration and planning, scope of operation, and movement in recent years toward both vertical and horizontal integration. The family, the backbone of the peasant enterprise, has lost much of its economic function as the unit of production.

Equally as important and interesting as the historical processes and events leading to all this are the degree and particularly the areas of continuity from the past to the present in the countryside. Three of these areas are treated in this chapter. Further, I argue here that much of the continuity observed in Kislapos's social organization and in the concerns of its villagers is a result of two main factors: 1) the preadaptive nature of some social and cultural elements of the past for the new, changed conditions of collectivization, in particular the ability of older forms of social organization to take on many of the requirements of the new social forms, and 2) the explicit building of the new social organization on elements and groups of the old social order.

FAMILY, KINSHIP, AND RECIPROCITY

The elimination of the importance of landed wealth brought important changes in the family power structure of Kislapos. The dominion of the older generation over younger adult members and of men over women within the family gave way to greater equality as the system of land tenure was abruptly terminated and broader inheritance patterns were markedly affected. The elder generation experienced a sharp drop in power, since the loss of land meant the loss of most of the wealth they could pass on to their children and the loss of the economic enterprise in which they were the controlling figures. Initially this was compounded by the reduced earning potential of the elderly because of their age and limited skills and, after retirement, by low pensions. Other factors also reinforced this tendency. The continuing trend of young couples moving away from home, made easier by the increased availability of empty houses in the village because of greater migration to the cities and industry, a lower birthrate, and the reduced attraction of agriculture all decreased the hold of the elderly over the young, as did the vastly increased ability of the latter to earn an income independent of their parents even in the village.

On the other hand, the family has retained a focal position in the village's social organization and in the lives of both those staying in and leaving the village. It has remained central in the pattern of reciprocal ties that organizes much of village social interaction. This has been due largely to the continued importance of the houseplot enterprise in Hungarian agriculture. Numerous economic and social ties characteristic of the peasant past have counterparts in today's interfamily relations centering on family agricultural enterprises. Although mutual participation and aid in family celebrations and crises could have persisted in reduced form without this economic component (which clearly has a large social overlay), it is clear that patterns of economic ties have served only to reinforce these other relations. The family obviously has been well preadapted for the maintenance of the ties made possible by the houseplot enterprise.

This should hardly be surprising, since one of the purposes of the household enterprise was to serve as a palliative for villagers losing their land to the collective, as a possibility for limited private farming. In fact, the early organization of farm work and the payment for services rendered, as well as the terms of membership, were designed to keep the family a productive unit within the cooperative enterprise; they largely maintained the family power structure and division of labor. Though much of this early organization of farm work and the terms of membership have been superseded, the sexual division of labor typical of pre-collective days is seen even today both within and outside the farm. Many of the more prestigious "heavy" tasks are now done on the farm instead of at home, however, by men with work-saving machines the possession and handling of which still offer prestige.

The family has experienced other changes as well. It has turned in on itself to a greater degree than in the past. The wider circle of kin with whom frequent interaction was maintained, and upon whom villagers often depended for aid, has given way to a smaller circle of familial interaction. This is reflected in circumscribed visiting patterns, the extension of the trend of picking close relatives for koma-s, and the reduction in the numbers involved in family celebrations. Although more distant relatives are still consulted when a wider circle of connections will help in solving a problem or in carrying out a task, and their presence is expected at important occasions like marriages and funerals, they are less important than in the past. One factor in this has been the earlier transition from joint to stem families and the decreased personal contact with more distant relatives that this implied.

The main reason for this concentration seems to be the greater emphasis placed now by parents on the lives and desires of their children. Whereas in the past the lives of the older generation were deemed central, today parents and grandparents who were already adults in precollective days center their concerns on their children. With far larger incomes than they could have had in the past, they often maintain past consumption patterns and spend their money on houses, cars, household appliances, and furniture for their children. Lacking pride in their own way of life, those engaged in agricultural work strive to obtain a "better" existence for their children outside agriculture. Their considerable material sacrifices ease the way for their children, while helping to maintain family ties with children who move to the city. The devaluation of traditional agricultural labor through the policies of the past, the loss of the independence maintained by landownership, the attraction of the cities, and the expansion of industry have pushed many to find importance and meaning not in their own lives but in the accomplishments, comforts, and status of their children.

HIERARCHY AND POWER

With land reform, the policies of the late 1940s and early 1950s, and the completion of the collectivization drives in the early 1960s came the end of the importance of landed wealth in the countryside. Political power based on this resource was largely nonexistent by the late 1940s, though landed wealth still finds lingering expression today in the greater education and slightly higher social status of descendants of wealthy and middle peasants. However, the old system of hierarchy based on wealth was completely replaced by a new hierarchy largely manned by the former poor and closely connected with the Communist Party.

Successful collectivization introduced another new local leadership, one manned largely by the middle peasantry and even by a few wealthy peasants of the past or their children. Any lasting success for a new collective required the inclusion of the middle peasantry; their enhanced position was brought about by the explicit building of the new cooperative farms on the base of the middle peasantry and on kin ties. In the ensuing competition for good positions and work opportunities, leaders have extended the hold of the middle peasantry by often making use of particularistic norms of the past, selecting relatives and friends for good positions. Losers have been disgruntled; but at first the commitment of members to making this new enterprise work, the relative smallness of the farms (creating a feeling of closeness), the relative lack of differentiation in pay and authority, and the kin ties themselves in the farms kept concerns about hierarchy within bounds.

However, as the organizations grew through merger, their scale of operations increased, and specialization and technology received more emphasis, greater degrees of hierarchy were introduced. The ideology of the new social order and the ideals of the cooperative movement came into conflict with some of the exigencies of that new order. In particular, the egalitarianism promoted by socialism and the democratic principles laid down in the bylaws of the cooperative conflicted with the centralized chain of command in the Hungarian political and economic structures. Concern with hierarchy and the dissatisfaction with leadership was almost inevitable, especially in light of the position of the leadership as both the elected representatives of the membership and the transmitter of policy directives from above. By establishing ties with the party and with members of higher administrative and political organs, some leaders were able to increase their own personal power in this situation. Though this was sometimes done at the cost of a drop in local popularity, it was often balanced by the increased patronage available to dispense to relatives and others in favor.

The inevitability of concern with hierarchy has been increased by elements of the traditional value system. Despite the universalistic claims made by villagers, reciprocity and other particularistic norms are still widespread in Kislapos and no doubt in the rest of the countryside. Dissatisfaction with the leadership stems as much from the personally unfavorable application of particularistic norms as it does from the absence of universalistic ones. Traditional concerns with subservience and independence have also found voice in the disaffection with those in power and have made acceptance of any hierarchy more difficult. Moreover, the copying of less than ideal past models of leadership by some in power, the large number and variety of expectations for leaders held by villagers, and the relative absence in the local population of persons with the higher education, technical knowledge, and administrative skills desired in leaders make dissatisfaction all the more likely.

SOCIAL PERCEPTUAL CONCERNS

There are many reasons for the continued salience of hierarchy in villagers' thinking. Besides those already discussed, there are three other important areas: work and thriftiness, sociability, and cultivation.

The high value placed on work in the past has been strongly reinforced by the work organization of the cooperative farm. Members work largely in each other's presence, and to a great degree their collective earnings depend on each other's labor. They are acutely conscious of others' efforts, are concerned about them, and are in a position to oversee them.

Associated themes of leaders doing little work and of less honorable routes to success have been strengthened by the concerns with hierarchy mentioned above and by the conditions of the 1950s, which bred strong fears of tale-bearing and two-facedness.

Though villagers no longer save to buy land, the purchase of material goods for themselves or for their children has taken on much greater importance. The status associated with these goods and the necessity to skimp and save to obtain them have kept thriftiness a salient dimension in village thinking.

Given the size of the village, the frequent interaction of villagers both in farm and nonfarm settings, and the new egalitarianism, there is no reason to be surprised that the past concern with sociability has been maintained. The high value traditionally placed on learnedness, the increased schooling of villagers' children, the growing dissatisfaction with the peasant self-image, and the expectations for the leadership in the face of perceived equality have all kept cultivation a salient perceptual category, too.

THE FUTURE

Several broad trends promise further changes in village social organization and social perception. These include the outmigration of children from the village and their increased education; greater mechanization and specialization within the collective farm; and the continuing integration of the village into the larger collective farm and into contemporary urban culture. Probably the greatest factor will be the eventual replacement of the present generation, which grew up in precollective days, with a younger, better educated generation that has grown up under far different conditions and has increasingly taken on the values of an urban, less traditional setting.

Much will change, including the agricultural methods and organization themselves. We have already seen some of the trends of rationalization, centralization, and the increasing importance of universalistic norms within the farm.

As the number of workers in Hungarian agriculture continues to decrease, as the knowledge and technical skills required in agriculture become more and more specialized, as more complex machinery is introduced both to increase production further and to compensate for the continuing drop in the number of agricultural workers, in short, as traditional farming is replaced by modern forms more reminiscent of industry, those who fill positions in the farm will increasingly be highly trained workers and specialists. Because of their years away from the village and their adoption of many urban, nonvillage values, a good number will place greater emphasis on leisure time and other interests and will not be willing to maintain significant houseplot enterprises. Although these houseplots will continue to be an important element in Hungarian agriculture, and the government will, no doubt, encourage villagers to maintain them and to produce more, it may be that the houseplot and the family as an economic unit of production will no longer form a focal point around which kinship and other relations of reciprocity will revolve.

This movement away from the houseplot enterprise will undoubtedly lead to still greater variation and less rigidity in the sexual division of labor within the family. It will also help maintain the trend away from wider kin ties and toward closer family relationships, a trend also encouraged in Lapos by outmigration, which leaves steadily fewer distant kin within the village. The shift in the emphasis within the family toward affect will also continue. But as local parents become more educated, and more reconciled to skilled positions in agriculture as jobs worthy of prestige and self-esteem, as they denigrate themselves less because of their work, and as more villagers come to occupy nonfarm or other skilled jobs and maintain their residences in the village (as in many other villages, where there are more nonagricultural positions), there is likely to be a lessening of the heavy emphasis placed on the plans and lives of children. Certainly there will be less encouragement for children to migrate or to find a way of life very different from that of their parents. This will hardly spell a return to the power relations and socialization patterns of the past; it is likely to produce family ties like those in the city, where children are important but their success is not the prime prestige element in the village or the center of villagers' lives. One can hope, although this is by no means certain, that villagers' own work, hobbies, and interests, not just the pursuit of material gain, will come to occupy that position. Close ties with children, living both within the village and elsewhere, will be maintained.

Some of the social perceptual concerns of the villagers will be further modified, others will continue just as strongly. As a new generation takes its place in the collective farm it is likely that the importance of the traditional value of independence (as opposed to subservience) will decrease. Because of this, because of the greater recognition administrative tasks will receive as "real work," and because of the increased presence of individuals who command skills more widely accepted than before as uniquely necessary for their positions, some of the emphasis placed on themes of hierarchy and the dissatisfaction with local leadership and work assignments will probably decrease.

The emphasis on work as the measure of a man will probably decrease somewhat as tasks grow more complex and harder to oversee by those not directly involved and as the emphasis on leisure grows.

Sociability will probably remain important, partly because of Lapos's small size. It is likely that ties of friendship will gain in importance, particularly as economic ties of reciprocity lose their central position. The work organization of the farm, the development of new interests, and the continuing reduction in kinship ties will facilitate these trends.

One's cultivation may decrease somewhat in importance as the general level of education increases, although it is unclear just what will happen regarding the importance of demeanor.

Unlike larger, better-situated villages and the countryside in general, where families have participated more actively in the prospering mix of agriculture and industry, Kislapos as a community faces problems in the future. The low priority in regional planning of increasing services to such a small community will cause the pattern of outmigration to continue for at least several years. Most of those now older than thirty-five will probably remain in Kislapos, while the younger leave, even if only for Kistó. Many elderly individuals and couples will die or move in with their children elsewhere. The population will continue to drop rapidly, although some of the loss may be offset by an increase in the number of Gypsies. In time, as the number of workers decreases (and if, as is likely, the Gypsies do not take agricultural jobs), Kislapos as a separate production unit within the collective farm may be absorbed by a neighboring community. Despite Lapos's precollective reputation for good farming and the present financial success of its collective farm, the possible severe population losses of the next decade or two lead some to think the village may die.

Whatever does happen to Kislapos, it is clear that the series of transformations triggered by post-World War II events and policies in the Hungarian countryside is not yet complete. The future promises a further working out of these transformations, producing changes that, if not as momentous as those that have occurred so far, may in the end be nearly as fundamental.

Glossary

The following is a list of some of the more important Hungarian words that appear in the text, with brief definitions. See the chapter numbered in parentheses for a more detailed treatment of each term.

arató:	harvester (especially wheat harvester) for a share of the harvest (2)
cigány:	1. Gypsy; 2. two-faced, flattering, insincere (10)
cigánykodni:	to be two-faced, flattering, insincere (10)
cseléd:	year-round hired hand (2)
forint:	new Hungarian currency, introduced in 1946, whose official exchange value in recent years has ranged twenty–thirty to one U. S. dollar (5)
gazda:	1. head of the household; 2. farmer (3)
gazdasszony:	head woman in the family (3)
gimnázium:	academic secondary school
háztáji:	collective farm houseplot (6)
hold:	measure of land: 1 *hold* equals 1.42 acres equals 0.57 hectare (2)
jegyző:	pre-World War II village notary/secretary (2)
kaláka:	traditional village work group of relatives, neighbors, in-laws, and friends (3)
kántor-tanító:	combination church cantor, village school-teacher (2)
kisbirtokos:	smallholder (2)
kert:	garden (3)
koma:	1. the godfather of one's child; 2. a male for whose children one is a godparent; 3. a male's male childhood friend (3)
középparaszt:	middle peasant (2)
magángazdálkodó:	private farmer (9)
megjelenés:	bearing, demeanor (9)
meny:	daughter-in-law (3)

művelt:	cultivated, refined, learned (9)
műveltség:	cultivation, refinement, learnedness (9)
nagygazda:	wealthy peasant (2)
napszámos:	day laborer (2)
nász:	the parents-in-law of one's child (3)
násznagy:	1. the host at a wedding, usually the godfather of the groom; 2. the witness for the groom at a wedding (3)
nincstelen:	landless (2)
nyoszolyóasszony:	the maid of honor or hostess at a wedding (7)
pengő:	Hungarian currency until 1946
protekció:	patronage, influence, personal connections (5)
részes munkás:	share worker (for a share of the harvest) (2)
sógor:	brother-in-law and by extension any male relative by marriage in the same generation as ego (7)
sógornő:	sister-in-law and by extension any female relative by marriage in the same generation as ego (7)
summás:	hired hand for periods of two to six months on large estates (2)
tanya:	isolated farmstead (1)
tanyázás:	nightly gatherings of males in barns for conversation or card playing (3)
tekintély:	authority, prestige (9)
törpebirtokos:	smallholder (2)
virilista:	one of the wealthiest tax-paying individuals in prewar villages, thus automatically eligible for a seat on the village council (4)
vő:	son-in-law (3)

Bibliography

Andorka, Rudolf
  1975 Az ormánsági születéskorlátozás története [The history of birth limitation in the Ormánság]. Valóság 18[5]: 45–61.
  1979 A magyar községek társadalmának átalakulása [The transformation of Hungarian village society]. Budapest: Magvető Kiadó.

Bailey, F. G.
  1977 Morality and Expediency: The Folklore of Academic Politics. Chicago: Aldine.

Bailey, F. G., ed.
  1971 Gifts and Poison. Oxford: Basil Blackwell.

Bango, J. F.
  1976 Some Social-Historical Aspects in the Development of Hungarian Cooperative Farming. Journal of Rural Cooperation 4[2]: 129–153.

Barth, Fredrik
  1969 Introduction. *In* Ethnic Groups and Boundaries. Fredrik Barth, ed. Boston: Little, Brown. Pp. 10–38.

Beck, Sam
  1976 The Emergence of the Peasant-Worker in a Transylvanian Mountain Community. Dialectical Anthropology 1: 365–375.

Berend, Iván T., and György Ránki
  1973 The Horthy Regime, 1919–1944. *In* A History of Hungary. Ervin Pallényi, ed. Budapest: Corvina Press. Pp. 451–534.

Berényi, Andrásné
  1975 Nagy Rozália a nevem [My name is Rozália Nagy]. Budapest: Gondolat.

Bodrogi, Tibor, ed.
  1978 Varsány: tanulmányok egy éjszak-magyarországi falu társadalomnéprajzához [Varsány: ethnographic studies of the society of a northern Hungarian village]. Budapest: Akadémiai Kiadó.

Boissevain, Jeremy
  1974 Friends of Friends: Networks, Manipulators and Coalitions. Oxford: Basil Blackwell.

Brandes, Stanley
  1977 Ethnic Stratification in Andalusia: The Case of the Gypsies. Paper presented at the 76th Annual Meeting of the American Anthropological Association, Houston, Texas.

Clébert, Jean-Paul
  1967 The Gypsies (originally published in 1961 as Les Tziganes). Charles Duff, trans. Harmondsworth, England: Penguin.

Cole, John W.
1976a Field Work in Romania: Introduction. Dialectical Anthropology 1: 239–250.
1976b Familial Dynamics in a Romanian Worker Village. Dialectical Anthropology 1: 251–266.

Csalog, Zsolt
1976 Kilenc cigány [Nine Gypsies]. Budapest: Kozmosz Könyvek.

D'Andrade, Roy G.
1974 Memory and the Assessment of Behavior. *In* Measurement in the Social Sciences. T. Blalock, ed. Chicago: Aldine-Atherton. Pp. 159–186.
1976 A Propositional Analysis of U.S. American Beliefs about Illness. *In* Meaning in Anthropology. Keith H. Basso and Henry A. Selby, eds. Albuquerque: University of New Mexico Press. Pp. 155–180.

Donáth, Ferenc
1976 A kisparaszti mezőgazdaság [Small peasant agriculture], 1945–1949. *In* A magyar mezőgazdaság a XIX–XX. században [Hungarian agriculture in the nineteenth and twentieth centuries], 1849–1949. Péter Gunst and Tamás Hoffmann, eds. Budapest: Akadémiai Kiadó. Pp. 401–472.
1977 Reform és forradalom [Reform and revolution]. Budapest: Akadémiai Kiadó.

Enyedi, György
1978 Kelet-Közép-Európa gazdaságföldrajza [The economic geography of East-Central Europe]. Budapest: Közgazdasági és Jogi Könyvkiadó.

Erdei, Ferenc
1940 Magyar falu [The Hungarian village]. Budapest: Athenaeum Nyomda.
1964 A mezőgazdasági népesség gazdasági-társadalmi viszonyainak alakulása a felszabadulás után [The development of the agricultural population's socioeconomic relations since the liberation]. *In* Tanulmányok a mai faluról [Studies of the contemporary village]. Sándor Zsarnóczai, ed. Budapest: Kossuth Könyvkiadó. Pp. 11–51.
1971 Város és vidék [City and countryside]. Budapest: Szépirodalmi Könyvkiadó.

Fazekas, Béla
1976 A mezőgazdasági termelőszövetkezeti mozgalom Magyarországon [The cooperative farm movement in Hungary]. Budapest: Kossuth Könyvkiadó.

Fél, Edit, and Tamás Hofer
1969 Proper Peasants: Traditional Life in a Hungarian Village. Viking Fund Publications in Anthropology, no. 46. Chicago: Aldine.
1973 Tanyakert-s, Patron-Client Relations, and Political Factions in Átány. American Anthropologist 75: 787–801.

Foster, George
1961 The Dyadic Contract: A Model for the Social Structure of a Mexican Peasant Village. American Anthropologist 63: 1173–1192.

Francisco, Ronald A., Betty A. Laird, and Roy D. Laird, eds.
1979 The Political Economy of Collectivized Agriculture: A Comparative Study of Communist and Non-Communist Systems. New York: Pergamon Press.

Franklin, S. H.
1969   The European Peasantry: The Final Phase. London: Methuen.
Griffiths, Brian
1976   Inflation: The Price of Prosperity. London: Weidenfeld and Nicolson.
Gunst, Péter
1976   A mezőgazdaság fejlődésének megrekedése a két világháború között (az 1920–30-as években) [The stagnation of agricultural development between the two world wars (in the 1920s and 1930s)]. *In* A magyar mezőgazdaság a XIX–XX. században [Hungarian agriculture in the nineteenth and twentieth centuries], 1849–1949. Péter Gunst and Tamás Hoffmann, eds. Budapest: Akadémiai Kiadó. Pp. 275–400.
Gyenes, Antal
1975   Decision Making in the Hungarian Cooperatives from a Sociological Point of View. Journal of Rural Cooperation 3[2]: 101–110.
Gyimesi, Sándor
1965   A parasztság és a szövetkezeti mozgalmak [The peasantry and the cooperative movements]. *In* A parasztság Magyarországon a kapitalizmus korában [The peasantry in Hungary in the age of capitalism], 1848–1914, vol. II. István Szabó, ed. Budapest: Akadémiai Kiadó. Pp. 616–652.
Haraszti, Miklós
1978   A Worker in a Worker's State. Michael Wright, trans. New York: Universe.
Hegedüs, András
1970   Változó világ [Changing world]. Budapest: Akadémiai Kiadó.
1971   A szocialista társadalom struktúrájáról [On the structure of socialist society]. Budapest: Akadémiai Kiadó.
Hofer, Tamás
1968   Anthropologists and Native Ethnographers in Central European Villages: Comparative Notes on the Professional Personality of Two Disciplines. Current Anthropology 9: 311–315.
Horváth, Zoltán
1965   A községi önkormányzat és a parasztság [Community self-government and the peasantry]. *In* A parasztság Magyarországon a kapitalizmus korában [The peasantry in Hungary in the age of capitalism], 1848–1914, vol. II. István Szabó, ed. Budapest: Akadémiai Kiadó. Pp. 565–615.
Hull, Clark L.
1943   Principles of Behavior. New York: Appleton-Century-Crofts.
Ignotus, Paul
1972   Hungary. London: Ernest Benn.
Illyés, Gyula
1967   People of the Puszta (originally published in 1937 as Puszták Népe). G. F. Cushing, trans. Budapest: Corvina Press.
Jain, Shail
1975   Size Distribution of Income: A Compilation of Data. Baltimore: Johns Hopkins Press.
Jávor, Kata
1978   Kontinuitás és változás a társadalmi és tudati viszonyokban [Continuity and change in the conditions of society and consciousness]. *In* Varsány: tanulmányok egy éjszak-magyarországi falu társadalomnéprajzához

[Varsány: ethnographic studies of the society of a northern Hungarian village]. Tibor Bodrogi, ed. Budapest: Akadémiai Kiadó. Pp. 295-373.

Jones, Edward E., and Richard E. Nisbett
  1971 The Actor and the Observor: Divergent Perceptions of the Causes of Behavior. *In* Attribution: Perceiving the Causes of Behavior. Edward E. Jones, David E. Kanouse, Harold H. Kelley, Richard E. Nisbett, Stuart Valins, and Bernard Weiner, eds. Morristown, N.J.: General Learning Press. Pp. 79-94.

Karcz, Jerzy F., ed.
  1967 Soviet and East European Agriculture. Berkeley: University of California Press.

Karolyi, Michael
  1956 Memoirs of Michael Karolyi: Faith without Illusion. Catherine Karolyi, trans. London: Jonathan Cape.

Katona, Imre
  1962 Types of Work Groups and Temporary Associations of Seasonal Labour in the Age of Capitalism. Acta Ethnographica 11: 31-84.

Kemény, István
  1974 A magyarországi cigány lakosság [The Gypsy population of Hungary]. Valóság 17[1]: 63-72.

Kerblay, Basile
  1971 Chayanov and the Theory of Peasantry as a Specific Type of Economy. *In* Peasants and Peasant Societies. Teodor Shanin, ed. London: Penguin. Pp. 150-160.

Kideckel, David A.
  1976 The Social Organization of Production on a Romanian Cooperative Farm. Dialectical Anthropology 1: 267-276.

Kovats, Charles E.
  1977 The Path of Church-State Reconciliation in Hungary. *In* Eastern Europe's Uncertain Future. Robert R. King and James F. Brown, eds. New York: Praeger. Pp. 301-311.

Kulcsár, Viktor
  1976 A változó falu [The changing village]. Budapest: Gondolat.

Kunszabó, Ferenc
  1970 Social Strata and Interest Relations. *In* Social Aspects of Rural Life in Hungary. Research Institute of Agricultural Economics, bull. 28: 51-78.

Levy, Marion J., Jr.
  1966 Modernization and the Structure of Societies: A Setting for International Affairs, 2 Vols. Princeton: Princeton University Press.

McArthur, Marilyn
  1976 The Saxon Germans: Political Fate of an Ethnic Identity. Dialectical Anthropology 1: 349-364.

Márkus, István
  1971 Kifelé a feudalizmusból [Outward from feudalism]. Budapest: Szépirodalmi Könyvkiadó.

Mieczkowski, Bogdan
  1975 Personal and Social Consumption in Eastern Europe. New York: Praeger.

Moldova, György
 1974 Az Őrség panasza [The Őrség's lament]. Budapest: Magvető Könyvkiadó.
Neuberg, Paul
 1973 The Hero's Children. New York: William Morrow.
Orbán, Sándor
 1972 Két agrárforradalom Magyarországon: demokratikus és szocialista agrárátalakulás [Hungary's two agrarian revolutions: democratic and socialist agrarian transformations], 1945–1961. Budapest: Akadémiai Kiadó.
Ortutay, Gyula, ed.
 1977, 1979 Magyar néprajzi lexikon [Hungarian ethnographic dictionary], vols. I, II (of 5). Budapest: Akadémiai Kiadó.
Randall, Steven G.
 1976 The Family Estate in an Upland Carpathian Village. Dialectical Anthropology 1: 277–285.
Robinson, William F.
 1973 The Pattern of Reform in Hungary: A Political, Economic and Cultural Analysis. New York: Praeger.
Salzmann, Zdenek, and Vladimir Scheufler
 1974 Komarov: A Czech Farming Village. New York: Holt, Rinehart and Winston.
Sampson, Steven
 1976 Feldiora: The City Comes to the Peasant. Dialectical Anthropology 1: 321–347.
Sanders, Irwin T., ed.
 1958 Collectivization of Agriculture in Eastern Europe. Lexington: University of Kentucky Press.
Sárkány, Mihály
 1978 A gazdaság átalakulása [The transformation of the economy]. *In* Varsány: tanulmányok egy észak-magyarországi falu társadalomnéprajzához [Varsány: ethnographic studies of the society of a northern Hungarian village]. Tibor Bodrogi, ed. Budapest: Akadémiai Kiadó. Pp. 63–150.
Sas, Judit H.
 1973 Életmód és család: az emberi viszonyok alakulása a családban [Lifestyle and family: The development of human relations in the family]. Budapest: Magyar Tudományos Akadémia Szociológiai Kutató Intézetének Kiadványai.
Shweder, Richard A.
 1977 Likeness and Likelihood in Everyday Thought: Magical Thinking and Everyday Judgment About Personality. Current Anthropology 18[4]: 637–658.
Simonffy, Emil
 1965 A parasztföld és a tagosítás [Peasant-owned land and the consolidation]. *In* A parasztság Magyarországon a kapitalizmus korában [The peasantry in Hungary in the age of capitalism], 1848–1914, vol. I. István Szabó, ed. Budapest: Akadémiai Kiadó. Pp. 207–264.

Sozan, Michael
1976 Sociocultural Transformation in East Central Europe: The Case of the Hungarian Peasant-Worker in Burgenland. East-Central Europe 3[2]: 195–209.

Szabad Föld
1970 September 20. Budapest.

Szabady, Egon
1972 Changes in Hungarian Society during 1945–1970. *In* Hungarian Sociological Studies. The Sociological Review Monograph, no. 17. Paul Halmos, ed. Pp. 59–89.
1974 Hungary. *In* Country Profiles. New York: Population Council. (Appeared in July 1974 as a brief monograph in the Population Council's series of periodic country profiles; repr. in the Hungarian Studies Newsletter, Fall 1974[6]: 5–15.)

Szelényi, Iván
1977 Regional Management and Social Class: The Case of Eastern Europe. Informationen der Arbeitsgemeinschaft für interdisziplinäre angewandte Sozialforschung 1977[1/2]: 16–36, 1977[3/4]: 121–131.

Szilágyi, Vilmos
1971 A párválasztás és családalapítás problémái [The questions of choosing a spouse and founding a family]. *In* Család és házasság a mai magyar társadalomban [Family and marriage in contemporary Hungarian society]. Pál Lőcsei, ed. Budapest: Közgazdasági és Jogi Könyvkiadó. Pp. 78–103.

Varga, Gyula
1965 A Cooperative Village. The New Hungarian Quarterly 6[19]: 16–34.

Varga, István
1965 A közterhek [Taxes]. *In* A parasztság Magyarországon a kapitalizmus korában [The peasantry in Hungary in the age of capitalism], 1848–1914, vol. II. István Szabó, ed. Budapest: Akadémiai Kiadó. Pp. 246–318.

Volgyes, Ivan
1973 Hungary in the Seventies: The Era of Reform. Current History 64 [May]: 216–219, 232.
Manuscript. Modernization, Social Stratification and Elite Development in Hungary.

Zsarnóczai, Sándor, ed.
1964 Tanulmányok a mai faluról [Studies of the contemporary village]. Budapest: Kossuth Könyvkiadó.

Zsigmond, Gábor
1978 Az 1960–70-es évek fordulójának családtípusa [The family type of the late 1960s and early 1970s]. *In* Varsány: tanulmányok egy éjszakmagyarországi falu társadalomnéprajzához [Varsány: ethnographic studies of the society of a northern Hungarian village]. Tibor Bodrogi, ed. Budapest: Akadémiai Kiadó. Pp. 151–171.

Index